The prices and rates listed in this guidebook were confirmed at presstime. We recommend, however, that you call establishments before traveling to obtain current information.

ISBN: 0-7627-1238-4
ISSN: 1078-5493

Cover photo: PhotoDisc
Cover design: Lana Mullen
Text design: Nancy Freeborn/Freeborn Design
Illustrations by Mauro Magellan and Duane Perreault

Manufactured in the United States of America
Eighth Edition/First Printing

Recommended
COUNTRY INNS®

THE SOUTH

Alabama / Arkansas / Florida / Georgia / Kentucky / Louisiana
Mississippi / North Carolina / South Carolina / Tennessee

Eighth Edition

by Carol and Dan Thalimer

The Globe Pequot Press

GUILFORD, CONNECTICUT

To Sara Pitzer,
who laid the groundwork

Contents

Introduction

ince the first edition of this book was published in 1987, it has been called *Recommended Country Inns* but has included urban inns as well as rural bed-and-breakfasts. Some definitions are in order. What's an inn and what's a bed-and-breakfast? In general, we think of an inn as having a restaurant, other amenities such as sports facilities, and somewhere between ten and one hundred rooms, with the vast majority having between twenty-five and fifty rooms. A stay there may or may not include breakfast in the overnight rate. We generally think of a bed-and-breakfast as having ten or fewer rooms and no restaurant. Naturally, it usually does include breakfast in your stay. Unfortunately, not every establishment fits neatly into either of these categories, so we've devised a third classification: B&B inn. This describes a property that may be small but has a restaurant or a property that's large but doesn't have a restaurant.

In a few cases, you'll find establishments that clearly fit the bed-and-breakfast definition. We've kept them in this book to give some states adequate coverage. You'll also find a few inns with more than one hundred rooms: We've included them because we think they have the intimate appeal of a smaller property. If you miss some of your favorites in this edition, it's probably not because they're closed but because we've moved them to a new companion book, *Recommended Bed & Breakfasts: The South*, also published by The Globe Pequot Press.

There are other changes to this new edition: In each chapter some of the inns are designated as a Top Pick, and these outstanding properties have a more thorough description than the others. Sprinkled throughout each chapter you'll also find an amusing anecdote; a recipe; more information about an inn, city, or region; or attractions you shouldn't miss.

SETTING THE STANDARDS

The inspection and requirements an inn must meet before guides such as Mobil and AAA accept them are rigorous and standardized. It may mean that the toilet paper is folded into a triangle. An escape from standardization, however, is what drove some of us into searching for inns in the first place. As a traveler, one of the main ways you can keep a wave of sameness from overtaking the inn world too is by letting innkeepers know specifically what you like about their facilities and what doesn't matter. If you truly want the most expensive little bottles of shampoo and hand lotion (known as "amenities" in the hospitality business), say so. If you think they're beside the point, say that, too. One of the best inns in the South will never make it into a standardized guide. In each of its bathrooms you'll find a full-size bar of Ivory soap. Period. No little baskets and bottles. The issue here isn't whether these things are good or bad but whether they matter to you or not. You must speak up or the formal check-sheet of a guide rating will decide for you.

Something else you are bound to notice: The cost of staying at inns has gone up. This is not a result of greed on the part of the innkeepers; it simply reflects an increase in the cost of maintaining a nice inn. If we want private baths as well as pitchers of wildflowers on our breakfast tables, we have to expect to pay for them. If we want Ritz-quality linens as well as muffins made by hand in small batches from old family recipes, we have to expect to help bear the cost.

That's why you can now stay in most motel chains for a lot less than it costs to stay at most inns. The price of a motel is right, but of course the individuality and charm of small inns is missing. Sometimes you still want something special, more personal; when you wake up in the morning you don't want to struggle to remember where you are. That's where inns come in.

As you travel, you are bound to find some wonderful inns that are not in this guide. That's not because we're discriminating against them; it's either because we haven't been able to visit yet or because we don't know them. If you find a must-not-miss inn, let us know. We always follow up on readers' recommendations and have found some of our favorite inns that way.

Sometimes, in spite of our best efforts to choose only very stable inns for this book, an inn changes, declines in quality, and disappoints a reader. We hope it won't happen to you, but if it does, let us know about that, too.

Your comments and questions are invaluable in guiding our travels.

—Carol and Dan Thalimer

How to Use This Inn Guide

*W*orking on the theory that most of us know our alphabet better than our geography, we have arranged the listings in this book alphabetically. The ten Southern states are listed in alphabetical order, as are the towns within each state and the inns (by name) within each town. The maps at the beginning of each chapter show you where the inns are geographically.

CAVEATS

Rates: Often they are complicated, and they change. We have tried to indicate general ranges here, but you should always discuss rates when you make reservations. They may have gone up, or, as it happens, you may qualify for a discount that you don't know about.

Forms of payment: Innkeepers love cash. Every inn in this book will gleefully accept your folding money or traveler's checks. These days most inns accept Visa and MasterCard, as well as personal checks. Some accept other credit cards, too. We have mentioned under "Rates" if an inn does not accept credit cards or personal checks; nevertheless, when you are making your reservations, it is always a good idea to ask because, as with everything else, these things change, sometimes without notice.

Children: Life used to be so simple. An inn could specify whether children were accepted or not and could even specify what ages were appropriate to the inn. A couple of legal discrimination-against-children battles have changed that in many places. That doesn't change the fact that some inns are not suited to small children. Some have priceless fragile antiques that could be destroyed by one toddler's misstep; others have lofts, balconies, mountaintop locations, and other features that make the places down-right dangerous for children. Moreover, some inns don't have cribs or extra beds to accommodate a child in a room with adults. Don't ever just show up with a child at an inn. It's simply not fair to you, the child, or the innkeeper. Talk it over when you call for reservations.

Pets: In the South few inns accept pets. In some cases, it may be because the long warm season and frequent humidity are as pleasing to fleas as they are to sunbathers. More likely, prohibiting pets is a local health regulation, or the owners aren't prepared to have strange pets among their priceless antiques and Oriental rugs. In smaller properties that are actually in the owner's home, there may be family pets. Local laws may or may not restrict them from the kitchen and/or guest areas, so if you are extremely allergic to pets, be sure to check whether there are any in residence. Assume that pets are not accepted unless otherwise noted.

Smoking and fireplaces: In response to the public furor over smoking and secondhand smoke, more and more places, including large properties, have adopted a "no smoking indoors" policy as a matter of course. In addition, many insurance companies have genuine concerns about fire hazards in fine old frame homes and historic buildings and refuse to grant insurance if smoking is allowed or if wood-burning fireplaces are used. Therefore it is best to assume that in all but the largest properties, smoking will be permitted only outdoors. Larger properties, which are really small hotels, may offer smoking and nonsmoking rooms and permit smoking in the bar. If smoking—its presence or absence—is important to you, ask about it when you make reservations. Smoking policies are definitely in a state of flux, so what we've indicated here may not be the policy by the time you decide to visit.

Many older properties have drop-dead gorgeous fireplaces but don't use them at all for insurance reasons. We've tried to indicate those as "decorative fireplaces." We also indicate the presence of gas-log fireplaces, some with an electric switch starter, as well as the few wood-burning fireplaces that are available. Likewise, if a working fireplace is important to setting the scene for a romantic or just-plain relaxing getaway, be sure to ask. In fact, although many inns have at least one guest room fireplace, very few have a fireplace in every guest room, so it's very important to let the innkeeper know that you want one before he/she assigns you a room.

Wheelchair access: Increasingly, inns are finding ways to accommodate wheelchairs, but in some old buildings what they are able to do is limited. Discuss your particular needs with the innkeeper.

Air-conditioning, television, and telephones: Most inns in the South are air-conditioned these days. The only ones that don't have air-conditioning are those at high altitude, where you sleep under blankets even in July and are more apt to be looking for a heater than a cooler. As for television and telephones, there's absolutely no consistency. Some inns have one or the other, some both, some neither. We've listed those facts about each inn in the category "Rooms" in the basic information.

Business travel: Increasingly, business travelers are staying at inns instead of at hotels and motels. To attract corporate business some inns are adding such features as fax and copy service, in-room telephones with dataports, private lines, and/or voice mail, and desks. We have noted such features in the basic information following each inn profile. Since the needs for each business traveler differ, we urge you to ask about any features you need. Often an inn can supply them even if they are not advertised.

Booze: One of the most charming features of many small properties has often been the late afternoon/early evening wine-and-cheese reception where you can get to know the innkeepers and your fellow guests. Liquor laws are becoming tougher and tougher on the ability to serve liquor (even for free) without an expensive or impossible-to-get liquor license; insurance liability is causing further restrictions. Inns that have offered this amenity in the past may have had to exchange the wine for something nonalcoholic.

The laws about serving alcohol in the South vary from state to state and from county to county within the states. You can drive the better part of a day in some states—North Carolina, Kentucky, and Arkansas especially—and never get out of dry counties. Some states, such as South Carolina, sell no alcohol on Sunday, except in "open" tourist areas. Others, like North Carolina, don't sell alcoholic beverages until after 1:00 P.M. Some inns, in such states as Tennessee, are in areas that forbid the sale of liquor by the drink but allow the sale of bottled liquor, even though they are in dry counties. We have tried to indicate what to expect at each inn, but if an evening cocktail or wine with dinner is important to you, we suggest that you travel with your own supply. Make sure that you understand the inn's policy before taking alcoholic beverages into any public area. In the South, we use the phrase "brown bagging" to mean bringing spirits of your own into a public place like a restaurant.

Reservations: Make them. You go to inns for personal attention and the feeling of being a special guest. Your responsibility is much the same as it would be if you were going to visit friends. You don't show up without warning. Many bed-and-breakfast inns are in a person's home, and there may be no extra staff. If you aren't expected, there may be no one home.

Shared baths and nonattached baths: Shared baths are more common in small bed-and-breakfasts than in inns and B&B inns. We've tried to indicate properties that have any shared baths. Some make a policy of renting only one of the rooms that share a bath at a time unless it would be shared by a family or adults traveling together so that in effect you do have a private bath. In a few cases at older properties, you may have to go out in the hall to get to a private or shared bath, so some inns provide bathrobes. Unless you're absolutely sure that the inn provides robes, if you're likely to be sharing a bath or having to go out in the hall, it's always a good idea to travel with robes.

Special functions: Many properties are used for other functions, such as luncheons, weddings, corporate meetings, and so forth. Some have restaurants and shops, so the public may be wandering through as well. The smaller the property, the more disruptive these other activities may be, so you may want to ask about what else may be going on.

Breakfast: Breakfast can range from true continental (a roll, juice, and coffee) to a vast plantation breakfast that includes enough food for your entire day's sustenance. We've tried to indicate what type of breakfast to expect, but the morning meal may depend on the whims of the chef. Most inns will try to accommodate any special dietary restrictions if given advance notice.

Feedback: If you have any particularly good or not-so-good experiences when visiting any of these properties, we'd like to know about them before we do our next update. We're also interested in suggestions for wonderful inns that aren't included so that we can visit them before the next edition. Please drop a note to the publisher, and it will be forwarded to us.

Disclaimer: When studying this guide, please keep in mind that because of the long research, writing, and publishing time involved, some of these inns may no longer be in business. In addition, features and policies at other properties may have changed drastically for the better or worse. This guide is simply meant to give you some ideas about inns you might want to investigate further.

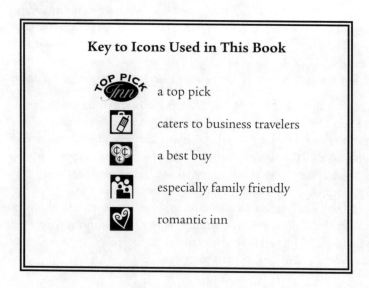

Recommended

COUNTRY INNS®

THE SOUTH

Alabama

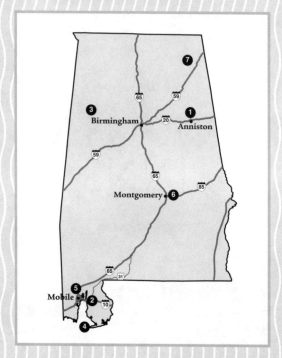

Arkansas

Alabama

Numbers on map refer to towns numbered below.

Arkansas

Numbers on map refer to towns numbered below.

* A Top Pick Inn

The Victoria, A Country Inn
Anniston, Alabama 36201

INNKEEPERS: Beth and Fain Casey

ADDRESS/TELEPHONE: 1604 Quintard Avenue (mailing address: P.O. Box 2213, Anniston 36202); (256) 236–0503 or (800) 260–8781 (reservations only); fax (256) 236–1138

WEB SITE: www.thevictoria.com

E-MAIL: thevic@mindspring.com

ROOMS: 3 suites in main house, 56 rooms in adjacent hotel, 1 guest house; all with private bath, telephone with dataport, cable television, clock radio, hair dryer, iron and ironing board, some with whirlpool, some with refrigerator, antiques, and fireplace.

RATES: $79 to $175 hotel, double. Suites $149 to $319. Inquire about guest house rates. Bountiful breakfast buffet daily. Two rooms fully equipped for handicapped. No-smoking rooms available.

OPEN: Year-round.

FACILITIES AND ACTIVITIES: Full cocktail service, dining room serves dinner Monday through Saturday for guests and the public by reservation; swimming pool, Wren's Nest Gallery. Nearby: Anniston Museum of Natural History, antiques shops, Cheaha State Park, and Silver Lakes Golf Course on the Robert Trent Jones Trail. Passes to YMCA.

BUSINESS TRAVEL: Dataport in room.

When you need the kind of escape that makes the real world seem far away and unimportant, try The Victoria, an inn property that fills almost an entire square block in Anniston. The heart of the inn is the rejuvenated 1888 mansion that was once home to several important families in Anniston. But this is not just an old home that's been "fixed up." An architect, some developers, and a general contractor collaborated to preserve the existing structure and add additional spaces for outdoor activities and lodging.

Inside, on the first floor, are dining spaces, a piano lounge, and a glassed-in veranda. In one of many nice touches, the piano lounge is in what was originally the music room. These rooms are furnished and decorated with parquet floors, elaborate draperies, carved mantels, and crystal chandeliers in a style appropriate to the exterior of the building. The food fits the mood, too.

The Victoria's meals keep earning raves. The continental-style cuisine features subtle sauces and uses lots of fresh vegetables and fruits in imaginative ways. The inn has a good wine list and staff knowledgeable enough to help you make appropriate choices.

Although there are three luxury guest rooms furnished with antiques on the second floor of the old house, most of the inn's rooms are in a new hotel building that was designed to blend in with the older structures. Unlike hotels, however, the rooms in this addition are all decorated differently, featuring mostly cool, light colors and comfortable furnishings of pine, wicker, glass, and brass.

We were personally taken with the staff, all of whom struck us as being enthusiastic and unusually professional in demeanor. The entire staff seems to be thoroughly versed in the history of the inn, interesting things to do and see in the area, and simple directions for getting around.

Given the extent of the landscaped grounds, the swimming pool, and the patios on the property, you could enjoy a complete escape and not go anywhere else at all.

HOW TO GET THERE: From I–20, take the Oxford-Anniston exit 185 and go north on Highway 21/431 (Quintard Avenue) for 4 miles. The Victoria is on the left side of Quintard.

Bay Breeze Guest House
Fairhope, Alabama 36533

INNKEEPERS: Bill and Becky Jones

ADDRESS/TELEPHONE: 742 South Mobile Street (mailing address: P.O. Box 526); (334) 928–8976; fax (334) 929–2389

WEB SITE: www.bbonline.com/al/baybreeze/

ROOMS: 4 suites, 1 guest room; all with private bath, cable television, ceiling fan; cottage suites with telephone, small kitchen. No-smoking inn. 1 room and 1 suite are handicapped accessible.

RATES: $105, single or double; $135, suites; full breakfast in main house; breakfast extra for cottage suites. $20 each additional person in suites. All major credit cards accepted. Unable to accommodate children.

OPEN: Year-round.

FACILITIES AND ACTIVITIES: Private pier, decks, and beach on Mobile Bay; three acres of flowers. Nearby: Walking distance to downtown historic Fairhope, restaurants, and shops.

BUSINESS TRAVEL: Suites have telephone and excellent light and work area; fax available.

This B&B inn sits on a three-acre site right on the shores of Mobile Bay. The grounds are filled with mature shrubs and trees that give you a feeling of being in the woods. The stucco building was built in the 1930s and has been variously remodeled and enlarged over the years. It works beautifully as an inn.

The entire downstairs—a sitting room with fireplace, glassed-porch bay room, living room, and kitch-en—is devoted to guests. (The Joneses have private quarters upstairs.) Most of the furnishings in the main house are family heirlooms going back as far as five generations. The mix of wicker, stained glass, and hooked and Oriental rugs  produces a homey feel no designer could duplicate.

The cottage suites are newer. They have pickled, white pine walls; old brick floors; vaulted ceilings; and lots of generously sized windows. One of these cottages is well equipped for the handicapped, with wide spaces to accommodate a wheelchair, grab bars in the proper places in the bathrooms, and flexible shower wands. The cottages are decorated with just the right combination of antiques, Oriental rugs, new sofas, and good beds.

HOW TO GET THERE: From I–10, take U.S. Highway 98 toward Fairhope and exit right onto Scenic/Alternate Highway 98 at the WELCOME TO FAIRHOPE sign. At the third traffic light, turn right onto Magnolia Avenue. Go 4 blocks and turn left on South Mobile Street at the municipal pier. Bay Breeze Guest House is about a mile farther, on the right.

Rose House Inn

Fayette, Alabama 35555

INNKEEPERS: Diane and Dennis Fisher

ADDRESS/TELEPHONE: 325 Second Avenue N.W.; (205) 932–7673 (ROSE) or (800) 925–ROSE; fax (205) 932–3250

WEB SITE:
www.rosehouseinn.com

E-MAIL: diane@rosehouseinn.com

ROOMS: 10, all with private bath, cable television, telephone, ceiling fan; one with whirlpool bath; two with decorative fireplace; some with VCR; well-behaved children welcome; limited wheelchair access. No-smoking inn.

RATES: $55 to $90 single or double, including continental-plus breakfast; additional person $10. Ask about Valentine packages. Credit cards accepted.

OPEN: Year-round.

FACILITIES AND ACTIVITIES: Large living/dining/kitchen common area with TV and VCR. Nearby: Downtown Fayette, antiques shopping, Fayette Art Museum, Fayette County library, Guthrie Smith Park, fishing, golf, tennis.

BUSINESS TRAVEL: Work space, two telephone lines, voice mail; computer and fax access.

One of the oldest houses in town, the Rose House Inn is the only property in Fayette that is individually listed on the National Register of Historic Places. Built on four acres in 1898 by Edward Rose, it is an excellent example of a Queen Anne Victorian cottage with characteristics such as the telltale wraparound porch, a hexagonal turret with a bell-shaped tower, and imbricated woodwork on some of its gables.  The newly constructed Rose Cottage blends well with its sister; in addition to a porch, it also boasts a tower.

You Say TomAto, I Say Tomahto You Say Cupola, I Say Belvedere

What we twenty-first-century folks might think of as a purely decorative addition perched on the roof of a historic house, barn, or other structure was really an early method of air-conditioning. Heat rises, which is why old houses had high ceilings on every floor—so that the heat would rise above the height of the people. By the time the heat collected on the upper floors or in attics, however, the temperature could be unbearable. An opening in the roof would allow some of the heat to escape.

But how to put an opening in the roof without letting in the elements? Little covered rooms with windows all around that could be raised during hot weather solved the problem. If the additions are square, they're called belvederes; if they're dome shaped and on a round base, they're called cupolas. Of course, the more opulent the house, the larger and fancier the belvedere or cupola was likely to be. Although most belvederes and cupolas were simply big enough to do the job, others are large enough to hold a roomful of furniture and people. During cold weather, the belvedere was probably the warmest place in the house, so a room big enough to be furnished as a sitting room was a very comfortable place to be. As an added benefit, the belvedere provided wonderful views.

Tastefully decorated, mostly in Victorian-era antiques, the interior ambience is that of the turn of the twentieth century. Many guests are particularly interested in the large collection of Thomas Kinkade lithographs.

Each guest room has its own distinctive personality and is tastefully decorated with period antiques. The queen among the rooms, the Honeymoon Suite, boasts a king-size canopy bed and a two-person whirlpool tub.

Breakfast is a substantial meal of fruits and juices, some kind of muffins—such as the specialty sausage-cheese muffins—cereals, grits, eggs, and hot beverages.

Located only 2 blocks from downtown, the inn is within easy walking distance of restaurants, shops, and businesses. In fact, this convenience to downtown makes the inn popular with business travelers, and the Fishers know how to treat them right.

HOW TO GET THERE: At the intersection of Highway 43 and Highway 18, turn right on Highway 18 West. Pass through three traffic lights. After the third light, turn on Second Avenue N.W. and proceed until you approach a four-way stop. The Rose House Inn is on the left before the four-way stop sign.

The Beach House 💙 Bed and Breakfast
Gulf Shores, Alabama 36542

INNKEEPERS: Carol and Russell Shackelford

ADDRESS/TELEPHONE: 9218 Dacus Lane; (334) 540–7039 or (800) 659–6004

WEB SITE: www.bbchannel.com

ROOMS: 5, all with private bath.

RATES: Peak Season (Friday before Mother's Day to Thursday after Labor Day), Long Weekend or Short Week Plans $500 to $695, Full Week Plan $1,000 to $1,390; Off Season (Friday after Labor Day to

Thursday before Mother's Day), Long Weekend or Short Week Plans $450 to $585, Full Week $900 to $1,170 (which means the seventh night is free). Rates are double occupancy and include breakfast, snacks, beverages, afternoon wine and cheese; credit cards are not accepted; single deduct $25.

OPEN: Eleven months (usually closed from mid-December to mid-January, but dates change, so be sure to ask).

FACILITIES AND ACTIVITIES: Use of the living room, kitchen, porches, and hot tub. Smoking outside only. Nearby: Historic Fort Morgan and Mobile Bay are only a few miles to the west; the towns of Gulf Shores, Orange Beach, and Foley with shopping, restaurants, amusement parks, museums, theaters are only a few miles to the east. Take the auto ferry across the bay to Dauphin Island, Bellingrath Gardens, or the casinos of Biloxi. A variety of golf courses include the nationally ranked Kiva Dunes. Also bicycling, boating, fishing, hiking, horseback riding, sailing, and tennis nearby.

BUSINESS TRAVEL: 35 miles from Mobile, 33 miles from Pensacola; suitable for very small meetings.

For us, there is no better place to be rejuvenated than at the beach. The delightful Beach House Bed and Breakfast, a B&B inn near Gulf Shores on the Alabama Gulf coast, fulfills our every requirement and desire—even things we hadn't previously realized we wanted. Owners Carol and Russell Shackelford provide an intimate, friendly atmosphere with lots of amenities to spoil you outrageously. Their philosophy is to balance "leaving you alone" with "taking care of you." The biggest decision you'll have to make is whether to relax in one of the hammocks, soak in the hot tub, go to the beach, or leave the property for sight-seeing, shopping, or dinner.

Perched on high dunes directly on the shores of the Gulf of Mexico, the rambling, three-story Beach House sits on the last lot before the Bon Secour National Wildlife Refuge, which guarantees that the vast stretch of dune-backed beach next door will never be developed. This provides you with solitude when you want it. Although the house is only seven years old, the tin-roofed exterior is reminiscent of the grand beach houses built early in the twentieth century. A huge screened porch wraps around the front of the first floor. This is a perfect place to get out of the sun and get to know your hosts and fellow guests. Outdoor stairs lead to the hot tub deck, where you can soak away your tensions—a particularly popular place to go at night to enjoy the canopy of stars. A smaller second-floor screened porch is another popular retreat. Wicker seating, hammocks, and hanging chairs provide numerous choices for unwinding.

Inside, the Beach House is filled with modern amenities. Ample use is made of pine, ceramic tile, and beaded board. Round timbers rise through all floors of the house like the masts of old sailing ships. The living room/kitchen is a large open room with a wall of windows looking out onto the Gulf. Comfortable seating invites guests to settle in, and a large library table is a great place to play games or put together a puzzle. What you happily won't see are televisions and telephones. In fact, the Shackelfords advertise their home as a "no phone, no TV, no shoes zone." Instead they provide kites and floats, beach chairs, and even flip-flops. (If you absolutely can't live without television, you can request to have one put in your room.)

All five luxurious guest rooms have their own distinct personality, indicated by their names: Nags Head, Cape May, Key West, Cumberland Island, and West Indies. All boast fabulous views, pine floors, Oriental rugs, and ceiling fans (air-conditioning is used in particularly hot weather). Private baths are large; some have tub/showers, others have huge walk-in showers, but all are amply supplied with plush towels and bathrobes. Beds are king- or queen-size and feature mattresses topped with plump feather beds, down pillows, and luxury linens. The two suite-size rooms on the third floor feature seating areas and private Jacuzzis; one has a private deck.

Firmly believing that a one-night stay simply isn't sufficient in which to unwind and get all the benefits of the ocean, beach, and fresh salt air—as well as the inn itself—the Shackelfords require a minimum three-night stay.

HOW TO GET THERE: From I–10 (exit 44), follow Alabama Route 59 south to Gulf Shores. At the fourth traffic light after the bridge over the Intracoastal Waterway, turn right (west) on Route 180 (Fort Morgan Parkway). Continue approximately 11 miles. When you see the Meyer Real Estate office on the left, continue approximately 7/10 mile and turn left on the Veterans Road. Take the second left, onto Dacus Lane. At the end of Dacus Lane, The Beach House is on the right, atop the dunes.

Malaga Inn
Mobile, Alabama 36602

INNKEEPER: Julie Beem

ADDRESS/TELEPHONE: 359 Church Street; (334) 438-4701 or
(800) 235-1586; fax (334) 438-4701 ext. 123

ROOMS: 40, all with private bath, television, and telephone; some with
refrigerator. Some with wheelchair access. No-smoking rooms available.

RATES: $69 to $79 rooms; $135 suites; includes coffee, continental
breakfast, and daily newspaper; each additional adult $10; all meals
extra.

OPEN: Year-round.

FACILITIES AND ACTIVITIES: Cocktail lounge, swimming pool. Nearby:
Located in historic district of downtown Mobile; within walking dis-
tance of the Museum of the City of Mobile, Mobile Civic Auditorium,
Conde-Charlotte House Museum; Oakleigh Period House Museum, The
Cox-Deasy House, The
Minnie Mitchell
Archives, The Fine Arts
Museum of the South,
Fort Conde Military
Museum; short drive to
Bellingrath Gardens
and Home and USS
Alabama Battleship
Memorial Park.

Although Malaga looks pretty much like a hotel now, it started
out as two three-story town houses built in 1862 by two
brothers-in-law. Had the outcome of the Civil War been different, they might still stand as two town houses. Instead, the two homes have
been restored, beginning in 1968 with a patio and garden and space for new
accommodations between them.

Twenty of the guest rooms are in the restored homes. Some of these still
have the original wallpaper and hardwood floors. One has the remains of a
fine marble fireplace. The rooms are furnished comfortably with both traditional furniture and some good antiques. The other twenty rooms, in the
newer addition, are more elaborate but perhaps less interesting because they
have less history. Many of the rooms overlook the courtyard, a pretty, spa-

cious, tiled area with a fountain and lots of plants.

With forty rooms, you can't expect highly personal treatment, but the inn's staff is very friendly and helpful in the tradition of old Southern gentility.

HOW TO GET THERE: Traveling east on I-10, take the Canal Street exit. Cross Canal to Jackson Street and follow it to Church. Turn left on Church. Traveling west on I-10, take the Government Street exit from Bayway through the Bankhead Tunnel. Follow Government Street to Claiborne, turn left, go to Church Street, and turn left again. From I-65 take I-10 east and follow the directions for traveling east on I-10. You will come to the inn almost immediately.

Red Bluff Cottage
Montgomery, Alabama 36104

INNKEEPERS: Anne and Mark Waldo

ADDRESS/TELEPHONE: 551 Clay Street (mailing address: P.O. Box 1026); (334) 264–0056 or (888) 551–2529; fax (334) 263–3054

WEB SITE: www.bbonline.com/al/redbluff

E-MAIL: RedBlufBnB@aol.com

ROOMS: 4, of which 1 is a two-room suite; all with private bath. No-smoking inn.

RATES: $65 to $85 including full breakfast. Children welcome; crib available. Credit cards accepted.

OPEN: Year-round.

FACILITIES AND ACTIVITIES: Guest refrigerator and coffeemaker, children's fenced-in play yard, gazebo. Nearby: Restaurants, Alabama State Capitol, historic sites, Jasmine Hill Gardens, Montgomery Museum of Fine Arts, Alabama Shakespeare Festival Theatre. In walking distance of downtown.

BUSINESS TRAVEL: Phones with dataports; access to copier, fax machine, and Internet.

Red Bluff Cottage is a new building, built especially as a B&B inn in 1987. The guest rooms are all on the ground floor, with the kitchen, dining room, living room, den, and music room on the second floor, which makes the guest rooms quiet and the public rooms exceptionally light and airy, looking out over the yard and gardens.

The flower gardens are an important part of Red Bluff Cottage; guest rooms are filled with fresh flowers, and seasonal blooms adorn the breakfast table. Anne has been a passionate gardener for years.

The Waldos' personal passions influence the look of the rooms inside the inn as well. In the music room, a harpsichord, a piano, and a recorder testify to the talent in the family—no guarantee that you'll hear a little concert during your stay, but it does happen.

In the guest rooms, you see furniture that's been in the family for years: the bed Anne slept in as a child, her Grandmother Sims's little rocker, and an old leather trunk from Mark's great-aunt in Wisconsin, which contained invitations to firemen's balls dated 1850.

But artifacts of family past don't mean much unless you enjoy the present family. Every time we see them, we find something more to talk about. They're simply nice people to know.

HOW TO GET THERE: Take exit 172 off I-65. Go toward downtown (east) on Herron Street 1 block. Turn left on Hanrick Street. Parking is on the right off Hanrick by the inn's rear entrance.

The Lodge on Gorham's Bluff
Pisgah, Alabama 35765

INNKEEPERS: Bill, Clara, and Dawn McGriff

ADDRESS/TELEPHONE: 101 Gorham Drive; (256) 451-3435; fax (256) 451-7403

WEB SITE: www.gorhamsbluff.com

E-MAIL: reservations@gorhamsbluff.com

ROOMS: 6 rooms, all with private bath, single- or double-whirlpool tub, telephone by request, clock, desk, ceiling fan, working fireplace; 4 with private shuttered porches; wheelchair access only to common areas and dining room; not suitable for children younger than 12.

RATES: $120 to $175 including full breakfast; additional person $10. Ask about the Celebration Package, which includes dinner, champagne, chocolates, and flowers.

OPEN: Year-round.

FACILITIES AND ACTIVITIES: Restaurant, living room and dining room with fireplace, den with TV, guest kitchen, porches, decks, gazebo, lawn games. Nearby: Hiking trails, bicycling, fishing at West Lake or in Tennessee River.

BUSINESS TRAVEL: Desk and telephone.

This sounds like a tall tale, but it's for real. In 1992 Bill and Clara McGriff and their daughter Dawn set out to develop a complete town on 186 acres they owned on a 1½-mile bluff overlooking the Tennessee River in the foothills of the Appalachian Mountains. They started with a few houses, shops, a wedding pavilion, and a performance amphitheater.

Next came the lodge, sitting high atop Sand Mountain with its long back porch overlooking spectacular views. Now don't get the idea that this is a rustic mountain log cabin with knotty-pine paneling. Rather, it's built in the style of a grand Southern mansion, with columned verandas wrapping around both the first and second floors and a belvedere perching on top. Inside, common rooms feature cream-colored clapboard walls, hardwood floors, and enormous fieldstone fireplaces. Oriental carpets and traditional furnishings give a touch of elegance.

Six spacious guest rooms boast king- or queen-size beds, whirlpool tubs, sitting areas or separate sitting rooms, and gas-log fireplaces. Hardwood floors gleam in the light admitted through tall windows and French doors out onto the private, shuttered verandas. Carefully chosen furniture, rich fabrics—often handcrafted—and interesting art and accessories give each guest chamber a feeling of both elegance and intimacy. Deserving of special mention are the Owens and Roden Rooms, which have cathedral ceilings with exposed beams, double-size whirlpool tubs, and separate sitting rooms.

Breakfast features a buffet of fresh fruits and juices, egg dishes or a casserole, cheese grits, and biscuits. Gourmet four-course dinners are served in the restaurant seven nights a week for an additional fee.

A visit to Gorham's Bluff might become a permanent residence. The new town is built in the tradition of the small towns that thrived in the United States at the turn of the twentieth century. Three hundred and fifty residential home sites are grouped into six neighborhoods and are all in close proximity to the town green, post office, shops, and meetinghouse. A workshop district attracts artists who live and work there. There's even an assisted-living facility. Prescribed setbacks, building heights, roof pitches, and overhangs ensure a consistent look. Swimming pools, garden pavilions, tennis courts, parks, and lakes are spread throughout the community.

HOW TO GET THERE: From Pisgah, follow Jackson County Road 58 for $2^{2}/_{10}$ miles. Turn left onto County Road 357 and go $1^{2}/_{10}$ miles. Turn left onto County Road 457. Follow it $^{7}/_{10}$ mile and turn right onto Main Street.

Heartstone Inn and Cottages
Eureka Springs, Arkansas 72632

INNKEEPERS: Cheri and Rick Rojek

ADDRESS/TELEPHONE: 35 Kingshighway; (501) 253–8916 or (800) 494–4921; fax (501) 253–5361

E-MAIL: heartinn@ipa.net

ROOMS: 7 rooms, 3 suites, and 2 cottages, all with private bath, clock radio, cable television. Suites and cottages have VCR, refrigerator, coffeemaker. Smoking outside only.

RATES: $75 to $139, single or double; includes full breakfast. Inquire about winter discounts and packages. Children 10 years of age and older welcome. Credit cards accepted.

OPEN: Year-round, except January.

FACILITIES AND ACTIVITIES: Video library, gift shop, on-site massage/reflexology therapist available by appointment. Located in the historic district, within walking distance of downtown Eureka Springs tourist activities; golf privileges at private course. Nearby: Restaurants.

The Heartstone Inn gets its name from a large, flat, vaguely heart-shaped stone that the original owners found on the property. They played with the heart theme, using the phrase "Lose your heart in the Ozarks" and a heart-shaped logo in their brochure. The doors have heart-shaped welcome signs. The stone that justifies it all rests in the front garden, surrounded by flowers.

The Heartstone Inn has new owners, Cheri and Rick Rojek. Rick spent thirteen years in the hospitality industry, cutting his teeth with such giants in lodging as Westin, Ritz-Carlton, and Doubletree. The Rojeks tired of the corporate lifestyle and decided that running an inn or bed-and-breakfast would be the best of the hotel business. They searched from California to Florida before falling in love with Eureka Springs and the Heartstone Inn.

Their philosophy is simple: make guests feel as if they are at home. They do their best to anticipate guests' needs and pride themselves on providing first-class service without being intrusive.

SpaWafers: Sweet Memories of Eureka Springs

SpaWafers began as a tasty European treat at luxurious old-world health spas in 1856. Spa visitors looked forward to nibbling on the delicacies while enjoying lively conversation and the fragrance of the sweet delicious wafers filling the air. The crispy wafers were much loved by such historical notables as Edward VII and composer Johann Strauss. It was only natural that when Eureka Springs became a popular spa resort in this country that visitors would want the wafers to enhance their experience. The only American producer of these international gourmet treats is Eureka Springs's Forest Hills Restaurant, which conforms to the strictest European standards and uses a specially designed oven it had shipped from Europe.

Created in creamy chocolate and vanilla hazelnut flavors, each wafer is embossed with a special design unique to Eureka Springs. Each colorful box contains six original sweet and crispy wafers. Naturally when you visit Eureka Springs you'll want to take home several boxes for yourself and for gifts. When you run out, you can order more by logging on to www.SpaWafers.com.

The B&B inn is pretty. It's an Edwardian house, painted pink, with a white picket fence and lots of bright pink geraniums and roses all around.

Most of the rooms are furnished with elegant antiques, though a couple are done in country style. One of the newer touches is an especially elegant Jacuzzi suite. The fairly steady addition of such outdoor niceties as decks and a gazebo means there are always glorious places for special gatherings such as weddings.

In the dining room is a Pennsylvania Dutch hex sign in which tulips and hearts, the symbols for faith, hope, charity, love of God, and smooth sailing, make up the pattern.

In the living room is a collection of ceramic English cottages and ceramic pieces decorated with pictures of cottages. This pottery, English Torquay, is very expensive and hard to find. The collection has attracted a lot of publicity in the past.

The Heartstone Inn has enjoyed a good bit of "discovery," applause from magazines and newspapers and other innkeepers for doing such a good job. We think guests can be assured that the fine tradition of hospitality at the inn will continue.

Guests feel pampered by breakfasts including strawberry blintzes, coffee cake, and several kinds of fruit. Only fresh ingredients are used.

HOW TO GET THERE: From the west, take the first 62B exit off Route 62. From the east, take the second 62B exit. Follow 62B through town until it becomes Kingshighway.

The Olde Stonehouse B&B Inn
Hardy, Arkansas 72542

INNKEEPER: Peggy Volland

ADDRESS/TELEPHONE: 511 Main Street; (870) 856–2983 or
(800) 514–2983; fax (870) 856–4036

E-MAIL: oldestonehouse@centurytel.net

ROOMS: 6 in stone house, 2 two-room suites and 1 minisuite in cottage, all with private bath, clock radio, TV, VCR, movies, coffee service. Suites also feature a small refrigerator, fireplace, and whirlpool tub. Telephone available on request. No-smoking inn.

RATES: $79 to $125, double; includes full breakfast and evening desserts with beverages. Credit cards accepted. Ask about special theme packages and murder mystery weekends.

OPEN: Year-round.

FACILITIES AND ACTIVITIES: Player piano, organ, musical instrument collection, bicycles, across the street from the Spring River. Nearby: Restaurants, shopping; swimming and sunbathing at Spring River Beach; 1 mile to Cherokee Village golf, horseback riding, and marina boat rentals. Vintage car museum, Veterans Museum, Country Music Theater.

BUSINESS TRAVEL: Fax, copy machine, dataports, corporate rates.

This B&B inn occupies two very different buildings. The main house is stone, built in 1928, and has in its common area a wonderful fireplace made with local rocks. The Shaver Cottage is older, built in 1905, and is a simple frame building that looks as if it belongs somewhere on the prairie.

These are the kinds of accommodations that don't demand anything except your relaxation. You don't have to move cautiously around delicate fine antiques; you can just appreciate being surrounded by things that are older and were meant to be used. For example, Aunt Jenny's Room, in the main house, has a cathedral ceiling, a white iron bed with a quilt, and the original claw-foot tub in the bath.

Grandpa Sam's and Uncle Buster's have more masculine decor. One big old window of etched glass depicts a voluptuous nude woman. Now, this ain't exactly the stuff of the prairie!

For that matter, neither are the rockers built for two on the front porch of the stone house. The point here is that nothing is constrained by what history "ought to be," and everything is interesting.

Peggy is active in local preservation and historic activities. She understands the town's history—it's always been a resort town, about two and a half hours from Memphis, Springfield, and Little Rock—and she knows the stories of all the buildings on the property.

She also understands that there are differing eating habits these days and offers breakfasts that let you be as "good" or as "bad" as you wish. Choose fresh fruit and homemade granola with yogurt or a baked apple pancake with turkey sausage, for instance.

One weekend of each month, October through May, is a murder mystery weekend. Romance, golf, and fly-fishing packages are available, too.

HOW TO GET THERE: Highway 62/63/412 runs directly through Hardy; in town it becomes Main Street.

Edwardian Inn
Helena, Arkansas 72342

INNKEEPERS: John D. Crow, owner; Simon W. Herbert, innkeeper

ADDRESS/TELEPHONE: 317 Biscoe; (870) 338-9155; fax (870) 572-9105

WEB SITE: www.bbonline.com/ar/

E-MAIL: JohnC@Ipa.net

ROOMS: 12, including 4 on ground floor; all with private bath; 1 with wheelchair access. Smoking outdoors only.

RATES: $65 to $195, single or double; includes full breakfast.

OPEN: Year-round.

FACILITIES AND ACTIVITIES: Conference room. Nearby: Restaurants, antiques shops, Delta Cultural Center, Mississippi Riverfront Park; St. Francis National Forest with two lakes for hiking, fishing, and swimming.

BUSINESS TRAVEL: Located in downtown Helena. Rooms with direct-dial phone with computer capabilities, good work space or desk, excellent lighting. Card tables and fax available.

A very rich man built the Edwardian Inn for his family home in 1904. And even though he went broke, lost it, and a lot of bad things happened to it over the years, it is perfectly obvious (now that the restoration is done) that it is a fabulously expensive building and a wonderful B&B inn.

Everyone notices the woodwork first. The first floor has something called *wood carpeting*. It was parqueted in Germany from strips not more than 1 inch wide, mounted on canvas, and shipped to Helena in rolls. The wainscoting on the walls is elaborately carved. Barleytwist balusters adorn the banister of the oak stairway.

The rooms are correspondingly lovely, with high ceilings and outstanding period antiques. Many businesspeople stay here regularly.

Although the entire setting is more elaborate than most of us are accustomed to at home, the sociability of the innkeeper and the quiet good taste of the decor make it all feel very comfortable—an easy place to be.

There is a second-floor sitting room in addition to the downstairs common rooms. And, even though the inn is right downtown, you can watch raccoons, birds, and squirrels playing right outside the window.

In the morning, guests have homemade rolls, whatever fruit is fresh in season, and coffee in the sunny little latticed breakfast room. The innkeeper takes pride in serving breakfasts that are not ordinary and in adding special touches, such as using real cloth napkins.

HOW TO GET THERE: Take 49B into Helena and follow it up a hill directly to the inn, which is painted deep yellow.

1890 Williams House ♥
Bed & Breakfast
Hot Springs, Arkansas 71901

INNKEEPERS: Karen and David Wiseman

ADDRESS/TELEPHONE: 420 Quapaw; (501) 624–4275 or
(800) 756–4635; fax (501) 321–9466

WEB SITE: www.1890williamshouse.com

E-MAIL: bnb@1890williamshouse.com

ROOMS: 5, plus 2 suites; all with private bath and cable TV, some with
two-person whirlpool tub, small refrigerator, coffee pot, VCR, CD
player, robes. No-smoking inn. Children 12 years and older welcome.

RATES: $99 to $155, single or double. Ask about corporate rates;
includes full breakfast. Wedding, honeymoon, and anniversary packages. Credit cards accepted.

OPEN: Year-round. Sometimes closed in January, depending on weather.

FACILITIES AND ACTIVITIES: Nearby: Restaurants, art galleries, shopping, national park hiking trails, Hot Springs thermal baths, Oaklawn
Park Race Track, three lakes for boating, fishing, and swimming; golf.

Many innkeepers say that guests want good beds and good
breakfasts and that their inns are popular because they provide
custom-made beds and excellent food. While all of this is true at
the 1890 Williams House, we think there is more to it than that.

Start with the building. You won't find many Victorian brownstones in
Hot Springs. The doctor who built it in 1889 had the stone hauled in. In the
ensuing years, it's been through some hard times, but the Wisemans have
refurbished it well. You can't help being impressed by the turret and tower with
notched battlements on the outside, the wraparound upstairs and downstairs
verandas, and the lovely woodwork and the black marble fireplace inside.

Guests will enjoy the charm and elegance of the 6,500-square-foot inn
with seven guest rooms and suites—five in the main house and two in the
carriage house and each furnished differently with antiques. Located in the
main house, two particularly popular rooms are the rounded Parlor Suite
and West Chamber. Both feature queen-size beds, separate sitting parlors,
and cable television. Romantics love the big two-person whirlpool tub in the
Carriage Suite, Parlor Suite, and Carriage Chamber or the china tub for two
in the Guest Chamber.

But to us, the real attraction is the innkeepers. Take David's penchant for refurbishing and fixing things. Just ask him about the work they've done since they took over the inn in 1996—the woodwork that has been stripped and restored, the old car-

pets that were torn up to reveal magnif-icent hardwood floors, Karen's marvelous flea market finds that now add so much to the decor, and even the addition of a general store in the cottage that contains items they have found, refurbished, and now offer for sale.

In the kitchen, Karen prepares an array of mouthwatering dishes, such as her stuffed croissants, blueberry-filled French toast, hash-brown omelette, and different quiches.

Karen and David's almost instinctive sharing of the myriad duties involved in running a successful inn—while always being ready to answer guests' questions and impart their significant knowledge of the area—make them perfect examples of what it takes to be effective innkeepers.

Another nice extra is a sheet for guests entitled "How a Thermal Bath Is Taken in Hot Springs National Park." It tells you exactly what happens. In addition, the Wisemans keep ice and jugs of mineral-spring water in a refrig-erator at the bottom of the stairs outside the kitchen so that you can sip the waters even if you don't go to the baths. If you like a little more fire in your water, they offer complimentary wine, as well.

HOW TO GET THERE: From the north on I-40, take Route 7 and follow it into Hot Springs. This is a drive of about two hours, longer than it looks on the map because the road winds through mountains. In Hot Springs turn right off Route 7 onto Orange Street. Go 3 blocks to the corner of Orange and Quapaw, where you will find the inn. From the south on I-30, take Route 7 for 22 miles into Hot Springs and stay on 7 until you come to Orange. Turn left onto Orange and go to Quapaw.

Wildflower Bed and Breakfast
Mountain View, Arkansas 72560

INNKEEPERS: Lou Anne Rhodes and Bill Tunnelberger

ADDRESS/TELEPHONE: Court Square, 100 Washington (mailing address: P.O. Box 72); (870) 269-4383 or (800) 591-4879; fax (870) 269-4383

WEB SITE: www.bbonline.com/ar/wildflower

E-MAIL: wildflowerbb@yahoo.com

ROOMS: 7 rooms and suites, all with private bath, some with queen beds; 1 is a three-room suite with kitchenette, living room, and sleeping loft. Smoking outside only.

RATES: $69 to $94, double; single $10 less; $10 each additional person. Includes full breakfast buffet. Children welcome. Ask about packages.

OPEN: Year-round.

FACILITIES AND ACTIVITIES: Located on historic Court Square—where folk musicians gather informally to pick with one another. Nearby: Restaurants, Blanchard Springs Caverns, Ozark Folk Center, swimming in Sylamore Creek, many mountain-music programs, fishing, Buffalo National River, canoeing, kayaking.

his B&B inn was once known as the Commercial Hotel. That was its name since 1918, when it was built to accommodate commercial travelers. The former owners, the Budys, decided that the name didn't really reflect the kind of inn they were running—hence the change. But changing the name won't eclipse the spirit of the old place. An unusual diary is kept at the Wildflower. It contains entries from people who stayed at the inn when it was the Commercial Hotel.

One entry reads, "Vera and Laren Waggoner honeymooned here January 1, 1920." Another man wrote that he boarded here in 1929 for $5.00 per month, with meals. And a woman wrote that it was nice to see the lobby clean and white—she remembered that it always used to be thick with cigar and cigarette smoke.

The entries are accumulating—from a traveling salesman who stayed here regularly during World War I, from vacationers who stopped only a few times but always loved the place, and from people who stayed here for one reason or another as children and have not been back until now.

The inn they are remembering isn't elaborate now. Never was. Never presumed to be. When the Budys took it over, it was a battered old boarding-

house, like a fat lady in a tight corset, structurally sound but sagging at the edges. In restoring it and returning it to operation as an inn, they added such niceties as central air-conditioning and heat, lots of nice pale-blue carpeting, and good clean paint. They kept the original furniture and iron beds. Today they're antiques.

Current innkeepers Lou Anne and Bill continue to increase the level of quality, comfort, and pampering with fluffy towels, soft linens, good bedside lighting, and an eclectic traditional decor. Several smaller rooms have been combined to create larger rooms or suites, and a large parlor and dining room have been added to the guest common areas. A television/sitting room complete with a VCR and a selection of games and puzzles, and comfy chairs in which to relax, is available to guests on the second floor.

We haven't mentioned the inn's most unusual feature yet. How would you like to have your own group of folk musicians that get together most nights on your front porch to do a little pickin'? One of the town traditions is for musicians to gather each night and play together. The big wraparound porch at Wildflower has become their favorite place to gather. One group likes the inn so much that it has changed its name to the Wildflower Porch Band. As long as the weather doesn't get too cold, this is where they can be heard most any weekend night. If you like folk music, here's a great way to have a wonderful weekend and be entertained at the same time.

HOW TO GET THERE: From the east, follow Highway 9, 5, and 14 to where it becomes Highway 5 and 14 (Main Street). Go to Court Square and turn right. From the west, Highway 66 goes into Mountain View directly to the square. From the north, Highway 9 goes to the square. The B&B is on the corner across from the square.

Margland Bed and Breakfast Inns
Pine Bluff, Arkansas 71601

INNKEEPER: Wanda Bateman

ADDRESS/TELEPHONE: 703 West Second Avenue; (870) 536-6000 or (800) 545-5383; fax (870) 536-7941

ROOMS: 22, all with private bath, cable television, and telephone; 8 with whirlpool tubs. Margland Two is equipped for handicapped access with elevator and ramp. Smoking in designated areas.

RATES: $85 to $110, double; includes extended continental breakfast.

OPEN: Year-round.

FACILITIES AND ACTIVITIES: Exercise room, swimming pool. Nearby: Restaurants; murals on Main Street showing Pine Bluff history; Marks' Mills Battle Site, Martha Mitchell Home, Pine Bluff/Jefferson County Historical Museum, Pine Bluff Regional Park, Pioneer Village, Arkansas Railroad Museum. Forty-five minute drive from Little Rock Regional Airport.

BUSINESS TRAVEL: Fax and copier available; good light and work space in rooms; discounts.

Margland comprises four century-old homes clustered in a residential area of Pine Bluff. The homes have their own individual personalities and don't look like public lodgings at all because they are treated so much like other homes in the neighborhood, with window boxes, fenced lawns, chairs on the porch, lace curtains at the windows, and crape myrtle growing along the street. The houses are called Margland One, Two, Three, and Four. In all four, the rooms are designed with obvious attention to detail. Guests have a choice of rooms decorated in a variety of styles. Many of the furnishings are fine an-tiques, and interesting collections cover many surfaces in the houses. Three suites have loft bedrooms to which you ascend via a spiral staircase.

Outside, the yards for each of the four houses open to each other and there are sitting spaces under the trees in the landscaped gardens, beautifully

delineated with terraces of old brick salvaged from the properties during renovations.

A gazebo behind Margland Two is a nice sitting area, and in good weather it's delightful to take your breakfast in the garden outside Margland One, although service is available also in the formal dining room. Breakfast at Margland is described as "extended continental," and it is often extended quite a bit, especially in response to guests' special requests.

At Margland Three, the kidney-shaped swimming pool, which serves all four homes, is also set off with a wall of old brick and a slate-paved sunning area that integrates the pool into the landscape.

HOW TO GET THERE: From U.S. Highway 65 at Lake Pine Bluff, take Cherry Street to West Second Avenue. Turn left. The inns are in the fourth block. You will receive a map when you make reservations.

Select List of Other Alabama and Arkansas Inns

Alabama

Lakepoint Resort
104 Lakepoint Drive
Eufaula, AL 36027
(334) 687-8011 or (800) 544-5253

Rustic lodge; 101 rooms and suites, 29 cottages, some with fireplace; restaurant, pool, golf, tennis, lake, marina.

DeSoto State Park Lodge
265 County Road 951
Fort Payne, AL 35967
(256) 845-5380 or (800) 568-8840

Rustic lodge; 25 rooms, 22 cottages, some with fireplace; restaurant, pool, tennis.

Lake Guntersville State Park Lodge
1155 Lodge Drive
Guntersville, AL 35976
(256) 571-5440 or (800) 548-4553

Rustic lodge; 100 rooms and suites, 35 cottages, some with fireplace; two restaurants, pool, golf.

Joe Wheeler State Park Lodge
4401 McLean Drive
Rogersville, AL 35652
(256) 247-5461 or (800) 544-5639

Rustic lodge; 75 rooms and suites; restaurant, pool, golf.

Twin Pines Resort and Conference Center
1200 Twin Pines Road
Sterett, AL 35147
(205) 672-7575 or (800) 858-6858

Rustic; 46 rooms and suites, some with fireplace; restaurant.

Arkansas

5 Ojo Inn B&B

5 Ojo Street
Eureka Springs, AR 72632
(501) 253-6734 or (800) 656-6734

Century-old Victorian with wraparound porch; 10 rooms, some with fireplace, all with whirlpool.

The Anderson House Inn

201 East Main
Heber Springs, AR 72543
(501) 362-5266 or (800) 264-5279

Williamsburg-style inn with century-old appeal; 15 rooms; full breakfast; cooking school and murder-mystery weekends, fly shop.

Inn at the Mill

3906 Greathouse Springs Road
Johnson, AR 72741
(501) 443-1800 or (800) CLARION

1835 mill; 48 rooms, some with whirlpool bath; restaurant, bar.

The Inn at Mountain View

307 Washington Street
Mountain View, AR 72560
(870) 269-4200 or (800) 535-1301

Rustic Victorian; 10 rooms; country breakfast; murder-mystery weekends.

Florida

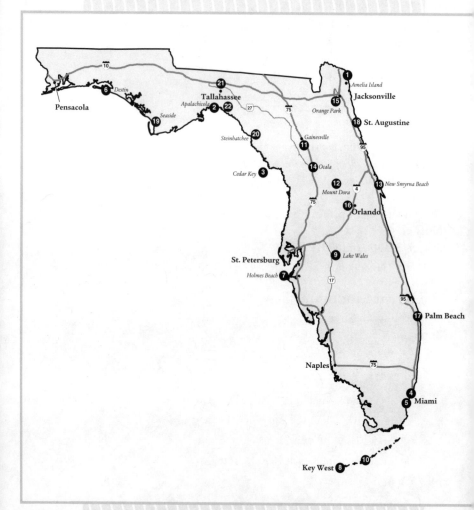

Pensacola

Destin **6**

Seaside

19

Apalachicola **2** **22**

Tallahassee

21

Steinhatchee **20**

Cedar Key **3**

10

27

75

Gainesville **11**

Ocala **14**

Mount Dora **12**

75

4

Orlando **16**

Amelia Island

Jacksonville **1**

15

Orange Park

St. Augustine **18**

95

New Smyrna Beach **13**

St. Petersburg

Holmes Beach **7**

Lake Wales **9**

17

Naples

75

Palm Beach **17**

95

Miami **4**
5

Key West **8**

10

Florida

Numbers on map refer to towns numbered below.

A Top Pick Inn

The Bailey House ♥
Amelia Island, Florida 32034

INNKEEPERS: Tom and Jenny Bishop

ADDRESS/TELEPHONE: 28 South Seventh Street; (904) 261–5390 or (800) 251–5390; fax (904) 321–0103

WEB SITE: www.bailey-house.com

E-MAIL: baileyhs@bellsouth.net

ROOMS: 10; all with private bath, king or queen beds, telephone, and cable TV; some with whirlpool tubs or extra beds; 1 with kitchen.

RATES: $115 to $175, single or double, including full breakfast. Credit cards accepted.

OPEN: Year-round.

FACILITIES AND ACTIVITIES: Verandas; bicycles available. Nearby: Fort Clinch, public beaches, restaurants, shopping, galleries, water sports, tennis, golf, horseback riding.

BUSINESS TRAVEL: Telephone and modem connection in guest rooms; fax on-site.

*A*lthough beautifully furnished with antiques and Victorian-style reproductions, The Bailey House has a homey, lived-in feeling.

The Bishops have a fine collection of antique furnishings, but they arranged it carefully so that no room seems too full, and you never feel as if you're bumping into knickknacks everywhere you turn. The Bishops have worked steadily at upgrading everything about The Bailey House, which is listed on the National Register of Historic Places.

Each of the ten guest rooms has its own special features: a king-size bed with a hand-carved headboard in the Rose Room; an antique footed tub (and separate shower) in the Country Room; and an imported marble fireplace and two-person whirlpool in the French Garden. Oriental rugs throughout tie everything together.

Breakfast is spread on the marble-topped buffet in the dining room bay window for guests to help themselves to in the morning. In addition to the usual coffee, juices, fruits, and homemade granola, the Bishops feature bran muffins with nuts and raisins. For other meals, the Bishops can recommend many excellent restaurants within walking distance of the inn.

HOW TO GET THERE: From I–95 or U.S. 17, take Route A1A to Amelia Island. Stay on A1A. In Fernandina Beach on Amelia Island, A1A becomes Eighth Street. Turn left onto Centre Street and left again onto Seventh Street. The Bailey House is on the left corner at Seventh and Ash Streets.

Elizabeth Pointe Lodge
Amelia Island, Florida 32034

INNKEEPERS: David and Susan Caples

ADDRESS/TELEPHONE: 98 South Fletcher Avenue; (904) 277–4851 or (800) 772–3359; fax (904) 277–6500

WEB SITE: www.ElizabethPointeLodge.com

E-MAIL: Eliz.pt@worldnet.att.net

ROOMS: 25, all with private bath and oversized marble tub, telephone, and television; some with Jacuzzi. Wheelchair accessible. No-smoking inn.

RATES: $160 to $240; includes full breakfast and morning newspaper. $20 per additional person in room. Children 5 and under free. Some rooms can be combined to form suites; inquire about rates. Credit cards accepted.

OPEN: Year-round.

FACILITIES AND ACTIVITIES: Light lunches, dinners, and snacks. Full beach privileges, bicycles, 24-hour room service. Nearby: Restaurants, tennis, golf, horseback riding, boating, and deep-sea fishing. Walking distance to Fort Clinch; short drive to Fernandina Seaport.

BUSINESS TRAVEL: Located 30 minutes from Jacksonville. Telephone in room; fax, telecommunications, audiovisual equipment, copy machine, and secretarial services available; conference room. Special packages for small conferences and retreats.

*T*his is a new beachfront inn built in the 1890s Nantucket shingle style. It has guest rooms furnished with a nautical theme; common areas furnished with antiques; a great stone fireplace; 13 miles of quiet, uncrowded Atlantic Ocean beaches; and a highly personable staff. Dunes separate the house and the beach.

The Capleses have managed to give the inn interesting nooks and crannies . . . and a feeling that the building has always been right where it is. The guest rooms have a nautical feel but are much more spacious than you'd find in anything that floats. For example, one of the rooms with large windows facing the sunset has hardwood floors brightened with pastel area rugs and a mahogany armoire containing hanging space, drawers, the television, and a full mirror. The bed is a bright green, pencil-post reproduction. A white wicker rocker and live plants make the space cheery, while nautical photos and a porthole window to one side of the bed continue the nautical theme.

If you come here for a low-key vacation, you can do all the beach things most folks like, or you can read on the porch. You can sit by the fireplace, surrounded by books, handmade quilts, and antiques, or you can get physical with golf, tennis, boating, and fishing. Whatever you want can be arranged with little effort on your part right from the inn.

Unlike many inns, this one works well with children. Shelves with kids' books and toys are placed low to be reached easily.

If you let yourself relax, you might end up doing some kidlike things yourself—drinking lemonade, learning to make fishnets by hand, or searching for sand crabs with a flashlight on the beach at night.

HOW TO GET THERE: From I-95, take the Amelia Island/Fernandina Beach/Route A1A exit just inside the Florida border, near Georgia. Go east on A1A for 15 miles—you will cross the bridge onto the island. Continue on Route A1A to the fifth stoplight and the intersection with Centre Street. Turn right on Atlantic Avenue and go east 2 miles to the second red light. Turn right on Fletcher. The inn is on the left.

The Fairbanks House
Amelia Island, Florida 32034

INNKEEPERS: Bill and Theresa Hamilton

ADDRESS/TELEPHONE: 227 South Seventh Street; (904) 227-0500 or (888) 891-9882; fax (904) 277-3103

WEB SITE: www.fairbankshouse.com

E-MAIL: fairbanks@net-magic.net

ROOMS: 6 rooms, 3 suites, 3 cottages, all with cable television, telephone, hair dryer, coffeemaker, and iron and ironing board. 6 have whirlpool tubs. None are handicapped accessible. Completely nonsmoking inn, including the grounds.

RATES: $150 to $250 year-round, including full gourmet breakfast and social hour. Bicycles, beach chairs, beach towels, and beach umbrellas available at no additional cost. Two-night minimum on nonholiday weekends and 3-night minimum during holidays and special events. Ask about special packages. Children 12 and older are welcome.

OPEN: Year-round.

FACILITIES AND ACTIVITIES: Swimming pool, bicycles. Nearby: Walking distance to historic downtown, restaurants, shopping, tennis courts; short drive to marina, beach, horseback riding, 4 golf courses, Amelia Island Museum of History, pre–Civil War Fort Clinch, carriage rides through historic district.

A trip to the beach usually means sand in your shoes, salt in your hair, sunburn on your nose, and a room or two in a touristy condo—unless you visit Amelia Island, which is bustin' out all over with small inns in restored old buildings. The Fairbanks, opened in 1994, is one of the best.

This B&B inn is housed in a restored 1885 Italianate Victorian, built by Confederate veteran Maj. George Rainsford Fairbanks, with all the trimmings of that era: a 15-foot square tower, dormers, bay

windows, gables, chimneys, and romantic balustraded balconies. In renovating the house, the former owners, the Smelkers, tried to be faithful to its original style and decorate and furnish it appropriately.

The quality inside matches the exterior: 12-foot-high ceilings, fancy moldings, heart-of-pine floors, and dramatic colors. The living spaces are filled with crystal chandeliers, Eastlake and French antiques, and Oriental rugs. And there's an upstairs luxury suite in the tower that makes you willing to be the crazy aunt who's been kept there for years.

In a setting this formal you might expect to feel formal yourself, but you don't. That has a lot to do with the tastefulness of the arrangements—furniture isn't crowded into spaces too small for it, and surfaces are not cluttered with too many knickknacks.

Gourmet breakfasts served on fine china are pull-out-all-the-stops affairs, including such exotic choices as orange pecan French toast with caramel sauce. On the other hand, you can also arrange ahead of time for breakfasts accommodating dietary restrictions.

The house sits on an acre of land, which allows plenty of space for a swimming pool, a spacious brick courtyard, and lots of blooming plants. Also on the grounds, three cottages with kitchen and living and dining rooms provide extra seclusion and privacy.

HOW TO GET THERE: From I-95, take exit 129 onto A1A. Follow A1A onto the island and turn left on Cedar Street. The inn is at the corner of Cedar and Seventh Streets.

Florida House Inn 💙
Amelia Island, Florida 32034

INNKEEPERS: Bob and Karen Warner and Janine Rowe

ADDRESS/TELEPHONE: 20 and 22 South Third Street; (904) 261–3300 or (800) 258–3301; fax (904) 277–3831

WEB SITE: www.floridahouse.com

E-MAIL: flahseinn@net-magic.net

ROOMS: 15, all with private bath; some with shower only, some with tub/shower, some with whirlpool and separate shower; some rooms open onto one of the porches; some rooms have a fireplace; all with television, telephone, clock radio. Bedding ranges from twin to king-size beds.

RATES: $79 to $179, double occupancy; includes full breakfast and free newspaper. Additional guests in the room are charged $10. During the week in the off-season (parts of December, January, and February), stay two nights and get a third night free (does not include stays that include a Friday or Saturday).

OPEN: Year-round.

FACILITIES AND ACTIVITIES: Pub, restaurant, guest laundry facilities, concierge. Smoking is permitted only in outdoor areas and the pub. Nearby: Beaches, horseback riding on the beach from Sea Horse Stables, Fort Clinch State Park, diving, snorkeling, nature preserves and trails, bicycling and jogging trails, boating, fishing, golf course, hiking, tennis, museums, galleries, shopping, theater.

BUSINESS TRAVEL: Business center with secretarial services, fax, and copier; meeting and banquet facilities.

*T*his fine old inn is located behind a whitewashed picket fence in the heart of the historic district of Fernandina Beach on popular Amelia Island. The charming frame building—graced with smatterings of gingerbread, long windows flanked by shutters, and delightful verandas with ornate porch railings—has been welcoming lodgers for more than 140 years. Listed on the National Register of Historic Places and featured in *Best Places to Stay in Florida,* this quaint inn is located in an 1857 building, which originally opened as an inn serving passengers on the Florida Railroad, making it the oldest lodging property in the state.

The current reincarnation of the inn offers every modern comfort and convenience without sacrificing the historic character. Today the space is divided into fourteen spacious and comfortable bedrooms and one suite, all featuring private baths. Ten rooms boast working fireplaces, two feature old-fashioned claw-foot tubs, and six offer whirlpool tubs. Furnished with antiques and period reproductions and decorated with quilts and handmade rugs, the cheery rooms feature romantic four-poster beds or quaint iron beds, a telephone, and a television.

Common areas where guests can mingle and get to know one another or find a private place to read a good book include the elegant formal parlor, the vast courtyard, or the clubby pub with its fireplace. Our favorite place to while away some time and catch the gentle breezes is the brick-paved courtyard shaded by the sprawling branches of a gigantic 200-year-old live oak tree or one of the rear porches overlooking the courtyard.

In addition to a full hot breakfast served to guests each morning, the inn also offers a full-service restaurant featuring boardinghouse-style dining. Lunch—which costs only $6.98 for fried chicken, another meat entree, four or five vegetables, biscuits, corn bread, dessert, and iced tea—is served Monday through Saturday. Sunday brunch ($8.98) features egg dishes, grits, home-fried potatoes, sausage gravy, fried chicken, ham, vegetables, fresh fruit, breads, desserts, and tea. Dinner ($11.98) includes all the lunch items and more and is served Tuesday through Saturday. Large tables seat twelve, so you get to know your fellow guests and other visitors to Amelia Island.

The inn's location is ideal for exploring the historic 30-square-block Victorian seaport village and the harbor area, which first lured swashbuckling pirates to the island, and the shrimp docks. The wide, spectacular Atlantic beaches are less than 2 miles away.

HOW TO GET THERE: From I–95, take exit 129 and travel east on A1A over the large bridge that leads to Amelia Island. A1A becomes Eighth Street. When the divided 4-lane road becomes 3 lanes with a center turn lane, continue to the third traffic light, which is the intersection of Atlantic and Centre Streets. Turn left and go 2 blocks, passing the large courthouse. Turn left onto Third Street. The inn is ½ block on the left. Look for the fluttering flags depicting the various governments under which Amelia Island has served.

The Coombs House Inn
Apalachicola, Florida 32320

INNKEEPERS: Pamela Barnes and Anthony Erario

ADDRESS/TELEPHONE: 80 Sixth Street; (850) 653–9199; fax (850) 653-2785

WEB SITE: www.coombshouseinn.com

E-MAIL: coombsstaff@coombshouseinn.com

ROOMS: 19, all with private bath, cable television, telephone with dataport; some with whirlpool tub and/or refrigerator, private entrance to veranda. Carriage House with living room, kitchen, bedroom, and bath. No-smoking inn.

RATES: $79 to $199 including full breakfast, wine-and-cheese reception on weekends and holidays; each additional person $15. Well-behaved children welcome. Credit cards accepted.

OPEN: Year-round.

FACILITIES AND ACTIVITIES: Mountain bikes, tandem bike, beach chairs, towels, umbrellas. Nearby: Historic district, Apalachicola River, beaches of St. George Island and Cape San Blas, restaurants, shops, museums, nightlife.

The Coombs House Inn is a romantic Victorian bed-and-breakfast that occupies two century-old mansions in the historic district of Apalachicola. Guests will appreciate the charm and historical authenticity as well as a comfortable, homey atmosphere. Although the main house is larger and more opulent, both are filled with antiques, oil paintings, and Oriental carpets from all over the world. Just a few architectural details of note include beautiful cypress spindles reproduced from a nineteenth-century railway bridge, large leaded-glass bay windows, hardwood floors, and the original hand-carved oak stairway in the main house.

Each guest room has a seamlessly installed private bathroom and is tastefully appointed with antique furnishings, Damask-patterned fabrics, imported English chintz draperies, and colorful Asian carpets. Ten boast decorative fireplaces.

The aroma of Pamela's homemade muffins and breads draws guests to the main house each morning for a delicious breakfast in the mansion's original dining room. This delightful meal is accompanied by fresh-baked "Surprise Dishes."

Superbly situated for any type of sight-seeing, the Coombs House is within easy walking distance of the historic district as well as the Apalachicola River and is a short drive from the beaches. If you'd rather do nothing, the elegant public rooms and rocker-filled porches are excellent places to relax.

HOW TO GET THERE: The Coombs House Inn is located at the corner of U.S. 98/Coastal Highway and Sixth Street. Arriving from the west, it is on the right before you get to the commercial district. From the east, cross the Apalachicola River Bridge, go to the only flashing light in town, and turn left. Go 3 blocks, and the inn is on the left.

The Gibson Inn 🪙

Apalachicola, Florida 32329

INNKEEPER: Michael Koan

ADDRESS/TELEPHONE: 57 Market Street (mailing address P.O. Box 221); (850) 653–2191; fax (850) 653–3521

WEB SITE: www.gibsoninn.com

E-MAIL: info@gibsoninn.com

ROOMS: 31, all with private bath, ceiling fan, cable television, and telephone. Children welcome. Smoking rooms available. Pets permitted.

RATES: $75 to $135, including breakfast. Weekends $5.00 additional. Several discounts available. Credit cards accepted.

OPEN: Year-round.

FACILITIES AND ACTIVITIES: Restaurant, pub, verandas. Nearby: Historic district, shops, restaurants, Apalachicola River, beaches of St. George Island and Cape San Blas, bird-watching, tennis, canoeing, kayaking, biking, ecotours, sailing aboard the *Governor Stone* schooner, horseback riding, boating.

*W*here the Apalachicola River meets the bay and the mainland sits a quaint inn that exudes Old Florida charm. Wrapped with white verandas on two levels, the three-story blue-gray inn is topped with a tin roof and a belvedere. This is Florida the way it used to be.

Each guest chamber is different in size, shape, and decor, but each has Victorian flair. When we think Victorian, we often think dark and opulent with heavy bed draperies and window treatments, but the decor has been toned down to reflect the casual lifestyle of a river/beach community. Four-poster and canopy beds, antique armoires, and pedestal sinks set the tone, but light walls, tall windows with sheer curtains, ceiling fans, and exposed hardwood floors lend a more laid-back air. No matter which room you're assigned, you'll be delighted.

Apalachicola is an oyster, shrimp, and seafood heaven, so it's no surprise that local seafood is a specialty in the restaurant, with oysters, shrimp, and grouper prepared in a variety of delicious ways. Chef Adam Mitt's years in New Orleans give his cuisine a definite Cajun flavor.

Up until now, this area of Florida's panhandle has been known as the Forgotten Coast—but that's what makes it so appealing. Crowds, traffic, tacky shops, miniature golf courses, and amusement parks are blessedly absent. What you find instead is slow-paced life in a small town right out of the Victorian era. Historic homes ornamented with gingerbread line streets shaded with live oaks draped in swaying Spanish moss. Small boutiques and cozy seafood restaurants border the antebellum cotton and lumber wharfs. Beaches are just a short drive away. When you're not otherwise occupied, the rocker-filled verandas are the perfect place to while away some meaningful quiet time.

HOW TO GET THERE: The Gibson Inn lies right along the river on U.S. 98. From the west, take U.S. 98 into the commercial district and turn right on Third Street. Go 3 blocks. The inn is at the foot of the Gorrie Bridge.

Island Hotel
Cedar Key, Florida 32625

INNKEEPERS: Tony and Dawn Cousins

ADDRESS/TELEPHONE: 373 Second Street; (352) 543–5111 or (800) 432–4640; fax (352) 543–6949

WEB SITE: www.islandhotel-cedarkey.com

E-MAIL: info@islandhotel-cedarkey.com

ROOMS: 13, 11 with private bath, some with a claw-foot tub; double or queen-size beds; all rooms are air-conditioned, some also have ceiling fans; no in-room telephones or television. The hotel has limited suitability for children, so inquire first. Smoking is restricted to the bar and outdoor areas.

RATES: $75 to $125, single or double occupancy, including breakfast; $20 per additional person. Minimum stays during special events.

OPEN: Year-round.

FACILITIES AND ACTIVITIES: Gourmet restaurant, King Neptune Bar, wraparound porch. Nearby: Beach, fishing, boating, antiques and other shopping.

A pre–Civil War structure built in 1859 from seashell tabby with oak supports, the Island Hotel has withstood hurricanes and other natural and man-caused disasters for almost 150 years. Rustic and authentic, the venerable inn is listed on the National Register of Historic Places.

Island Hotel

It's not surprising that an inn that has survived more than 140 years of eventful history would have many interesting stories to tell. The crotchety old building, which has survived innumerable hurricanes, floods, storms, and even fires, contracts and expands with the seasons and moans and groans like an elderly person with aches and pains.

What began as Parson's and Hale's General Store had its purpose interrupted during the Civil War when Union troops, who occupied Cedar Key because it was a strategic port, torched almost the entire town. It is believed that the store was spared because it served as a barracks and warehouse for the Yankees. During its long history, offices of the Customs House and the Cedar Key Post Office were also located in the store, and it's even believed that for a short while the building was occupied by a brothel before becoming a hotel.

One of the most fascinating stories about the hotel involves a former longtime owner—Loyal "Gibby" Gibbs and his wife, Bessie. Unfortunately, Gibby died in 1962, and it's reported that Bessie had to store his ashes behind the bar until the tide changed so that she could scatter his remains at sea. When some locals found this somewhat tasteless, Bessie is said to have retorted, "Why not. That's where he was happiest!"

During the seventies, Jimmy Buffett was a frequent visitor and held many an impromptu concert in the Neptune Bar. He mentions Cedar Key in his song "Incommunicado."

Noted for its muraled walls, nostalgic ceiling fans, French doors opening onto the wide wraparound second-story porch, and the cozy King Neptune lounge bar, the Island Hotel is a perfect place to kick back and relax. Sit in a rocker to watch the sun set on the Gulf, or relax in the upstairs or downstairs hotel lobby (downstairs has a grand piano), where you can get to know your fellow guests and dine on gourmet seafood, especially Cedar Key specialties.

The thirteen individually decorated guest rooms in the old inn and the annex are simple but attractive—many with double or queen-size iron beds romantically draped with mosquito netting (for atmosphere, not necessity).

Those in the main building retain the charm of hand-cut walls and floors, while those in the annex feature tile floors. All rooms have private bathrooms—some with claw-foot tubs (bubble bath provided), others with showers or tub/shower combinations. All also have ceiling fans.

Although we always swear that we're going to eat lightly while we're on vacation, what can you do when the dining room is legendary. Chef Dawn's culinary skills are generally believed to be unsurpassed on the island. You'll get the day off to a good start with an ample breakfast, included in the overnight rate, which can be served in the dining room or on the screened porch. This delightful meal includes fresh brewed coffee served in a French press, juice, toasted homemade poppy-seed bread, and a house specialty entree. On weekends special gourmet breakfasts are available at an additional price.

Don't limit your culinary experiences at the Island Hotel to breakfast, though. At dinner, Chef Dawn's crab bisque is a specialty. Among other specialties you should try are *Escargot à la Jahn* (named for a former longtime chef); the Island Hotel Original Heart of Palm Salad, developed by former owner Bessie Gibbs during the forties; a dozen or more seafood dishes from fish in parchment paper to Cedar Key soft-shell crabs, stone crab claws, and oysters—all in season. Enjoy your meal in the casually elegant dining room or on the screened porch.

If you're looking for a place where you can totally relax, which has 140-plus years of history, and features a gourmet kitchen, pack your bags and head for Cedar Key and the Island Hotel.

HOW TO GET THERE: Cedar Key is 58 miles southwest of Gainesville at the end of FL 24. At the stop sign, turn left onto Second Street. The inn is 3 blocks on the left.

Mayfair House Hotel
Coconut Grove, Florida 33133

INNKEEPER: Amaury Peedra, general manager

ADDRESS/TELEPHONE: 3000 Florida Avenue; (305) 441-0000 or (800) 433-4555; fax (305) 443-4812

WEB SITE: www.mayfairhousehotel.com

E-MAIL: coryf@bellsouth.net

ROOMS: 179 rooms; all with private bath, hair dryer, cable television with VCR, central stereo system, telephone, minibar; 1 suite with Jacuzzi on the balcony.

RATES: $169 to $649, double occupancy; children 12 years of age or younger may stay in an adults' guest room at no additional charge. Extra charges apply for older children and adults staying in the room. Ask about Weekend Break rates, which are applicable for stays of 2 nights or more between Friday and Sunday inclusive and include breakfast and added value benefits such as complimentary use of sports and leisure facilities.

OPEN: Year-round.

FACILITIES AND ACTIVITIES: Room service, valet parking, concierge, fitness center, rooftop pool, and Jacuzzi with views of Biscayne Bay, restaurant, champagne bar, laundry service, car rental, facilities for the disabled. Nearby: Restaurants, movie theaters, boutique shopping, Key Biscayne beaches, Viscaya Museum, University of Miami.

BUSINESS TRAVEL: 10 miles from downtown Miami, 15 miles from the Miami airport; 8 meeting rooms; business-friendly rooms have dataport phones, fax facilities, and desks that are big enough on which to do some real work.

*L*ocated in the quaint shopping district of Coconut Grove across the street from the exciting Cocowalk, this superior, first-class, five-story inn comes as a surprise. Above the first floor of shops, an ivy-covered structure rises. It isn't immediately apparent whether it's a parking deck, an office building, a department store, or a hotel. You'll be well rewarded by finding out what's inside. Awarded four stars and four diamonds by the major hotel rating services, the Mayfair House Hotel offers unsurpassed service in exquisite surroundings. Beautifully appointed, the mahogany-furnished suites boast either a Japanese spa tub nestled on a private veranda hidden behind the ivy or a marble Roman bath. One suite also has a Jacuzzi on its balcony.

American contemporary cuisine is served in the exquisite white-linen restaurant, where seafood is a specialty. Begin your epicurean feast with an appetizer such as chardonnay-steamed white clams, garlic-grilled squid, or pan-fried lump crabcakes, then move on to an entree such as Florida snapper, grilled veal steak, grilled tenderloin of Sterling beef, or rosemary-roasted rack of lamb—but save room for the specialty desserts of the day.

The well-trained, friendly staff of helpful professionals, who help impart the feeling of an upscale inn, are always ready to give you directions to the many sights in the area, other places to eat, the best nightspots, or the quietest beach.

HOW TO GET THERE: I-95 becomes U.S. 1, which you will take south to Unity Boulevard. Continue south to Tigertail Avenue, turn right, and go to May Street. Turn left on May and go 1 block to Florida Avenue. Turn right on Florida; the hotel is on your right.

Hotel Place St. Michel
Coral Gables, Florida 33134

INNKEEPER: Stuart Bornstein, owner; Christian Horsley, manager

ADDRESS/TELEPHONE: 162 Alcazar Avenue; (305) 444–1666 or (800) 848–HOTEL; fax (305) 529–0074

WEB SITE: www.hotelplacestmichel.com

ROOMS: 27, including 3 junior suites; all with private bath and antiques.

RATES: $125 to $165 for rooms, $160 to $200 for suites, depending on season; includes continental breakfast, fruit on arrival, and morning newspaper.

OPEN: Year-round.

**FACILITIES AND ACTIVI-
TIES:** Restaurant St. Michel, piano bar, French deli. Nearby: Sight-seeing, shopping, fine dining, and nightlife in Coral Gables, Coconut Grove, Miami, and Miami Beach.

he friendly folks at this exquisite boutique hotel are fond of saying, "If you can't get to Paris or Provence this year, just book yourself into the Hotel Place St. Michel instead." Actually, your first impression will be that of the Spanish countryside. Built in 1926, the hotel had to adhere to the Spanish/Mediterranean–style architecture decreed by the city of Coral Gables at that time.

Inside, things take on a grander, but not overpowering, air. A barrel-vaulted ceiling accented with ornate plaster looms over a checkerboard floor.

Filled with English and French antiques as well as fresh flowers and lush greenery, the inn exudes elegance and charm.

Dan's favorite attraction is the 1926 Otis manual elevator, which is still in use. The hotel staff is happy to operate this slice of the past for you—this is definitely *not* a self-service elevator.

The cozy mahogany-paneled Stuart's Bar and Lounge is a popular piano bar and gathering place, where complimentary hors d'oeuvres accompanied by live piano entertainment are offered in the late afternoon. Performances on another grand piano set the romantic dinner mood in the elegant Restaurant St. Michel, where many a proposal has been offered. The award-winning restaurant, lauded for its French/continental cuisine, also serves breakfast and lunch. Charcuterie St. Michel is a French deli offering takeout.

Spacious guest rooms and junior suites feature French antiques and period reproductions as well as opulent floral fabrics in the bed coverings and window treatments. Junior suites include a spacious seating area.

The attentive staff sets the tone, which takes us back to the past when gentility and charm were the rule. If this type of ambience turns you on, as it does us, give this hidden jewel a try.

HOW TO GET THERE: Take I-95 to FL 836 and go west. Turn south on South Le Jeune Road and continue to Alcazar, where you will turn left (east). The inn is on the right.

Henderson Park Inn
Destin, Florida 32541

INNKEEPER: Susie Nunnelley

ADDRESS/TELEPHONE: 2700 Scenic Highway 98E; (850) 654–0400 or (800) 336–4853 (reservations only), fax (850) 654–0405

WEB SITE: www.hendersonparkinn.com

E-MAIL: innkeeper@hendersonparkinn.com

ROOMS: 36, all with private baths, most with refrigerator, icemaker, coffeemaker, microwave, telephone, cable TV, in-room safe, and bathrobes.

RATES: $95 to $334 in high season (summer), includes full Southern breakfast, a late afternoon cocktail hour around the gulfside gazebo, and evening turndown service; reduced rates fall through spring. Not set up to accomodate guests younger than 5. Some non-smoking rooms available.

OPEN: Year-round.

FACILITIES AND ACTIVITIES: The Veranda Restaurant; heated pool; complimentary beach chairs, umbrellas, and beach towel service in season; sundeck area. Limited room service. Nearby: Championship golf courses, charter deep-sea fishing boats, shopping, several state parks, Indian Temple Mound and Museum, U.S. Air Force Armament Museum, Focus Center Children's Museum, zoo, Gulfarium.

BUSINESS TRAVEL: Dedicated meeting facility with audiovisual equipment and complete food and beverage service can accommodate up to 50 persons; also business center with fax, computer, and modem lines.

*B*uilt only nine years ago, but resembling a stately old New England shingle-style inn with full-length verandas on the first and second floors, the beachfront Henderson Park Inn is on one of the most beautiful soft white-sand beaches on the Gulf of Mexico. As if it needed any added attractions, the inn is located on the eastern boundary of Henderson Beach State Park, ensuring a permanent undeveloped mile-long stretch of beach beyond the inn. Although we usually prefer historic properties, this thoroughly modern inn is so well done, we completely forgive it its lack of age. Combining the best of beachside charm and elegance with all the modern comforts and conveniences, the inn and its surroundings are the perfect antidote to the hectic everyday world.

Evoking a nostalgic ambience, lavish guest rooms are furnished with Victorian-era reproductions and accented with luxuriant fabrics for the bed coverings and window treatments as well as Impressionist art. Graceful and romantic bedchambers, many of which sport high ceilings, feature a king- or queen-size four-poster, canopied, or iron bed draped with fine linens. All rooms offer a private bath, most with a whirlpool tub. Some extra-special accommodations boast a fireplace as well.

You'll enjoy fine seafood specialties and eclectic continental cuisine in the inn's aptly named Veranda Restaurant, where you can choose a table by a wall of windows overlooking the beach and the Gulf or dine out on the veranda itself. The delightful dining room is where you will enjoy your complimentary breakfast and where you can sample from the lunch menu or share an elegant, romantic candlelight dinner with your loved one. Cocktails are served, and there is an impressive wine list. In season, you don't even have to leave the beach and get dressed for lunch; beachside menu service is offered.

HOW TO GET THERE: Take U.S. 331 south from I-10 to U.S. 98. Follow U.S. 98 west toward Destin, then follow Scenic Route 98 to the inn.

Harrington House Beachfront Bed and Breakfast
Holmes Beach, Florida 34217

INNKEEPER: Jo and Frank Davis

ADDRESS/TELEPHONE: 5626 Gulf Drive; (941) 778-5444 or (888) 828-5566; fax (941) 778-0527

WEB SITE: www.harringtonhouse.com

E-MAIL: harhousebb@mail.pcsonline.com

ROOMS: 16 rooms and 2 cottages, all with private bath, cable TV, desk, telephone, small refrigerator; some with ceiling fan, whirlpool tub, fireplace; 2 rooms with wheelchair access.

RATES: $129 to $249, double occupancy, including full gourmet breakfast and refreshments; 2-night minimum stay on holidays and weekends. Children older than 12 welcome. Credit cards accepted.

OPEN: Year-round.

FACILITIES AND ACTIVITIES: Beach, swimming pool (heated in winter), bicycles, kayaks, equipment and games, gift shop. Nearby: International cuisine, swimming, jet-skiing, sailing, shopping, Ringling Museum, Mote Marine Aquarium.

*Y*ou don't have to go to an anonymous, cookie-cutter motel or high-rise hotel, nor do you have to rent a condo or entire house, to get beachfront accommodations. At relatively undiscovered Holmes Beach on the Florida Gulf Coast's Anna Maria Island, bed-and-breakfast accommodations are offered in a charming restored 1920s multi-level stucco home, an adjacent 1940s one-story cottage, and a new beach house, located on one and a half acres directly on the Gulf of Mexico. The Harrington House is a place of casual elegance that exudes Old Florida charm.

Although every guest room is different, each is light and summery, with a soft romantic touch and a cozy feel of home. Most rooms are found in the main house, the remainder in the two cottages. Many boast French doors leading to balconies overlooking the pool and the Gulf. A variety of bedding sizes ranges from twins to kings created from two twins. Two of the most popular rooms are the Surfside, with its four-poster bed, wraparound walls of windows, and its own deck; and the Gulfside, with its wicker king-size bed, whirlpool tub, and deck.

What's important here isn't what the houses and decor look like, but everything you can do here. Watch stunning sunrises and sunsets. Listen to the soothing sounds of the ocean lapping against the shore. Walk all or part of the 7 miles of white-sand beach. Kayak with the dolphins. Take a tour of the island by bicycle. Splash in the pool. Soak up some rays on the beach. Revel in the gracious hospitality. But most of all, bask in the tropical surroundings and tranquillity.

Morning coffee is set out at 7:00 A.M. for early risers. A good stiff walk on the beach or a few laps in the pool will work up an appetite for a breakfast that might consist of stuffed French toast, eggs Benedict, omelettes, frittata, or pancakes with strawberries and whipped cream. A refrigerator well stocked with cold drinks is a welcome respite from the heat of the day. On those occasional chilly or overcast days, curl up by the fireplace in the great room, with its 20-foot, open-beam ceiling.

HOW TO GET THERE: From I-75, take exit 42 westbound. Stay on Manatee Avenue, Route 64, over the causeway to Anna Maria Island. Turn right onto County Road 789, Gulf Drive. The Harrington House is on your left on the beach side.

The Curry Mansion Inn 💟
Key West, Florida 33040

INNKEEPERS: Edith and Al Amsterdam

ADDRESS/TELEPHONE: 511 Caroline Street; (305) 294–5349 or (800) 253–3466; fax (305) 294–4093

WEB SITE: www.currymansion.com

E-MAIL: frontdesk@currymansion.com

ROOMS: 28, 4 in main house, 16 in modern addition, 8 in historic house across the street; ceiling fan, refrigerator; ask about small pets; no wheelchair access in mansion.

RATES: Deluxe rooms $150 off-season to $240 in-season, sitting-room suites $200 to $275, including complete breakfast with omelette station; all rooms nonsmoking.

OPEN: Year-round.

FACILITIES AND ACTIVITIES: Swimming pool, hot tub. Nearby: Duval Street, Mallory Square, Ernest Hemingway Home and Museum, Audubon House, Key West Lighthouse, Mel Fisher's Maritime Museum, restaurants, shops, bars, beach, golf, tennis, diving, fishing, North America's only living coral reef, seaplane adventures, sight-seeing boat, Key West Aquarium, Conch Tour Train, Old Town Trolley, bicycle and moped rentals.

BUSINESS TRAVEL: Fax and computer available.

*F*unky Key West is mainly comprised of small century-old cottages. An exception is the palatial three-story, multigabled Curry Mansion, a Classic Revival home completed in 1899. William Curry, a Bahamian immigrant who earned his fortune as a salvager—those scurrilous fellows who preyed on shipwrecks in Florida's pirate-infested waters—is believed to have been Key West's first millionaire.

Curry began building his home in 1855. Architectural details include a widow's walk, ornate trellises and balustrades, and columns, colonnades, and verandas. Curry didn't get to see the construction to its completion, however. His son Milton finished the house in 1899 and furnished it with eighteenth- and nineteenth-century antiques that still grace the parlor today.

How did Edith and Al Amsterdam, who were the successful proprietors of upstate New York's Casa Blanca, end up owning and operating an inn in Key West? In 1975 the Amsterdams brought their yacht into Key West's harbor and were going for a stroll when Edith spied the wedding-cake mansion. As luck would have it, it was for sale. The rest, as they say, is history. The bed-and-breakfast they created has been named the best in Key West six out of nine years and one of the nation's top ten by INNovations National Network Services.

The antique-filled bedchambers in the mansion were created from the original master suite, the children's room, and the nanny's room. A contemporary addition provides sixteen more rooms, which are similarly furnished and decorated; they just lack the architectural detailing of the main house. There are also another eight rooms in the historic home across the street.

Lucky guests in the opulent two-room Master Suite enjoy a king-size bed and a whirlpool tub. This is the perfect luxurious hideaway for honeymooners and other romantics. The long-ago children and their nanny surely didn't have it anywhere near as good as today's guests who stay in their former rooms, one of which now boasts a queen-size brass bed and the other of which features a queen-size canopy bed.

Haviland china and faux replicas of the Curry family's solid-gold Tiffany flatware create the backdrop for the elegant breakfast buffet, which is laden with freshly baked bagels, muffins, and pastries as well as fresh tropical fruit, cereals, and at least one hot specialty item. Every afternoon the Curry Mansion sponsors a complimentary cocktail party for its guests.

Although most guests like to hang out by the pool and hot tub, we all have to be careful about too much sun these days, so take advantage of some of the mansion's many public rooms, including the music room, the library loaded with Hemingway memorabilia, and the third-floor billiard room.

For those not fortunate enough to stay at the Curry Mansion, tours are offered from 10:00 A.M. to 5:00 P.M.

HOW TO GET THERE: When arriving in Key West via U.S. 1, bear right, following U.S. 1 south about 3 miles to Duval Street, and turn right. Go 10 blocks to Caroline Street and turn right. The Curry Mansion is a ¼ block on the left.

Chalet Suzanne
Lake Wales, Florida 33853

INNKEEPER: Vita Hinshaw

ADDRESS/TELEPHONE: 3800 Chalet Suzanne Drive; (863) 676-6011 or (800) 433-6011 (reservations only); fax (863) 676-1814

WEB SITE: www.chaletsuzanne.com

E-MAIL: info@chaletsuzanne.com

ROOMS: 30; all with private bath, private entrance, cable TV, telephone, clock radio, robes, fresh flowers, fruit, candy, and sherry. Seven with jetted tubs. Hair dryer, iron and ironing board, VCR, and coffeemaker available. Some rooms are wheelchair accessible.

RATES: $169 to $229, double; includes full country breakfast for two. Additional person $12 plus meals. No pets. Summer, honeymoon, and anniversary packages available. Credit cards accepted.

OPEN: Year-round.

FACILITIES AND ACTIVITIES: Daily lunch and dinner in award-winning restaurant; wheelchair access to dining room. Cocktail lounge, wine cellar open for sampling, gift shop, antiques shop, ceramics studio, pool, lake, soup cannery, airstrip. New in 2001: Chalet Suzanne Museum. Nearby: Golf, tennis, fishing, Cypress Gardens, Bok Tower Gardens.

BUSINESS TRAVEL: Conference facilities; access to fax; telephone in room.

*E*veryone who writes about this inn falters under the burden of trying to describe what they've seen—a collection of whimsical, odd buildings assembled over a number of years by Vita Hinshaw's mother-in-law. We've seen the words *Camelot, phantasmagoria, fairy tale,* and *magical,* in the reviews of writers trying to capture the mood of the place. Any and all will do. Staying here is a great giggle for anyone who doesn't like too many straight lines, who enjoys walks and walls that tilt, and who appreciates the kind of humor represented by a potted geranium atop the ice machine. The venerable old inn is showing some wear and tear, but it just adds to the charm.

We enjoyed the Orchid Room, a roughly octagonal space where sherry and fruit were set out on a small table between two comfortable chairs. Live plants and fresh flowers are scattered throughout the room and its bath, and the furniture was painted various shades of aqua, cream, and deep orchid. The bath has been updated and features a whirlpool-jet tub and new tile.

Chalet Suzanne is famous for its award-winning restaurant, in which the tables are all set with different kinds of china, silver, and glasses collected by the Hinshaw family over years of travel. Romaine soup, broiled grapefruit garnished with chicken livers, and the shrimp curry are all much-extolled selections, so we tried them all with a nice house wine dispensed in generous servings. We enjoyed everything, including being served by costumed waitresses in the Swiss dining room, where European stained-glass windows provide a focal point.

The innkeeper's late husband, Carl Hinshaw, made soups that became so popular that he started a cannery on the premises for people who want to take soup home. The soup is sold in better gourmet shops and was even taken to the moon by the Apollo astronauts.

So there you are, in a wacky, unreal environment, eating food that's been to the moon, served by waitresses dressed like Snow White, and you're sleeping in a room that looks like it came out of a fairy tale. How are you going to describe it? You're not—so simply enjoy.

HOW TO GET THERE: Chalet Suzanne is 4 miles north of Lake Wales on Chalet Suzanne Road, which turns off Highway 27. Signs clearly mark the turns.

Little Palm Island Resort and Spa
Little Torch Key, Florida 33042

INNKEEPERS: Ben Woodson, owner; Michel Neutlings, director

ADDRESS/TELEPHONE: 28500 Overseas Highway; (305) 872-2524, (800) 343-8567, or (800) 3-GET-LOST; fax (305) 872-4843

WEB SITE: www.littlepalmisland.com

E-MAIL: reservations@littlepalmisland.com

ROOMS: 28 one-bedroom, thatched-roof oceanfront bungalow suites, all with king-size bed, living room, private bath with whirlpool tub, indoor and outdoor showers, private veranda, ceiling fan, air-conditioning, coffeemaker, wet bar/minibar. Two exclusive Island Grand suites have his-and-her bathrooms and outdoor hot tub. Some rooms are handicapped accessible. No smoking. No telephones or televisions.

RATES: Four seasonal prices ranging from $550 to $1,200 in the lowest season to $795 to $1,695 in the highest, include launch service to and from the island, daily newspaper, and use of swimming pool, sauna, exercise room, kayaks and canoes, sailboards and instruction, Hobie day sailers, snorkel and fishing gear, beach lounges, towels, and floats. Suites will sleep four adults; additional persons, $100 per night. Full American dining plan is available for $140 per person per day; modified American plan $125 per person per day. Holiday meals may be subject to a meal plan surcharge. Wedding and other special packages available. Minimum stay requirement for weekends and holidays.

OPEN: Year-round.

FACILITIES AND ACTIVITIES: Full-service luxury spa, water sports, fishing tournaments, scuba diving and certification, snorkeling, fishing charters, backcountry and flats fishing, pontoon boat rental, natural-history backcountry ecotours.

BUSINESS TRAVEL: Ideal for small corporate meetings and retreats.

A mere five-acre private island located 3 miles offshore from Little Torch Key midway down the Keys, Little Palm Island's location at the entrance to Newfound Harbor and its fast-running tides created a white sandy beach and deepwater dockage sure to please any adventurer.

Accessible only by boat, the palm-ringed island's lush grounds are home to flamboyant bougainvillea, oleander, hibiscus, and other vibrant tropical blooms. Scattered among this profuse vegetation, and very subdued in contrast, are fourteen thatched-roof villas on stilts—like charming tree houses. Designed for seclusion,  each villa houses two luxurious ocean-view suites. The interior of each features a sitting room and bedroom decorated and furnished as a tropical retreat with bold, bright colors; plantation shutters; and ceiling fans and a luxurious bath with a Jacuzzi. You'll love the romantic mosquito netting draped over the bed. Although the villas are air-conditioned, with an average year-round temperature of 76.8 degrees, you'll prefer to enjoy the fresh air and natural breezes.

Our idea of a really strenuous day is breakfast on our deck, then spending some time on the pristine white beach with a good book, followed by a dip in the aquamarine Gulf waters or the lagoon-style freshwater pool with its tinkling waterfall, followed by a nap in a hammock strung between two palms, punctuated by a snack or a cool drink, and finally ending the day sitting on our private veranda sipping a frosty cocktail while contemplating the sunset—all the while serenaded by colorful birds and fanned by ocean breezes. Ah, it's all so exotic and seductive. Another day, maybe, we'll have a massage in the massage tree house, where fresh breezes and birdsong blow through the windows, or avail ourselves of some spa services.

An alternative activity might be standing on the main dock looking west to Loggerhead Key, where 2,000 rhesus monkeys live, or waiting quietly in the evening to see the endangered Key deer feeding on the hibiscus and the herbs in the kitchen garden. During the day, watch the wading birds such as the roseate spoonbill.

For those who are more active, there's plenty to do. They can snorkel or dive to explore Looe Key reef—one of the prettiest in the world—where the HMS *Looe* sank in 1744 after hitting it. Looe Key National Marine Sanctuary is rated as one of the top ten reefs in the world and is the only living reef in North America. Scuba and sailing certification courses are offered, as are fishing charters and pontoon boat rentals. Environmentalists will appreciate a visit to bird rookeries and wilderness sanctuaries in the backcountry of the Great White Heron National Wildlife Refuge.

The only problem we experience with all this inactivity is the calories that don't get burned off from the award-winning French cuisine accented with Caribbean flavors. Meals are served in the spacious, airy dining room on the terrace or, more romantic to us, right on the beach. Chef Adam Votaw creates a six-course gourmet feast each Thursday and is renowned for his Sunday brunch and holiday offerings. Because the island is so close to the mainland, folks come over by boat to dine at Little Palm Island (by reservation only). Every night reveals a new delicacy to savor, such as lobster and stone crab soup, smoked salmon parfait with Belgian endive and green apple, Chef Adam's signature rack of lamb, or crab cakes—all culminated by a mouthwatering dessert such as coconut cream–filled chocolate ravioli with praline sauce.

Is it any surprise that Little Palm Island has been named one of the twelve most romantic hotels in the country? Come find out for yourself.

HOW TO GET THERE: Take U.S. 1 from Miami through the Keys to Little Torch Key, then the launch to Little Palm Island.

Herlong Mansion
Bed and Breakfast Inn
Micanopy, Florida 32667

INNKEEPERS:
Julie and Lon Boggs

ADDRESS/TELEPHONE: 402
Cholokka Boulevard (mailing
address: P.O. Box 667); (352)
466-3322 between 8:00 A.M. and
9:00 P.M. or (800) HERLONG;
fax is the same.

WEB SITE: www.herlong.com

E-MAIL: info@herlong.com

ROOMS: 11, including rooms, suites, and cottages, all with private bath;
some with whirlpool tub, fireplace, coffeemaker, robes, private veranda
or porch, wheelchair access.

RATES: $89 to $189, double, including Southern gourmet breakfast; single $5.00 less; additional person $20. Children welcome. Credit cards
accepted. Ask about special packages.

OPEN: Year-round.

FACILITIES AND ACTIVITIES: Wraparound verandas. Nearby: 18 individually owned antiques shops, Smiley's Antique Mall with 200 vendors,
Micanopy Historical Museum, Payne's Prairie State Preserve, Lake
Wauberg, boating, fishing, camping, bird-watching, horseback riding,
Cross Creek (home of Marjorie Kinnan Rawlings). Short drive to
Gainesville (10 miles) and Ocala (30 miles).

BUSINESS TRAVEL: Fax and Internet access available.

This bed-and-breakfast is an eyepopper. The imposing building
you see today has a wide front veranda with four two-story
Roman Corinthian columns carved from wood. However, the
original was a two-story Victorian house with a detached kitchen that was
built about 1845. In 1910 the owners built a brick Classical Revival imitation
of a Southern colonial design all the way around it—sort of a house within a
house.

Inside, all the guest rooms and public areas, which have 12-foot-high ceilings, are exceptionally spacious. You can prowl through the place and inspect leaded-glass windows, ten fireplaces, inlaid floors of oak and maple, and glorious floor-to-ceiling windows in the dining room.

The guest rooms variously have canopy beds, private porches, claw-foot tubs, white wicker furniture, and gas-log fireplaces, depending on the room. They're all tasteful and pretty.

Then we have Inez. This resident ghost has become a topic of much interest. Over blueberry waffle breakfasts, the owners and guests discuss the peculiar and inexplicable little episodes that keep happening in one of the guest rooms. Could Inez also have something to do with strange noises coming from a room with a hidden outside entrance under the house? Nobody knows what the room was for. Bootleg liquor? Hiding runaway slaves? Insane aunts? Well, Inez has been busy enough that now you can even pick up a T-shirt at Herlong Mansion that says, I SAW INEZ.

HOW TO GET THERE: From I–75, take exit 73 and go east ½ mile. At the HISTORIC MICANOPY sign, turn right. The road ends in less than a mile in downtown Micanopy. The inn is 1½ blocks farther on your left.

Lakeside Inn 👥
Mount Dora, Florida 32757

INNKEEPER: James Barggren, general manager

ADDRESS/TELEPHONE: 100 North Alexander Street; (352) 383–4101 or (800) 556–5016; fax (352) 735–2642

WEB SITE: www.lakeside-inn.com.

E-MAIL: Via Web site.

ROOMS: 88 rooms and suites, all with private bath, cable television, telephone; smoking and nonsmoking rooms available; limited access for the disabled.

RATES: There are three seasons: January 1 through May 15, May 16 through September 30, and October 1 through December 31. On top of that, there are selected weekends when price is affected. Lakefront rooms and suites cost more than others. In general, weekday rates range from $125 to $205 and weekend and holiday rates from $175 to $235, single or double occupancy; includes continental breakfast. An occupancy charge of $10 per person is levied for additional persons in the room.

OPEN: Year-round.

FACILITIES AND ACTIVITIES: The Beauclaire dining room restaurant, Tremain's Lounge, room service, Olympic-size pool and towel service, tennis courts, croquet; Mount Dora trolley stops at the inn; variety of boat rentals by the hour or day, carriage rides; live entertainment mid-week through the weekend. Nearby: Antiques shopping, golf, Ice House Theater, concerts, exhibitions at the Mount Dora Center for the Arts, Royellou Museum, Gilbert Park, Palm Island Park, House of Presidents wax museum, Lakeridge Winery, Yalaha Bakery, horseback riding in Ocala National Forest.

BUSINESS TRAVEL: 25 miles north of Orlando; 5 meeting rooms and lobby can accommodate up to 125 for small meetings and retreats.

Follow the quiet lane lined with lampposts to the shores of central Florida's Lake Dora and go back in time to the Lakeside Inn of yesteryear. Beginning with a modest ten rooms in 1883, the original inn was expanded over many years until it reached its current size of eighty-eight rooms in the early 1930s. The 1920s, the Gatsby era, saw the inn's heyday. It is the ambience, traditions, and hospitality of the 1920s and 1930s that today's proprietors strive to evoke in this English country-style refuge. Permeated with history and infused with romance, this venerable hostelry has been a perennial favorite as a winter haven for all kinds of travelers.

Although this venerable old duchess is showing some wear and tear, we think it's a little bit of heaven to step onto the sweeping verandas cooled by paddle fans and comfortably furnished with colonial rockers, from which you can watch the stirring sunsets over the lake. In less-than-perfect weather, it's fun to gather in the ballroom-size lobby for fireside chats, games, and tea dances. Evenings are the time to enjoy vibrant conversation and vintage music in Tremaine's Lounge. Almost any time of day is perfect to dine on epicurean delights in The Beauclaire, the award-winning restaurant. Continental breakfast is included in the room rate, but you can also order more substantial breakfast items a la carte; a sumptuous brunch is served on Sunday. Light lunch items are served Monday through Saturday. Reservations are strongly recommended for dinner in The Beauclaire.

Guest rooms are sure to please whether they have two twin beds, one or two doubles, or a king-size bed. Parlor rooms boast a similar deluxe guest room with an additional connecting room, which serves as a cozy parlor. In most cases the parlor has a sofa bed to accommodate children or additional travelers. Naturally, the most sought-after rooms are the lakefront ones. One in particular boasts a private balcony with rocking chairs.

For the sports enthusiast, the pool is open year-round, and there are two lighted tennis courts, a croquet lawn, and boat rentals. The inn serves as the base for the Mount Dora annual sailing regatta, the oldest in the state. Angling for bass and catfish is a longtime tradition, and bird-watching is just as popular as it was when the inn was founded.

HOW TO GET THERE: Take U.S. 441 to FL 46, then exit west to FL 500A West. Follow FL 500A West (it becomes Highland Avenue). Turn left onto Fifth Avenue, then left on Alexander Street.

Riverview Hotel ¢¢¢
New Smyrna Beach, Florida 32169

INNKEEPERS: Jim and Christa Kelsey

ADDRESS/TELEPHONE: 103 Flagler Avenue; (904) 428–5858 or (800) 945–7416; fax (904) 423–8927

WEB SITE: www.riverviewhotel.com

E-MAIL: rvhotel@aol.com

ROOMS: 18, all with private bath, robes, television, telephone with data-port, ceiling fan; some with desk.

RATES: $90 to $100 rooms, $115 to $135 suites, $200 cottage for 4, all including expanded continental breakfast, use of bicycles, evening turn-down service.

OPEN: Year-round.

FACILITIES AND ACTIVITIES: Riverview Charlie's Seafood Grill, heated pool, gift shop, Intracoastal Waterway. Nearby: Beaches, fishing.

"This looks like Key West or the Caribbean," we said as we pulled up to this small historic hotel located on the Intracoastal Waterway. Multiple stories are enveloped in wraparound porches filled with rockers. Plantation shutters shade all the windows and doors but allow the soothing breeze to enter. A tin roof creates a pleasant patter when it rains. Tropical vegetation surrounds the building and pool.

As it turns out, our first impression was exactly what Jim and Christa want to convey. They lived for ten years in Marathon, Florida, in the Keys and looked for an inn that would let them retain the look and charm of the Keys as well as the laid-back way of life.

The elegantly restored hotel was built in 1885, and part of its appeal is that every room opens onto one of the verandas, so you're only a few steps away from a rocking chair and a delightful view of the Intracoastal Waterway or the tropical courtyard surrounding the pool.

Guest rooms are simple and reflect century-old charm. Most have plaster walls, although a few have beaded paneling. Victorian-era reproductions add just the right touch. Ceiling fans and bright tropical bedspreads create a cheery, beachy ambience. All the modern conveniences have been unobtrusively added, not the least of which is a private bath, and there are also a television and telephone.

In the morning luxuriate with a breakfast of fresh fruit, cereals, and muffins brought to your room. Then wander over to the pool or sit out on the dock to fish or watch the boat traffic. The ocean is only a few blocks away. If hunger strikes, Riverview Charlie's serves lunch and dinner. Depending on the weather, you can dine in the relaxed atmosphere indoors or on the deck overlooking the Intracoastal Waterway.

HOW TO GET THERE: Take I–95 to the New Smyrna Beach exit (84) at Route 44. Go east and follow the signs to the beaches. After you go over the Intracoastal Waterway on the high-rise bridge, take the first left at the traffic light on South Peninsula Avenue. Go straight past the stop sign until you come to the next traffic light. Turn left on Flagler Avenue. Turn left into the parking lot before reaching the bridge.

Seven Sisters Inn
Ocala, Florida 34471

INNKEEPERS: Bonnie Morehardt and Ken Oden

ADDRESS/TELEPHONE: 820 Southeast Fort King Street;
(352) 867–1170 or (800) 250–3496; fax (352) 867–5266

WEB SITE: www.7sistersinn.com

E-MAIL: sistersinn@aol.com

ROOMS: 13; all with private bath; 8 with fireplace; 1 on first floor with wheelchair access and equipped for handicapped. No-smoking inn.

RATES: $99 to $269, depending on season, single or double; additional person $25; includes full breakfast and five-course gourmet dinner, newspaper and afternoon tea. Inquire about senior and military rates. Not appropriate for children younger than 12.

OPEN: Year-round.

FACILITIES AND ACTIVITIES: Club room, smoking porches, bicycles. Nearby: Walking distance to restaurants, historic downtown, antiques and gift shops; short drive to Silver Springs Park, Appleton Art Museum.

BUSINESS TRAVEL: Scott Room has desk with private phone and computer setup; corporate rates.

The Seven Sisters Inn started as a family home in 1888. The rooms on the upper two floors are named for the seven sisters of the woman who renovated the building in 1985. The decor of each room reflects the interests of each of the sisters, and you'll find a picture of each lady somewhere in her room. Accommodations range from the truly lavish formal room fit for a king and queen to county casual. Lottie's Loft is one of the most whimsical rooms we've ever seen anywhere. The entire third floor has been transformed into a beach getaway. A wall of Welly blue glass forms a wavelike boundary to separate the stairwell from the main part of the room. The oversized whirlpool tub sits under a skylight and is bordered with black and white tiles embellished with fish. Beach umbrellas, beach chairs, beach toys, beach towels, and fabrics reminiscent of the seashore complete the scene. The only thing missing is the sand. The downstairs room that is equipped for the handicapped really works because a member of the family who lived here was handicapped.

Special weekends are offered, ranging from slick murder mysteries to scavenger hunts and chocolate extravaganzas. There often are wine-tasting weekends, cooking classes, Friday-night bistros, and theater packages, too.

In the morning, you'll be treated to a special breakfast. Unusual juices, such as pear nectar, are served, followed by fresh fruit and cream and specialties such as blueberry French toast.

Apparently things were too calm around the inn, so the innkeepers bought the historic house next door and added six more rooms. These are more exotic than those in the main house, reflecting the breadth of Bonnie and Ken's worldwide travels. Each bedchamber represents one of their favorite destinations: Argentina, Egypt, India, Paris, China, and Bali. All the furniture and accessories were purchased during their travels. These rooms boast hydro showers, fireplaces, whirlpool tubs, and much more.

When it originally opened, Seven Sisters Inn occasionally served candlelight dinners for small groups and dinner buffets for some of the special weekends. However, bowing to demand, the inn is now deep into the dinner trade. The new rates now include a five-course gourmet dinner in addition to the sumptuous breakfast. A pure B&B rate is also available for those who insist on going elsewhere for dinner.

HOW TO GET THERE: From I-75, take exit 69 onto State Road 40, which becomes Silver Springs Boulevard downtown. Turn right at Southeast Ninth Avenue and right again in the next block at Southeast Fort King Street.

The River Suites at Club Continental 💟 👥
Orange Park, Florida 32073

INNKEEPER: Karrie Massee Stevens

ADDRESS/TELEPHONE: 2143 Astor Street (mailing address P.O. Box 7100); (904) 264-6070 or (800) 877-6070; fax (904) 215-9503

WEB SITE: www.bbonline.com/fl/clubcontinental

E-MAIL: ccsinfo@bellsouth.net

ROOMS: 22, all with private bath, cable television, telephone, ceiling fan; some with refrigerator, microwave, fireplace, whirlpool tub, private balcony, wheelchair access. Pets allowed in 2 rooms. Some smoking rooms.

RATES: $75 to $160, including continental breakfast. Weekend Escape packages. Children welcome. Credit cards accepted.

OPEN: Year-round.

FACILITIES AND ACTIVITIES: Riverfront location, marina space by reservation, expansive grounds, 2 swimming pools, whirlpool, 7 tennis courts, restaurant, pub. Nearby: Antiques shopping, fishing, golf, parks, sporting events, theater.

BUSINESS TRAVEL: Ideal for corporate functions; conference rooms, fax, copier.

Club Continental is a place where you can get away from it all and do nothing or indulge in some laid-back activities. Located just 10 miles south of busy Jacksonville, this elegant estate is nevertheless a quiet oasis overlooking the widest part of the St. Johns River. We felt as if we'd been transported to an old-world Mediterranean estate.

The monumental villa that occupies the heart of the property was built in 1923 as the family residence of Caleb Johnson, founder of the Palmolive Soap Company. The architecture of the grand villa is Mediterranean stucco topped by a clay tile roof. In the manner of European estates, it is surrounded by extensive formal gardens and elegant courtyards as well as wide lawns shaded by giant oaks. Spanish moss wafts gently in the breeze.

Still lovingly preserved by Johnson descendants, the estate today operates as The River Suites at Club Continental—a quiet retreat in its own hushed world, one that offers a wide array of special privileges to members and overnight guests. Be sure to spend some time in the small hidden garden on the banks of the river, where a wall has been created using tiles autographed by celebrities. See whose inscription you can find. If you desire more active pursuits, swim some laps in one of the pools or play a few sets of tennis.

The original manor house, Mira Rio, contains opulent formal public rooms and seven guest rooms with old-world charm coupled with modern conveniences. The fifteen River Suites, in another building constructed to complement the original house and being of more recent vintage, boast even more amenities. These suites boast dynamic views of the St. Johns River, and many feature a fireplace and/or whirlpool tub. As you might imagine, these guest chambers are sought by honeymooners and those celebrating an anniversary or other special occasion, but you don't need an excuse to pamper yourselves in luxury.

At Club Continental, attention to detail is observed in many ways—not the least of which is the exquisite presentation of delicious classic continental cuisine in the dining room, where lunch and dinner are served Tuesday through Friday as well as brunch on Sunday.

HOW TO GET THERE: From I-295, take exit 3 in Orange Park. Go south 2 miles to Kingsley Avenue and turn left. Go 2 blocks to Astor Street and turn right to the inn.

The Courtyard at Lake Lucerne
Orlando, Florida 32801

INNKEEPER: Eleanor Meiner

ADDRESS/TELEPHONE: 211 North Lucerne Circle East; (407) 648–5188
or (800) 444–5289; fax (407) 246–1368

WEB SITE: www.orlandohistoricinn.com

E-MAIL: Via Web site

ROOMS: 30 in 4 buildings, all with private bath, television, and
telephone; some with steam shower and oversized whirlpool tub;
some with small kitchen. No-smoking building.

RATES: $89 to $225, single or double; includes continental buffet
breakfast, wine in room, and cocktail party.

OPEN: Year-round.

FACILITIES AND ACTIVITIES: Restaurant, courtyard gardens, reception
areas. Nearby: Lake Cherokee Historic District trail begins here; walking
distance to restaurants and downtown Orlando; health club facilities,
golf and tennis can be arranged; sailing on Lake Eola; 20-minute drive
to Walt Disney World, Splendid China, and other regional theme attractions.

BUSINESS TRAVEL: Located 5 minutes from business district. Telephone and good work space in room; fax, copy machine, and computer
setup available; conference facilities; corporate rates.

The accommodations at this gracious inn are contained in four separate historic buildings from three distinct eras grouped around a
20,000-square-foot semitropical garden. The Norment-Parry,
Orlando's oldest house, is Victorian; the Wellborn is an excellent example of
Art Deco architecture and decor; the I. W. Phillips House is a West Indies–style
manor house furnished in Edwardian and Eastlake antiques; and the Dr.
Phillip Phillips House is an impressive Neoclassical mansion. If you look at
the whole place at once, you are simply overwhelmed with color, design, and
antiques.

Since many of the rooms look onto the garden, let's start there. Orlando
is a good place to grow tropicals. What Eleanor Meiner's daughter-in-law,
Paula, has done with this garden enchants you. The lines are curved rather
than straight and stiff, the walks are old brick for a softer appearance, and
the plants are an astonishing collection of azaleas, bird-of-paradise, helico-
nia, bougainvillea, ginger, banana trees, 80-foot camphor trees, and scores of

other plants, familiar and rare.

You find more vivid colors in the guest rooms. For example, in the Norment-Parry, each of the six guest rooms, four of which have sitting rooms, has been decorated by a different architect, artist, or designer.

The jazzy Art Deco decor of the Wellborn gives the impression that a well-to-do family of the 1930s has simply stepped out for the day. A particularly sophisticated parlor in this house sports a black-and-white zebra print sofa sitting against a brilliant red wall. One of the honeymoon suites is in this house.

The I. W. Phillips House is furnished in Belle Epoque style. French doors open out to verandas overlooking the garden. The three luxury rooms feature double tubs and, in one, a steam room and whirlpool.

A conference room at the rear of the I. W. Phillips House opens from the downstairs reception room through pocketed mirror French doors.

The Dr. Phillip Phillips House, which was built in 1893, was reopened to the public in 1999 after extensive renovations. The downstairs is devoted to a fine-dining establishment and the two upstairs floors to guest rooms. Furnished with impressive antiques and fine artwork, these bedchambers feature oversized whirlpool tubs. A few rooms still spotlight original hardwood floors and fireplaces.

For all the glamour, the staff are pleasant, unpretentious, and very helpful. Once you get your senses calmed down and can appreciate one thing at a time, this is an easy place to be.

HOW TO GET THERE: From I-4 going east, take the Anderson exit. At the stop light at the top of the ramp, turn right. Go three lights and turn right onto Delaney Avenue. Take the first right onto Lucerne Circle North. Going west on I-4, take the Anderson Street exit, go four lights, turn right onto Delaney, and almost immediately take the first right onto Lucerne Circle North.

Palm Beach Historic Inn
Palm Beach, Florida 33480

INNKEEPERS: Sean and Jody Herbert

ADDRESS/TELEPHONE: 365 South County Road; (561) 832–4009;
fax (561) 832–6255

WEB SITE: www.palmbeachhistoricinn.com

E-MAIL: innkeeper@palmbeachhistoricinn.com

ROOMS: 9, plus 4 suites, all with private bath, refrigerator, cable television, telephone, and robes.

RATES: $85 to $175 in low season (May 15 through December 14), $150 to $325 the rest of the year; single or double occupancy, includes deluxe continental breakfast, morning newspaper, beach chairs, towels, and umbrellas.

OPEN: Year-round.

FACILITIES AND ACTIVITIES: Nearby: 1 block to the beach, 2 blocks to Worth Avenue; casual and gourmet dining, art galleries, antiques shops, specialty boutiques, golf, tennis, horseback riding, polo, croquet, jai alai, greyhound racing, performing arts, cruise ships, museums, zoo, planetarium, botanical gardens, water sports.

We admit it—we were starstruck by the glitz and glamour and rarified atmosphere of enchanting, tropical Palm Beach, especially the Henry Morrison Flagler Museum and the tony boutiques and galleries on Worth Avenue. Just about everything there might be way, way out of our price range, but it's oh so much fun to look. And never have we seen such a concentration of shiny Rolls Royces.

The good news is, you don't have to be a multimillionaire to stay in Palm Beach. Although there are plenty of hotels with astronomical prices, there is a secret little historic gem of a B&B inn where you can stay in luxury on a regular person's salary.

Located in a landmark Moorish-style building with numerous arches and a red tile roof, the inn has been carefully restored to preserve its structural integrity and refined elegance, while adding every modern convenience.

The look and feel of an intimate European parlor characterize the lobby. Spacious, high-ceilinged guest rooms are tastefully appointed with antiques and reproductions as well as opulent bed coverings and elegant window treatments. Beds, many of which are romantic four-posters, testers, or half-testers, range in size from doubles to kings. Several particularly spacious bedchambers and two-room suites feature a trundle bed, additional twin beds, and/or a sofa bed to accommodate additional travelers in your party, making them ideal for families or friends traveling together.

You'll get your day off to a good start with a sumptuous continental-plus breakfast served in your room and accompanied by the morning newspaper. Through careful attention to every service detail, the staff has your utmost comfort in mind. You'll feel like royalty when you stay at the Palm Beach Historic Inn.

HOW TO GET THERE: From I–95, exit at Okeechobee Boulevard East. From the Florida Turnpike, exit at 99, West Palm Beach. Drive east on Okeechobee Boulevard and cross over the bridge to Palm Beach onto Royal Palm Way. Turn right onto A1A and drive south to 365 South County Road. The inn is opposite the historic city hall.

Kenwood
St. Augustine, Florida 32084

INNKEEPERS: Mark, Kerrianne, and Caitlin Constant

ADDRESS/TELEPHONE: 38 Marine Street; (904) 824–2116 or (800) 824–8151; fax (904) 824–1689

WEB SITE: www.oldcity.com/kenwood

ROOMS: 10, plus 3 two-room suites and 1 three-room suite, all with private bath; none are handicapped accessible. No-smoking inn.

RATES: $85 to $200, double, includes continental breakfast; daily wine hour, cookies, sherry, coffee and tea, cold drinks, use of inn bicycles. Two-night minimum on weekends. Reduced and single rates available Monday through Thursday. Unable to accommodate children 8 and younger. Credit cards accepted.

OPEN: Year-round.

FACILITIES AND ACTIVITIES: Swimming pool. Nearby: Restaurants, St. Augustine historic sites and tourist activities; short drive to ocean beaches.

*K*enwood gets better and better. The story of this B&B inn is interesting. A number of years ago the building languished as a dilapidated boardinghouse. It was purchased by owners whose specialty was renovation, and they set about restoring it to soundness and safety, named it Kenwood, and started modest operations as an inn. When they went on to their next project, the new owners continued improving the property and ran Kenwood in their own laid-back style until health problems eventually forced them to give it up.

Then the Constant family entered the scene. Mark and Kerrianne were innkeepers in New England who, like so many visitors, got the St. Augustine I-wanna-stay bug. Caitlin, their daughter, was too young to do much innkeeping in New England, but she's rapidly growing into it all in St. Augustine. Kenwood is definitely a family project now.

The Constants are adding even more improvements at Kenwood. They've redone the courtyard and gardens to include a great variety of tropical plants and lots of colorful blooms. The swimming pool sits in the newly landscaped area like a summertime jewel.

Mark and Kerrianne brought many of their favorite antiques from New England and have mixed these antiques with comfortable couches and chairs in cool greens, creams, and rose. We especially like the way they've arranged furniture into several groupings so that people can gather in any one of several places at any time. It is not unusual to find three different, animated conversations going on.

We had a lot of conversation at breakfast, too, inspired mostly by Kerrianne's unusual offerings. We got into much "What do you think this is?" and "Oh, taste this, it's marvelous" as we nibbled our way through several generous trays full of goodies.

When we weren't talking about food, we were asking Kerrianne questions about her family in New York, and, this sounds awful, we were cracking up at how she could turn what should have been disastrous episodes into funny stories. It tells you something about Kerri's style that she did all this casually dressed.

Mark's approach is relaxed, too. We kept trying to move from the entrance to a far corner of the living room without walking on an especially lovely, pale Oriental carpet. Mark kept laughing at us and saying that in New Hampshire everyone walked over it with slush on their boots.

HOW TO GET THERE: From I–95 South, exit to Route 16 east. At the end of Route 16, turn right onto San Marco Boulevard. After the fifth set of lights, bear right onto Marine Street. The inn is 2 blocks on the right. From I–95 North, take exit 94 to Route 207. At the end of Route 207, turn left onto Route 1 North. At the first set of lights, turn right onto King Street. At the end of King Street, turn right and immediately bear right at the fork onto Marine Street. The inn is 2 blocks on the right. Parking is on Marine Street and in a private lot 1 block from the inn.

St. Francis Inn
St. Augustine, Florida 32084

INNKEEPER: Joe Finnegan

ADDRESS/TELEPHONE: 279 St. George Street; (904) 824–6068 or (800) 824–6062; fax (904) 810–5523

WEB SITE: www.stfrancisinn.com

E-MAIL: innceased@aug.com

ROOMS: 11 rooms and suites, 2-bedroom cottage, 3-bedroom cottage for groups only; all with private bath, telephone, cable television, hair dryer, iron and ironing board, clock radio, ceiling fan, queen- or king-size bed; some with electric fireplace, kitchenette, whirlpool tub, sleeper sofa.

RATES: $85 to $149 weekdays; $95 to $195 weekends, holidays, or special events for double occupancy; includes full breakfast, evening social hour, use of bicycles, and admission to the St. Augustine Lighthouse. Add $15 for each additional person. Several packages available. Credit cards accepted. No-smoking inn.

OPEN: Year-round.

FACILITIES AND ACTIVITIES: Swimming pool, courtyards, gardens, private parking. Nearby: Historic St. Augustine, Castillo de San Marcos, restaurants, museums, galleries, antiques shopping, boutiques, narrated trolley or horse-and-buggy tours, water sports, beaches, St. Augustine Lighthouse.

BUSINESS TRAVEL: 3-bedroom house for groups; 3 conference areas; audiovisual equipment; Internet access; fax, copier, and secretarial services; complete food and beverage service.

When we visited St. Augustine for the first time, we instantly fell in love with the restored old Spanish town, as almost everyone does who even passes through this country's oldest continuously inhabited city. With the exception of a few cheesy tourist traps, what's not to love? There are ancient (by New World standards) Spanish-influenced homes, churches, commercial buildings, and a fort as well as narrow, old brick-paved streets; charming restaurants; museums; galleries; and shops—all topped off by near perfect weather. There's even a beach nearby.

Although St. Augustine has many charming Victorian-era B&Bs, what could be more natural in America's oldest city than to stay in its oldest lodging, now a B&B inn? Located in St. Augustine Antigua, the restored historic district, the structure in which the St. Francis Inn is housed was originally constructed in 1791 by Señor Gaspar Garcia. As might be expected from a structure so old, the building has many eccentricities. For example, there are no right angles in the building because Señor Garcia's land at the junction of two drunken streets forced him to construct his house as a trapezoid rather than a rectangle.

Step through the wrought-iron fence and under the romantic archway into one of the inn's serene courtyards filled with lush banana trees, flaming bougainvillea, fragrant jasmine, and other exotic flora to experience old St. Augustine coupled with all the modern amenities discriminating travelers of the twenty-first century have come to expect. You'll literally feel all your cares slip away.

Public spaces and bedchambers are tastefully furnished—but not overdone—with simple antiques, tropical art, and Oriental carpets. Exposed ceiling beams, arched doorways and windows, fireplaces with ornate mantelpieces that were added later, and rough plaster walls characterize the public spaces.

Each bedchamber has its own distinct, old-fashioned personality. Rooms might be highlighted by stained-glass windows, a hammered-tin ceiling, a private balcony, or a claw-foot tub. Most feature queen-size beds, a ceiling fan, and an electric fireplace. Several boast a single- or double-size whirlpool tub. Two suites deserve special mention: Elizabeth's Suite features two rooms overlooking St. Francis Park, a fireplace in the bedroom, a double whirlpool tub, and a kitchenette. The Garcia Suite includes the same amenities, as well as a king-size bed. Located in the former cookhouse and slave quarters, the Cottage, which easily sleeps four, has two bedrooms and two baths.

Plan several leisurely days in St. Augustine so that you can indulge in short days of sight-seeing and long respites at the inn. In addition to the early-evening social hour with a wide variety of tasty treats, you'll want to relax in or around the pool and end your day (spring through fall) with warm breezes and the lilting notes of music performed in the candlelit courtyard. Sweet dreams are guaranteed.

HOW TO GET THERE: From the Visitor Information Center and Castillo de San Marcos, follow South Castillo Drive, which merges into Avenida Menendez. Follow it south to St. Francis Street and turn right. Go 3 blocks to St. Georges Street (you'll have passed The Oldest House in the second block). The inn is on the corner.

Josephine's French Country Inn
Seaside, Florida 32459

INNKEEPERS: Bruce and Judy Albert

ADDRESS/TELEPHONE: 38 Seaside Avenue (mailing address P.O. Box 4767); (850) 231-1940 or (800) 848-1840; fax (850) 321-2446

WEB SITE: www.josephineinn.com

E-MAIL: judy@josephineinn.com

ROOMS: 9, all with private bath, television, VCR, telephone, microwave, coffeemaker, refrigerator, and wet bar; 7 have a fireplace; rooms offer queen- or king-size beds; suites feature a full kitchen.

RATES: $200 to $240, includes breakfast.

OPEN: Year-round.

FACILITIES AND ACTIVITIES: Restaurant. Nearby: Art galleries, specialty shops, weekend entertainment, beach and water sports.

BUSINESS TRAVEL: Ask about business rates.

*I*f we hadn't known better ahead of time, we'd have been convinced that the stately Georgian-style mansion with the six soaring pillars across the front was an authentic plantation home. But we were in Seaside, Florida—one of this country's premier experimental planned communities and, in our opinion, an unqualified success. This captivating beach community, which you might recognize from the movie *The Truman Show,* is internationally recognized for its excellence in architectural design. Both *Life* and *Newsweek* magazines have called the small town's beautiful stretch of Gulf of Mexico beach the number-one beach in America.

Located in the heart of this paradise, the elegant, upscale, intimate inn is surrounded by storybook cottages and picture-perfect shops and galleries. Named one of the top inns in the country by *Country Inns* magazine, Josephine's is owned and operated by the Albert family, who offer you all the comforts of home with amenities you expect of a premier hotel.

Each pleasant, light, and airy guest room, named for an infamous character in French history, has unique charm accented by antiques, Battenburg lace, other fine fabrics, and decorative accents. Realizing that vacationers don't always want to go out for meals, the Alberts have equipped each room with a microwave, coffeemaker, and small refrigerator. On the occasional inclement day or late in the evening, you might enjoy the television and VCR, or you might want to while away the hours with a good book on one of the sprawling rocker-filled porches or in one of the common rooms.

You'll wake up with a smile, eager to start the day with a complimentary heart-healthy breakfast of fruits, cereals, yogurts, and signature breads along with a gourmet entree prepared by Bruce, which changes daily.

After a busy day or one spent doing absolutely nothing, enjoy four-star cuisine in the dining room, where romantic candlelight embellishes the richness of mahogany and fine antiques. Your hardest decision of the day might be making a choice from the world-class crab cakes or other seafood dishes, rack of lamb, or filet mignon. Signature dishes are adorned with scented herbs and edible flowers from the Alberts' nearby farm.

HOW TO GET THERE: From U.S. 98, take FL 395 south to FL 30A and turn west to Seaside. Follow the signs to the inn.

Steinhatchee Landing Resort
Steinhatchee, Florida 32359

INNKEEPERS: Dean and Loretta Fowler

ADDRESS/TELEPHONE: P.O. Box 789 (Highway 51 North);
(352) 498-3513 or (800) 584-1709; fax (352) 498-2346

WEB SITE: www.steinhatcheelanding.com

E-MAIL: SLI@INETW.NET

ROOMS: 21 cottages with 1 to 3 bedrooms; all centrally heated and
cooled and with one or more private baths, fully equipped kitchen with
dishwasher, coffeemaker, microwave, laundry, telephone, TV, VCR,
stereo system, barbecue grill, picnic table; some with fireplaces or wood-
stoves; some with whirlpool baths; some handicapped accessible.

RATES: June 25 to September 10, $165 for a 1-bedroom cottage to $350
for a 3-bedroom cottage; September 11 to May 30, $120 to $245;
slightly higher on holiday weekends, when there is a 3-night minimum.
During June, Florida residents can book 1-bedroom units for $500 per
week and 2-bedroom units for $700; July and August are the busiest
months; includes complimentary use of most recreational facilities and
continental breakfast. Ask about honeymoon and other packages, which
include flowers, candles, fruit, champagne, breakfast, and dinner. One
package includes the wedding and many extras.

OPEN: Year-round.

FACILITIES AND ACTIVITIES: Riverside swimming pool and hot tub,
archery range, outdoor barbecue area, basketball, volleyball, badminton,
jogging and nature trails, shuffleboard, bicycles, canoeing, bird-watching,
kiddie playground, fishing, tennis, horseshoes, fitness club, boat docks,
and pontoon boat (pontoon boat, and fitness club are extra). Corral facilities for those who bring their own horse. Nearby: Picturesque fishing village of Steinhatchee, Econfina River State Park, Wakulla Springs State
Park, Manatee Springs, Weeki Wachee Springs, Silver Springs, High
Springs, High Springs Station Museum, Poe Springs Park, Blue Springs,
St. Marks Wildlife Refuge, Suwanee River, Stephen Foster Cultural Center, Forest Capital State Museum, area historical museums, Horseshoe
Beach, Keaton Beach, antiques shopping, restaurants.

BUSINESS TRAVEL: 70 miles from Gainesville, 90 miles from Tallahassee; ideal for small business retreats; audiovisual equipment, food service.

*S*itting on thirty-five acres on the banks of the placid, coffee-colored Steinhatchee River, just 3 miles from the Gulf of Mexico, Steinhatchee Landing Resort contains twenty-one wood-frame, earth-tone, tin-roofed, two-story cottages set under the canopy of shade provided by ancient live oaks and nine other varieties of oak as well as palms, cedars, magnolias, and cypresses in such a way to preserve and protect the lush natural environment and create an intimate, old-fashioned neighborhood atmosphere. Narrow streets are routed around trees and other natural landmarks. Gazebos, wooden bridges, picket fences, fruit orchards, and vegetable and flower gardens transport guests to a quieter place in time. Fittingly, Steinhatchee Landing has been designated as one of eight destinations in the "AAA Audubon Natural Florida Journeys," a listing of places where visitors can learn about the state's ecosystem and wildlife.

Exuding nineteenth-century charm and beauty, the buildings, which include Victorian-style Georgia and Florida "Cracker" cottages, were designed in keeping with Florida heritage. All have screened porches, swings, rockers, and ceiling fans. Historic in concept but modern in amenities, they vary in size and design. An imposing Victorian-style house actually contains three apartments. Although for rent by the night, week, or month, most of the cottages are privately owned and therefore decorated and furnished according to their owners' tastes. Six of the cottages were known as the Spice Girls even before that music group skyrocketed to fame: Cinnamon, Vanilla, Clove, Saffron, Pepper, and Ginger. The Presidential Retreat, a large, homey house, is so named because former first couple Jimmy and Rosalynn Carter stayed there when they hosted a family reunion on the property several years ago. Another cottage boasts three bedrooms and a private screened pool. Every cottage also features a kitchen, living room, and dining room or dining area.

Although it's incredibly easy to do absolutely nothing without a trace of guilt, those who desire a little more activity find myriad choices. Very family-friendly, the resort offers opportunities for swimming, boating, fishing, and much more. Scalloping lends itself to family fun because the shelled seafood is found in shallow, clear water, providing easy targets for children. In fact, the Marine Fisheries Commission reports that the Steinhatchee River surpasses all others in Florida in its scallop population. In addition, bird-watching and nature photography are popular pastimes.

HOW TO GET THERE: Steinhatchee Landing is located on State Road 51, 8 miles west of its intersection with U.S. 19. From north or south, the easiest travel route is I-75, west on U.S. 27, then U.S. 19 to State Road 51.

Governors Inn
Tallahassee, Florida 32301

INNKEEPER: Charles W. Orr, general manager

ADDRESS/TELEPHONE: 209 South Adams Street; (850) 681-6855 or (800) 342-7717 in Florida; fax (850) 222-3105

ROOMS: 40 rooms and suites, all with private bath, telephone, television, writing desk, robes.

RATES: $119 to $149 for rooms, $159 to $229 for junior suites, $179 to $189 for loft bedroom suites, $189 to $219 for suites, single or double occupancy; includes continental breakfast, morning newspaper, cocktail hour, and nightly turndown service; $10 for each additional person; football weekends and some special events require a minimum 2-night stay; rates may be higher during special-event periods.

OPEN: Year-round.

FACILITIES AND ACTIVITIES: Airport transportation service, valet parking, laundry/valet service, room service, access to a nearby fitness club with a pool and hot tub. Nearby: Old and New Capitols, Knott House Museum, Tallahassee Museum, Florida Caverns State Park, Natural Bridge Battlefield State Historic Site, Pebble Hill Plantation, Torreya State Park, Wakulla Springs State Park.

BUSINESS TRAVEL: Meeting space for up to 60; audiovisual equipment; in-room desks; fax and copy service; in-room telephones with dataports on request.

*V*isitors to the state capitol in Tallahassee, official and unofficial, were delighted when a historic commercial building located within sight of the capitol was converted into the intimate Governors Inn, which is the crowning touch in the Adams Street Commons project to reestablish a sense of history to the heart of the city. Restaurants, shops, brick streets and sidewalks, period streetlights, and planters overflowing with flowers and lush greenery round out the attractive project.

You'll know you're in for superior service the minute you pull up in front of the hotel and turn your car over to valet parking. Inside, the inn conveys the slow-paced flavor of a far simpler time coupled with all the modern amenities and services. Instead of a cavernous and often overly ostentatious lobby, there's a small registration area. You step down into a cozy two-story Florida Room where guests congregate for afternoon refreshments, continental breakfast each morning, or informal gatherings throughout the day. Those of you who don't live in Florida might mistake this description for a conservatory-like room filled with plants and blending almost imperceptibly with the outdoors. In the case of the Governors Inn, however, the Florida Room is more like a gentleman's library from the turn of the twentieth century. Richly paneled walls glow in the warm light of reading lamps, and tapestry- and leather-covered furniture provide comfortable seating.

Comfortable guest rooms, some of which are located in a modern addition, are reached by way of a picturesque hallway, the size of a small street, topped with original exposed heart-pine beams and well lit by skylights. Forty bedchambers and suites, which are named for former governors, feature hand-polished antiques such as black-oak desks and rock-maple armoires as well as all the modern creature comforts, such as queen- and king-size beds in many rooms and cable television. For a special event treat yourself to the lovely Spressard Holland Suite with its romantic four-poster bed, separate living room, and whirlpool bath.

We love the comfortable feel of the inn and appreciate its friendly staff. Although many of the guests are high-powered legislators, lobbyists, and others on government business, each and every guest—no matter how humble—is made to feel welcome and at home.

HOW TO GET THERE: From the airport, turn right onto Capital Circle (Route 263), go 1³/₁₀ miles to the light at Springhill Road, turn left and go 2 miles to the light at Orange Avenue, turn right and go 1³/₁₀ miles to South Monroe Street (Highway 61), and turn left and go 1⁷/₁₀ miles to downtown, where you will pass the state capitol on the left. Past the capitol, turn left at Jefferson Street, go 1 block to Adams Street, and turn right. Governors Inn is on the right.

Wakulla Springs Lodge ⊛

Wakulla Springs, Florida 32305

INNKEEPER: Bill Roberts, manager

ADDRESS/TELEPHONE: 550 Wakulla Park Drive; (850) 224–5950;
fax (850) 561–7251

WEB SITE: www.dep.state.fl.us/parks

ROOMS: 27, all with marble floors, private marble bath, and telephone.
One room with a king-size bed, five with queens, remainder doubles
and/or twins.

RATES: $69 to $90.

OPEN: Year-round.

FACILITIES AND ACTIVITIES: Restaurant. In the park: Glass-bottom
boat rides, swimming, snorkeling, picnicking, nature trails, hiking, bicycling. Nearby: Tallahassee, Florida Caverns State Park, Natural Bridge
Battlefield State Historic Site, Torreya State Park, Lake Jackson Mounds
State Archaeological Site, Thomasville, Georgia.

BUSINESS TRAVEL: Meeting rooms and restaurant can accommodate
up to 100 for meetings and retreats; glassed-in terrace for receptions.

f you're a fan of old movies as we are, you may recognize Wakulla
Springs, the world's largest and deepest freshwater spring, from the
classics *Tarzan, Creature from the Black Lagoon,* and *Airport 77.* We did,
and so we first went to Wakulla Springs State Park to see the springs and the
wildlife that lives in and around it. Imagine our pleasant surprise when we
discovered the historic Wakulla Springs Lodge, a two-story Moorish-style
inn built in 1937 by financier and railroad magnate Edward Ball.

Ball designed the lodge using many arches, hand-wrought iron, imported
Italian marble, and hand-made ceramic tiles. Little changed except for
improvements in safety and comfort, the lodge offers a nostalgic glimpse
into life in Florida in the 1930s. Today the inn is operated by the Florida
State University Center for Professional Development. The dining room is
renowned for its cuisine and is a favorite destination for locals to dine.

The huge lobby is characterized by exposed beams, gray-and-pink checkerboard marble floors, and a walk-in marble fireplace. It's the ceiling, however,
that is the most amazing. Kaiser Wilhelm, Germany's court architect, painted
the ceiling with flamingos, other wildlife, palms, and tropical scenes Ponce de
Leon might have seen when he explored Florida looking for the Fountain of
Youth in the mid-1500s, as well as many colorful stenciled designs. Large

walls of windows in the lobby and dining room overlook the springs. Check out Old Joe, a stuffed alligator who lives in a glass case in the lobby.

Each guest room with its private marble bath is filled with antiques and offers beautiful views of the park. Furnishings for most of the guest rooms are simple 1930s and '40s reproductions. Particularly large rooms have fancier furniture and a seating area.

The major attraction in the park, of course, is the incredible water-filled sinkhole, which was formed from the eroded bed of ancient limestone filled by natural springs. Archaeological evidence indicates that Florida's first human residents lived near the springs site as much as 12,000 years ago.

A part of any visit to the lodge and park is the thirty-minute glass-bottom boat ride along the Wakulla River and the springs, where you're sure to see alligators floating on logs or stretched out in the sun along the riverbanks, the large population of year-round birds, or some of the 2,000 waterfowl that make the park their winter migratory home. The crystal-clear waters don't seem nearly as deep as they are and reveal fish, water plants, and other surprises. On dry land, the park's 1,500 acres of mature upland hardwoods contain some of the state's champion trees.

HOW TO GET THERE: Wakulla Springs State Park is just 14 miles south of Tallahassee. Take U.S. 319 south from the capital city, and 2 miles beyond Capital Circle, take the left fork onto FL 61 and travel 7½ miles to FL 267. Turn left, and the park entrance is immediately on the right.

Old Joe

While you're staying at the Wakulla Springs Lodge, or even if you're just visiting the park or eating in the dining room, be sure to take a gander at Old Joe, a stuffed alligator in the lobby. He was an 11-foot alligator who inhabited the springs for many years—some say he was 300 years old. Usually found stretched out in the sun opposite the swimming area, he is said never to have bothered anyone. He became a mascot to the park because he was so much beloved by the locals, but he was killed by a poacher in 1966. The Fish and Wildlife Service had Joe stuffed and traveled with him to schools around the state for many years. Then it was decided that he should have a more dignified retirement; now he resides in a glass case at the hotel. On New Year's Eve, even Old Joe gets a party hat.

Select List of Other Florida Inns

Addison House

614 Ash Street
Amelia Island, FL 32034
(904) 277-1604 or (800) 943-1604

1876 home; 14 rooms, some whirlpool baths; full breakfast

The Clewiston Inn

108 Royal Palm Avenue
Clewiston, FL 33440
(941) 983-8151

Greek Revival inn; 48 rooms

Live Oak Inn

444-448 South Beach Boulevard
Daytona Beach, FL 32114
(904) 252-4667

Historic inn; 12 rooms; near Intracoastal Waterway

The Villa Bed and Breakfast

801 North Peninsula Drive
Daytona Beach, FL 32118
(904) 248-2020

Historic Spanish-style mansion; 17 rooms; pool, spa; near beach

Crown Hotel

109 North Seminole Avenue
Inverness, FL 34450
(352) 344-5555 or (888) 856-4455

Historic downtown hotel; 34 rooms; pool; English pub, restaurant

Heron House

512 Simonton Street
Key West, FL 33040
(305) 294-9227 or (800) 294-1644

New England Cape Cod/Key West conch house style; 21 rooms

Georgia

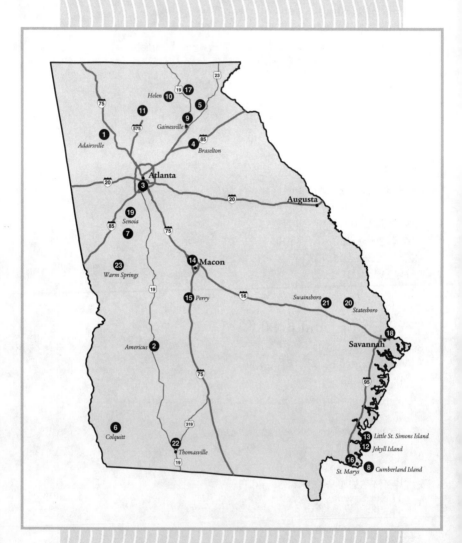

Georgia

Numbers on map refer to towns numbered below.

*A Top Pick Inn

Barnsley Inn and Golf Resort
Adairsville, Georgia 30103

INNKEEPER: Euan McGlashan

ADDRESS/TELEPHONE: 597 Barnsley Gardens Road; (770) 773-7480 or
(877) 773-2447; fax (770) 773-1779

WEB SITE: www.barnsleyinn.com

E-MAIL: smtp.barnsley@mindspring.com

ROOMS: 70 1- and 2-bedroom cottages, all with private bath, sitting
room, bedroom, fireplace, ceiling fan, porch, television, telephone with
dataport.

RATES: $255 to $900, double, including full breakfast. Some smoking
cottages. Children welcome. Ask about pets ($75 refundable fee). Credit
cards accepted.

OPEN: Year-round.

FACILITIES AND ACTIVITIES: 3 restaurants, 18-hole Fazio-designed golf
course, swimming pool, tennis courts, fitness center, health and
beauty spa, hiking trails, fishing ponds; horseback riding on Saturday
by reservation. Nearby: Chattanooga-Chickamauga National Battlefield, Kennesaw Mountain National Battlefield, Atlanta attractions,
hiking, biking.

BUSINESS TRAVEL: Ideal for meetings and retreats; 3 meeting rooms;
individual rooms have desk and telephone with dataport.

*T*he romance of the antebellum period is combined with the
charm of an English country cottage at Barnsley Gardens Inn and
Golf Resort, a retreat located on a historic estate of 1,300 acres.
Wrested from the Cherokee wilderness by Geoffrey and Julia Barnsley, the
mansion was built in 1842 and surrounded by English-style formal gardens.
A Civil War skirmish occurred on the property in 1864, but the house was
spared only to be partially destroyed by a tornado in 1906. The property had
deteriorated almost beyond redemption when it was rescued in 1988 by
Prince Hubertus Fugger and his wife, Alexandra, of Bavaria, Germany. Her-
culean efforts restored the gardens to near their former splendor and they
were opened to the public. One wing of the ruined manor house became a

small museum with exhibits relating to the history of the Barnsley family and the restoration of the gardens.

Not one to be satisfied with small successes, Prince Fugger decided the estate had much more to offer and created a magnificent resort. Today Barnsley Gardens opens its doors to a new millennium with a nineteenth-century inspired village complete with sumptuously appointed country cottages, picturesque streets, fine dining, and numerous sports options.

The exterior of each whimsical cottage is characterized by high peaked roofs, gables, porches, and gingerbread trim. Inside there are a sumptuously appointed sitting room, one or two bedrooms, one or two fireplaces, and a luxurious bath. Elegant fabrics, hardwood floors splashed with Oriental rugs, opulent wallpapers, fine moldings, and lots of windows combine with quality period reproductions to create an exquisite temporary abode perfect for a romantic getaway.

Barnsley Gardens offers several choices for fine dining: The Rice House, located in a historic house moved to the property, features traditional Southern dishes designed to suit contemporary tastes; the Woodlands Grill is a fine steak house; and the Bavarian Beer Garden offers more casual fare.

Woven into the rural idyll are superb recreational amenities: a Fazio-designed championship golf course, tennis courts, and fishing ponds. Just wandering the grounds, viewing the beautiful formal and informal gardens, and exploring the ruins is pleasure enough, but if you're searching for even more rejuvenation, the resort offers a full-service spa.

HOW TO GET THERE: From Atlanta, take I-75 north to exit 306 and follow the signs to the resort.

Windsor Hotel Americus
Americus, Georgia 31709

INNKEEPER: Marilyn Fallis, marketing consultant

ADDRESS/TELEPHONE: 125 West Lamar Street; (912) 924–1555 or (888) 297–9567; fax (912) 924–1555, ext. 113

WEB SITE: www.windsor-americus.com

E-MAIL: windsor@sowega.net

ROOMS: 53 rooms and 6 suites, all with private bath, ceiling fan, telephone, cable television with movies, clock radio, and coffeemaker.

RATES: $72 for standard guest rooms, $99 for junior suites, $109 to $189 for suites; children under 12 stay free in the same room with their parents. Credit cards accepted.

OPEN: Year-round.

FACILITIES AND ACTIVITIES: Grand Dining Room restaurant, Floyd's Pub. Nearby: Plains, Jimmy Carter National Historic Site, Andersonville, Andersonville National Cemetery.

BUSINESS TRAVEL: Function areas accommodate up to 200.

What attracted us to the Windsor Hotel in the first place was its whimsical castlelike appearance. Depending on your vantage point, you could envision yourself in Amsterdam, Austria, Germany, or some fairy-tale European kingdom, not in a small west-central Georgia town.

What brought this opulent pleasure palace to sleepy Americus? Strange as it may seem now, in the nineteenth century Americus was a popular winter destination for northern hunters and vacationers. In the midst of Victorian excess, a simple lodge or hotel simply wouldn't do. So in 1892 this extravagant five-story edifice was erected. Unfortunately, after many years of misuse and disuse, the hotel had deteriorated and was in danger of destruction when it was rescued by the town, rehabilitated to its present form, and opened as an inn in September 1991.

Although the interior is a little less exuberant than the exterior, it is characterized by a gorgeous three-story atrium trimmed in golden oak, marble floors, antique chandeliers, soaring columns, and a grand staircase that rises from the lobby and splits into twin staircases before completing its ascent to the restaurant and ballroom on the second floor. Very convenient for guests, the Americus Welcome Center is located off the lobby, as is the Tog Shop.

Our spacious, high-ceilinged junior suite retained a nostalgic feel with

period reproductions, suitable fabrics, a sitting area, ceiling fan, and plantation shutters, at the same time providing all the modern creature comforts. Standard guest rooms are similar to the junior suites, but without the seating area. The two most romantic accommodations are the two tower suites located in the round tower.

After a wonderful night's sleep, the next morning, a Sunday, we slept late and then went down to the historic restaurant for a gargantuan brunch. Tiny white tiles on the floor, dark furniture, and generous use of palms and other lush greenery served to authenticate the turn-of-the-twentieth-century ambience.

HOW TO GET THERE: From I-75, take either GA 27 or U.S. 280 west until they are joined by GA 49. Follow GA 49; as it enters Americus it is called Forsyth Street. Just past the post office, turn left at the light onto Lamar Street. The hotel is on the right.

Ansley Inn
Atlanta, Georgia 30309

INNKEEPERS: Curt Levy, manager; Morris Levy, owner

ADDRESS/TELEPHONE: 253 Fifteenth Street; (404) 872-9000 or (800) 446-5416; fax (404) 892-2318

WEB SITE: www.ansleyinn.com

E-MAIL: reservations@ansleyinn.com

ROOMS: 22, all with private bath; most with single or double whirlpool tub, hair dryer, iron and ironing board, telephone, cable television, clock radio, wet bar, coffeemaker; some with gas-log fireplace. Evening turn-down and in-room breakfast on request. Limited handicap access. Non-smoking inn except outdoors.

RATES: $129 to $189 for rooms and suites in the main house; $109 to $149 for rooms in the corporate wing; all include hot breakfast buffet, afternoon snacks, and beverages.

OPEN: Year-round.

FACILITIES AND ACTIVITIES: Concierge, free parking, free pass to Australian Body Works. Nearby: Woodruff Arts Center, Atlanta Botanical Garden, Piedmont Park, MARTA rapid rail Arts Station,tennis courts.

BUSINESS TRAVEL: Near midtown and downtown business districts; fax machine, computer ports in guest rooms.

*I*f we didn't already live in Atlanta and were traveling there, we'd love to stay at the lovely Ansley Inn. The philosophy of the owner and innkeeper of this B&B inn is to offer residential flavor with the service of a first-class hotel. The beautifully restored English Tudor mansion offers not only sumptuous accommodations but also impeccable service.

One of the things we find especially appealing is the inn's location in

Midtown's elegant, historic Ansley Park neighborhood, conveniently near the Woodruff Arts Center, where we spend a lot of time visiting the High Museum of Art and attending performances of the acclaimed Atlanta Symphony Orchestra and the Alliance Theater. In addition, the Atlanta Botanical Garden, Fourteenth Street Playhouse, and Piedmont Park are within easy walking distance.

Built in 1907, the magnificent yellow-brick house, with the addition of a corporate wing, spent many years as a boardinghouse before becoming this gracious inn. Now fully restored, the Ansley Inn is accented with antiques, burnished hardwood and gleaming Italian marble floors, massive fireplaces, crystal chandeliers, and Oriental rugs.

Each individually decorated guest chamber, named for an Atlanta street (in the main house), features a private bath. Most have a whirlpool tub, period and reproduction furnishings, a wet bar, telephone, and cable television. Many rooms boast gas-log fireplaces and four-poster rice beds. Those in the main house feature high or cathedral ceilings, large windows, and formal furnishings. Those in the corporate wing are more casual and intimate.

A lavish breakfast buffet including hot beverages, juices, assorted breads, cereal, and fresh fruit is served in the spacious, formal dining room. You can also order eggs any style, bacon, hash browns, and French toast. For special occasions you can request breakfast in your room. Coffee, a selection of teas, and juice are available in the dining room throughout the day and evening. In the late afternoon the tantalizing aromas of freshly baked cookies and popcorn draw guests to the cozy common room, with its beamed ceiling and fireplace surrounded by ceramic tiles. In good weather guests may want to take their breakfast or snacks out on the front terrace.

HOW TO GET THERE: From I–75/85, exit at Fourteenth Street and go east to Peachtree Street. Turn left and go 1 block to Fifteenth Street; bear right. The inn is just ahead on the right. Pull into the circular driveway to register; you will be directed to the parking lot.

The Spa at Chateau Elan
Braselton, Georgia 30517

INNKEEPER: Michelle Ufer-Herold

ADDRESS/TELEPHONE: 100 Rue Charlemagne; (678) 425–0900 or (800) 233–WINE; fax (678) 425–6000

WEB SITE: www.chateauelan.com

E-MAIL: chateau@chateauelan.com

ROOMS: 14, all with private bath, cable television, sound system, hair dryer, robes; some with whirlpool tub. No smoking. Not appropriate for children.

RATES: $170 to $250, including use of facilities. Meals, spa services, and sports options extra. Credit cards accepted.

OPEN: Year-round.

FACILITIES AND ACTIVITIES: Spa, restaurant, whirlpool, fitness equipment. On the resort grounds: Winery, gift shops, art gallery, 7 restaurants, golf, several swimming pools, conference center, tennis complex, equestrian center, bike and nature trails, paddle boats, ropes course.

*O*oh-la-la! Don't fret if you lovebirds can't jet to Paris. A decadent tryst at a French-style chateau and winery right outside of Atlanta awaits hedonistic couples. One of the jewels of the 3,000-acre estate, the intimate full-service European-style health spa only hints at the lavish enchantments you can lose yourselves in at this four-star resort. A long, sensual stay is a perfect way to experience the delights of the winery, restaurants, spa services, accommodations, sports facilities, and maybe even a special event or two. A stay at the spa coupled with an abundance of pampering is guaranteed to revitalize your bodies, spirits, love life, and anything else that needs rejuvenating.

The spa's unique guest rooms are whimsically decorated with a flair for differences in personal tastes and moods. Fanciful themes and features enhance your experience and appeal to your imagination. For example, the highlight of the exotic Oriental Room, a Far Eastern paradise, is an oriental-style deep-soak tub with Jacuzzi. A framed antique kimono and bonsai trees amplify the Oriental theme. At the other end of the spectrum, the Western

Room features a cannonball bed, wooden floors, and burlap curtains. Space-age features define the sophisticated Hi-Tech Room, which boasts black lacquer furniture, chrome, green and black marble, and a full-body massage recliner. Other themes include Vintage, Greek, Gatsby, Georgia, Lodge Loft, Art Deco, Victorian Wicker, Fox Hunt, Bacchus, and Country—each adorned to symbolize its name. Several boast Jacuzzis. The farther ahead you make your reservation, the more likely you can choose the room that best matches your individual tastes and dreams.

The spa offers all the latest spa equipment and services, including all types of massage (our favorite was hot-stone therapy), early fitness walks, and various types of aerobics, yoga, and relaxation techniques. Some services are geared specifically to men. Schedule spa services ahead of time, and be on time for your spa appointments—late arrivals don't get an extension of time.

Although accommodations, meals, and spa services can be purchased a la carte, there are seven overnight spa packages of various lengths ranging from $259 to $3,879, which consist of accommodations, specific spa services, and meals. Health-conscious cuisine is served in the spa's own restaurant, Fleur-de-Lis, but other options in your package allow you to choose from the Versailles Room in the inn or Cafe Elan in the chateau.

After an afternoon of relaxation and pampering in the spa, dress up (coat and tie for the gentleman) for a gourmet prix fixe dinner at Le Clos. The elegant restaurant serves a magnificent seven- or eight-course meal expertly coupled with the chateau's finest wines. After dinner, head over to Paddy's Irish Pub for drinks and entertainment.

On Saturday during the summer, Chateau Elan features musical concerts for your listening and/or dancing pleasure. Dancing cheek to cheek is particularly pleasurable after your cheeks have been smoothed with a facial.

Chateau Elan hosts numerous activities throughout the year, so call for more information if you want to coordinate your visit with one of them. Also check for Meet the Winemaker and Cooking Demonstration events. In addition, the resort hosts the Sarazan World Open Golf Tournament, and some kind of equestrian event occurs almost every weekend.

HOW TO GET THERE: Take I–85 north from Atlanta to the Braselton exit. Turn left and cross back over the interstate. The resort is on the left.

Glen-Ella Springs
Clarksville, Georgia 30523

INNKEEPERS: Barrie and Bobby Aycock

ADDRESS/TELEPHONE: 1789 Bear Gap Road; (706) 754-7295

WEB SITE: www.glenella.com

E-MAIL: info@glenella.com

ROOMS: 16 rooms and suites, all with private bath; some with fireplace; some with wheelchair access.

RATES: $125 to $195, single or double; includes full breakfast. Inquire about discounts for weeknights and stays of more than 3 nights.

OPEN: Year-round.

FACILITIES AND ACTIVITIES: Dining room, with wheelchair access, open to guests and public most days; reservations requested; available for private parties; brown bagging permitted. Conference room. Swimming pool, 17 acres with nature trails along Panther Creek, herb and flower gardens, mineral springs, garden house with living room for guest use, pavilion in meadow for special functions. Located in northeast Georgia mountains near historic sites. Nearby: Restaurants, golf, horseback riding, boating, rafting, tennis, hiking, Tallula Gorge State Park, Chattahoochee National Forest.

We think we're in love! Country inns are usually elegant or rustic. This one-hundred-year-old place is both. The suites are beautifully finished and furnished with fireplaces; refinished pine floors, walls, and ceilings; whirlpool baths; and such niceties as fresh-cut pansies floating in crystal bowls.

The fireplace in the lobby is made of local stone, flanked by chintz-covered chairs.

An especially nice swimming pool, surrounded by a posh, extra-wide sundeck, overlooks a huge expanse of lawn and gardens that ends in woods. Both the pool and the lawn are great for kids.

The dining room could be called "subdued country," but there is nothing subdued about the food. It is simply spectacular—some of the best in the South, compliments of Barrie and her kitchen staff.

We have eaten here more times than we can remember and have *never* had a bad (or even fair) meal—they have all been wonderful. Dan's fav-orite is the rack of lamb; Carol's is either the low-country shrimp and grits entree or the fresh trout sautéed and dressed with lime juice, fresh herbs, and toasted pecans.

You can get a copy of the *Glen-Ella Cookbook*, with some of the inn's best recipes, at the front desk, or you can order it by calling or writing the inn.

Every time we visit we find something new has been added—corporate-challenge obstacle course, state-of-the-art conference facility, upgraded rooms, etc.

And now there's one more bragging point for Barrie and Bobby: The hotel has been added to the National Register of Historic Places.

HOW TO GET THERE: From Atlanta, take I–85 north to I–985, traveling through Gainesville. Stay on this four-lane road past Cornelia and Clarkesville heading toward Clayton. It will become U.S. 441. After the stoplight at the Tom Arrendale Interchange (GA 365), go 7 miles and turn left on G. Hardman Road, then turn right back onto Historic Old 441. After ¼ mile turn left on Orchard Road and follow the signs for 3½ miles to the inn. From Clarkesville go north on Historic Old 441 for 8½ miles to Orchard Road. Follow the signs for 3½ miles.

Tarrer Inn
Colquitt, Georgia 31737

INNKEEPERS: Jerry and Mavis Phillips

ADDRESS/TELEPHONE: 157 South Cuthbert Street; (229) 758–2888 or (888) 282–7737; fax (229) 758–2825

WEB SITE: www.tarrerinn.com

E-MAIL: tarrer@surfsouth.com

ROOMS: 12, all with private bath, telephone, television, coffeemaker; some provisions for the disabled.

RATES: $89 to $105, including full breakfast.

OPEN: Year-round.

FACILITIES AND ACTIVITIES: Restaurant. Nearby: Spring Creek Park for bird-watching and fishing.

BUSINESS TRAVEL: Meeting rooms accommodate up to 300; full audiovisual equipment; guest room telephones have dataports; copy and fax service.

*U*nless you're from southwest Georgia, you might not know what a mayhaw is. We didn't when we first moved to Atlanta more than twenty years ago, but we were soon educated. A mayhaw is a tart, but delicate, swamp berry similar to a cranberry that can be made into jellies and sauces. This is important because Colquitt is the Mayhaw Capital of the World and the home of the annual Mayhaw Festival. The town also hosts a popular folk production called Swamp Gravy Tales. If you're in town for these events or just using it as a base from which to explore the southwestern corner of the state, the place to stay is the Tarrer Inn.

Built in 1866 as a boardinghouse, by the turn of the twentieth century the structure had become a full-fledged hotel known as the Hunter House. During this elegant period, white horse-drawn carriages picked up travelers from the train depot and brought them to the hotel in style. Restored to its former splendor, the inn continues the tradition of hospitality, recapturing the graceful nuances of days gone by with elegant surroundings updated with modern conveniences.

An elegant formal reception room is embellished with heavily carved Victorian sofas, chairs, a fainting couch, and ottomans covered in plush burgundy velvet dripping fringe. Opulent draperies, an ornate gilt mirror, Corinthian columns, Oriental carpets, and a tapestry complete this century-old vision.

Our favorite spot is the second-story porch, where we can sit in comfortable wicker chairs or rockers, fanned by slowly turning paddle fans while we watch the slow pace of life on the town square.

Each of the twelve guest chambers is appointed in a distinctive motif and furnished with exquisite antique treasures from the Victorian era. We particularly liked the hand-painted or faux-finished fireplace mantels, surrounds, and screens. Embroidered bed linens add another touch of elegance.

Although most of the rooms feature queen-size beds, a few have twin beds. Every room, however, has a private bath, television, and coffeemaker. Other amenities include fresh flowers and nightly turndown service with a chocolate left on your pillow.

As attractive as all these features are, there's one more reason to stay at the Tarrer Inn: the wonderful food. Noted for its fine dining—rich in the traditions of Southern cooking—the inn's dining room serves lunch Wednesday through Friday, dinner Thursday and Friday, and brunch Sunday. Included in the room rate, your full breakfast will feature Southern delicacies such as pecan waffles and quiches.

HOW TO GET THERE: Colquitt is located at the intersection of U.S. 27 and GA 91. Follow the signs to the historic downtown commercial district and the courthouse square, where the inn is located on one corner.

Inn Scarlett's Footsteps
Concord, Georgia 30206

INNKEEPERS: K. C. and Vern Bassham

ADDRESS/TELEPHONE: 40 Old Flat Shoals Road; (770) 884–9012 or (800) 886–7355; fax (770) 884–9012

WEB SITE: www.gwtw.com

E-MAIL: gwtw@gwtw.com

ROOMS: 5 rooms and 5 cottages, all with private bath; some with fireplace, whirlpool tub, and porch. No-smoking inn.

RATES: $89 to $125, including full Southern breakfast.

OPEN: Year-round.

FACILITIES AND ACTIVITIES: Formal parlors, dining room, veranda, screened porch, extensive grounds, gift shop. Nearby: Conveniently located for exploring Macon, Columbus, and Atlanta.

BUSINESS TRAVEL: Fax on-site.

When it comes to *Gone With the Wind* (GWTW) obsession, few folks can hold a candle to K. C. Bassham, proprietress of Inn Scarlett's Footsteps, a bed-and-breakfast in the Old South tradition. K. C. told us that when she was six years old, she saw *the* movie for the first time with her grandfather and told him right then that she was going to live in a house like that someday. Since then she says she has seen the movie at least 700 times, all the while dressing up in hoop skirts any chance she got, and looking for her antebellum dream. She found it in a small town south of Atlanta—a magnificent redbrick, white-columned, 8,000-square-foot mansion that she has turned into her own GWTW world, complete with rooms named after the characters and a place to display her astounding collection

of memorabilia. Soon after the inn opened, K. C. and Vern began offering costumed balls and barbecues that were so successful, they bought another property to use as a special-events facility.

The manor house, built in 1905, features inlaid hardwood floors, 12-foot-high ceilings, and original chandeliers and ceiling medallions. Commodious rooms are furnished with antiques and reproductions. One downstairs parlor is devoted to K. C.'s GWTW collection—one of the largest in the world. If you're covetous of the items, you can pick up some collectibles in Miss Margaret's Carriage House gift shop.

Guest rooms are found in the main house and in four newly constructed cottages. The rooms are appropriately named for the major characters in the Southern opus. Boldest of the bedchambers, in deference to its namesake, is Scarlett's Room. A portrait of our heroine hangs over the mantel, where several collector plates are displayed. Don't be disconcerted by the full-size mannequin of Scarlett dressed to kill. Vibrant colors, a queen-size four-poster bed, and a clawfoot tub help create just the right mood. Rhett's Room, by contrast, is more masculine. English antiques reflect his European travel and sophistication. The room showcases movie stills and a top hat tossed rakishly on one of the two high beds. Melanie's Room, which features a dainty iron bed, is pretty and pastel, reflecting her gentle spirit. Ashley's Suite, which depicts his military experience with an authentic uniform and portraits of favorite generals, has the added comfort of a sitting room with an additional daybed. Mr. Gerald's Room is decorated around an equestrian theme, reminiscent of his love of horses and jumping, and overlooks the horse pastures.

New since we last visited are four guest cottages: Aunt Pitty's Parlor, Mammy's Retreat, Miss Ellen's Chamber, and Dr. Mead's Quarters, each with a queen-size bed, whirlpool tub, television, and porch. Miss Ellen's is subdued in decor in deference to her refined background and personality. Aunt Pitty's features pastels, lace, and wicker. Mammy's is decorated with that famous red petticoat in mind and has an iron bed and rocking chairs. Completely over the top is Wedding Belle's Cottage, a popular honeymoon suite. This 1890s three-room cottage is as flamboyant as Belle Watling, with its gas-log fireplace beside the four-poster bed and another fireplace beside the red heart-shaped whirlpool tub.

More Fun at Inn Scarlett's Footsteps

If you're a dyed-in-the-wool *Gone With the Wind* fan, who knows what other-worldly experience you might have at Inn Scarlett's Footsteps. The innkeepers report that characters from the story have appeared to some guests. Some claim to have seen ladies and gentlemen in antebellum apparel floating down the grand staircase. One lady reported that Rhett, cigar in hand, appeared and kissed her on the cheek. Another group of ladies had a slumber party in Rhett's Room and sipped White Russians while waiting for him to appear.

HOW TO GET THERE: Drive south from Atlanta on I-75. At Griffin, go south on U.S. 19/41 to Zebulon. In Zebulon, turn right (west) at the traffic light onto GA 18 and follow it through Concord ⁴/₁₀ mile past the R. F. Strickland building. The bed-and-breakfast is on the right and is identified by a sign. From I-85 South, take I-185 South to GA 18 and go east. Look for the bed-and-breakfast just at the edge of town.

Greyfield Inn 💙
Cumberland Island, Georgia

INNKEEPER: Brycea Meyer

ADDRESS/TELEPHONE: For reservations contact the business office at 8 North Second Street, Box 900, Fernandina Beach, Florida 32035-0900; (904) 261-6408; fax (904) 321-0666

WEB SITE: www.greyfieldinn.com

E-MAIL: seashore@greyfieldinn.com

ROOMS: 17 rooms; only 9 rooms have private en-suite bath; 2 others have adjoining bath; the remainder share baths; the only shower is in an outside bathhouse; rooms vary in size and have twin, double, queen- or king-size beds.

RATES: $275 to $450; all double occupancy; includes three meals, naturalist's tour, bicycles, and ferry transportation to and from Fernandina Beach. Weekends require a 2-night minimum. Credit cards accepted. Children older than 5 are welcome.

OPEN: Year-round.

FACILITIES AND ACTIVITIES: Dining room, bar, bicycles, nature jeep tours, beach and beach equipment. Nearby: Intracoastal Waterway, historic sites, museum, fishing.

BUSINESS TRAVEL: Ideal for small corporate meetings and executive retreats.

*A*s writers, isolated Cumberland Island and the exclusive Greyfield Inn have always presented us with a great dilemma: Do we tout their many attractions to our readers, or do we keep the best-kept secrets on the East Coast all to ourselves? Well, that decision was taken out of our hands when John F. Kennedy Jr. chose the supersecluded spot for his top-secret wedding to Carolyn Bessette. Since then, pictures and information about the island and the inn have been splashed around the world. Fortunately, restrictions on visitation to the island keep it peaceful and untamed.

Healthy dunes, oceans of sea oats, long stretches of deserted beach, and dense, scrubby maritime forests characterize Cumberland Island—one of the most pristine islands in America. For almost one hundred years, the Manhattan-size island was owned by the wealthy Thomas Carnegie family, and on this sanctuary they built several mansions for themselves and their nine children in the late 1800s. Among the homes were Dungeness (since destroyed by fire), Plum Orchard, and Greyfield. Greyfield was built in 1901 for Lucy and Thomas's daughter, Margaret Ricketson. In 1972 the family donated all but 1,300 acres of the island and all but one of the mansions to the

United States, and it was designated as a National Seashore to preserve and protect the island from development. The island is operated by the National Park Service and access is only by ferry. Visitation is severely limited to 300 day-trippers and campers per day. The National Park Service ferry operates between the island and St. Marys, Georgia, once or twice a day, depending on the season. (The inn operates its own ferry, which makes three exclusive runs between the island and Fernandina Beach on Amelia Island, Florida.)

The family maintains Greyfield on the acreage they retained, and Margaret's daughter, Lucy Ferguson, opened up her home as an inn in the 1960s as an elite refuge from the hectic everyday world. Lucy's children and grandchildren operate the inn now as if they were welcoming old friends into their home. Expect eccentric charm, but not a decorator look. The inn is furnished with family heirlooms and antiques, many of them original to the house, and some of them suffer from the passage of time and exposure to the salt sea air.

Although it isn't visible from the house, endless vistas of deserted beach are only steps away through a stand of scrub growth that protects the inn from all but the most severe storms. For nonbeach time, our favorite place to relax is on the spacious front veranda. Heavily shaded by deep overhangs, sheltered by ancient live oaks, and cooled by a gentle sea breeze, the veranda is furnished with comfortable rockers and two immense porch swings.

For most of its existence Greyfield was not air-conditioned, and therefore the inn was closed each August. Recent addition of air-conditioning permits the inn to remain open year-round. Guests in the know realize that winter is a particularly pleasant time for a getaway at Greyfield. Fires blaze from the living room and dining room fireplaces, encouraging guests to gather around after a blustery walk on the beach. Cooler temperatures make vigorous hiking, biking, and long walks on the beach more pleasant; the bug population has all but disappeared; and there are even fewer visitors. Storms often deposit a wealth of shells on the deserted beaches.

Fine dining is integral to the Greyfield experience, and all meals are included. A full country breakfast is served in the dining room each morning. Lunches are prepared picnic style and packed into knapsacks or baskets for you to take with you. Depending on your choice of activities for the day, you might feast at the beach, near the ruins of Dungeness, or on the front veranda. If you've been off at the beach or exploring the island, be sure to be back in time to get cleaned up for hors d'oeuvres before dinner. The evening meal is a more formal affair, served in the dining room with candlelight and flowers, and gentlemen are requested to wear jackets. The centerpiece of the gourmet meal might be seafood, Cornish hen, lamb, or beef, but it will be accompanied by homemade breads and fresh vegetables and topped off by a mouthwatering dessert. The wine list, although limited, is excellent. At other

Cumberland Island National Seashore

We plead guilty. We and other travel writers tend to use the phrase "get away from it all" somewhat cavalierly to mean any junket away from home or to describe any place that's not a big city. Very few wilderness areas exist anymore that can be accurately described this way.

One of the exceptions is Cumberland Island, the largest of Georgia's barrier islands known as the Golden Isles. Imagine an island the size of Manhattan with only a handful of widely scattered buildings on it, a place where there are no paved roads and few service vehicles, a haven where there's no store or tourist trap and only one indoor overnight accommodation, the Greyfield Inn.

Why go there? For paradise on Earth. Miles and miles of deserted, wide, hard-packed beach are backed by gentle dunes, anchored by gently waving sea oats, where shorebirds and loggerhead turtles make their homes. You're likely to see small herds of wild horses galloping down the beach or armadillos scuttling across the crushed seashell roads. Deer, bobcats, alligators, birds, and other wildlife are more plentiful than people.

You have three options for visiting the island: Take a day trip, camp out, or stay at the inn. But plan ahead—only 300 visitors are allowed to experience Eden each day, so you need reservations for the National Park Service or inn ferry, the only way to get there. Campers need to make reservations far in advance. Actual campsites can't be reserved, however, so you may end up with a spot at the semideveloped campground or a primitive campsite far removed from everything. For campers and day-trippers: No matter how long you're staying, take everything you need. There are no stores or food outlets.

Day-trippers are at a disadvantage because they can see so little of the island in such a short time—especially if they spend much time on the beach—so we recommend several days to a week of camping or staying at the inn.

For information about Cumberland Island National Seashore, call (912) 882-4335; for day ferry reservations call (912) 261-6408.

times during the day, the inn maintains a well-stocked bar in the old gun room, where guests help themselves on the honor system.

Some things to know before you go: The only telephone is a radio-phone to the mainland and is reserved exclusively for emergencies. There are no stores on Cumberland Island, so bring everything you think you will need. The inn shop stocks a limited supply of sunscreen, film, cigarettes (for outdoor smoking only), over-the-counter medications, and insect repellent. Pack according to the season and weather and bring some rain gear. Ferries depart to and from Greyfield only three times a day, so plan accordingly.

If you've been searching for a place where it's more than OK to do nothing, this is it.

HOW TO GET THERE: Get specific directions when you make your reservations—you can only get to the inn via their ferry from Fernandina Beach on Amelia Island, Florida.

The Dunlap House
Gainesville, Georgia 30501

INNKEEPERS: David and Karen Peters

ADDRESS/TELEPHONE: 635 Green Street; (770) 536–0200 or (800) 276–2935; fax (770) 503–7857

WEB SITE: www.dunlaphouse.com

E-MAIL: innkeepers@dunlaphouse.com

ROOMS: 9, all with private bath, clock radio, robes, and cable television; some with sitting area, four-poster bed, fireplace; some with wheelchair access. No-smoking inn.

RATES: $85 to $155, double; includes full breakfast and refreshments on arrival. Ask about corporate rates and discounts. Children welcome. Credit cards accepted.

OPEN: Year-round.

FACILITIES AND ACTIVITIES: Nearby: Restaurants, Helen and tourist activities, North Georgia mountains, Lake Lanier, Quinlan Art Center,

Road Atlanta, Riverside Academy, Brenau College, Lake Lanier Rowing Venue, Atlanta Falcons facility, Mall of Georgia.

BUSINESS TRAVEL: Excellent work area and dataport in most rooms. Fax, direct-dial computer access, and printer available.

The Dunlap House has become an "innkeepers' choice"; that is, we get letters from other innkeepers telling us how much they've enjoyed staying at the Dunlap House. That's high praise.

Dunlap House is an elegantly renovated 1910 house listed on the National Register of Historic Places. The furnishings are period reproductions that include many pale pine pieces. The overall effect is bright and light, not the darkness we sometimes associate with historic homes.

In the front lobby area, a few small round tables with chairs make a good place to have a social drink in the evening if you bring your own. And the white wicker-furnished porch is our choice of locations for the full breakfast of fresh fruit; hot muffins or bread; French toast, eggs, or casseroles; fruit juice; and coffee or tea. Some people prefer breakfast on a tray in their room, but we like being outside with those healthy plants.

As for dinner, Rudolph's on Green Street is a neighboring restaurant in an old English Tudor–style house with a solid granite foundation and exposed beams in the living room. The offerings include standards such as prime rib of beef and fresh Georgia trout, as well as some more elaborate continental entrees, including veal prepared a couple of different ways.

HOW TO GET THERE: From I-985, take exit 6 to Gainesville. Stay on the same road to the corner of Ridgewood Avenue and Green Street. Turn left at the light and park behind the inn.

The Lodge at Smithgall Woods
Helen, Georgia 30545

INNKEEPER: Philip Mastin

ADDRESS/TELEPHONE: 61 Tsalaki Trail; (706) 878–3087 or (800) 318–5248; fax (706) 878–0301

WEB SITE: www.smithgallwoods.com

E-MAIL: sgwoods@stc.net

ROOMS: 14 in 5 homes and cottages, all with private bath, telephone, cable television, robes, toiletries; some with outdoor hot tub; 1 handicapped accessible. No-smoking inn.

RATES: $179 to $479, including three meals daily and evening hors d'oeuvres. Special packages available. A tax-exempt portion of your bill is directed toward the Smithgall Woods Foundation to support conservation efforts. Special advance arrangements must be made to accommodate guests younger than 18. Credit cards accepted.

OPEN: Open to individual guests one week per month year-round.

FACILITIES AND ACTIVITIES: Verandas, exercise room, washer/dryer on-site, massage by appointment, hiking trails, access to Dukes Creek Falls, managed trout fishing, interpretive nature programs, bird-watching and wildlife viewing. Nearby: Helen and Cleveland, Appalachian Trail, hiking, water sports, golf, horseback riding, mountain biking, shopping.

BUSINESS TRAVEL: Ideal for corporate retreats, workshops, and seminars; complete array of audiovisual equipment, fax, copier, modem.

*D*eep in the north Georgia mountains lies one of the state's most special retreats. And one of Georgia's best-kept secrets. On the day before Thanksgiving, we followed the winding drive along the sparkling stream and at the end of our journey emerged from the heavy stands of hardwoods, pines, and rhododendrons to find a magnificent rustic mountain retreat. One man's dream has resulted in a true getaway.

Charles Smithgall, a broadcaster from Atlanta, amassed almost 6,000 acres in the north Georgia wilderness and built a rustic house on it. Later he built and moved into a larger log house and constructed several smaller log cabins for his adult children. Eventually he sold the entire complex to the state for use as the Smithgall Woods Dukes Creek Conservation Area, which is operated by the Georgia Department of Natural Resources as a Heritage Preserve.

Here you're far removed from outside traffic, noise, and other distractions so you can focus on the natural surroundings and indulge in hiking, wildlife observation, interpretive ecology, Native American history, and fly-fishing on one of Trout Unlimited's "Top 100 Trout Streams in the U.S." The clamor of the city is replaced by a calming symphony of bird songs, rushing water, and the whisper of leaves rustling in a soft breeze. The lodge combines a wilderness backdrop with all the comforts and rustic allure of a private estate.

The facility boasts five cottages within short walking distance of each other. Beautifully decorated with regional art and cozily furnished with homey pieces, each cottage features a great room and one or more bedrooms as well as a stone fireplace or woodstove, fully equipped kitchen, washer/dryer, and a spacious porch and/or deck. Each guest room is appointed with a comfortable bed or beds, thick comforters, luxurious lounge chairs, desk and telephone, and an armoire in which the television is hidden. Oriental carpets and wildlife and botanical prints create a warm and welcoming ambience. Laurel and Garden Cottages are romantic private retreats for one couple. They feature a bedroom, kitchen, sitting room with a woodstove, and an outdoor hot tub located on a very private deck.

All guests enjoy three meals a day of superb regional cuisine and obliging, discreet hospitality. Dining is a celebration of fresh ingredients grown at area farms. A small on-site garden provides herbs and vegetables, as well as flowers for the tables. Meals are group experiences with all your fellow guests. Depending on the weather, dining may be indoors or on the expansive decks overlooking the stream. You can request a portable picnic if you're going to be away from the lodge at lunchtime.

The only negative to the Lodge at Smithgall Woods is that it isn't open to individual guests all the time. Because of the facility's unusual location and special attributes, it is ideal for corporate retreats and is used for that purpose three weeks of each month. It is usually open to the general public on weeks surrounding holidays such as Thanksgiving, Christmas, and Valentine's Day.

HOW TO GET THERE: From Atlanta, take GA 400 North until it ends. Keep going straight onto Long Branch Road. Turn right on GA 115/52 and continue into Cleveland. Proceed approximately 3 miles and turn right onto GA 75-Alternate. Go 5⁶/10 miles to the entrance on the right.

The Woodbridge Inn
Jasper, Georgia 30143

INNKEEPERS: Brenda and Joe Rueffert

ADDRESS/TELEPHONE: 44 Chambers Street; (706) 253–6293; fax (706)
692–9061 or (706) 253–9061

WEB SITE: www.woodbridgeinn.net

ROOMS: 18, all with private bath, telephone, and television.
Pets welcome. No-smoking inn.

RATES: $50 to $95, single or double; breakfast not served. Children free.

OPEN: Year-round.

FACILITIES AND ACTIVITIES: Lunch on Wednesday and Sunday; dinner
every night except Sunday; full bar service. Swimming pool. Nearby:
Short drive to restaurants; tennis and golf; Amicalola Falls State Park
hiking; Carter's Lake swimming, sailing, and fishing; Amicalola River
and Talking Rock Creek white-water canoeing.

The following is one guest's view of the inn's food: "I went to the
restaurant early. A cheery man with a black mustache was digging
flower beds around the front porch of the inn. Seeing my camera,
he said, 'Take my picture,' and struck a bunch of comic poses.

"While I was tasting a wonderful seafood chowder that the waitress had
recommended and eating crackers topped with a homemade cheese-spread
from a crock on the table, I asked who the funny man working out front was.

"That's Joe, the owner and the chef," my waitress said.

"Made me nervous. How was he going to cook my dinner if he was outside with a shovel? Especially something as out-of-the-ordinary as venison
fillet in a pepper-and-cognac sauce or sweetbreads with mushrooms? Not to
worry. I finally decided on the sautéed sweetbreads, and somehow Joe got
back into the kitchen and shortly produced the best calf sweetbreads I've ever
tasted. They were lightly browned and delicately crisp on the outside, perfectly moist and tender inside, mixed with whole sautéed mushrooms that
were still firm and juicy and a splash of light wine sauce. Everything was so
good that I ate slowly for a long time."

Accolades like this are not unusual at the Woodbridge Inn. Guests tend
to linger over dinner, hating to leave the dining room to go to their rooms.

The dining room is in a historic old hotel that was built in the mid-1800s. The guest rooms are in a separate, newly built lodge a few steps away on the side of a hill with a magnificent view of the mountains.

The lodge is contemporary with siding that matches the exterior of the restaurant. The rooms have either patios or balconies, depending on whether you're on the first floor or on one of the other two floors. Inside they're quiet and simple but luxurious, with ceiling fans and Broyhill furniture. One room has spiral steps going up to a sitting area with a sofa so that guests don't feel confined to a bedroom. Another nice touch is a coffeemaker in each room. The owners have recently finished six more rooms in the old hotel over the restaurant.

HOW TO GET THERE: Jasper is in the mountains, about an hour-and-a-half drive north of Atlanta. From the south, take I–75 to 575, then follow the signs into Jasper. From the north, take U.S. 53 off I–75 into Jasper. In Jasper, go north on Main Street. Cross over a small wooden bridge on the right and go into the parking lot.

Jekyll Island Club Hotel
Jekyll Island, Georgia 31527

INNKEEPER: Kevin Runner

ADDRESS/TELEPHONE: 371 Riverview Drive; (912) 635–2600 or (800) 535–9547; fax (912) 635–2818

WEB SITE: www.jekyllclub.com

E-MAIL: jiclub@technonet.com

ROOMS: 157 guest rooms and suites, all with private bath—some whirlpool baths—television, VCR, clock radio; some fireplaces, balconies, porches.

RATES: $109 to $149 for a standard single, $119 to $209 for a double,

$169 to $329 for specialty rooms and suites. In general, room rates are per room based on double occupancy. Bed-and-Breakfast Getaway packages are available for $59 to $79 Sunday through Thursday or $69 to $89 Friday and Saturday per night per person. Modified American Plan is available for $54 and Full American Plan for $72—both per person per night.

OPEN: Year-round.

FACILITIES AND ACTIVITIES: 4 food outlets, elevator, concierge; staff fluent in 5 languages; private Surfside Beach Club, heated outdoor pool, 9 tennis courts (1 indoor, 5 lighted), laundry, dry cleaning; tours of the property, bicycle rental, complimentary transportation throughout the island. Nearby: Summer Waves water park, indoor/outdoor tennis, 63 holes of golf, deep-sea fishing, biking, horseback riding, carriage rides, historic tours, 20 miles of bicycling and jogging paths, miniature golf, dolphin watch tours.

BUSINESS TRAVEL: 6 miles off the coast of Georgia, 12 miles from Brunswick and its airport, between Savannah and Jacksonville, Florida, airports. Ideal for small corporate meetings and retreats; 10 meeting rooms provide space for banquets up to 160 and receptions for up to 400 guests; some secretarial services.

No matter how sophisticated a traveler *you* might be, you're probably not so jaded that you'll escape being impressed by relaxing in luxury at what was once one of the most exclusive clubs in this country. In fact, the entire island was an elite playground for the fabulously wealthy. In the nineteenth century one hundred millionaires purchased the 1½-mile-wide 9-mile-long island off the coast of Georgia. They used it as a winter hunting retreat and for other recreational pursuits when they weren't in residence at their mansions.

The group commissioned the construction of a vast, rambling, sixty-room clubhouse with a grand dining room, lounge, library, other public rooms, and sweeping verandas on the Intracoastal Waterway side of the island, and it opened to its first guests in January 1888. In 1896 Sans Souci, an adjacent building of six large apartments (the island's first condominiums), was added, and an annex attached to the clubhouse was constructed in 1901. Between 1888 and 1928 many member families built their own "cottages" nearby. Ranging up to 8,000 square feet, these mansions had one eccentricity—they had no kitchens because everyone ate at the clubhouse.

The membership, however, began to dwindle during the Depression, and then the U.S. government requested that the resort not be used during the entirety of World War II. In 1947, the state of Georgia purchased the entire island and the club. The state attempted to operate the clubhouse, Sans

Souci, and Crane Cottage as a resort complex, but sadly it closed in 1972. In 1978 the 240-acre club district was designated a National Historic Landmark and a massive restoration began, making it the largest revitalization project in the Southeast. Beginning in 1986, a total of $20 million has been invested in restoring the club and its leaded art glass, ornate woodwork, and Rumsford fireplaces,  and it has reopened as a hotel. In the spring of 2001, two mansions were opened for additional accommodations.

As one of today's discerning guests at the Jekyll Island Club, you can revel in a combination of natural beauty, elegant architecture, upscale amenities, and superb personal service akin to those enjoyed by the original millionaires.

Luxuriate in turn-of-the-twentieth-century appointments such as Victorian fireplaces in some guest chambers and custom-made mahogany period reproduction furnishings—two-poster beds, armoires, chairs and sofas, and desks and tables—enhanced by rich fabrics, plush carpeting, and modern private baths. Some rooms have whirlpool baths, televisions, VCRs, clock radios, and multiple-dataport telephones. Good taste and attention to detail combine to redefine the meaning of being pampered. These features and amenities have earned the resort four stars and four diamonds from the major rating organizations and inclusion in the National Trust for Historic Preservation's Historic Hotels of America.

Dining options include gourmet continental cuisine with an emphasis on seafood in the opulent Grand Dining Room, delicatessen/bakery fare at Cafe Solterra, and fast-food and snack items at both the Surfside Beach Club and the Poolside Bar and Grill in season. J. P.'s Pub offers an intimate environment for cocktails and conversation. In good weather you'll want to take your drink out onto one of the vast verandas.

While you're on the island, be sure to take a guided tour of the historic district. The district includes Faith Chapel and several of the cottages, which contain impressive collections of decorative arts as well as historical photographs and documents related to the club era.

HOW TO GET THERE: From I–95, take exit 29/U.S. 17 east to the Jekyll Island Causeway and cross to the island. Follow the signs to the hotel.

The Lodge on Little St. Simons Island

Little St. Simons Island, Georgia 31522

INNKEEPERS: Maureen Ahern, resident manager; Bo Taylor, innkeeper.

ADDRESS/TELEPHONE: Little St. Simons Island (mailing address: P.O. Box 21078); (888) 733–5774 or (912) 638–7472; fax (912) 634–1811

WEB SITE: www.LittleStSimonsIsland.com

E-MAIL: lssi@mindspring.com

ROOMS: 2 in main lodge with private bath; 4 in River Lodge, all with private bath; 4 in Cedar House, all with private bath; 2 in Michael Cottage share bath; 3 in Helen Cottage share 2 baths. Amenities include robes, botanical soaps and lotions, hair dryer. All cottages have a screened porch or deck overlooking the marshes or maritime forest.

RATES: $375 to $550; includes all meals, wine with dinner, island activities, and ferry service. Minimum 2-night stay. Inquire about longer-stay and off-season discounts as well as exclusive full-island reservations for family get-togethers, weddings, and corporate retreats for $5,000 a night.

OPEN: Year-round.

FACILITIES AND ACTIVITIES: Bar in lodge; collection of books about native birds, plants, animals, and marine life; spring-fed swimming pool, stables, sunrise horseback rides, horseshoes, ocean swimming, 7-mile pristine undeveloped beach, birding, naturalist-led explorations, beachcombing, shelling, fishing, canoeing, kayaking, hiking, biking, fly-fishing schools, sea turtle monitoring and protection program.

This is truly a special place. It is a 10,000-acre barrier island still in its natural state except for the few buildings needed to house and feed thirty guests. You can get there only by boat. Such creature comforts as nice bathrooms and ice machines have been added, but they rest unobtrusively in the natural scene.

When we visited, we felt welcomed as though we'd been visiting there for years.

You will marvel at how much you can do in a short time. The permanent staff includes three naturalists. One of the naturalists loaded us into a pickup truck and drove us around the island to help us get oriented. We walked through woods and open areas and along untouched ocean beaches. We saw our first armadillo. We gathered more sand dollars than we'd ever seen in one place before. We saw deer, raccoons, opossums, and more birds than we could identify. Serious bird-watchers plan special trips to Little St. Simons to observe the spring and fall migrations.

We even rode horseback with one of the naturalists to view some eagle and stork nesting sites.

When we weren't out exploring the island, we played boccie ball, swam, and just soaked up some rays. In the evening we sat in front of the fire in the lodge, chatting with the other guests.

One of the best meals we had while we were there was roast quail, served with rice pilaf and little yellow biscuits. After dinner, with no thought of television, we retired to the comfortable bed in a simple, pleasant room and fell asleep instantly. It's no wonder that the island receives so many accolades: *Condé Nast* "Best Small Hotel in North America" and the 2000 Readers Choice Award among them.

HOW TO GET THERE: When you make your reservations, you will receive instructions on where to meet the boat that takes you to the island.

1842 Inn
Macon, Georgia 31201

INNKEEPER: Nazario Filipponi

ADDRESS/TELEPHONE: 353 College Street; (478) 741–1842; reservations (800) 336–1842; fax (478) 741–1842

WEB SITE: www.1842inn.com

E-MAIL: the1842inn@worldnet.att.net

ROOMS: 21, all with private bath, telephone, and television; some with whirlpool and fireplace; some with wheelchair access.

RATES: $220 to $260, double; single $170 to $210; includes continental breakfast and other inn courtesies.

OPEN: Year-round.

FACILITIES AND ACTIVITIES: Beverages from bar at nominal charge, meeting rooms. Nearby: Restaurants, easy access to Macon Historic District walking tours, Cherry Blossom Festival in March. Access to private dining and health clubs and country club for swimming, tennis, and golf; horse-drawn carriage rides.

BUSINESS TRAVEL: Located 5 minutes from business district. In-room computer and modem setup; excellent work surface; limited secretarial service; copier and fax available. Conference facilities on-site for up to 20 (60 using nearby property).

*S*carlett's Tara might not exist, but if you are looking for a very good substitute, the 1842 Inn is a good bet. Every time we visit, we fall in love with this place all over again.

This B&B inn started with a strong-minded owner who was determined to get the restoration done right, then work on service. The new owner and manager have taken it from there.

When you start with a Greek Revival antebellum house of this beauty, it's hard to see how anyone could go wrong; but when the earlier owners bought the property, the house had passed its glory years, was divided into apartments, and had fallen into disrepair.

Such a building has a continuing life (life implies growth and change) as its fortunes wax and wane over the years. Originally it was smaller, with only four columns. About the turn of the twentieth century, the house was enlarged, columns were added, and elaborate parquet floors were laid over the original heart-of-pine floors.

Now, fully restored, this main house is connected by a courtyard to a Victorian cottage that was moved from Vineville Avenue to the rear of the inn and refurbished to provide additional rooms. One wonders: In another generation, what next?

When you stay at the 1842, you may find the history interesting, but if you're like us, you want to know more about your creature comforts. They're all here, including full handicap facilities, blackout linings in the draperies for late sleepers, and walls that are insulated to keep your room quiet. Some rooms have a second television set in the bathroom so that you can watch while you enjoy the whirlpool.

The furnishings are a mix of fine antiques, period reproductions, Oriental rugs, and luxurious towels and linens. The beds are all king- or queen-size period reproductions with custom-made mattresses.

The inn offers all the services of a fine European hotel: continental breakfast delivered to your room with flowers and a paper, turndown service with mints on the pillow, shoe shines while you sleep, and robes in guest rooms.

The inn has begun winning coveted awards from other inn guides—which shall remain nameless in this guide!

One of the most pleasant touches is the addition of "formal evening hospitality." This means really elaborate hors d'oeuvres and beverages in the parlors, with piano music, to separate the workday from evening relaxation.

HOW TO GET THERE: From I-75, take exit 164 (downtown and Hardeman Avenue). Turn left coming from the north, right from the south. Go two traffic lights to College Street and turn left. The inn is past two traffic lights on the left.

Henderson Village
Perry, Georgia 31069

INNKEEPER: Stuart McPherson

ADDRESS/TELEPHONE: 125 South Langston Circle; (912) 988-8696 or (888) 615-9722; fax (912) 988-9006

WEB SITE: www.hendersonvillage.com

E-MAIL: info@hendersonvillage.com

ROOMS: 28 rooms and suites, all with private bath, cable television, sound system, hair dryer, iron and ironing board, ceiling fan, robes; some with fireplace and/or whirlpool tub. Smoking areas limited.

RATES: $145 to $245, including country breakfast. Children welcome. Credit cards accepted.

OPEN: Year-round.

FACILITIES AND ACTIVITIES: Formal gardens, heated swimming pool, farm and exotic animals, hunting, horseback riding, clay-pigeon shooting. Nearby: Georgia National Fairgrounds and Agricenter, Hawkinsville Harness Training Facility, Andersonville Trail, Andersonville National Historic Site, Jimmy Carter National Historic Site.

BUSINESS TRAVEL: Separate conference facilities and the wide variety of sporting activities make this an ideal choice for small corporate meetings and retreats.

Here in Georgia's heartland, an aggregation of grand nineteenth-century Southern homes and simple tenant cottages create lovely Henderson Village, located at what was once a stagecoach intersection. Some of the structures are in their original locations; others have been moved from elsewhere to create the village. Sprawling verandas and white columns evoke the grace of the Old South. Twenty-eight guest rooms and suites are exquisitely decorated to reproduce the fascination of that period. Today, however, the guest accommodations boast all the modern amenities, and some feature a fireplace and/or a whirlpool bath. At Henderson Village, exquisite accommodations, divine cuisine, and outdoor pursuits combine for an idyllic getaway sure to please everyone.

Naturally, the accommodations in the houses are more elaborate than those in the tenant cottages, but don't sell the cottages short. Ours had wood plank walls, a double fireplace separating the bedroom area from the sitting area, a gargantuan bathroom, an iron king-size bed, and simple bed coverings, window treatments, and art. Its private porch was a delightful place to relax as dusk began to fall. The guest chambers in the houses boast high ceilings, elaborate moldings, and more sumptuous furnishings, window treatments, and artwork.

Almost as appealing as the accommodations are the grounds. Sweeping lawns are shaded by ancient trees. Serpentine brick paths lead to rolling pastures and formal gardens and fountains. Step through the gate in the picket fence to the elegant swimming pool with its twin gazebos to shade you on a hot summer day. Moonlight carriage rides are offered Saturday between 7:00 and 9:30 P.M., weather permitting.

Henderson Village is surrounded by 8,000 acres of prime hunting land. Those so inclined can hunt Booner and Crocket bucks, quail, and boar. Other outdoor pursuits include clay-pigeon shooting, fishing, and horse-back riding. For those more interested in just observing animals, a small farmyard contains a donkey, a llama, and other creatures.

Fine cuisine is an integral part of the Henderson Village experience. The resort's award-winning European chef serves excellent Southern continental cuisine. Breakfast, which is included in the overnight rate, can be served in the privacy of your room or in the Langston House Restaurant, which is also open for gourmet meals in the evening.

HOW TO GET THERE: From Atlanta, take I-75 south toward Macon and then take the I-475 Bypass around the city. On the south side of Macon, rejoin I-75 and continue on it to exit 127. Turn right off the exit and travel approximately 1 mile. Turn right into Henderson Village at the intersection of Highways 26 and 41.

Riverview Hotel
St. Marys, Georgia 31558

INNKEEPERS: Jerry and Gaila Brandon

ADDRESS/TELEPHONE: 105 Osborne Street; (912) 882-3242; fax (912) 729-6158

WEB SITE: www.stmaryswelcome.com

ROOMS: 18, all with private bath and television.

RATES: $45, single; $55, double; includes tax and continental breakfast.

OPEN: Year-round.

FACILITIES AND ACTIVITIES: Breakfast and lunch Monday through Friday, dinner Monday through Saturday (5:00 to 10:00 P.M.), Sunday brunch; wheelchair access to restaurant. Lounge (closed Sunday), self-guided tours of St. Marys historic district. Nearby: Crooked River State Park and King's Bay Submarine Base; hour's drive to Okefenokee Swamp; access to Cumberland Island by ferry.

*Y*ou can't tell an inn by its name. We've seen places called inns that were motels, and here's a place called a hotel that's really an inn. Sitting on the banks of the St. Marys River, across the street from the ferry to Cumberland Island National Seashore, the Riverview has a sitting room, a veranda with rockers, and an old-fashioned lobby with big brown-and-white tiles on the floor. The rooms are furnished, without frills or ruffles, with heavy country-style furniture.

The Brandon family (Jerry and Gaila) renovated the 1916 building in old-time style and furnished it with simple country furniture appropriate for the campers, bicyclists, and hikers who tend to gather in St. Marys.

If you are here before a ferry is scheduled to leave for Cumberland Island, the lobby will probably be full of knapsacks and backpacks, whose owners are eating in Seagle's Restaurant in the hotel, along with everybody else in town.

The restaurant has been renovated with wood siding, Irish green accents, a gallery for local artists, and some original brick walls exposed for the old-fashioned flavor. The restaurant, which is leased out, is not operated by the Brandons, but they do fix an expanded continental breakfast for their guests and will provide picnic lunches that you can take on the ferry or on a hike.

The food is fantastic! We thought the stuffed shrimp were surely the best thing possible until we tasted the fried rock shrimp, which are sweeter than regular shrimp and were fried in a delicate homemade batter resembling tempura. If you ask ahead of time, you can enjoy equally good food on your trip to Cumberland Island or Okefenokee Swamp by asking the Brandons' staff to pack a picnic for you.

If you're just exploring Georgia, you'll like St. Marys. It's historic but handles its tourism in a low-key way. The local people don't get all gussied up for it.

HOW TO GET THERE: From I–95, take Route 40 east straight into St. Marys and down to the water. The inn is on the right.

Spencer House Inn
St. Marys, Georgia 31558

INNKEEPERS: Mary and Mike Neff

ADDRESS/TELEPHONE: 200 Osborne Street; (912) 882–1872;
fax (912) 882–9427

WEB SITE: www.spencerhouseinn.com

E-MAIL: spencer@eagnet.com

ROOMS: 13, plus 1 suite; all with private bath, telephone, clock radio,
cable television, ceiling fan.

RATES: $80 to $130 for rooms, $145 for the suite; includes breakfast
buffet and afternoon peach iced tea; $15 for each additional person;
holidays and special events require a minimum stay.

OPEN: Year-round.

FACILITIES AND ACTIVITIES: Parlor, breakfast room, elevator. Nearby:
Orange Hall, Toonerville Trolley of cartoon fame, 38 National Register
of Historic Places sites, McIntosh Sugar Mill tabby ruins; tennis, golf at
Osprey Cove and Laurel Island Links, deep-sea fishing, sea kayaking;
Cumberland Island National Seashore, Okefenokee National Wildlife
Refuge, Georgia's Golden Isles; Amelia Island, Florida.

BUSINESS TRAVEL: 35 minutes from Jacksonville, Florida, airport.

*Y*ou'll love the first- and second-story verandas of this B&B inn, just
as we do. It's perfect for relaxing with a book and a cool drink, eating breakfast in good weather, getting to know your fellow guests,
or just people watching as tourists come and go through the quaint historic
district of St. Marys.

Capt. William T. Spencer, the collector of customs in St. Marys from
1871 to 1873, built this gracious Victorian structure as a hotel in 1872. Over
the intervening years it served many purposes or sat abandoned. Today,
fully restored and painted a cheerful pink, the building has returned to its
original use. Original moldings, high ceilings, heart-pine floors, many windows, antiques and period reproductions, and appropriate fabrics add
warmth and beauty.

Different guest room sizes and configurations, as well as a variety of furniture and fabrics, ensure that every guest chamber has its own distinctive
personality. While retaining the charm of yesteryear, each room features
modern conveniences, such as a private bath with a claw-foot tub or shower,
television, and telephone. An elevator provides easy access to all three floors.

A generous full breakfast is served buffet style in the breakfast room each morning and will feature one of the chef's daily specials, such as cranberry-pecan bread pudding, a frittata, or other specialty. Although the bright, cheery breakfast room is delightful, we prefer to take our breakfast out on one of the verandas.

Mary and Mike are only too delighted to sit down with their guests to give advice about area sight-seeing and help them get tickets on the Cumberland Island ferry, reserve tee times, or make restaurant reservations. For an additional fee they'll be glad to prepare a picnic lunch for you to take to the wilds of Cumberland Island or the Okefenokee Swamp.

St. Marys is the departure point for the National Park Service ferry to Cumberland Island. Because the ferry leaves in the morning, many who are going to camp out on the island for several days arrive in St. Marys the night before to enjoy a night of luxury and comfort at the Spencer House Inn before going on to their primitive camp site. On the day of their return, others immediately check in to the inn from the late-afternoon ferry to celebrate their return to civilization. Our personal recommendation is to do both.

HOW TO GET THERE: From I–95, exit onto State Route 40. As you enter St. Marys, Route 40 becomes Osborne Street. The inn is on the left at the corner of Bryant and Osborne. Parking is at the side of the inn or on the street.

The Stovall House
Sautee, Georgia 30571

INNKEEPER: Ham Schwartz

ADDRESS/TELEPHONE: 1526 Highway 255N; (706) 878–3355

WEB SITE: www.georgiamagazine.com/stovall

ROOMS: 5, all with private bath; 1 with wheelchair access. No smoking inside.

RATES: $56 single; $84 double; includes continental breakfast. Children of all ages welcome; under age 4 free; children ages 4 to 18 $11.

OPEN: Year-round.

FACILITIES AND ACTIVITIES: Restaurant serves dinner Thursday through Saturday 5:30 to 8:30 P.M.; Sunday brunch 11:00 A.M. to 2:00 P.M.; reservations recommended; brown bagging permitted, wheelchair access to dining room. Massage therapist studio on-site. Located in the northeast Georgia mountains. Trout fishing in creek on property; bird-watching. Nearby: Lakes, rivers, creeks, waterfalls, and state parks for fishing, hiking, rock climbing, snow skiing (in season); Sautee-Nacoochee Arts Center, Art Gallery, and History Museum.

*T*his inn is the quintessential family homestead—rolling fields, a big white house with the kind of front porch people really sit on, and a lively assortment of kids and animals.

Ham is a zany, enthusiastic innkeeper who has brought a home of the 1800s back to life by restoring, renovating, decorating, and then welcoming guests as family. He says that he wants the place to feel like home away from home.

Not that many of us have homes with mantels and doors handmade of walnut, working fireplaces in all the downstairs rooms, heart-of-pine floors, and an original telescoping bed (the first Hide-A-Way) made in 1891.

Ham's particular genius is being able to blend his passion for restoration with a sense that history is about living, not about museums. Stovall House is on the National Register of Historic Places and has won two important awards for restoration. But you enjoy the inn not for its awards but for how it feels to stay here. Guests often plan birthday and anniversary celebrations here.

Just being in a room can be a celebration. In some of the upstairs rooms, you can go to sleep watching stars and wake up to see the sun rise through skylights strategically placed in the dormers.

Even though people celebrate romantic milestones at the inn, you don't have to live on love alone while you are here. The food is good—and fresh!

The menu features homemade soups, fresh vegetables fixed in as many different ways as Ham and the staff can think of, and such delicacies as pan-fried trout. The restaurant was named one of the top fifty restaurants in Georgia by the publication *Georgia Trend*.

Ham is deeply involved behind the scenes in the restoration of the old Nacoochee School, which dates back to the 1800s, and its development as an arts and community center. It has performances of everything from the Savannah Symphony to children's theater. Ham has enjoyed performing in some of the plays himself.

17 Hundred 90 Inn
Savannah, Georgia 31401

INNKEEPERS: Dick and Darlene Lehmkuhl, owners

ADDRESS/TELEPHONE: 307 East President Street; (912) 236-7122 or (800) 487-1790; fax (912) 236-7123

WEB SITE: www.17hundred90.com

E-MAIL: 1790inn@email.msn.com

ROOMS: 14, all with private bath, telephone, cable television, clock radio, VCR, hair dryer, and a small refrigerator; king- or queen-size beds; some with gas-log fireplace. No-smoking inn.

RATES: $119 to $189; includes continental breakfast and complimentary bottle of wine. Credit cards accepted.

OPEN: Year-round.

FACILITIES AND ACTIVITIES: Restaurant and cocktail lounge. Nearby: Savannah historic district, River Street, shopping, fine dining, nightlife; beaches of Tybee Island.

The first night we stayed at the 17 Hundred 90 Inn, Carol woke up in the middle of the night with the feeling that someone else was in the room. When she opened her eyes, a woman in a long dress and with her hair in a bun was standing beside the bed peering down at us. She instantly evaporated into thin air, so obviously she was just curious and meant us no harm. When we related our tale over breakfast with owner Dick Lehmkuhl the next morning, instead of thinking we were crazy, he reassured us, "That's only Anna Powell, the first owner; she's our resident ghost. Your room is the one from which she jumped out the window to her death when her sailor boyfriend jilted her." We've stayed in the same room ever since, but she's never visited us again. Dick says other ghostly manifestations, such as lilting piano music when no one is playing the piano, occasionally delight guests.

Upstairs you'll find luxury, Old South charm, and gracious pampering in the splendidly appointed guest rooms, which are filled with antiques, period reproductions, and appropriate wall coverings and fabrics. Gas-log fireplaces add romance to twelve of the rooms. One of our favorites is the largest, with its king-size bed on a dais and its spacious sitting area, but some romantics prefer the two rooms with mirrored ceilings.

As much as we love the spacious, high-ceilinged guest rooms, the heart of the inn is the cellar. Here you'll find the gastronomic delights of one of Savannah's most popular restaurants and cocktail lounges, where the intimate atmosphere is enhanced by low ceilings, brick walls, and dim flickering light cast by the glow of blazing fires in the twin walk-in fireplaces. *Gourmet* magazine has called the dining room the most elegant in Savannah. *Georgia Trend* magazine singled out the restaurant and lounge as the in place to be for "financiers, businesspeople, and professionals," and, we might add, politicians. *Gourmet* Diners Club has honored the establishment with its Silver Spoon award for several years. During a stay at the inn, no matter how long or short, treat yourselves to a dinner of continental cuisine accompanied by fine wines in the restaurant. Another night, you might get back to the inn in time for complimentary hors d'oeuvres in the lounge. So generous are they that you won't even have to worry about dinner that evening.

The full gourmet breakfast served in the Garden Room typically includes a casserole, wonderful banana-nut bread, fresh fruit, juice, and coffee or tea. Later in the day the Garden Room becomes a popular lunch spot for Savannahians.

Outside your door is the Savannah historic district, which you can explore on foot for days.

HOW TO GET THERE: I–16 ends as it merges into Montgomery Street. Pass the Civic Center on the right and go 2 more blocks to York Street and turn right. Go 7 blocks and turn left onto Lincoln. The inn is at the corner of Lincoln and President Streets. Parking is on the street.

Ballastone Inn 💟

Savannah, Georgia 31401

INNKEEPER: Jean Hagens

ADDRESS/TELEPHONE: 14 East Oglethorpe Avenue; (912) 236–1484 or (800) 822–4553; fax (912) 236–4626

WEB SITE: www.ballastone.com

ROOMS: 13, plus 3 suites; all with private bath, telephone, television, and VCR; 11 with working fireplace and some with whirlpool tub; some with wheelchair access.

RATES: $195 to $225 standard, $285 to $315 superior, and $375 to $415 suites ($60 more during high season and for special events such as St. Patrick's Day); includes full breakfast, high tea, hors d'oeuvres, brandy, chocolates and parking.

OPEN: Year-round.

FACILITIES AND ACTIVITIES: Full-service bar, landscaped courtyard. Located in Savannah historic district. Nearby: Restaurants, antiques shops, Savannah riverfront, historic sites.

BUSINESS TRAVEL: Located 5 minutes from business district. Telephone in room; fax available. Inquire about corporate rates.

he Ballastone Inn is the kind of place that indulges the whims and idiosyncrasies of even the most crotchety traveler. Each time we stay at this B&B inn we're impressed with the good humor and ease with which the staff carry in extra luggage, rearrange schedules, and hasten check-in for a group of what we consider unusually demanding guests.

A few other nice things the staff will do for you include serving your breakfast at whatever time you choose—either in your room, in the tea or main parlor, or in the courtyard—and arranging everything from restaurant reservations and theater tickets to sight-seeing tours and airline flights. They'll even polish your shoes if you leave them outside your door at night.

Like many other old buildings in Savannah, the inn has been restored with special attention to authenticity, using Scalamandré fabrics and Savannah Spectrum colors. The colors were developed by chipping old buildings down to the original paint and matching it.

The most impressive thing about the inn is the absolute faithfulness with which the fabric, carpet, and eighteenth- and nineteenth-century furniture and art have been combined to fit the period of the house.

To give you a better idea of the rooms, consider the one called Scarlett's Retreat, a popular room at the Ballastone. It has an English canopy bed, a small sitting area, and a gas fireplace. The walls are painted spruce green and the drapes and bedding blend softly in more shades of green and white. The hardwood floors are set off with Oriental rugs.

The Ballastone now serves a full breakfast (you select what you want and where you want it served the night before), high tea at 4:00 P.M. each day, hors d'oeuvres at 6:00 P.M., and chocolates and brandy at bedtime.

HOW TO GET THERE: Take I–16 east to its end in downtown Savannah, where it merges into Montgomery Street. Turn right at the second stoplight onto Oglethorpe Avenue. Go 4 blocks to Bull Street. The inn is next to the Juliette Gordon Low House.

East Bay Inn
Savannah, Georgia 31401

INNKEEPER: Ronnie Jones

ADDRESS/TELEPHONE: 225 East Bay Street; (912) 238–1225 or (800) 500–1225; fax (912) 232–2709

WEB SITE: www.eastbayinn.com

E-MAIL: info@eastbayinn.com

ROOMS: 28, all with private bath, telephone, television, and coffeemaker.

RATES: $99 to $189; includes deluxe continental breakfast, morning newspaper, evening wine and sherry, and turndown service with a sweet treat.

OPEN: Year-round.

FACILITIES AND ACTIVITIES: Restaurant; elevator. Nearby: Savannah's historic district, fine dining, shops, theater, nighttime entertainment; beaches of Tybee Island.

BUSINESS TRAVEL: Fax and copy service; meeting planning services; meeting and banquet facilities ideal for small groups.

Charm, romance, an atmosphere reminiscent of nineteenth-century Savannah; elegant surroundings; personalized service; and a location just off River Street and the bustling waterfront make the East Bay Inn an extremely attractive place to stay in the city's historic district. This is a great place to people watch—especially during the three-day St. Patrick's Day celebration.

During the 1880s the building in which the inn is located was a cotton warehouse with offices on the third floor. Later the downstairs was occupied by a drugstore and then abandoned for many years. In 1984 it was fully restored and adapted for use as an inn. The structure maintains its original crown moldings, hardwood floors, and Savannah bricks.

All public areas and the twenty-eight intimate guest rooms are furnished with antiques and period reproductions, porcelains, antique maps, Oriental rugs, and artwork by Audubon and Catsby. Well-proportioned, high-ceilinged guest rooms, some with exposed brick walls, feature a queen-size four-poster rice bed and offer all the modern conveniences; such as a private bath, telephone, cable television, and coffeemaker. In this well-run small hotel, the friendly staff are always ready to help you in any way and to answer questions and make suggestions about their favorite city.

A continental-plus breakfast is served each morning, and this is a good opportunity to get to know your fellow guests. So is the relaxed social hour in the evening, when wine and sherry are served. Skyler's Restaurant serves Asian gourmet cuisine.

HOW TO GET THERE: I-16 ends and merges into Montgomery Street. Pass the Civic Center on the right as well as Elbert, Liberty, and Franklin Squares. Turn right onto West Bay Street and go 7 blocks. The inn is on the right opposite Emmett Park. Off-street parking is available next to the inn.

The Eliza Thompson House
Savannah, Georgia 31401

INNKEEPERS: Carol and Steve Day

ADDRESS/TELEPHONE: 5 West Jones Street; (912) 286-3620 or (800) 348-9378; fax (912) 238-1920

WEB SITE: www.elizathompsonhouse.com

E-MAIL: ElizaT.H.@aol.com

ROOMS: 25, all with private bath, telephone, television, hair dryer, makeup mirror, iron and ironing board; one room with whirlpool tub; one handicapped-accessible room. No-smoking inn.

RATES: $109 to $260 per room; includes deluxe continental breakfast and daily wine-and-cheese reception. Dessert and coffee from 8:30 to 11:30 P.M. each evening. Children welcome.

OPEN: Year-round.

FACILITIES AND ACTIVITIES: Located in the Savannah historic district. Nearby: Walking distance to restaurants, antiques shops, Savannah riverfront, historic sites.

BUSINESS TRAVEL: Desks in some rooms; dataports in all rooms; fax available.

*J*ust down the street from our favorite breakfast and lunch spot, Mrs. Wilkes' Boarding House, is one of Savannah's wonderful B&B inns, The Eliza Thompson House. This 1847 town house and carriage house have been lovingly restored to their original grace and beauty, including the courtyard, which has been landscaped with Old South formality, including fountains, and the parlor, where guests may sip sherry and relax with one another after the day's activities.

Carol and Steve Day, the owners, have added such niceties as delivering breakfast to your room on a silver tray, providing a modified breakfast of coffee and fresh breads if you have to leave early, ironing the bed linens, providing good reading lights by the beds and, most recently, nine new marble bathrooms.

The mix of guests is interesting—travelers en route to farther places, tourists exploring Savannah, and an increasing number of men and women who find inns more congenial than motels when they're in Savannah on business. It makes for good conversation.

If you like Civil War lore, you'll be interested in hearing about how Eliza Thompson (the house was built for her in 1847), a beautiful red-haired widow, entertained here in traditional gracious Southern style and feared that Sherman would destroy her home when he marched into Savannah.

HOW TO GET THERE: From the north, exit from U.S. 17A; turn left onto Oglethorpe. Go to the second light and turn right on Whitaker. Go to Jones and turn left. From I-95, take I-16E and then the Montgomery Street exit. Immediately turn right (at the Civic Center) onto Liberty. Take Liberty to the first stoplight at Whitaker. Go right on Whitaker for 3 blocks, then turn left on Jones. A small sign identifies the inn.

Foley House Inn
Savannah, Georgia 31401

INNKEEPER: Phil Jenkins

ADDRESS/TELEPHONE: 14 West Hull Street, Chippewa Square;
(912) 232–6622 or (800) 647–3708 outside Georgia; fax (912) 231–1218

WEB SITE: www.foleyinn.com

E-MAIL: foleyinn@aol.com

ROOMS: 18 rooms; all with private bath, telephone, television, VCR;
some with whirlpool bath; some with fireplace. Limited smoking;
restrictions on children.

RATES: $175 to $290 single or double occupancy; includes full breakfast, afternoon and evening refreshments; minimum stay may be
required.

OPEN: Year-round.

FACILITIES AND ACTIVITIES: Nearby: Savannah historic district, casual
and fine dining, shopping, nightlife, Forts Jackson and Pulaski, beaches
of Tybee Island; golf, bicycle rental, boating, tennis.

BUSINESS TRAVEL: Savannah airport is 15 miles away; all guest room
phones have a dataport.

One of out favorite innkeepers is the new host at the Foley House Inn. For many years, Phil Jenkins did an absolutely superb job as the owner/innkeeper of the magnificent 1842 Inn in Macon. We were devastated when we heard he'd sold it, but our dismay turned to delight when we learned he's decided to devote his considerable talents to another fine inn.

Honored by *Vacation Magazine* as one of the Ten Most Romantic Inns in the country, by *National Geographic Traveler* as one of the Twenty-five Top Southern Inns, and featured on the Home and Garden Television Network in *Great Homes Across America*, Foley House Inn occupies a pair of elegant 1896 Federal-style town houses. Restored in the most minute detail, every cornice, joist, and sill has been renewed by a master craftsman.

Each of the eighteen spacious guest rooms and suites is an individual masterpiece, handsomely appointed with period furniture, hand-colored engravings, and Oriental rugs. All the rooms in the main house are blessed with a four-poster bed and a gas-log fireplace. Fifteen of the rooms boast a fireplace. Many chambers are enhanced by a whirlpool bath, but all offer telephone and television as well as a VCR, on which you can play movies borrowed from the inn's extensive film library. Guest rooms in the main inn are decorated in the opulent Victorian style, while those in the carriage house display a more casual country look.

A hearty full breakfast can be served in the privacy of your room, or you might prefer to join your fellow guests in the stunning lounge or, in good weather, out in the courtyard. If you're staying several days, a sweet breakfast of such dishes as waffles or French toast is alternated with a more traditional breakfast of quiches, omelettes, or other egg dishes. Two events are eagerly looked forward to in the afternoon: When a formal afternoon high tea including cakes and other sweets is cleared away, hors d'oeuvres follow. Be sure to arrange your daily schedule to get back to the inn in time to enjoy one

Foley House Inn Tidbits

- During the 1800s it was believed that gargoyles could ward off evil spirits, so the original owners used gargoyles to adorn several fireplaces.

- The exquisite parlor chandelier is from the set of *Gone With the Wind*, as is the candelabra at the foot of the stairway.

- Some believe that the restless spirit of Honoria Foley, the original owner, stills dwells in the house.

- During the restoration of the two houses that make up the inn, a human skeleton was found in the wall between the two. No one has been able to solve the mystery of who it was or how it got there.

- If you had an eagle eye out when you saw the movie *Forrest Gump,* you may recognize Chippewa Square in the heart of Savannah's historic district as the place where parts of the movie were filmed. Gracious Foley House Inn overlooks this lovely square.

or both of these repasts. Either or both will surely cut down on the amount of dinner you need. Late in the evening, cordials and a fine selection of wine are available to wind up the day.

HOW TO GET THERE: I-16 ends and merges into Montgomery Street. Immediately after you pass the Civic Center on the right, turn right onto West Oglethorpe Street. Go 3 blocks and turn right onto Whitaker Street. Go 2 blocks and turn left at West Hull Street. Foley House is on the northwest corner of Chippewa Square.

The Forsyth Park Inn
Savannah, Georgia 31401

INNKEEPERS: Rick and Lori Blass

ADDRESS/TELEPHONE: 102 West Hall Street; (912) 233-6800; fax (912) 233-6804

WEB SITE: www.forsythparkinn.com

E-MAIL: innkeeper@forsythparkinn.com

ROOMS: 9, plus 1 cottage; all with private bath, television, and telephone; some with Jacuzzi and working fireplace.

RATES: $115 to $230, single or double; includes continental breakfast, wine and hors d'oeuvres, turndown service with cordials and dessert. Credit cards accepted. No children under 8, except in cottage.

OPEN: Year-round.

FACILITIES AND ACTIVITIES: Courtyard and garden with fountain. Some tours pick up at the inn. Located in Savannah historic district, opposite Forsyth Park. Jogging, tennis courts, playgrounds for children, picnic area, and touch garden for the blind in the park. Nearby: Restaurants, historic sites, Savannah riverfront, historic lighthouse, forts, beaches.

*A*ptly named, this wonderful old mansion sits on a landscaped corner lot directly across the street from Forsyth Park, Savannah's largest and most opulent square, where there are fountains, walking paths, and gardens as well as recreational facilities to tempt you. Forsyth Park is also the staging area for Savannah's world-renowned St. Patrick's Day Parade. We particularly like to stroll through the park, stopping often to enjoy the flowers. It's also a great place to people-watch.

The meticulously restored home itself boasts a welcoming veranda outside and 16-foot-high ceilings, tall windows, and ornate wood architectural details inside. It is elegantly furnished with antiques, including a grand piano in the parlor. Guest rooms feature period antiques, four-poster king- or queen-size beds, fireplaces, antique marble baths, and all the modern amenities.

Beauty is only skin deep, however, and the difference between a simply OK stay and a really exceptional one lies in the level of service and pampering you get. Be assured that the Forsyth Park Inn specializes in indulging its guests, whether it's the evening wine and hors d'oeuvres hour in the parlor or on the patio or the turndown service with cordials and dessert. The innkeepers are only too happy to provide an early breakfast for those who have to leave early or to recommend restaurants and sight-seeing attractions.

The inn attracts many business travelers who are tired of staying in cookie-cutter motels or hotels and is particularly popular with women business travelers who appreciate the friendliness and security.

In addition to its proximity to Forsyth Park, the inn is within walking distance of the riverfront, shopping, restaurants, and entertainment.

HOW TO GET THERE: At Savannah take the U.S. 16 exit off I-95. Go north on Montgomery Street to Liberty. Turn right on Liberty. Continue to Whitaker, which is one-way. Follow Whitaker to Hall Street. The inn is on the corner.

The Gastonian ♥
Savannah, Georgia 31401

INNKEEPER: Anne Landers

ADDRESS/TELEPHONE: 220 East Gaston Street; (912) 232–2869 or

(800) 322–6603; fax (912) 232–0710

WEB SITE: www.gastonian.com

E-MAIL: gastonianinn@aol.com

ROOMS: 14, plus 3 two-room suites; all with fireplace, television, and telephone; many with whirlpool tub; 1 with wheelchair access. No-smoking inn.

RATES: $250 to $395, single or double; includes full sit-down Southern breakfast, afternoon tea and/or wine, late evening desserts, and nightly turndown service.

OPEN: Year-round.

FACILITIES AND ACTIVITIES: Sundeck, hot tub, off-street lighted parking, garden courtyard. Nearby: Restaurants, carriage tours of historic district, Savannah riverfront shops, museums, beach, wildlife refuge.

he Gastonian, an extensively restored B&B inn known as one of the most romantic inns in the Southeast, comprises two 1868 historic buildings sitting side by side and a two-story carriage house, joined by a garden and an elevated walkway.

The guest rooms are filled with English antiques, exotic baths, Persian rugs, and fresh flowers. The most outrageous bath is in the Caracalla Suite (named for a Roman emperor); it has an 8-foot Jacuzzi, sitting on a parquet platform draped with filmy curtains, next to a working fireplace. The fixtures here are of solid brass. In another room, they are of sculptured 24-karat gold. Each bath is unique and styled to complement the theme of its room—French, Oriental, Victorian, Italianate, Colonial American, or Country. All the inn's water runs through a purification system, which means that you have to go easy on the bubble bath.

The public rooms are equally lavish, furnished with English antiques, satin damask drapes, and Sheffield silver.

Recently, the interiors have been painted; the gardens replanted; and a new phone system, commercial laundry, and reservation system have been added. However, the most important feature, the ambience of this ultra-romantic inn, has remained.

HOW TO GET THERE: From I-95, take I-16 to Savannah. Take the Martin Luther King exit and go straight onto West Gaston Street. The inn is at the corner of East Gaston and Lincoln Streets.

The Kehoe House
Savannah, Georgia 31401

INNKEEPER: Martha Geiger

ADDRESS/TELEPHONE: 123 Habersham Street; (912) 232–1020 or (800) 820–1020; fax (912) 231–0208 or (912) 231–1587

WEB SITE: www.kehoehouse.com

ROOMS: 13, plus 2 suites; all with private bath, telephone, cable television, clock radio, hair dryer, robe; some with private porch and/or sitting area; 1 room wheelchair accessible; not suitable for children. No-smoking inn.

RATES: $195 to $275, includes a full gourmet breakfast as well as English afternoon tea and hors d'oeuvres, nightly turndown, and daily newspaper; more for St. Patrick's Day weekend; 2-night minimum required for stays with Friday, Saturday, or Sunday arrival from October 1 through May 1. $35 for additional person.

OPEN: Year-round.

FACILITIES AND ACTIVITIES: Elevator, honor bar, 24-hour concierge service, laundry service, limited room service. Nearby: Walking distance to historic Isaiah Davenport House, Savannah's historic district, casual and fine dining, shopping, nightlife; beaches of Tybee Island; Forts Jackson and Pulaski; golf, tennis.

BUSINESS TRAVEL: Entire fourth floor used as conference room, small boardroom; full secretarial services; corporate rates Sunday through Thursday.

This magnificent redbrick Victorian mansion, built in 1892 on Columbia Square, was unusual in being a single house in turn-of-the-twentieth-century Savannah when town houses were the rule. Listed on the National Register of Historic Places, the three-story Kehoe

House operates as a luxurious, intimate European-style B&B inn concentrating on exceptional personal pampering, which has earned it four stars and four diamonds from the major hotel rating services.

We've watched this property since it was a boarded-up derelict, hoping against hope that it would be saved and convinced that it would make a perfect inn or bed-and-breakfast. We'd idly wonder how much it would cost to purchase and fix up, but we knew without even asking that the answer was way more than we could ever afford or even borrow. Imagine our delight when we learned that such a project was in the works. Over several more trips to Savannah, we watched the progress with fascination and pleasure.

Now gleaming wall paneling, woodwork, and floors set off exquisite antiques, period reproductions, important artwork, Oriental carpets, and elegant fabrics in the public spaces and commodious guest chambers. Sumptuous guest rooms are found in the main house; two suites and a common parlor are found in the town house next door.

Some of the extraordinarily beautiful guest rooms feature canopy beds and/or private or shared upstairs porches. Generally considered the most romantic of the guest accommodations, the Limerick Suite boasts a four-poster bed and overlooks Columbia Square.

A full gourmet breakfast is served each morning and consists of eggs any style; bacon; grits; fresh fruits and juices; and freshly baked muffins, biscuits, and pastries. As if that weren't enough, a daily special is offered, which might be French toast with link sausage, eggs Benedict, omelettes, or whatever strikes the chef's fancy.

HOW TO GET THERE: I–16 ends and merges into Montgomery Street. Pass the Civic Center on the right and go 2 more blocks to York and turn right. Go 7 blocks and turn left onto Lincoln, then right onto President. The inn is on the corner of Habersham and President Streets. Parking is either off-street or on State Street.

Magnolia Place Inn
Savannah, Georgia 31401

INNKEEPERS: Kathy Medlock, Rob and Jane Sales

ADDRESS/TELEPHONE: 503 Whitaker Street; (912) 236-7674;
outside Georgia, (800) 238-7674; fax (912) 236-1145

WEB SITE: www.magnoliaplaceinn.com

E-MAIL: info@magnoliaplaceinn.com

ROOMS: 13 rooms in main house (1 with fireplace, 6 with Jacuzzi), 1
suite with Jacuzzi and fireplace, and 3 row houses; all with private bath
and telephone.

RATES: $145 to $325, single or double; includes full breakfast, high tea,
and evening dessert cordials. Special-occasion packages available. Children under 12 in row houses only.

OPEN: Year-round.

FACILITIES AND ACTIVITIES: VCRs and film library; gardens. Located
in Savannah historic district, overlooking Forsyth Park, which offers
jogging, tennis courts, playground for children, picnic area. Nearby:
Restaurants, within walking distance of riverfront.

BUSINESS Located 5 minutes from business district. Telephone in room
with direct dial for modems; fax available. Corporate rates.

This B&B inn has a verified ghost who's been known to open and
close doors and make other noises in distant rooms, turn on televisions and air conditioners, and move things around. According
to legend, the ghost of Magnolia Place is the original owner, a cotton magnate
who lost his fortune when the boll weevil hit and who committed suicide by
falling down the steps. Others say he died of an overindulgence of oysters.
Either way, staff members say the ghost is a strong and positive presence.

But ghost stories aside, the real attraction of Magnolia Place is in its exotic
furnishings, your luxurious accommodations, and the top-notch service.

Some examples: Jacuzzis and gas fireplaces in some of the rooms, English
antique furnishings, and prints and porcelains from around the world. The
butterfly collection in the parlor is famous. Also, the staff can arrange private tours of Savannah if you'd rather not be herded along with a group.

The parlor, where high tea with imported teas, wine, and benne seed
cookies is served in the afternoon, used to be a ballroom. Its fireplace is
rimmed with tiles from Portugal, hand painted to look as though two rose
trees rise from pots at floor level and "grow" up so that their bloom-laden

branches nearly meet under the mantel. Around the room, pieces of Japanese cloisonné and Chinese porcelains catch your eye.

The three row houses each feature a living room, full kitchen, two bedrooms, private baths, and small courtyards. These accommodations are ideal for families.

If you ask for a dinner recommendation, the staff will mention Elizabeth on Thirty-Seventh—a well-known gourmet restaurant in a century-old home nearby—the Pink House, or Bistro Savannah.

While you're at dinner, the staff at the inn are busy turning down your bed and placing pralines and madeira in your room, checking on your supply of Neutrogena amenities, and handling any personal requests you've made for extra service.

Personal attention like this attracts corporate and international travelers and celebrities, discreetly unidentified, as well as tourists. Best we can figure, the ghost hangs around, too, because he can't find such good service anywhere else.

HOW TO GET THERE: From I-95, take I-16 east onto Montgomery Street. Turn right on Liberty Street and then right on Whitaker. Coming from Charleston, take 17 north over the Savannah River Bridge. Immediately turn right on Oglethorpe and follow it to Whitaker. Turn right on Whitaker. Park behind the inn.

Olde Harbour Inn
Savannah, Georgia 31401

INNKEEPER: Russ Mitchell

ADDRESS/TELEPHONE: 508 East Factors' Walk; (912) 234-4100 or (800) 553-6533; fax (912) 233-5979

WEB SITE: www.oldeharbourinn.com

E-MAIL: info@oldeharbourinn.com

ROOMS: 24 suites, all with private bath, fully equipped kitchen, cable television with HBO, telephone, clock radio.

RATES: $129 to $199 for studios and living/dining room suites; $169 to $229 for balcony or 2-bedroom loft suites; includes continental breakfast, cordials in the afternoon, and nightly turndown service with a treat.

OPEN: Year-round.

FACILITIES AND ACTIVITIES: Kitchens, breakfast room, library. Nearby: Savannah's historic district, fine dining, shops, theater, nighttime entertainment; beaches of Tybee Island.

One of the things we liked so much about staying at the Olde Harbour Inn is its proximity to River Street and the busy waterfront. From our tiny balcony, we loved watching the bustling little tugboats guiding the gigantic ships up the Savannah River and the paddlewheel tour boat setting out, as well as getting a bird's-eye look at the tourists and town folks on River Street's Riverfront Plaza. The Olde Harbour Inn is an ideal vantage point during Savannah's fabled St. Patrick's weekend, but make reservations way, way in advance—a year ahead wouldn't be too soon.

Built in 1892, this three-story, bluff-side B&B inn is steeped in Savannah history. Originally the offices, warehouse, and shipping center of the Tide Water Oil Company, the structure has had many lives. The failure of a developer's dream turned into a boon for the traveling public in Savannah. Several years ago the structure was restored and modified as condominium apartments. With such an advantageous location, it's hard to understand how they failed to sell, but they did, permitting the building to be converted into an all-suites hotel.

Unusual elements of the original construction have been retained, including beams fashioned from various parts of old sailing vessels and gray bricks that were the first compressed bricks used in Savannah. Every luxurious accommodation—all of which overlook the river—is either a studio apartment or a full apartment with a fully equipped kitchen, living/dining area, and one or more bedrooms, some in lofts. Each is furnished in appropriate period reproductions.

Public spaces include the sunny Marine Room, where a deluxe continental breakfast of hot biscuits, muffins, fresh fruit, cereals, juices, and hot beverages is served; the elegant Grand Salon, where guests gather in the late afternoon for candlelight wine, sherry, and hors d'oeuvres; and the comfortably furnished library, which is well stocked with books, magazines, and newspapers.

All of Savannah's historic district is at your doorstep.

HOW TO GET THERE: I–16 ends and merges into Montgomery Street. Go past the Civic Center on the right as well as Elbert, Liberty, and Franklin Squares, then turn right onto West Bay Street. Go 10 blocks and turn left onto the Lincoln ramp. Follow the ramp down and turn right onto Factors' Walk. The inn's entrance is on the left.

Planters Inn
Savannah, Georgia 31401

INNKEEPER: Natalie Alman

ADDRESS/TELEPHONE: 29 Abercorn Street; (912) 232–5678 or (800) 554–1187; fax (912) 232–8893

WEB SITE: www.plantersinnsavannah.com

E-MAIL: plantinn@aol.com

ROOMS: 60 rooms and suites, all with private bath, telephone,and television; some with fireplaces.

RATES: $115 to $185; includes continental breakfast, afternoon wine, newspaper, turndown service, valet service. Credit cards accepted. Discounts for AARP and AAA.

OPEN: Year-round.

FACILITIES AND ACTIVITIES: Elevator, valet parking, bicycle rental, access to a health club. Nearby: Walking distance of historic district, restaurants, shops.

BUSINESS TRAVEL: Conference facilities, hospitality suites, secretarial services.

*A*lovely small B&B inn restored to its 1912 glory, the Planters Inn successfully blends the warmth and charm of an intimate inn with the services of a grand hotel. An award-winning landmark building on lovely Reynolds Square in the heart of Savannah's historic district, the inn was created and recently refurbished with lavish attention to detail.

The inn features a sumptuous pink-marble lobby with intricate moldings, soaring columns, and immense gilt-frame mirrors. Elegantly furnished with comfortable period sofas and wing chairs done in copies of period fabrics, the lobby is the gathering place for breakfast and afternoon tea—affording the opportunity to meet and mingle with your fellow guests.

We loved our spacious and luxurious guest chamber, which, like all the others, features high ceilings, a private bath, Baker period furnishings, and lavish bed and window coverings done in reproductions of the finest Old Savannah-style textiles. Individually decorated, some of the guest rooms boast four-poster rice beds and comfortable seating areas.

Depending on your appetites, two options are available for breakfast. A complimentary continental breakfast buffet, which was more than ample for us, is set out in the hospitality suite. For those with bigger appetites, a more elaborate breakfast is available from room service at an additional fee. After a strenuous day of sight-seeing and checking out other inns, we literally collapsed in the lobby in time for afternoon wine.

Among the other amenities at the inn are newspapers delivered to the room and evening turndown service with a sweet left on your pillow. Bicycle rentals and access to a health club satisfy those who yearn for physical exercise in addition to their sight-seeing, shopping, and dining pleasures.

With the Planters Inn as your home base, you're only steps from Savannah's bustling riverfront, where renovated cotton warehouses now contain quaint shops, casual and fine dining establishments, and nightlife.

HOW TO GET THERE: I-16 ends and merges into Montgomery Street. Go past the Civic Center on the right as well as Egbert, Liberty, and Franklin Squares. Turn right onto West Bay Street and go 6 blocks to Abercorn, where you will turn right. The inn faces Reynolds Square. Parking is on the street or across the street in a parking garage.

The President's Quarters
Savannah, Georgia 31401

INNKEEPERS: Stacy K. Stephens and Hank Smalling

ADDRESS/TELEPHONE: 225 East President Street; (912) 233-1600 or (800) 233-1776; fax (912) 238-0849

WEB SITE: www.presidentsquarters.com

E-MAIL: info@presidentsquarters.com

ROOMS: 10 rooms, plus 9 suites; all with private bath, ceiling fan, small refrigerator, television, VCR, telephone, robes, hair dryer, and clock radio; some with Jacuzzi and/or steam shower; some with gas-log fireplace, balcony, loft bedroom, private entrace. 16 rooms and suites wheelchair accessible; 1 room designed for the physically challenged. Restricted smoking.

RATES: $137 to $185 for rooms, $185 to $250 for suites, based on double occupancy; includes continental-plus breakfast, afternoon refreshments, nightly turndown service, newspaper, complimentary fruit and bottle of wine. Additional $20 per person above the age of 10. Honeymoon, anniversary, and St. Patrick's Day packages; off-season specials. Children of all ages welcome. Credit cards accepted.

OPEN: Year-round.

FACILITIES AND ACTIVITIES: Room service, elevator, pool, outdoor hot tub. Nearby: Savannah's historic district, casual and fine dining, shopping, nightlife; Fort Pulaski; beaches of Tybee Island.

BUSINESS TRAVEL: Writing desk and dataport; dining areas in the George Washington and Woodrow Wilson suites are appropriate for small board meetings; Corporate Cabinet Club membership for frequent business travelers.

*J*ust to orient you, this mirrored pair of back-to-back brick Federal-style town houses, built in 1855 on Oglethorpe Square in the heart of what is now Savannah's huge historic district, was the backdrop for one of the scenes in the television miniseries *Roots*. The prestigious Owens-Thomas House museum, noted for its superior Regency architecture, is next door.

Inside, well-proportioned rooms, which feature ceilings as high as 13 feet, are filled with antiques and period reproductions and embellished with appropriate Savannah-style fabrics. Only a small amount of space is devoted to the cozy lobby, where breakfast and afternoon refreshments are set out daily, with seating in the beautifully landscaped courtyard. The rest is dedicated to luxurious guest rooms and suites.

Each guest chamber is dedicated to a president, and each is accented with portraits, photos, handwritten notes, and other memorabilia relating to that president. Beds, which range from double to king size, may be four-poster,

Pampered at the President's

On our way to a weekend stay at The President's Quarters, we had car trouble and were stuck on I-95 for three hours at night. After thousands of cars had passed us without stopping, a friendly University of Georgia student came to our rescue. By the time he called for a tow and we got to the inn, it was about midnight, and we were frustrated and exhausted. The kindly night staff had lit our fireplace and, as soon as we were settled in, served us hot tea, cakes, and liqueur. That's the kind of pampering you can expect at this B&B inn.

canopy, or old-fashioned high beds. Every room boasts a gas-log fireplace, cable television, and a VCR. Plush terry-cloth robes are provided as well. Select rooms offer a ceiling fan, Jacuzzi tub and/or steam shower, and a queen-size sofa bed. Some rooms have the added attraction of a balcony or courtyard. The fourth floor offers loft suites.

Three additional rooms have been created in a guest house next door. Each luxurious accommodation is embellished with original colors and woodwork as well as ornate painted ceilings and features an oversize whirlpool tub and steam shower.

A sumptuous continental-plus breakfast of homemade sweet breads, Belgian pecan waffles, quiches, banana pancakes, breakfast casseroles, granola, and fruit can be served in your room, in the formal parlor, or in the courtyard. We always make plans to be back at the inn in late afternoon to enjoy the popular deluxe afternoon tea, which consists of cakes, warm hors d'oeuvres, cheeses, wine, and other refreshments. Then we can have a light dinner later in the evening. The President's Quarters also offers nightly turndown service with Savannah sweets and port or sherry, newspapers, valet service, twenty-four hour concierge, and off-street parking—a rarity in the historic district.

HOW TO GET THERE: I-16 ends and merges into Montgomery Street. Go 2 blocks past the Civic Center on your right and turn right onto York. Go 6 blocks to Oglethorpe Square. Just past the square on York, turn left into the parking lot. The inn is on the east side of the square.

The River Street Inn
Savannah, Georgia 31401

INNKEEPER: Jack Bussert

ADDRESS/TELEPHONE: 115 East River Street; (912) 234-6400 or (800) 253-4229; fax (912) 234-1478

WEB SITE: www.riverstreetinn.com

ROOMS: 86; all with private bath, television, telephone, coffeemaker.

RATES: $149 to $219, double occupancy; includes afternoon refreshments, morning newspaper, evening sweet. Children under the age of 16 stay free in the parents' room using existing bedding.

OPEN: Year-round.

FACILITIES AND ACTIVITIES: Elevator, billiard room, restaurants, lounge, use of nearby athletic club, concierge service. Nearby: Savannah's historic district, fine dining, shops, theater, nighttime entertainment; Fort Pulaski; beaches of Tybee Island.

BUSINESS TRAVEL: Meeting and conference facilities for up to 150; secretarial services available.

Because of its location right in the heart of the action fronting on Factors' Walk and overlooking River Street, Riverfront Plaza, and the busy Savannah River waterfront, we think The River Street Inn is an ideal headquarters for visiting Savannah's historic district. We love being only steps away from casual and fine dining, shopping, and nightlife. We can pop downstairs to Huey's for New Orleans–style beignets (square doughnuts covered with powdered sugar) or to Savannah Sweets nearby to stock up on to-die-for pralines.

Built in 1817 as a place to sample, grade, store, and export cotton, the structure was enlarged by adding three stories in 1853. As a result, a series of alleys and walkways were created between the bluff above and the building. Known as Factors' Walk after the factors who graded the cotton, these alleys and bridges are one of the River Street Inn's most unusual features. Best of all, the intimate hotel preserves the charm of the past with the amenities and conveniences of the present.

Beautifully restored, the structure has been reincarnated as a delightful inn where you'll find gleaming pine floors, intricate moldings, and exposed brick. Gracious high-ceilinged, well-appointed guest rooms, which range in decor from sea captain to English chintz, are furnished with antiques and period reproductions. Many feature a queen-size four-poster bed, decorative fireplace, hardwood floors with Oriental rugs, brass bathroom fixtures, French balcony, and floor-length windows providing an impressive view of the Savannah River.

Get your day off to a fun-filled start by going downstairs to Huey's for breakfast. We think beignets and coffee are more than adequate, but if you're hungrier, you can get a made-to-order breakfast. By afternoon, what with sight-seeing and shopping, you're bound to be dragging. Just get yourselves back to the inn for a pick-me-up of wine and hors d'oeuvres.

Dining options include the previously mentioned Huey's, which serves breakfast, lunch, and dinner with a Cajun flair, and Tubby's, which specializes in seafood and serves lunch and dinner.

HOW TO GET THERE: The inn is easily accessible from I–16 and I–95 as well as U.S. 17 and U.S. 17A via Montgomery Street. Turn right at West Bay Street and go ½ mile to the gazebo at Emmet Park. The inn is on the left, with its entrance and parking on the East Bay Street level.

The Veranda 💙 🏠
Senoia, Georgia 30276

INNKEEPERS: Bobby and Jan Boal

ADDRESS/TELEPHONE: 252 Seavy Street; (770) 599-3905 or (877) 525-3436; fax (770) 599-0806

ROOMS: 9 rooms, all with private bath, fresh flowers, clock radio, hair dryer, robes, turndown with a surprise on your pillow; most rooms have a decorative fireplace, desk, and queen-size bed; one room with king-size bed. Smoking outside on veranda only.

RATES: $125 to $155 double, $85 to $125 single; includes full Southern breakfast, afternoon refreshments, and evening desserts. Children are welcome as long as accompanying adults realize that the inn is not childproof and that they will be responsible for damages. Credit cards accepted.

OPEN: Year-round.

FACILITIES AND ACTIVITIES: Gift shop; popcorn and chocolate chip cookies and hot and cold beverages are available twenty-four hours a day. Nearby: Restaurants, antiques shopping, Callaway Gardens, Little White House National Historic Site, Warm Springs, Franklin D. Roosevelt State Park, Pine Mountain Trail, Atlanta attractions, Riverwood Movie Studio.

BUSINESS TRAVEL: Desk in some rooms; special corporate rates for single business travelers Monday through Thursday.

Bobby (female) and Jan (male) are congenial, voluble hosts who make their guests feel like valued friends or family members visiting them in their home. We especially like to get Jan aside to tell us about his vast and varied kaleidoscope and ornate walking stick collections, which are displayed around the inn. We'd never realized there could be so many kinds—and there's a story behind every one. You'll be so enthused about kaleidoscopes that you'll surely want to buy one or more in the gift shop to take home for your own pleasure or to give as gifts. Check out Jan's kaleidoscope Web site at www.kaleidoscopeshop.com.

But back to the inn. Built in 1906 as the Hollberg Hotel, the Neoclassical structure with the wraparound porch supported by classic Doric columns has been restored and returned to its original use. Besides being listed on the National Register of Historic Places, the inn has been featured in dozens of television programs and magazine and newspaper articles and received many awards.

Located on a large corner lot with gardens to admire or while away some time in, the inn features spacious rooms with high ceilings. One of the twin parlors is set up as a music room with a working 1860 Estey reed organ and a Wurlitzer player piano with numerous music rolls. Needless to say, this room is a popular gathering place where complete strangers get to know one another through rollicking sing-alongs. If you'd like things a little more decorous, retreat to the sitting room in the upstairs hall, which you'll find amply stocked with books and games; to an old-fashioned swing on one of the porches; or to a stone bench in the garden.

Guest rooms, which are furnished with simple antiques more reminiscent of a warm, comfortable boardinghouse than a "don't-touch-me" house museum, all offer private baths. Some boast decorative fireplaces. Of particular interest are the Honeymoon Suite, which has a Jacuzzi, and the front bedrooms, which can be closed off to create a suite for a family or friends traveling together.

A full Southern breakfast, included in the room rate, is served in the formal dining room. Afternoon tea and evening desserts are served here to guests as well.

HOW TO GET THERE: From GA 85, turn west onto Seavy Street. The inn is at the corner of Seavy and Barnes Streets. Alternately, from GA 16 turn north at Broad, which becomes Seavy.

The Historic Statesboro Inn and Restaurant
Statesboro, Georgia 30458

INNKEEPERS: Garges family

ADDRESS/TELEPHONE: 106 South Main Street; (912) 489-8628 or (800) 846-9466; fax (912) 489-4785

WEB SITE: www.statesboroinn.com

E-MAIL: frontdesk@statesboroinn.com

ROOMS: 16, including 2 suites; all with private bath, telephone with dataport, television, ceiling fan, coffeemaker, iron and ironing board; some with private porch, fireplace, and/or whirlpool bath.

RATES: $85 to $125 for rooms; $120 to $150 for suites; includes full breakfast. Corporate rates; some weekend packages. Credit cards accepted.

OPEN: Year-round.

FACILITIES AND ACTIVITIES: Restaurant, bar, several common rooms and porches. Nearby: Georgia Southern University museum, Herty Nature Trail, Raptor Center, historical and architectural walking tours, Botanical Garden, tours of Braswell Foods and Sunny South Pecans.

BUSINESS TRAVEL: Telephone dataports in rooms; fax and copy services available; reception, banquet, and conference facilities for large groups.

*K*ing Cotton built these two gracious side-by-side century-old mansions, which today provide elegant accommodations as well as superb dining. Elegantly restored, the inn is listed on the National Register of Historic Places. Exterior architectural elements of note include wraparound porches, small second-story porches, and screened-in porches. Inside, you'll admire the 14-foot-high ceilings and burnished floors and woodwork. The gardens are beautiful year-round and provide additional places to relax in the company of others or alone.

The main house contains most of the guest rooms and one suite; the sister house contains three additional rooms and a second suite. Lavish use of floral patterns and lace as well as antiques and period reproductions characterize the guest chambers and suites, most of which boast high or cathedral ceilings. Not surprising, the Honeymoon Suite is particularly romantic and features a whirlpool bath. The Executive Suite boasts two rooms, a private porch, and a queen-size hide-away bed, making it ideal for larger parties traveling together.

The well-known restaurant specializes in continental cuisine, featuring steaks, chops, seafood, and homemade breads and desserts. A generous full breakfast is served to guests, and the dining rooms are open Wednesday through Saturday for dinner. Reservations are strongly recommended.

HOW TO GET THERE: From I–16, turn north onto U.S. 301/25, which runs through town. The inn is 1 mile north of Georgia Southern University.

Coleman House
Swainsboro, Georgia 30401

INNKEEPERS: Connie and David Thurman

ADDRESS/TELEPHONE: 323 North Main Street; (912) 237-9100; fax
(912) 237-8586

WEB SITE: www.colemanhouseinn.com

E-MAIL: Via Web site

ROOMS: 10 rooms, all with private bath, cable television, ceiling fan,
telephone; children welcome; ask about pets; no wheelchair access.

RATES: $55 to $85, including full breakfast and refreshments; each
additional person $10. Credit cards and traveler's checks accepted.

OPEN: Year-round.

FACILITIES AND ACTIVITIES: Formal and informal parlors, dining
room, verandas and porches. Nearby: Fishing, golf, tennis, antiques
shopping; Savannah and coastal beaches.

BUSINESS TRAVEL: Telephones with dataports

*A*nyone who has ever seen the "painted ladies" in San Francisco
in person or in photographs will appreciate both the architecture and the paint job of the Coleman House. Built between
1901 and 1904, it is one of the best examples of the Queen Anne style in the
state. Painted in the traditional manner associated with the style, this majestic three-story residence has cream as the predominant color with subdued
rust, blue, and brown trim colors accentuating the moldings, eaves, columns,
and porch railings.

Previous owners did such a magnificent job of restoring the thirty-two-
room house—listed on the National Register of Historic Places—they
received an award from the Georgia Trust for Historic Preservation.

Inside we found the anticipated 12-foot-high ceilings and intricate moldings as well as eleven fireplaces. One of the architectural elements that make
this house so special, however, is the fact that it features burl-pine floors. In
fact, it is one of only three surviving houses in Georgia with such floors.

What really caught our immediate attention when we stepped inside was
the central hall, which is 55 feet long. As you can imagine, this magnificent
space is often the scene of weddings and other special functions. Just to give
you an idea of the immensity of the mansion, it covers 10,000 square feet.

All of the ten bedrooms feature private baths with a claw-foot tub, decorative fireplace, and period antiques and accessories. Because the beds are antiques, most of them are double size, but several rooms have queens or twins. There is an eleventh sleeping room without its own bathroom that can be rented in conjunction with the adjoining room, in essence making it a two-bedroom suite. This arrangement is ideal for a family or friends traveling together.

An immense wraparound porch with polygonal gazebo-like turrets complete with conical roofs and finials, as well as several upstairs porches, offer guests places to socialize or enjoy some solitude. The grounds themselves invite you for a leisurely stroll.

Since we last visited, several of the downstairs rooms have been incorporated into a restaurant, which serves lunch Monday through Friday, dinner on Friday, and a popular brunch on Sunday. You can enjoy your full breakfast, which might include bacon and eggs, waffles, or pancakes, in the breakfast room or out on the veranda. Dinner can be prepared for overnight guests on request for an additional fee.

HOW TO GET THERE: Take I–16 to exit 21. Turn north on U.S. 1 and go approximately 14 miles to Swainsboro. Go straight through to where U.S. 1 and U.S. 80 cross. Stay on U.S. 1 for 2½ blocks. The inn is on the right.

Melhana,
The Grand Plantation Resort
Thomasville, Georgia 31792

INNKEEPERS: Fran and Charlie Lewis

ADDRESS/TELEPHONE: 301 Showboat Lane; (229) 226–2290 or (888) 920–3030; fax (229) 226–4585

WEB SITE: www.melhana.com

E-MAIL: info@melhana.com

ROOMS: 29, plus 9 suites and honeymoon cottage; all with king- or queen-size beds and private bath (two are down the hall), bathrobes, television, desk; some with fireplace, whirlpool bath. The entire interior of the facility is nonsmoking.

RATES: Rooms and suites $285, Presidential suite $1,000; includes breakfast, afternoon tea, and use of recreational facilities. Ask about special packages. Discounted rates are available from October 1 through December 30.

OPEN: Year-round.

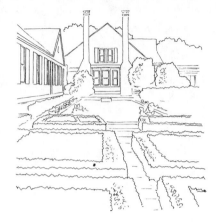

FACILITIES AND ACTIVITIES: Complimentary airport shuttle service, heated pool, clay tennis court, croquet, fitness facility with personal trainer available by appointment, massage available by appointment, horse-drawn carriage rides on weekend evenings or by appointment. Plans in the works for an etiquette school, cooking school, visiting chef's program, and live theater productions. Nearby: Historic Thomasville—the Rose City, Tallahassee, golf courses, skeet shooting, quail hunts in season, horseback riding, Birdsong Nature Center, Tall Timber Research Station, Maclay Gardens State Park, the Museum of History and Natural Science.

BUSINESS TRAVEL: Computer dataport, multiline phone with conferencing capabilities; 24-hour concierge to assist with faxes, express mail, and special business needs; ideal for meetings and small corporate retreats; four meeting rooms with audiovisual equipment, one with complete satellite hookup; corporate rates available.

We've all been told for years that the Old South with its traditional grand plantations was literally "gone with the wind." In actuality, hidden behind hedges, pine forests, and endless fields, America's greatest concentration of surviving working plantations—between seventy and one hundred—stretches between Thomasville, Georgia, and Tallahassee, Florida, which is why this region of Georgia is known as the Plantation Trace. Until recently, all but the grandiose Pebble Hill Plantation, which is open for tours, were a well-kept secret. Happily, now you can experience for yourselves the gracious, luxurious, romantic Old South way of life. Melhana Plantation is a truly magical place where your everyday cares will melt away in its luxurious surroundings.

The heart of the sprawling pink Greek Revival mansion was built in 1825, and it has been added onto various times over its long life, creating the graceful manor house you see today. Seven exquisite guest rooms and four opu-

Historic Thomasville

Find true Southern elegance among the stately oaks and pines and thousands of rose bushes in Thomasville—the Rose City. In the last twenty years of the nineteenth century, great weather, reputed curative powers for consumption and other respiratory illnesses, abundant game and game birds (along with the development of the modern shotgun), and the fact that the railroads' southern routes ended in Thomasville made the area an astoundingly popular resort destination. During Thomasville's heyday Northern socialites flocked to the area from fall through spring rather than chance the malaria epidemics in Florida. Grand hotels, seasonal vacation "cottages," and plantations blossomed. Due to the immense wealth and varied tastes of the Northern visitors, an astounding array of architectural styles are represented in Thomasville.

More than fifty historic homes from the Winter Resort Era still grace Thomasville's streets, and south of the city, more working plantations survive than anywhere else in this country. Several historic homes are open for tours or operate as bed-and-breakfasts, and you can tour the house, outbuildings, and grounds at magnificent Pebble Hill Plantation.

Begun in 1922 and held each April, the Thomasville Rose Show and Festival features more than thirty fun-filled activities, including an elegant plantation ball.

lent suites grace the manor house—now known as the Pink House. Each high-ceilinged guest chamber is uniquely furnished and decorated to ensure its own distinct personality, but each is appointed with lovely antiques and/or period reproductions, as well as opulent fabrics and every possible amenity, such as down comforters. Hibernia Cottage, a honeymoon hideaway in the fanciest creamery we've ever seen, guarantees complete seclusion for newlyweds or other romantics, and twenty-six other guest chambers have been fashioned out of the many splendid Greek Revival outbuildings.

Another treat at the plantation is the Showboat. What looks like a typical Southern mansion on the outside reveals a theater inside where the first private screening of *Gone With the Wind* was shown in 1939. Today the Showboat—completely paneled in pecky cypress—is used for screenings, productions, meetings, receptions, and other events. The grounds contain extensive gardens; a walled vegetable garden, a winter garden, sunken garden, marble goldfish pond with koi, and endless borders blooming flamboyantly depending on the season. Peacocks and hens strut their stuff for your entertainment. In good weather the wicker-filled veranda has its appeal; in inclement weather the delightful, formal Hogan and Hanna Rooms provide an elegant background for afternoon tea or a before-dinner drink.

White-gloved waiters serve you with elan in the princely Chapin Dining Room restaurant, which serves innovative, updated cuisine. Reservations and jackets for gentlemen are required.

HOW TO GET THERE: Follow U.S. 319 (Tallahassee/Thomasville Road) south from Thomasville 4 miles; watch for the sign on your right.

Hotel Warm Springs
Warm Springs, Georgia 31830

INNKEEPER: Gerrie Thompson

ADDRESS/TELEPHONE: 47 Broad Street; (706) 655-2114 or (800) 366-7616; fax (706) 655-2406

E-MAIL: hotelwarmsprings@alltel.net

ROOMS: 14 rooms and suites; all with private bath, television, and clock radio.

RATES: $70 to $145, includes full Southern country breakfast and evening social hour with soft drinks. Honeymoon package available. Senior, corporate, state, and federal discounts. Children of all ages welcome. Credit cards accepted. No handicapped-accessible rooms. No-smoking inn.

OPEN: Year-round.

FACILITIES AND ACTIVITIES: Formal parlor, social parlor, small garden with fountain and old-fashioned double swing, soda fountain/ice cream parlor, three gift shops. Nearby: Town, shops, and restaurants of Warm Springs, FDR Little White House National Historic Site, Franklin D. Roosevelt State Park, Pine Mountain Trail, Callaway Gardens, golf, tennis, hiking, covered bridge, national fishery, swimming..

BUSINESS TRAVEL: Ideal for small meetings and retreats.

*W*hat's the big attraction in Warm Springs? Well there are many—several of which are connected with Franklin D. Roosevelt, who built and maintained a home there. This became the Little White House during his presidency so that he could have easy access to the beneficial mineral waters for relief from his polio. But Warm Springs today is so much more; besides that, it's a very convenient base from which to explore west-central Georgia.

Drive into the tiny crossroads that is Warm Springs and you'll be transported back to the 1930s and 1940s when FDR often came to town to stay at his Little White House. The town nearly died on April 15, 1945, when the president expired at his home there. When his funeral train pulled out of town, Warm Springs went into a deep slumber from which it did not awaken until the late 1980s, when a group of entrepreneurs renovated many of the downtown buildings for use as gift and antiques shops and restaurants catering to visitors from all over the world who come to visit the Little White House National Historic Site.

Gerrie Thompson, one of the most intrepid of these entrepreneurs, restored the three-story, buff-colored brick hotel to its 1941 appearance. Usually the first person you'll see when you step into the lobby, with its 16-foot-high ceilings and black-and-white tile floor, is Gerrie behind the original reception desk. Not only is she probably on the phone taking reservations, but she's also probably engaged in creating some craft masterpiece to sell in the hotel's gift shop. There's also a soda fountain and ice cream parlor where you can taste Gerrie's homemade peach ice cream.

This is all the casual visitor to the Hotel Warm Springs will see, but a serene world awaits overnight guests upstairs. The second-floor mezzanine serves as a large, gracious formal sitting room where guests are encouraged to congregate. There's also a small, casual game room/social parlor where guests can watch television, work on a gigantic jigsaw puzzle, or play cards or checkers. The third-floor mezzanine serves as the breakfast room.

Spacious, simple guest chambers are filled with Roosevelt memorabilia, antiques, collectibles, and the unadorned furniture of the 1930s and '40s. Modern amenities include a private bath, queen-size bed, and television. Some bathrooms have original re-enameled claw-foot tubs with reproduction antique showers. The Moncrief Room is furnished entirely with heirlooms from Gerrie's family—the prize item being the hundred-year-old iron bed. In addition to a bedroom and separate parlor, the Presidential Suite boasts original oak furniture made in Eleanor Roosevelt's Val-Kill Shop. A red, heart-shaped double Jacuzzi dominates the Honeymoon Suite. Gerrie has developed a special package for honeymooners that includes a night in the suite along with champagne, chocolates, strawberries, fresh flowers, and breakfast in bed.

HOW TO GET THERE: Hotel Warm Springs sits at the crossroads of U.S. 27 and GA 85 west.

In FDR's Day

Longtime residents still remember the 1930s and '40s, when FDR's chauffeur-driven convertible would pull up to the drugstore located downstairs in the Hotel Warm Springs so the president could get a Coke without getting out of the car and so he could linger and chat with the townsfolk. As likely as not little Fala, the Scottie, would be bounding around in the backseat, giving his master licking kisses from time to time. This was the heyday of Warm Springs and a boon for the Hotel Warm Springs, where Secret Service agents, journalists, and visiting dignitaries would stay when FDR was in town.

In FDR's day, the hotel management decided that with such august guests and national and international scrutiny, the staff should be dressed in a more dignified manner than they had been heretofore. It was decreed that all the waitresses were to wear crisp white uniforms. Unfortunately, some details got lost in the translation. First of all, when the uniforms arrived they were all one size, but they were handed out anyway. You can just imagine how ridiculous that looked on the thin, medium, and heavy alike. Then the waitresses were directed to check out electric irons so they could take care of their uniforms at home. No one had bothered to find out that the girls were from homes so poor that they had no electricity. That problem was finally solved by allowing them to iron their uniforms at the hotel before they started their shift. Get Gerrie to tell you all about it.

Select List of
Other Georgia Inns

Smith House Inn
84 South Chestatee
Dahlonega, GA 30533
(706) 867-7000 or (800) 852-9577

1884 Victorian home and carriage house operating as an inn since 1922; 16 rooms; continental breakfast; famous family-style restaurant, gift shop.

Fieldstone Inn and Conference Center
3379 U.S. 76
Hiawassee, GA 30546
(706) 896-2262 or (800) 545-3408

Casually elegant inn on the shores of Lake Chatuge; 62 rooms and 4 suites; restaurant, pool, fitness center, tennis courts, hot tub, dock, lawn games, meeting facilities.

Catherine Ward House Inn
118 East Waldburg Street
Savannah, GA 31401
(912) 234-8564

1886 Italianate mansion; 10 rooms and suites; courtyard; full breakfast.

Hamilton-Turner Inn
330 Abercorn Street
Savannah, GA 31401
(912) 233-1833 or (888) 448-8849

French Second Empire–style; 14 guest rooms and suites; working fireplaces; full Southern breakfast and afternoon tea.

The Marshall House
123 East Broughton Street
Savannah, GA 31401
(912) 644-7896 or (800) 589-6304

Restored landmark property in the center of the historic district; 68 rooms; restaurant; jazz lounge.

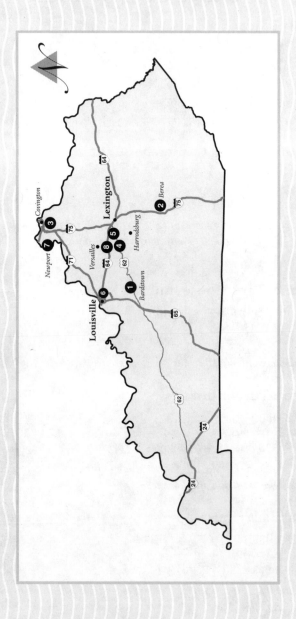

Kentucky

Kentucky

Numbers on map refer to towns numbered below.

* A Top Pick Inn

Jailer's Inn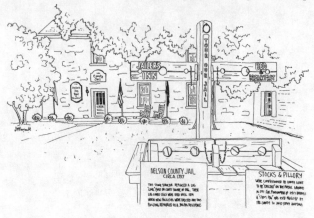

Bardstown, Kentucky 40004

INNKEEPER: C. Paul McCoy

ADDRESS/TELEPHONE: 111 West Stephen Foster Avenue;
(502) 348–5551 or (800) 948–5551; fax (502) 349–1837

WEB SITE: www.jailersinn.com

E-MAIL: cpaul@jailersinn.com

ROOMS: 6, all with private bath, clock radio. Most with cable TV, ceiling fan. 2 with Jacuzzi, fireplace, wheelchair access.

RATES: $65 to $115, single or double; includes full breakfast. Children welcome. Credit cards accepted.

OPEN: Closed January.

FACILITIES AND ACTIVITIES: Nearby: Restaurants, whiskey distilleries, My Old Kentucky Home State Park, Bardstown Historical Museum, Stephen Foster Drama, Shaker Village; 35 miles from Louisville.

his B&B inn was a jailer's residence until 1987. Fran and Challen McCoy, Paul's parents and the former innkeepers, purchased it in June 1988 and opened the prison section for tours almost right away. At that time, they didn't know it had been built by Fran's great-great-uncle. The front building, known as the "old" jail, was built in 1819 of native limestone. It had two cells and an "upstairs dungeon" for prisoners. The

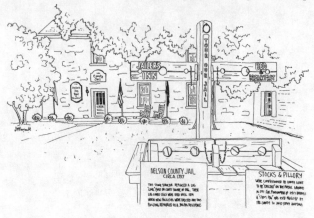

NELSON COUNTY JAIL
CIRCA 1797

STOCKS & PILLORY

stone building behind this, built in 1874, was known as the "new" jail. Once it was operating, the front building became the jailer's home.

Fran and Challen turned the "old" jail into an inn decorated with antiques and Oriental rugs, except for the former women's cell, which is done entirely in prison black and white and contains the two original bunks plus a waterbed. The floor is tiled in a black-and-white geometric pattern, the mirror over the sparkling white sink has a white frame, and a picture on the white brick wall has a black frame.

A much prettier room, the favorite of many guests, is the Garden Room, which looks out over the courtyard and is decorated in aqua green with wicker and wrought iron and lots of flowers. The Garden Room bedspreads are cross-stitched quilts in floral patterns. The courtyard is a favorite gathering place for savoring your full Southern breakfast, chatting with other guests, and trying to envision how it was as a work yard, with prisoners crushing limestone, and where they were visited by their relatives, or as the site of the county gallows.

The Victorian Room, a feminine room with flowered wallpaper, a tall mirrored vanity, lace-edged bed covers, and old-fashioned flowered hats on a stand in the corner, pleases guests, too.

HOW TO GET THERE: The inn is just off Court Square in downtown Bardstown. Highway 31-E runs directly to the square.

The Mansion Bed & Breakfast
Bardstown, Kentucky 40004

INNKEEPERS: Dennis and Charmaine Downs

ADDRESS/TELEPHONE: 1003 North Third Street; (502) 348–2586 or (877) 909–2586; fax (502) 349–6098

WEB SITE: www.bardstownmansion.com

E-MAIL: ddowns@bardstown.com

ROOMS: 7, plus 1 cottage; all with private bath; 2 with 2-person whirlpool tub.

RATES: $100 to $130, double occupancy; includes gourmet breakfast and fresh flowers; $15 for each additional person; children older than age 10 are welcome. Credit cards accepted.

OPEN: Year-round.

FACILITIES AND ACTIVITIES: Nearby: Historic Bardstown, the second oldest city in Kentucky.

A "truly dignified, aristocratic and striking example of Greek Revival architecture" is the way the National Register of Historic Places describes the 1851 Greek Revival Johnson villa that houses The Mansion Bed & Breakfast. Filled with history, stunning inside and out, exquisitely furnished and decorated, and surrounded by lush gardens, The Mansion is the very epitome of what a gracious B&B inn should be.

From the moment you step through the columned portico and enter the vast entry hall, you'll be wowed by the grandeur. Admire the original solid-brass chandelier with Waterford crystal prisms, the 10½-foot-tall gold-leaf mirror, and the 1876 rosewood Steinway square piano, then gaze up the stairwell of the freestanding elliptical staircase, which is the only one in Kentucky that turns first to the right instead of the left. The handrail is solid cherry, the steps are ash, and the spindles mahogany. Original mantels with fluted pilasters and fluted friezes grace the parlors.

Overnight guests are treated to a deluxe continental breakfast elegantly served in the formal dining room using china, silver, crystal, and fine linens.

In the well-proportioned bedchambers, high ceilings, Victorian-era antiques, and hand-crocheted bedspreads, dust ruffles, and pillow shams make every one inviting. Among the concessions to modern-day life are private baths and king-size beds—many of them romantic four-poster iron canopy beds draped with fabric. Located up under the eaves with cozy alcoves created by the sloping ceilings, two rooms have an additional twin bed, making them suitable for those traveling with an additional person. A former summer kitchen has been transformed into a snug cottage, which is particularly popular with those desiring a little additional privacy.

The equally beautiful three-acre grounds put on a colorful display spring through fall. In spring the estate is awash in the pastels of dogwood, pear, and apple blossoms. Summer showcases the feathery mimosa blooms, while fall is ablaze with brilliant maples.

HOW TO GET THERE: Follow U.S. 31 south from Louisville to Bardstown. U.S. 31 becomes North Third Street.

Boone Tavern Hotel of Berea College

Berea, Kentucky 40404

INNKEEPER: Dee Hudson

ADDRESS/TELEPHONE: College post office, Box 2345 (Main and Prospect Streets); (859) 985–3700 or (800) 366–9358; fax (859) 985–3715

WEB SITE: www.berea.edu/Publications/Boone-Tavern.html

ROOMS: 58, all with private bath, television, telephone.

RATES: $65 to $100, double occupancy; $10 for each additional guest in the room. Because the student employees of the hotel are working for their tuition, tipping is not permitted.

OPEN: May be closed in January for renovations.

FACILITIES AND ACTIVITIES: Restaurant, campus tours, college activities such as lectures, art exhibits, concerts, theater productions, and sports. Nearby: Churchill Weavers, Appalachian Museum, Whitehall State Shrine, Boonesborough State Park, Bybee Pottery, Kentucky Horse Park, Shakertown, The Red Mile racetrack, Fort Harrodsburg, Cumberland Falls State Park.

BUSINESS TRAVEL: 42 miles from Lexington off I–75; meeting rooms accommodate up to 100 persons.

Can you imagine being expected to house, feed, and entertain 300 guests in your home over the period of one summer? Just the thought of such an undertaking makes us shudder, but in 1908 that's exactly what Nellie Frost, the wife of the Berea College president, did. After this ordeal, she suggested to her husband that perhaps the college should build a guest house to accommodate future college visitors. We can almost feel her sigh of relief when the college did just that. The result is this elegant, white three-story hotel with immense columned porticos.

Beginning with its opening in 1909, the Boone Tavern Hotel has been operated by the college's hospitality management students as part of Berea College's extensive work-study program in which students work in lieu of tuition payments.

A gilt-framed portrait of the sixteenth president by Fred Walker peers down from over the graceful white fireplace and surveys the warm, magnificent Lincoln Lounge, which is fur-

nished with camelback sofas and other pieces befitting such a sumptuous room.

Guest rooms are well appointed and furnished with reproduction American traditional furniture created by students in the woodworking department and accessorized with student handiwork weavings and other crafts. Each features a private bath.

Although the hotel is an ideal place to stay when visiting the college or any of dozens of near-by attractions, the food served in the dining room, where three meals are served daily, has won the hostelry much of its acclaim. Considered a perfect blend of elegance and down-home Southern hospitality, the dining room serves simple Kentucky-style meals of meat and vegetables as well as specialties such as lamb chops and steaks. Be sure to try the spoonbread (a corn bread soufflé) and chess pie. Many traditional dishes were developed by Richard T. Hougen, who managed the dining room from 1940 to 1976. Some favorites are Chicken Flakes in a Bird's Nest, Jefferson Davis Pie, Cinnamon Kites, and Boone Tavern Cornsticks. You can take home these and other recipes by purchasing one or more of Hougen's cookbooks. Reservations are required for meals, and although breakfast and lunch are casual affairs, dressy casual attire is required for dinner.

College tours depart from the hotel and include the Berea College Museum, which emphasizes the rich history and culture of Appalachia and the fascinating history of Berea College itself, and the Log House Craft Gallery, which showcases the fine woodworking and crafts skills of Berea College students and other local artisans as well as the Wallace Nutting Collection of Early American Furniture.

HOW TO GET THERE: Berea College is located at the junction of U.S. 25 and U.S. 21.

Berea College Crafts

The unique Appalachian heritage of Berea College dates to 1855, when the school was founded by forward-thinking John G. Fee as the South's first nondenominational interracial college on land donated by Cassius M. Clay. Clay described the college as a "historic monument to human equality."

The college's long-established student crafts program traces its roots to a practical and utilitarian beginning. "Homespun Fairs" were held on the campus as early as 1896. At these fairs, parents sold hand-woven items to help finance their children's education. The woven items became so popular that looms were established on the campus so that the students could learn weaving skills. Woodcraft, begun in the late 1800s, provided tables, chairs, and other furniture needs for the college.

Eventually these extracurricular activities were incorporated as departments of the college. The weaving department produces couch throws, baby blankets, place mats, and napkins. Fine furniture is handcrafted, with most pieces being of Colonial design. Contemporary pieces can be made to order, however. Students in the department have also produced wooden puzzles and marble games as well as candleholders; a variety of cutting boards and chopping blocks; and the popular wooden board game, skittles.

Broom-making has been a college craft since about 1920. Each handmade broom is unique in style and color as the blending of native wood handles and natural and multicolored broomcorn results in a one-of-a-kind product.

New in the last few years are the ceramics and wrought-iron programs. Potters produce vases and a variety of bowls, mugs, casseroles, and pitchers. Functional, well-designed wrought-iron articles include fireplace sets, boot and shoe scrapers, and hanging plant brackets.

All Berea craft items are available at the Log House Craft Gallery, Boone Tavern Gift Shop, retail outlets in Berea, and by catalog.

The Amos Shinkle Townhouse
Covington, Kentucky 41011

INNKEEPERS: Don Nash and Bernie Moorman

ADDRESS/TELEPHONE: 215 Garrard Street; (859) 431–2118 or (800) 972–7012; fax (859) 491–4551

WEB SITE: www.amosshinkle.net

ROOMS: 7, 3 in main house, 4 in carriage house; all with private bath and television. Smoking and no-smoking rooms available.

RATES: $95 to $165, double; $10 less, single; includes full breakfast. Children under 6 free in room with adults.

OPEN: Year-round.

FACILITIES AND ACTIVITIES: Located in historic district across the bridge from downtown Cincinnati. Meeting space for groups up to 15. Nearby: Walking distance to restaurants; Ohio River recreation, boating, cruises.

This is the house the entrepreneur Amos Shinkle and his family lived in during the Civil War while his castle was being finished. A tour brochure for the historic district calls the structure a "modest Italianate home." Compared to a castle, maybe. But unless you are accustomed to castle life, you'll find The Amos Shinkle Townhouse posh.

The ceilings in this B&B inn are 16 feet high, with Rococo Revival chandeliers, plaster moldings, and cornices. Beyond the front entry a mahogany staircase, still with the original murals on the walls and crown moldings that continue on the second-floor landing, ascends to guest rooms furnished with antiques. The master bedroom has a fireplace, a four-poster bed, and a maroon-tiled bath with a crystal chandelier and a whirlpool tub.

Downstairs, comfortable couches and chairs clustered near the fireplaces make elegant places to read or chat. You're welcome to play the baby grand piano, too.

In the carriage house, behind the main house, are simpler rooms decorated in Early American style. This building served as stable quarters in the 1800s. The horse stalls have been turned into sleeping accommodations for children.

A brick-and-grass courtyard between the two buildings includes places to sit under umbrellas when the weather is nice. During the growing season, pots of geraniums, petunias, and black-eyed Susans brighten the area. Tall hollyhocks and mature shrubs soften the austere lines of the carriage house.

Quite apart from the visual and architectural interest of the town house, staying here evokes a sense of old Southern hospitality. Be sure to spend some time talking with the resident innkeeper, Bernie Moorman. He used to be the mayor and maintains active involvement with the community. He likes to tell guests how special the area is historically and culturally, and he'll do almost anything to make sure you like it here. Bernie says everyone at the inn will help you arrange everything from restaurants to tickets for the horse races.

Even breakfast reflects their willingness to cater to your schedule. You order, from a full menu, anytime from 7:00 to 9:30 A.M. during the week or 8:00 to 10:00 A.M. on weekends. Your eggs, pancakes, French toast, or whatever come to you cooked to order. Be sure to try the goetta, a regional sausagelike dish of cooked ground pork, pinhead oatmeal, and spices. Bernie says their goetta, made by Dick Fink, is the best in the area.

If you are a baseball fan, the Cincinnati ballpark is only a ten- to fifteen-minute walk (or a four- to five-minute car trip) from the house.

HOW TO GET THERE: From I–75/71 take exit 192 onto Fifth Street, which is one-way going east. Drive 9 blocks to where Fifth Street ends at Garrard Street. Turn left and go 2½ blocks north. The inn is on the left.

Beaumont Inn
Harrodsburg, Kentucky 40330

INNKEEPERS: C. M. (Chuck) and Helen W. Dedman

ADDRESS/TELEPHONE: 638 Beaumont Drive; (859) 734–3381 or (800) 352–3992; fax (859) 734–6897

WEB SITE: www.beaumontinn.com

ROOMS: 33, all with private bath, telephone, and television. No-smoking rooms available.

RATES: $90 to $125, double; single $20 less; includes continental breakfast.

OPEN: Mid-March to mid-December.

FACILITIES AND ACTIVITIES: Lunch and dinner. Swimming pool, tennis courts, shuffleboard, walking trails, gift shops. Nearby: Boating, fishing, and swimming on Herrington Lake; golfing; Keeneland Race Track; Shaker Village; Old Fort Harrod State Park.

BUSINESS TRAVEL: Well-equipped conference facilities; corporate rates; telephone in room.

Harrodsburg is in the heart of Kentucky's horse country, an area crammed with historic sites and gorgeous scenery, but the truth is that a lot of people go to the Beaumont Inn mainly to eat. The inn's food and service are famous.

When you make your dinner reservations, you have a choice of four seatings Wednesday and Thursday, five seatings Friday and Saturday, and one seating for brunch on Sunday. A bell rings right on the appropriate hour to announce dinner, and you are immediately shown to a table with your name on it. We have it on very credible authority that roast beef and the ham, which is aged two years, are fantastic choices. An appetizer such as the cream of celery soup is included in the cost of the meal. Then it seems that the food keeps coming for an hour.

After your salad, the server will bring your entree and a tray full of serving dishes from which you will be served such side selections as mashed potatoes and gravy, lima beans, corn pudding, and mock scalloped oysters. The server will return several more times to offer seconds and refill the basket of biscuits.

For dessert, try the crisp meringue shell filled with vanilla ice cream and fresh strawberries.

You'll barely have time to stroll around the grounds admiring the lush greenery and take a quick look at some of the antiques inside the inn after dinner before it's time to turn in. Then it will be breakfast time, and the whole incredible flow of food starts all over again, with an overwhelming

number of choices, including a stack of the lightest, tastiest batter corn cakes you ever sunk a tooth into. The full breakfast is $6.00 extra, but you still get the continental breakfast, too, if you want it.

HOW TO GET THERE: In Harrodsburg, turn left off South Main at the United Presbyterian Church onto Beaumont Avenue and then right onto Beaumont Drive.

Shaker Village of Pleasant Hill
Harrodsburg, Kentucky 40330

INNKEEPER: James C. Thomas, CEO/President

ADDRESS/TELEPHONE: 3501 Lexington Road; (859) 734–5411 or (800) 734–5611 for reservations; fax (859) 734–7278

WEB SITE: www.shakervillageky.org

E-MAIL: diana@shakervillageky.org

ROOMS: 81 in 15 buildings; all with private bath, television, and telephone. Inn especially suited for children.

RATES: $70 to $200, double; breakfast extra. Children 17 and younger free with adult. Credit cards accepted.

OPEN: Year-round except Christmas Eve and Christmas Day.

FACILITIES AND ACTIVITIES: Breakfast, lunch, dinner open to guests and public by reservation in Trustees' Office Dining Room. Shaker Village preserves 33 original nineteenth-century buildings as they were used by the community of Shakers living in the village; they are open for tours. Craft stores, Shaker craft and farming demonstrations, meeting facilities. Nearby: Cruises on the *Dixie Belle* riverboat, Fort Harrod State Park, *The Legend of Daniel Boone* outdoor drama, Herrington Lake, Pioneer Playhouse, hiking, horseback riding trails, 20 stalls for overnight boarding of your own horse.

"That's the closet," our guide said. We were in one of the guest-rooms, and she was pointing to a strip of heavy pegs along the wall. The Shakers hung everything, from their clothes to their utensils and chairs, on such pegs. Guests at Shaker Village do the same.

The rooms are furnished in the same sparse, simple style of the Shakers: rag rugs; streamlined, functional furniture; trundle beds; plain linens. Only the modern bathroom, telephone, and television set in each room make it different than it originally would have been.

Like other communities of plain people, the Shakers made up in the bounty of their table for what they lacked in knickknacks. The Shaker town menu, which says, "We make you kindly welcome," does the same. Shakers, wherever they lived, adopted the food of the area. In Kentucky, this means fried chicken, country ham, fried fish, roast beef, and large sirloin steaks. Fresh vegetables (some from the garden on the premises) and salads are passed at the table, as are breads fresh from the bakery. The smell of baking bread distracts you much of the day at Shaker Village. And for dessert, Shaker lemon pie tops off everything. It's an unusual lemon pie, made with a double crust and whole sliced lemons, plus eggs and sugar, because the Shakers didn't waste anything—not even lemon peels.

Although the meal is bountiful, the dining rooms in the old Trustees' Office resemble the guest rooms in their simplicity. The wood floors are polished and clean but unadorned. The tables and chairs are typical, functional Shaker design, and the place settings are plain white dishes. It adds up to a fascinating, almost-insider's view of unusual people whose way of life is almost gone except in this re-creation.

Many special events, including weekends of Shaker music and dance, are held during the year. You can write or call for a yearly calendar to help you plan a trip according to your interests.

HOW TO GET THERE: The entrance to Shaker Village is off U.S. Route 68, 7 miles northeast of Harrodsburg and 25 miles southwest of Lexington. Signs mark the drive clearly.

Gratz Park Inn
Lexington, Kentucky 40507

INNKEEPER: Liz Holmes

ADDRESS/TELEPHONE: 120 West Second Street; (859) 231–1777 or
(800) 752–4166 for reservations only; fax (859) 233–7593

WEB SITE: www.gratzpark.com

E-MAIL: gratzinn@aol.com

ROOMS: 36; plus 6 suites; all with private bath, telephone, cable television, clock radio, hair dryer. Some handicapped-accessible and non-
smoking rooms.

RATES: $110 to $149 during low season, $130 to $215 in high season
(April, July, and October), double occupancy; includes evening turndown, fresh flowers in the room, cookies and bottled water, daily
newspaper Monday through Friday; rate for each additional person is
$10. Children younger than age 12 are free in the room with the par-
ents; minimum stay required for special events. Credit cards accepted.

OPEN: Year-round.

FACILITIES AND ACTIVITIES: Elevator, fine dining restaurant and
pub. Nearby: Universities, downtown business district, historic residential districts; convention center, sports arena, race course, Kentucky Horse Park; antiques shopping, art galleries, casual and fine
dining, nightlife, performing arts, museums; water sports, golf, hiking,
horseback riding.

BUSINESS TRAVEL: Most rooms and all suites have a desk; all have
dataports. Meeting facilities accommodate up to 50.

*I*magine our surprise when we were chatting with the manager during our stay at this gracious historic Southern inn to learn that it
was originally built as the first medical clinic west of the Allegheny
Mountains. Whatever its origins, the 1916 Federal-style structure has made
a very successful transition to an elegant inn where such luminaries as
Sharon Stone, Albert Finney, Nick Nolte, and Ashley Judd have stayed.

In addition to our luxurious guest room, the elegant public spaces, the
scrumptious food, and the personal attention, one of the other things we

liked so much about the Gratz Park Inn, Lexington's only historic inn, was its desirable location in the heart of downtown's historic district, known as Gratz Park. We could stroll around the compact district admiring the beautiful old homes, then take a short walk to the commercial district centered around Triangle Park, with its dramatic wall of cascading fountains—especially striking when lit at night—to restaurants, shops,  the Convention Center, and the Rupp Arena. The University of Kentucky and Transylvania University are within walking distance, and it's just a short hop by car to Keeneland Race Course, the Kentucky Horse Park, and world-renowned horse farms.

At the inn, antiques and artwork highlight the nineteenth-century ambience. The cozy lobby's original hardwood floors, beautiful antiques, and fireplace make it a popular gathering place. Each spacious guest room is decorated differently, but each features antique reproductions, including a mahogany four-poster bed, regional artwork, and all the modern conveniences. Why, you can even hook up your laptop and log on to the Internet.

An ample continental breakfast is served each morning, coffee is always available in the lobby, and lunch (weekdays) and dinner (Tuesday through Saturday) are served in the inn's restaurant, Jonathan at Gratz Park, where the cuisine is Southern with a gourmet twist. Try the fried oyster–stuffed beef fillet with mushroom gravy, barbecued tuna with white cheddar grits and asparagus, or seafood Burgoo (a Kentucky dish) of shrimp, Little Neck oysters, and crawfish simmered with potatoes, corn, okra, and black-eyed peas.

HOW TO GET THERE: Convenient to both I-25 and I-27, from I-75 take exit 113 south onto Paris Pike south. As you get into town, the street name changes to Broadway. Continue to Short Street and turn left. Continue to Limestone and turn left. Follow it to West Second Street and turn left. The hotel is on the left.

Inn at the Park 💙
Louisville, Kentucky 40208

INNKEEPERS: John and Sandra Mullins

ADDRESS/TELEPHONE: 1332 South Fourth Street; (502) 637–6930 or (800) 700–PARK; fax (502) 637–2796

WEB SITE: www.innatpark.com

E-MAIL: innatpark@aol.com

ROOMS: 7, all with private bath, television and telephone; some with balcony, fireplace, whirlpool tub. Outdoor smoking areas available.

RATES: $89 to $169, double or single; includes full breakfast and snacks. Credit cards accepted. Not appropriate for children.

OPEN: Year-round.

FACILITIES AND ACTIVITIES: Located in Old Louisville neighborhood near Central Park. Nearby: Walking distance to restaurants; University of Louisville; Bellarmine and Spalding Colleges; Louisville Zoo; antiques shops on Bardstown Road; Ohio River Cruises on the historic *Belle of Louisville* stern-wheeler.

BUSINESS TRAVEL: Located 5 minutes from downtown Louisville, 10 minutes from Louisville International Airport. Telephone and desk in room; fax and copy service available.

One of the most striking features of this B&B inn, which started out as an 1886 mansion with Richardsonian Romanesque architecture, is an absolutely awesome staircase. It's the kind you expect Scarlett to come sweeping down. Also the inn has 10,000 square feet of space, hardwood floors, 14-foot-high ceilings, marble fireplaces, crown moldings, second- and third-floor balconies, and a perfect location right by Central Park in the historic district, Old Louisville. You can take walking tours right from the inn. If you do, you'll realize that the inn looks almost new since it was completely restored in 1985—not old and needing attention, as old buildings sometimes look as time passes.

The inn has developed a reputation as a great spot for a romantic getaway, and couples often book months in advance to get the room and date they want. The place looks romantic, decorated with warm Victorian colors, designer linens, and a combination of antique and reproduction furnishings. Some of the rooms have four-poster king-size beds that look romantically old and feel comfortably contemporary. (People apparently just weren't as big in earlier days as we've become now. Or else they didn't mind sleeping cheek to cheek.)

For business travelers who care more about utility than romance, the rooms also have desks and telephones that make a convenient work setup.

For the more romantically inclined, we suggest you check out the two new suites in the Carriage House with their whirlpool tubs and fireplaces.

And for guests in both categories, there are some really nice, out-of-room amenities, including complimentary beer, wine, and soft drinks plus a "munchies" cabinet in the Butler's Pantry.

But breakfast is a high point of staying here. You have a choice of juice, the inn's homemade granola, yogurt, home-baked breads and muffins—all that goes into a generous continental breakfast—in addition to a choice of two different entrees each day.

HOW TO GET THERE: From I-65, take exit 135A onto West St. Catherine Street. Drive west to Fourth Street and turn left. Go 2 blocks to 1332 South Fourth Street.

Old Louisville Inn
Louisville, Kentucky 40208

INNKEEPER: Marianne Lesher

ADDRESS/TELEPHONE: 1359 South Third Street; (502) 635–1574

WEB SITE: www.oldlouinn.com

E-MAIL: info@oldlouinn.com

ROOMS: 11, including 1 suite; all with private bath (one down the hall); suite with whirlpool bath and fireplace.

RATES: $95 to $195, single or double; includes full breakfast. Credit cards accepted.

OPEN: Year-round.

FACILITIES AND ACTIVITIES: Located in the Old Louisville neighborhood. Nearby: Walking distance to restaurants; University of Louisville; Bellarmine and Spalding Colleges; Louisville Zoo; antiques shops on Bardstown Road; Ohio River Cruises on the historic *Belle of Louisville;* Churchill Downs, Slugger Museum.

This B&B inn, all 12,000 square feet of it, was originally built in 1901 as a private home for the president of the Louisville Home Telephone Company. Apparently, that newfangled invention paid off in the early days, too!

The building was restored in the 1970s. It's in a section of Old Louisville where most of the homes are equally large and elaborate. If you're interested in architecture and history, you'll like staying here.

For one thing, 12,000 square feet and three stories makes a lot of room for things with aesthetic appeal: carved mahogany columns, murals on 12-foot-high ceilings, and a good-size lobby. Everything seems to have a story, and Marianne likes telling her guests about the place.

The inn has a parlor with a fireplace and lots of books; a game room has everything from an "antique" Monopoly set to television. But you probably will want to spend more time in the neighborhood, looking at the old homes and perhaps taking the walking tours. The Old Louisville Neighborhood Council has produced a tour booklet and has done a wonderful job of describing the buildings in the area and explaining their significance. The tour for Third Street (where the inn is located) alone contains thirty-three entries.

After a day of walking, you will be grateful to retreat to your room, maybe to soak in a tub in one of the marble baths with original fixtures. (They've been modernized to include showers.) Your bed will be covered with an antique quilt, in keeping with the neighborhood you've toured.

Breakfast, on the other hand, is contemporary and includes granola, fruit, and yogurt if you want it, served with freshly squeezed orange juice. Some mornings you may be offered omelettes or Belgian waffles. The inn is famous for its popovers.

Given the size of the inn, it's important to mention that the place is professionally run. This isn't someone's little hobby; this is a serious, well-established inn, and if you stay here, you can expect to be treated to professional hospitality.

HOW TO GET THERE: From I–65, take the St. Catherine exit. Stay in the left lane and turn left on Third Street. Go 3 blocks; the inn will be on the left. Pull in the drive and stop at the side door to check in. You will be directed to off-street parking behind the carriage house.

Cincinnati's Weller Haus
Newport, Kentucky 41073

INNKEEPERS: Valerie and David Brown

ADDRESS/TELEPHONE: 319 Poplar Street; (859) 431–6829

WEB SITE: www.wellerhaus.com

E-MAIL: innkeepers@wellerhaus.com

ROOMS: 5 in 2 buildings, all with private bath and television; 2 with whirlpool tub for 2.

RATES: $89 to $158, double; $10 less, single; includes full breakfast and afternoon snacks. Seasonal packages available. Credit cards accepted.

OPEN: Year-round.

FACILITIES AND ACTIVITIES: Gardens. Located in historic district across the river from downtown Cincinnati. Common kitchen. Nearby: Restaurants, Newport Aquarium, Cincinnati Stadium.

Here is small-town America, past and present. Two Victorian Gothic houses sit side by side, with a black iron fence dividing lawn from sidewalk. The American flag flies from a porch. Perennials bloom in a small garden out back.

The two houses constitute one homestead-style B&B inn. The main house is gray with blue-and-white striped awnings. The great room in this house has a cathedral ceiling. Guests check in and also have breakfast here.

Breakfast is not just a grab-a-doughnut affair, either. It's a full breakfast with homemade muffins, coffee cakes, and breads, served in high Victorian style.

In the buff-colored brick house next door, guests gather in an ivy-festooned kitchen where even the ceiling is covered with ivy-patterned wallpaper. You can get drinks here, use the microwave oven, and make tea or coffee. Guests often

get to know one another sitting around the kitchen table. It doesn't matter which house your room is in, you may use the common areas in both places. Guests going back and forth have worn a footpath across the lawn.

Throughout both houses you find good collections of antique porcelains, pattern glass, linens, and the like, along with comfortable antique furniture. Because the spaces remain uncluttered, however, none of this is overpowering.

One of the nicest accommodations is Margaret's Porch Suite, two rooms furnished in the Art Deco style of the 1920s, with bold colors. The suite has a private entrance, porch, and very comfortable whirlpool tub for two. Of course the Dream Suite is the special-occasion spot, with its Eastlake furniture and a big whirlpool tub. A simpler room, Nancy's Garden Room has a Steamboat Gothic brass bed, with stenciled flowers over the doors and windows. Such touches make an impression on guests.

HOW TO GET THERE: From I-471, take exit 5 toward Newport and Bellevue onto Dave Cowens, which is also Kentucky Highway 8. Turn right. The Ohio River will be on your left. After a few blocks this road becomes Fairfield Avenue. Turn right on Washington Street. Go 2 blocks to Poplar Street and turn right. The inn is at 319 Poplar.

Bed and Breakfast at Sills Inn
Versailles, Kentucky 40383

INNKEEPERS: Tony Sills and Glen Blind

ADDRESS/TELEPHONE: 270 Montgomery Avenue; (859) 873-4478 or (800) 526-9801; fax (859) 873-7099

WEB SITE: www.sillsinn.com

E-MAIL: SillsInn@aol.com

ROOMS: 12 rooms and suites, all with private bath, cable television, VCR, stereo CD player, and telephone; most with whirlpool tub; some with sitting room, porch, and/or deck.

RATES: $99 to $179, single or double occupancy; includes full gourmet breakfast, complimentary snacks, newspaper; $20 for each additional person. Credit cards accepted; AAA discount offered during certain periods. Children are not encouraged.

OPEN: Year-round.

FACILITIES AND ACTIVITIES: Porch, library, 2-person whirlpools. Nearby: Antiques shops, Nostalgia Station Toy and Train Museum, Bluegrass Railroad Museum, Buckley Wildlife Sanctuary, Jack Jouett House, Labrot and Graham Distillery, Shakertown Village at Pleasant Hill, Keeneland Race Course, Kentucky Horse Park.

BUSINESS TRAVEL: 10 minutes from Lexington, in downtown Versailles; all rooms have a work area and telephone with dataport. Some meeting space; copy and fax service.

*U*ltra romantics will find many things to love about the Sills Inn. First of all, most of this B&B inn's superb rooms are located in an elegant three-story 1911 Queen Anne Victorian mansion with its big, inviting wraparound porch. Second, nine of the nostalgic accommodations boast a two-person whirlpool tub—some heart shaped. And not to be neglected, we must mention the food, the attentive staff, and the location in historic downtown Versailles.

High ceilings, tall windows, opulent Victorian-era antiques, and king- or queen-size beds characterize the guest rooms in the main house. The Tara and Victorian suites in the main house feature gorgeous sitting rooms, and the Penthouse suite has a private deck. The English, French, and Oriental suites in the modern annex boast sitting area, private porches, and a wet bar with a microwave and refrigerator. Considered the most romantic of all, for one thing because it is the most secluded, the French suite features a crystal chandelier, French antiques, king-size bed, two-person whirlpool and two-person shower, and a private porch.

Breakfast is a substantial affair served in the formal dining room or on the delightful sunporch. Fresh fruit and juices as well as freshly baked muffins accompany an entree such as Eggs del Sol, eggs Benedict, baked stuffed French toast, or spinach soufflé.

One of the things we love about the inn is the lobby library, which is packed with books on Kentucky history, horses, and genealogy and an astounding collection of 1,500 cookbooks. Items with a horse theme as well as local arts and crafts are for sale in the sunporch gift shop.

HOW TO GET THERE: Exit from I-75 at exit 115 and head west on KY 922. Turn west (right) on New Circle Road, then turn west (right) on KY 60 at exit 5-B (it is approximately ten minutes to Versailles). Follow the business route to downtown, and at the courthouse turn left onto Main Street. At the second traffic light turn left at Montgomery Avenue. The inn is 2 blocks ahead on the right. Pull into the driveway and park in the back.

Select List of Other Kentucky Inns

Otter Creek Park Lodge

850 Otter Creek Park Road
Brandenberg, KY 40108
(502) 583-3577

Rustic, secluded lodge; 22 rooms, 12 cabins; restaurant.

Kenlake Hotel and Cottages

542 Kenlake Road
Hardin, KY 42048
(270) 474-2211 or (800) 325-0143

Rustic lodge overlooking Kentucky Lake; 48 rooms, 34 cottages; restaurant, pool, indoor tennis center and outdoor courts; boat rentals, water sports, golf.

Kentucky Dam Village Inn

KY 641
Gilbertsville, KY 42044
(270) 362-4271 or (800) 325-0146

86 rooms in rustic lodge, 72 cottages; restaurant; lake, beach, water sports, pool, boat rentals, golf, stables, tennis.

Louisiana

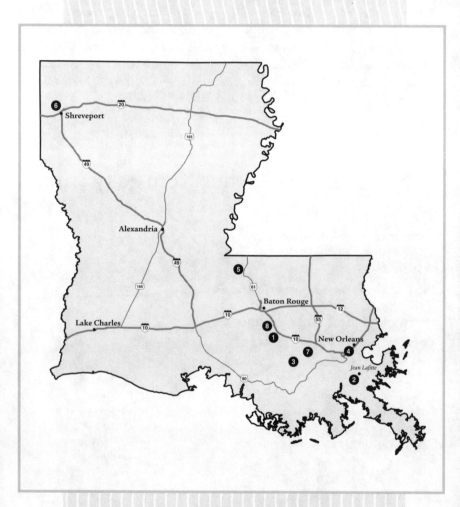

Louisiana

Numbers on map refer to towns numbered below.

* A Top Pick Inn

Tezcuco Plantation
Burnside, Louisiana 70725

INNKEEPER: Annette Harland

ADDRESS/TELEPHONE: Burnside (mailing address: 3138 Highway 44, Darrow 70725); (225) 562–3929; fax (225) 562–3923

WEB SITE: tezcuco.com

E-MAIL: tezcuco@eatel.com

ROOMS: 23 cottages, all with private bath and television; some with kitchen and fireplace.

RATES: $65 to $165, single or double; includes tour of plantation house and grounds, bottle of wine, and full Creole breakfast. $20 for each extra adult; $12.50 for each child.

OPEN: Year-round.

FACILITIES AND ACTIVITIES: Victorian-style restaurant, antiques-and-gift shop. Nearby: Restaurants, tour plantation homes and historic sites, Mississippi River, swamp tours, outlets.

*T*ezcuco Plantation tries to give guests a feeling of what it would have been like to live on a working sugar plantation in the 1800s. The original plantation house is an antebellum raised cottage (cottages were a lot bigger in those days) built about 1855 from cypress grown and cut on the property and from bricks made in the plantation's kiln.

Three of the original out-buildings remain. The others, long since gone from the grounds, have been replaced by moving in appropriate ones found on other plantations.

The overnight cottages are restored slave quarters, doubtless improved since slaves lived in them, with ruffled curtains, air conditioning, antique furnishings and artifacts, pecky cypress paneling, and the work of Louisiana artists on the walls.

Altogether there are thirty buildings on the plantation now, including a children's playhouse, a greenhouse and potting shed, an old shop with antique tools, a Civil War museum, and an African-American museum. Guests sit in rockers on the porches of the little cottages, chatting back and forth from cottage to cottage in the old-time way.

For dinner, the people at Tezcuco will certainly suggest that you drive a couple of miles to Bittersweet Plantation to Lafitte's Landing Restaurant, where John D. Folse, a chef much admired in the area, serves up wonderful, rich, and well-seasoned gourmet meals in his historic building.

On the grounds, the Tezcuco Plantation Restaurant is open from 11:00 A.M. to 3:00 P.M. to serve lunch. The offerings range from such comfortably familiar dishes as shrimp salad to more exotic choices, including fried alligator.

HOW TO GET THERE: Tezcuco is between Baton Rouge and New Orleans, near I-10. Coming from the north or the south on I-10, take exit 179 onto LA 44 south to Burnside. The plantation is 1 mile north of Sunshine Bridge on LA 44. Write for brochure with map.

Victoria Inn and Gardens
Jean Lafitte, Louisiana 70067

INNKEEPERS: Dale and Roy Ross

ADDRESS/TELEPHONE: 4707 Jean Lafitte Boulevard; (504) 689-4757 or (800) 689-4797; fax (504) 689-3399

WEB SITE: www.VictoriaInn.com

E-MAIL: info@VictoriaInn.com

ROOMS: 11, plus 3 suites; all with private bath and television with VCR, telephone, iron, hair dryer; suites have two-person whirlpool tubs and coffeemakers in rooms; one room handicapped accessible. No smoking in guest rooms.

RATES: $95 to $149, single or double; includes full breakfast.

OPEN: Year-round.

FACILITIES AND ACTIVITIES: Located on the Pen, a lake. Pier and covered dock with bar; pedal boat, sailboat, sailboard, and pirogue (motorless swamp boat) rentals; 9 acres of landscaped grounds, salt water swimming pool in lake surrounded by cypress plank deck, picnic tables; tea (hot or iced) is served each afternoon, complimentary drinks on arrival. Large library of videos. Fishing and sailing charters and swamp tours by seaplane can be arranged. Nearby: Restaurants; swamp tours, Gulf and inland fishing charters, Sunday "Fais do-do" at Bayou Barn. Tours to New Orleans (about one hour away) and plantations can be arranged.

Only 20 miles from New Orleans, Jean LaFitte is a little bayou town that surprises you with its simplicity and offers a completely different view of Louisiana. There's nothing much here but a few restaurants, places to rent boats, and down-to-earth, friendly Cajun people.

Victoria Inn sits on nine acres of landscaped grounds overlooking the Pen, a fishing lake in which crabs became trapped or "penned"—hence the name.

The buildings—two West Indies/Creole plantation houses and a converted carriage house—fit in with the overall simplicity of the region. Some of the guest rooms are named for what grows in the gardens: Magnolia, Jasmine, Rose, Ivy. The rooms are light, sunny, and brightly decorated. In the Magnolia Suite, for instance, the walls are a cheerful peach. In the sitting room, a loveseat sits in front of a small white wicker table. In the bedroom, a white Battenburg lace spread and a canopy of netting set off the antique bed. And the Ivy rooms are gardenlike in their combination of ivy-patterned fabrics, white wicker, and house plants.

What you eat when you crawl out of that bed in the morning reflects the local Cajun influence. You might choose among "mosquito toast" with bacon, a pecan waffle and bacon, and a crabmeat omelette, all served with fruit compote and juice. Whatever you choose, it will be beautifully presented on good china with white linens and fresh flowers. If you get up before most people, you may find coffee as early as 6:00 A.M. These early morning hours may be the best time for walking along the Pen, watching for the large variety of waterbirds that stay here.

If you are animal lovers like we are, the innkeepers have one cat, two dogs, two horses, ducks, and chickens to help you deal with your separation anxiety.

HOW TO GET THERE: The inn is on a country road in Jean Lafitte. You will receive a map and directions by mail, fax, or e-mail when you make reservations.

Madewood Plantation House
Napoleonville, Louisiana 70390

INNKEEPER: Christine Gaudet

ADDRESS/TELEPHONE: 4250 Highway 308; (504) 369-7151 or (800) 375-7151 (for reservations call 10:00 A.M. to 5:00 P.M.); fax (504) 369-9848

WEB SITE: www.madewood.com

E-MAIL: madewoodpl@aol.com

ROOMS: 6 rooms, 2 suites; all with private bath and hair dryer; 1 with wheelchair access. Smoking only on porches.

RATES: $195 single, $225 double, $275 to $285 triple; includes full breakfast and candlelight dinner.

OPEN: Year-round except Thanksgiving Eve and Day, Christmas Eve and Day, and New Year's Eve and Day.

FACILITIES AND ACTIVITIES: Dinner. Nearby: Mississippi River tour boats and tours of plantation homes such as Nottoway and Oak Alley, Attakapes Landing at Lake Verrett, and Bittersweet Plantation, home of chef John Folse's Lafitte's Landing Restaurant.

Madewood feels like a house in the country. A fancy one, admittedly, a Greek Revival mansion with six white columns, but a house in the country nonetheless. Irises grow around the sides of the porches; you can see fields in every direction; pear trees on the property produce fruit for the inn; and the parking area is shaded by established old trees.

The mansion itself is filled with antiques, Oriental rugs, and crystal chandeliers. It has recently been painted and completely refurbished, but Madewood still feels like a home rather than a museum.

Upstairs, one room has been preserved as a dressing room–bathroom, complete with an old scoop-shaped metal bathtub that would have had to be filled and emptied with a bucket. It makes you appreciate the modern bathrooms now available to guests.

Old clothes are displayed in one of the tour bedrooms, laid out and hanging as though someone were just about to put them on.

You get a simpler sense from the rooms in the old slave cabin, a rustic little building with a working fireplace and tufted quilts on the beds.

At the rear of the house, the original open-hearth kitchen for the plantation home is still intact, set up with odd tables and chairs, an antique wash-

ing machine, and assorted pieces of cooking equipment so that you can imagine what it must have been like when meals for the family and guests were prepared there.

Wherever you stay, be sure you arrange to have Yvette or Clem cook dinner for you. They are cooks who can tell you exactly what's in a dish—they just can't give you exact amounts. They stir things until they "feel right" and cook them until they "look right." Their menu includes chicken pies and shrimp pies, gumbos, corn bread, green beans, bread pudding, and Pumpkin Lafourche, a casserole of apples, raisins, pumpkin, sugar, butter, nutmeg, cinnamon, and vanilla.

Complimentary wine and cheese are served before dinner. Dinner includes an after-dinner drink in the parlor, where there's one of the tiniest old pump organs we've ever seen. A self-service honor bar is available for those who would like a drink during the day or later in the evening.

HOW TO GET THERE: From I-10, take exit 182, cross Sunshine Bridge, and follow bayou plantation signs to Highway 70, Spur 70, and southern Highway 308. The inn faces the highway.

The Cornstalk Hotel
New Orleans, Louisiana 70115

INNKEEPERS: Debi and David Spencer

ADDRESS/TELEPHONE: 915 Royal Street; (504) 523-1515; fax (504) 522-5558

WEB SITE: www.travelguides.com/bb/cornstalk

ROOMS: 14, all with private bath, telephone, cable television, iron and ironing board, clock radio; some with decorative fireplaces.

RATES: $75 to $185, double occupancy; includes continental breakfast and newspaper; higher rates and minimum stays required during special events such as Sugar Bowl, Mardi Gras, JazzFest, and the like. Credit cards accepted.

OPEN: Year-round.

FACILITIES AND ACTIVITIES: Nearby: In the midst of the French Quarter—only a block from Bourbon Street—with casual and fine dining, nightspots, shopping, zoo, aquarium, riverboats, museums.

Built in the early 1800s, Cornstalk was the home of Judge François Xavier-Martin, the first chief justice of the Louisiana supreme court and author of the first history of Louisiana. It is reported that Harriet Beecher Stowe was staying here when the sights at the nearby slave market inspired her to write *Uncle Tom's Cabin*.

Obviously, the house has been enlarged and remodeled several times to achieve its current appearance—mostly Greek Revival but with a battlemented tower. It is one of the most distinctive and photographed small inns in the French Quarter and has appeared in several movies.

Once inside the grand entrance hall lobby, you'll enter a quiet, more dignified world where brilliantly glowing crystal chandeliers reflect antique mirrors and ornate rosette scrolls, cherubs, and medallions float across the

The Famous Cornstalk Fence

A real French Quarter landmark, The Cornstalk Hotel's famous fence never ceases to attract locals and visitors. Richly detailed ripe ears of corn shucked on their stalks seem ready to be harvested. Pumpkins form the base of the massive iron columns, which are entwined with pumpkin vines, leaves, and morning glories.

The story of the fence is that when an early owner brought his young bride to New Orleans from Iowa, she was terribly homesick for the waving fields of corn back home. To help her adjust to her new home, he had the fence made in graceful iron so that she could always see something of her native land.

ceiling. Spacious, high-ceilinged guest rooms boast elegant antique furnishings such as carved and tester beds, as well as chandeliers, decorative fireplaces, and opulent fabrics.

You may enjoy your continental breakfast of pastries, muffins, juice, and hot beverages, accompanied by the morning newspaper, in your room, on the front veranda, or the second-story balcony.

HOW TO GET THERE: Exit from I-10 at Bernard Avenue and proceed south to Royal. Turn right and follow Royal to the inn.

Delta Queen 💚
New Orleans, Louisiana 70130

INNKEEPERS: Various captains of the Delta Queen Steamboat Co.

ADDRESS/TELEPHONE: Robin Street Wharf, 1380 Port of New Orleans Place; (504) 586-0631 or (800) 543-1949; fax (504) 585-0630

WEB SITE: www.deltaqueen.com

ROOMS: 87 staterooms, all with private bath.

RATES: Approximately $200 per night per person; includes 3 meals daily, snacks, and entertainment, depending on the season and itinerary.

OPEN: Year-round.

FACILITIES AND ACTIVITIES: Betty Blake and Forward Cabin Lounges, Orleans Room restaurant and theater, Texas Lounge bar, gift shop.

BUSINESS TRAVEL: Ideal for small executive retreats or incentive groups.

*A*t one time more than 11,000 steam-powered paddle wheelers plied the inland waterways that served as highways in the 1800s. Today only a few of these extraordinary boats remain, and most of those are used as sight-seeing tour boats. Only three—one a genuine antique, the other two of new construction—offer overnight accommodations. Listed on the National Register of Historic Places and included as one

River Terms

When you're onboard the *Delta Queen* for your first cruise, don't let your terminology show you up as a neophyte.

- First of all, it's a *boat,* not a ship.

- When you come into a town, the place you tie up to is called a *landing,* not a dock.

- Sometimes in a very small town with no port facilities, the crew will simply throw a line around a convenient tree stump; that's known as *choke a stump.*

- *Mark Twain* was actually the pen name of Samuel Clemens. He took the name from the soundings being taken as the boat entered shallow water.

- A *tow* is a string of barges being pushed, not pulled, up and down the river.

- The *liar's bench* was just outside the pilothouse and is where the captain, pilot, and other crew members gathered to swap tall tales about the river. When Samuel Clemens/Mark Twain was a captain and pilot himself, this is where he heard or told many of the stories that later made him famous.

- Being able to *draw the river* is a requirement of every riverboat captain and pilot. Not only must they draw the course of every stretch of river on which they are licensed, but they must also be able to indicate on the map every sand bar or other obstacle—all from memory.

- Accompanying every cruise is a *riverlorian,* a historian and expert about the river, who gives lectures and informal chats about steamboats in general and the terrain, flora and fauna, and history of the current stretch of river being passed.

of the National Trust for Historic Preservation's prestigious Historic Hotels of America, the *Delta Queen* is even a post office with its own postmark.

Fed on Twain stories and movies such as *Showboat*, we wanted to re-create the ambience of the steamboating paddle wheel era—the soul-stirring patriotic fervor, the slow pace of another era—for ourselves when we took our first cruise aboard the *Delta Queen*. That trip from New Orleans to Vicksburg and back to New Orleans created indelible, precious memories and friendships. All our expectations were surpassed. We totally agree with the company's slogan that a voyage aboard the *Delta Queen* is an "antidote to overstimulated lives." The soft swoosh, swoosh of the great steam pistons driving the enormous paddle wheel lulls you into a complete sense of well-being and detachment.

Constructed in 1926, the *Delta Queen* had a varied past as a shuttle, military ferry, and restaurant.

Then the Greene Line Steamers of New Orleans had the bright idea of providing overnight accommodations on the Mississippi River, sometimes called the American Nile. The *Delta Queen* was completely overhauled and refurbished (using many parts salvaged from its twin the *Delta King*) and put into service. For many years river cruising in America was a well-kept secret reserved for the wealthy, but gradually the news got out. Today cruising the Mississippi, Ohio, Tennessee, Arkansas, Atchafalaya, Cumberland, Red, Illinois, Black, Old, and Kanawha Rivers and the Intracoastal Waterway has become so popular that the company has built two other paddle wheelers.

Gleaming teak handrails line the decks, Tiffany windows sparkle in the brilliant sunlight or in the soft glow of lamp light, and crystal chandeliers sway gently as the vessel proceeds at her languid, almost silent, 5-mile-per-hour pace. Your surroundings are like those of a warm yet elegant nineteenth-century Victorian home, with rich paneling and a grand teak and brass staircase. Public spaces and most staterooms are filled with period furnishings—many of them genuine antiques—and opulent velvet- and tapestry-covered upholstered pieces. The small number of public rooms enhances the intimacy. You really get to know your fellow passengers and the crew.

Your cruise, whether it be three days or twelve days, includes three sumptuous meals a day, including a fabulous five-course dinner each night, late-night snacks, other snacks and treats throughout the day, professional showboat-style entertainment nightly, lectures, craft lessons, and calliope concerts. Drinks and shore excursions at many of America's most charming river cities and small towns are extra.

HOW TO GET THERE: You may board the *Delta Queen* at any of dozens of cities from New Orleans to Minneapolis/St. Paul or Pittsburgh to Galveston. Specific directions will be given with your cruise documents.

Hotel Maison de Ville and the Audubon Cottages
New Orleans, Louisiana 70130

INNKEEPER: Jean-Luc Maumus, managing director

ADDRESS/TELEPHONE: 727 Rue Toulouse; (504) 561–5858 or (800) 634–1600; fax (504) 528–9939

WEB SITE: www.maisondeville.com

E-MAIL: maisondeville@travelbase.com

ROOMS: 23 guest rooms, suites, and cottages; all with private bath, hair dryer, cable television with movies, modem phone jack, iron, and ironing board. No-smoking inn.

RATES: $215 to $245 rooms, $595 to $725 cottages; includes continental breakfast with a fresh rose, newspaper. Not appropriate for children.

OPEN: Year-round.

FACILITIES AND ACTIVITIES: The Bistro at Maison de Ville restaurant, swimming pool, 24-hour front desk, concierge. Nearby: French Quarter museums, casual and fine dining, nightspots, antiques shopping, boutiques; also not far away from aquarium, zoo, river cruises, Garden District.

hen we saw the inviting courtyards with their lush tropical flowers and greenery at the hotel and at the cottages, we could easily believe that in 1821 John James Audubon had produced a portion of his vast *Birds of America* series while he was living in one of the dwellings now named for him and that Tennessee Williams had worked on several of his plays in the courtyard of the main inn, where he stayed in Room 9. What glorious inspiration we would derive from these idyllic surroundings!

Maison de ville means *town house* in French, and the main part of this intimate hotel is just that—a three-story dwelling erected sometime between 1800 and 1820 after a massive French Quarter fire destroyed the previous structure and most of those in the area. Four original slave quarters, which had been built at least fifty years before (mid-1700s), did survive and serve as additional guest quarters today.

Nestled in a quintessential French Quarter setting wrapped around a hidden courtyard, the inn offers gracious accommodations as well as a renowned restaurant. The exterior is distinguished by a second-floor balcony made of the requisite ornate iron. Luxurious guest rooms feature antique furnishings such as ornately carved canopy beds, feather bedding, paintings and period accessories, and marble bathrooms with brass hardware. Modern conveniences include two-line phones with dataports, television, VCR, and hair dryer. Some rooms overlook Toulouse Street while others open onto the courtyard. The nearby cottages boast two bedrooms and two baths with a living room and dining room as well as their own courtyard and swimming pool.

Unless you stayed out partying too late the night before, you'll awaken eager to explore the French Quarter. Before you set off you'll want to savor the ample continental breakfast, which can be served in the privacy of your room or in the courtyard. Little touches say so much about an establishment. Your breakfast is served with a fresh rose in addition to the *Wall Street Journal* and the *Times-Picayune*.

Named New Orleans's Best Bistro by the Zagat Survey and the winner of numerous awards from *Wine Spectator, Gourmet, Bon Appétit,* and the *Times-Picayune,* the Bistro at Maison de Ville restaurant features creative nouvelle Creole cuisine in a jewel of a setting. Red banquettes, bentwood chairs, white table linens, ceiling fans, beveled-glass mirrors, and Impressionist paintings provide an intimate setting reminiscent of a Paris bistro. Menu items, which include traditional French favorites and New Orleans culinary selections, include Bistro Crawfish Remoulade, grilled Louisiana shrimp with sauce piquante, or andouille orzo jambalaya, and the signature crème brûlée for dessert. Lunch and dinner are served daily, and reservations are recommended.

HOW TO GET THERE: From I–10, take exit 235-A (Orleans Avenue/Vieux Carre). Follow the ramp to Basin Street, staying in the left lane and making a U-turn at the sign NORTH RAMPART VIA TOULOUSE STREET/FRENCH QUARTER. From Basin Street turn right onto Toulouse Street, which cuts across Rampart Street. Follow Toulouse until you cross Bourbon Street. The hotel is on the left.

Hotel Provincial
New Orleans, Louisiana 70116

INNKEEPERS: Clancy, Verna, and Bryan Dupepe

ADDRESS/TELEPHONE: 1024 Rue Chartres; (504) 581–4995; outside Louisiana (800) 535–7922; fax (504) 581–1018

WEB SITE: hotelprovincial.com

E-MAIL: info@hotelprovincial.com

ROOMS: 94 rooms and suites; all with private bath, telephone, cable television, hair dryer, iron and ironing board, voice mail, dataports; some with wheelchair access.

RATES: $99 to $325, single or double, including 24-hour coffee and newspaper; breakfast extra. Children under 17 free in same room with parents. Credit cards accepted. Special value rates in June, July, August, and December.

OPEN: Year-round.

FACILITIES AND ACTIVITIES: Beignet Cafe open 7:00 A.M. to 10:00 P.M. for guests and public, bar, wheelchair access. Swimming pool, off-street parking. Located in the French Quarter 2½ blocks from Jackson

Square and Bourbon Street. Nearby: Restaurants, antiques shops, jazz, historic tours, aquarium.

BUSINESS TRAVEL: Meeting rooms for up to 60; phones have dataports.

*O*bviously an inn with ninety-four rooms isn't a cozy little hostelry just like home, but people seem to feel at home in Hotel Provincial's public spaces, such as the courtyard, and easily connect with other guests. The fact that the inn has been in the Dupepe family since its opening more than four decades ago gives it a wonderful nontouristy feeling—as though you were visiting a prosperous friend or relative.

And it's not just the guests; the staff also always seems to have a few minutes to talk—asking how you're liking your stay, suggesting their own personal favorite sights around town, or getting you a serving of Creole gumbo from the restaurant, "just to try." By the way, if you haven't had a really good bowl of Creole gumbo lately, this is the place to get one. The quality of the cafe's food is superb, and now it's open for breakfast, lunch, and dinner. The cafe is supervised by a master chef whose offerings range from French bistro to New Orleans specialties. Local people flock to the cafe in addition to the guests from the inn. Calling it a cafe, seems to us, is a misnomer. This is not an eatery with checked tablecloths but a very elegant white-linen establishment with chandeliers, gilt framed mirrors, and the like.

The intimate hotel is actually a collection of low buildings, town houses, former slave quarters, and old commercial buildings—nothing high-rise—unified by restoration and courtyards. Four of the five buildings are listed on the National Register of Historic Places and surround spacious tropical courtyards, two of which have swimming pools.

Each individually decorated, spacious bedchamber is furnished with Creole antiques and French-style reproductions, which give the room a warm and relaxing ambience. Chandeliers or fans hang from the high ceilings; ornate plaster or wood moldings, period wallpaper patterns, chair rails, and paintings adorn the walls. Beautiful, romantic beds range from half-testers to highly carved headboards to brass. Magnificent bed coverings and window treatments and elegant seating areas complete the picture. Everyday comforts such as cable television and a clock radio are beautifully integrated into the rooms.

HOW TO GET THERE: Exit I-10 at the Orleans Avenue/Vieux Carre exit. Follow the right curve onto Basin Street and turn left onto Conti Street. At the first intersection, turn left onto Rampart Street. Go 7 blocks and turn right onto St. Philip Street. Go 5 blocks and turn left onto Rue Chartres. The hotel is in the middle of the block.

Lafitte Guest House
New Orleans, Louisiana 70116

INNKEEPERS: Edward G. Doré and Andrew J. Crocchiolo

ADDRESS/TELEPHONE: 1003 Bourbon Street; (504) 581-2678 or (800) 331-7971

WEB SITE: www.lafitteguesthouse.com

E-MAIL: lafitteguesthouse@travelbase.com

ROOMS: 14, all with private bath and telephone, television, sleep (white noise) machines. Not handicapped accessible.

RATES: $129 to $219, single or double; includes continental breakfast and wine and cheese each evening.

OPEN: Year-round.

FACILITIES AND ACTIVITIES: Off-street parking, $10 per night. Located in the French Quarter. Nearby: Restaurants, antiques shops, jazz, historic tours.

When Lafitte was built in 1849, it was a single-family home. Today, as a guest house, it still feels more like a home than a hotel. We've attended meetings in the parlor and swear that something about the Victorian furniture, Oriental rugs, and elegant red

velvet draperies made us all more cooperative than we would have been in an ordinary meeting room.

The guest rooms are decorated in period furnishings and have a kind of low-key calm that is a refreshing retreat from the outside activity of the Quarter. Many of them have the original black marble mantels over their fireplaces. Several have four-poster beds with full or half testers. The rooms in the main house are somewhat larger than those in the former slave quarters. Their slave quarters rooms have simpler furnishings and exposed brick walls that lend another kind of charm to a room, and, if anything, the sense of privacy is even greater in these rooms.

We especially liked the staff. Their approach is informal; instead of a conspicuous desk for checking in, they use an unobtrusive antique table set well back in the hall so that when you come in the front door you see the Victorian parlor before you see anything resembling a hotel front desk. Even at the busiest times on the busiest days, the staff always has time to answer questions and provide helpful little extras.

New Orleans has so many good restaurants that recommending just one seems wrong. The inn staff all know a lot about city restaurants and tours and will talk to you about your own particular tastes, then make suggestions about where to eat and what to do. You can also exchange experiences and recommendations with other inn guests during the daily cocktail period from 5:30 to 7:00 P.M. over wine and cheese. As if that weren't enough, you'll also find a book of menus to browse. If this seems like a lot of emphasis on food, it is. As the innkeeper says, "Some people come just to eat!"

It is exciting to walk up and down Bourbon Street in the evening, full from a good meal, listening to the different music coming from each establishment along the way and enjoying the high spirits of the tourists and performers as they acknowledge one another.

HOW TO GET THERE: The inn is in the French Quarter. Bourbon Street is between Dauphine and Royal.

Park View Guest House
New Orleans, Louisiana 70116

INNKEEPER: Nick Ransom

ADDRESS/TELEPHONE: 7004 St. Charles Avenue; (504) 861-7564 or (888) 533-0746; fax (504) 861-1225

WEB SITE: www.parkviewguesthouse.com

E-MAIL: info@parkviewguesthouse.com

ROOMS: 22 rooms; 14 with private bath, all with telephone and cable television.

RATES: $95 to $159; includes continental breakfast and champagne happy hour; $10 for additional guests in the room.

OPEN: Year-round.

FACILITIES AND ACTIVITIES:
Nearby: Next door to Audubon Park and Zoo; on the St. Charles trolley line with easy access to the French Quarter museums, casual and fine dining establishments, nightspots, shopping, riverfront, aquarium.

*L*ocated right on the St. Charles trolley line adjacent to the Audubon Park and Zoo and near Tulane and Loyola Universities, the stately three-story B&B inn, which looks as if it began life as an impressive private residence, was actually built as a hotel for the Cotton States Exposition in 1884. Listed on the National Register of Historic Places, it is the longest continuously operating hotel in New Orleans and offers guests a taste of a less hurried era.

An architectural gem, the corner property features many-pillared wraparound verandas on the first and second floors. These porches and balconies are favorite spots for guests to gather. Temple pediments and dormers characterize the third floor.

In impeccable condition, the inn's interior showcases high ceilings, hardwood floors accented by colorful Oriental carpets on the first floor, and burgundy carpet on the upper two floors. The twenty-two guest rooms are light and airy and furnished with elegant antiques. Fourteen guest chambers feature a private bath, while the remainder share baths. Each room has a phone and a few have television.

The nightly rate includes a continental breakfast of croissants, juice, and hot beverages served in the formal dining room.

HOW TO GET THERE: Take I-10 to downtown and exit onto the Pontchartrain Parkway. Take the parkway to the St. Charles Street exit and turn right onto St. Charles Street Southwest. Follow it to the inn, which is on the left.

St. Charles Guest House
New Orleans, Louisiana 70130

INNKEEPERS: Joanne and Dennis Hilton

ADDRESS/TELEPHONE: 1748 Prytania Street; (504) 523-6556; fax (504) 522-6340

WEB SITE: www.stcharlesguesthouse.com

E-MAIL: dhilton111@aol.com

ROOMS: 38; 26 with private bath; some with decorative fireplace; alarm clocks on request.

RATES: $35 to $95 double occupancy; includes continental breakfast; each additional person in the room is $10; a minimum stay is required during special events such as JazzFest, New Year's Eve, and Mardi Gras.

OPEN: Year-round.

FACILITIES AND ACTIVITIES: Swimming pool, extensive library.

When we visited this unpretentious pensione-style B&B inn filled with nooks and crannies and eccentricities, we realized it certainly would not be for everyone. But for those who want to visit New Orleans on a shoestring, stay in a historic property, and meet some very interesting folks in the bargain, this could be a match made in heaven.

Although the guest house has been welcoming guests for more than forty years, Joanne and Dennis have been operating it for more than twenty years, and you can tell by their enthusiasm how much they love it. Dennis says their purpose in life is to offer safe, clean, affordable accommodations—and they've succeeded admirably.

The guest house, which is actually located in three adjoining century-old Garden District homes, is so well known worldwide that it welcomes around 4,000 guests annually—many of them students, artists, writers, academics, world travelers, and others on a budget. Accommodations range from backpacker rooms at $35 per night to queen-bedded rooms with private bath at $95, with a variety of other accommodations in between. (A backpacker room isn't a hostel-style dormitory room as we feared, but rather a simple room with a double bed, no bathroom, and no frills that is available on a first-come, first-served basis.) Self-described as low-tech, the quaint, eclectically furnished rooms have high ceilings, the simple necessities, and no telephones or televisions. There are pay phones in each house. We were left with the impression of a jumble of wallpaper patterns that were, perhaps, picked up at sales or flea markets, but the sense is also one of comfort and friendliness.

In good weather guests frolic in or around the pool. When the weather is less than ideal, they can borrow a book from the thousands located on bookshelves throughout the buildings. In the late afternoon fixings for tea or coffee are set out along with some kind of goodies.

Located 1 block off the St. Charles trolley line, the inn is convenient to the French Quarter, zoo, aquarium, and other New Orleans attractions.

HOW TO GET THERE: Take I–10 to downtown and exit onto the Pontchartrain Parkway to the St. Charles Street exit. Turn right onto St. Charles Street Southwest. Turn left on Jackson and go 1 block to Prytania and turn right. Follow it to the guest house, which is on the left.

The Soniat House Hotel
New Orleans, Louisiana 70116

INNKEEPERS: Rodney and Frances Smith

ADDRESS/TELEPHONE: 1133 Rue Chartres; (504) 522–0570 or (800) 544–8808; fax (504) 522–7208

WEB SITE: www.soniathouse.com

E-MAIL: Via Web site

ROOMS: 33 rooms and suites, all with private bath and upscale amenities. One suite has 2 baths; many have a whirlpool tub.

RATES: $195 to $325 for rooms, $350 to $650 for suites, double occupancy; $11 for continental breakfast; $19 for valet parking. Discounts in July, August, and mid-December. Two rooms are handicapped accessible. Largely nonsmoking.

OPEN: Year-round.

FACILITIES AND ACTIVITIES: Courtyard, honor bar, upscale amenities. Nearby: French Quarter museums, St. Louis Cathedral, casual and fine dining, shopping, tours, carriage tours, riverboat tours, nightlife.

BUSINESS TRAVEL: Telephone with dataport; desks in some rooms; many businesspeople like to work in the sitting room off the lobby, where there is a computer for guest use.

We love so many of New Orleans's small hotels, inns, guest houses, and bed-and-breakfasts, it may be hard in reading the descriptions to tell which ones are really far above the others, so let us help you—this one is really special.

Considered by many worldwide to be New Orleans's finest small hotel, this thirty-three-room gem is located in a quiet residential section of the French Quarter, but it is still convenient to the action. The superb, intimate inn combines Creole style with Greek Revival detail to transport you back to the New Orleans of the 1830s, when the grand town house was built by Joseph Soniat du Fossat, the son of one of the earliest leading New Orleans families. Thirteen children, in-laws, grandchildren, and the attendant staff explain the ample size of the house.

From the moment you enter the stone carriageway, which leads to a small registration area and a cozy sitting room, you'll be enchanted. An aura of adventure and romance hovers over the handsome house. You won't be surprised to learn that the inn has been named one of the Ten Best Small Hotels in America by *Condé Nast Traveler*.

In the Creole fashion, the original house turned its back on the street; a carriageway led to the courtyard, where the life of the house took place. Built of red brick, the structure rises two stories with symmetrically arranged windows. Ample dormers open up the attic level. The main entrance, with its elegant paneled doorway flanked by sidelights and slender columns, was on the second floor. In the 1860s, when the fashion for ornate cast iron swept through the French Quarter, the extensive second-story gallery, with some of the most elaborate ironwork in the area, was added.

Creole houses seldom wasted interior space on stairs, so the graceful spi-

ral staircase rises from the courtyard to an open gallery that feeds into the second-story rooms.

On the second floor, the great central hall is embellished at each end by decorative doorways. The handsome rooms off this hallway are noted for their fine cornices and plaster ceiling medallions. Accommodations are impressive, with English, French, and Louisiana antiques the Smiths have collected during more than twenty-five years of world travel. Bedsteads, many of which have massive headboards, canopies, or half testers, were carved by New Orleans's finest cabinetmakers. Custom fabrics are chosen for each room to give it an individual style. Oriental carpets enhance the polished hardwood floors, and paintings by contemporary New Orleans artists enliven the walls. Fine antique books, lamps, and conversation pieces are carefully arranged throughout each room. Some guest chambers boast a balcony and/or whirlpool bath.

The management prides itself on attention to detail, with extra touches such as high-quality soaps, extra-luxurious bed linens, a wine cellar, and an honor bar. Some special luxuries include 200-count cotton percale bed linens, goose down pillows, and extra reading pillows. Your bed will be turned down at night. Whether your visit involves business, pleasure, or both, the staff is ready to meet your needs.

One of the two lush and exotic courtyards contains a babbling fountain and a lily pond next to which you might choose to be served a continental breakfast (extra charge) of Southern buttermilk biscuits, homemade strawberry preserves, sweet butter, freshly squeezed orange juice, and rich Creole coffee on a silver tray. You can also be totally decadent and have breakfast in your room. In the evening, the courtyard by candlelight is a romantic place for a before- or after-dinner drink.

HOW TO GET THERE: Take the Esplanade exit from I–10 and turn toward the river to Rue Chartres. Turn right; the hotel is 2 blocks on the right.

The Terrell House
New Orleans, Louisiana 70130

INNKEEPER: Bobby Hogan

ADDRESS/TELEPHONE: 1441 Magazine Street; (504) 524–9859 or (800) 878–9859; fax (504) 529–9859

WEB SITE: www.lacajun.com

E-MAIL: info@lacajun.com

ROOMS: 9, all with private bath, telephone, and television; carriage house rooms with wheelchair access.

RATES: $85 to $165, single or double; includes full breakfast and evening cocktail. Credit cards accepted. Adults-only inn. Special golf packages available.

OPEN: Year-round.

FACILITIES AND ACTIVITIES: Library of books about New Orleans and Louisiana, secluded courtyard. Nearby: Fine restaurants, the French Quarter, the New Orleans Convention Center, the Riverwalk shopping-dining-entertainment center, St. Charles Avenue and the Garden District (where most antiques shops in the city are located), docks for the *Delta Queen* and other riverboats.

he Terrell House was built in 1858 by a wealthy New Orleans cotton merchant. It has twin parlors, marble fireplaces, gaslight fixtures, guest rooms that open onto balconies, and an outstanding courtyard.

As for the furniture, we'd heard about it from other innkeepers before we even visited. The inn is furnished with an excellent quality collection (much of it rosewood) of New Orleans furniture of the 1850s. Many pieces are by Prudent Mallard, and there are also numerous antiques that were purchased by a former owner.

While the inn is steeped in the past, the innkeepers have also kept modern comforts in mind, upgrading all the baths with pedestal sinks and tile floors and adding a hot tub in the courtyard.

Another nice feature of the inn is its location in the Lower Garden District. Magazine Street is wonderful. It's undergone restoration and is full of antiques shops and restaurants. This neighborhood is quieter than the French Quarter; it's where the local people shop and eat away from the tourist area. Taxis are easy to find and inexpensive.

You can get as much or as little advice and attention as you want from the innkeepers. They know all about tours, tourist attractions, and interesting spots off the beaten path. Of course they know all about restaurants, too.

Bobby Hogan is a P.G.A. golf professional, so he has special knowledge for golf players, too.

HOW TO GET THERE: From I-10 East, take the Canal Street exit and turn right toward the river. Go 10 blocks to Magazine Street; turn right on Magazine to the 1400 block. From I-10 West, take the Poydras Street exit. Go 10 blocks to Magazine Street and turn right to the 1400 block.

Barrow House
St. Francisville, Louisiana 70775

INNKEEPERS: Shirley Dittloff and Christopher Dennis

ADDRESS/TELEPHONE: 9779 Royal Street (mailing address: P.O. Box 2550); (225) 635-4791; fax (225) 635-1863

WEB SITE: www.topteninn.com

E-MAIL: staff@topteninn.com

ROOMS: 5, plus 3 suites in 2 buildings; all with private bath, television, iron and ironing board, hair dryer; telephone on request. Suites have access to a full kitchen.

RATES: $85 to $115, double; $130 to $160, suites; inquire about single rates. Includes continental breakfast, wine, and cassette walking tour of Historic District. Full breakfast available at $5.00 extra per person. Credit cards accepted. Well-behaved children are welcome.

OPEN: Year-round except December 20 to 25.

FACILITIES AND ACTIVITIES: Located in St. Francisville Historic District. Nearby: Eight tour plantations and historic sites, golf, cassette walking tour of Historic District.

*B*arrow House is made up of two buildings: an 1809 saltbox with a Greek Revival wing added in the 1860s that's decorated with period antiques and listed on the National Register of Historic Places, and, next to it, the Printer's House, which was built for the monks who founded the town. It dates from about 1780.

In the saltbox, the gorgeous antiques include a rosewood armoire by Prudent Mallard and a queen-size Mallard bed with a *Spanish moss* mattress. You don't have to sleep in that bed unless you want to, but one man, a doctor with a bad back, said it was the most comfortable bed he'd ever slept in.

Spanish moss was the traditional mattress filler used in Louisiana for 200 years. Shirley's informal tour of the house gives you a chance to learn how the mattress was made and to see all the fine antiques.

Similarly, the professionally recorded Historic District walking tour (with Mozart between stops) Shirley wrote guides you from Barrow House to twenty-three historic stops.

Some people don't want too much personal fuss. Shirley says that she has to know when guests would rather be left alone. You'll get whatever amount of attention you want—no more. Probably the ultimate privacy is in the rooms and suites at the Printer's House. Here, the Empire and Victorian suites are the very best accommodations. Wherever you stay, expect to leave happy.

HOW TO GET THERE: Barrow House is behind the courthouse in the St. Francisville Historic District. You will receive a map after you make reservations.

Myrtles Plantation
St. Francisville, Louisiana 70775

INNKEEPERS: John and Teeta Moss

ADDRESS/TELEPHONE: 7747 U.S. 61; (225) 635–6277 or (800) 809–0565; fax (225) 635–5837

WEB SITE: myrtlesplantation.com

E-MAIL: myrtles@bsf.net

ROOMS: 10; all with private bath featuring claw-foot tubs.

RATES: $95 to $195; includes continental breakfast and a historical tour of the house; $7.00 for ghost tour given Friday and Saturday nights after dark; limitations on children.

OPEN: Year-round.

FACILITIES AND ACTIVITIES: Restaurant. Nearby: Rosedown Plantation and Gardens, Greenwood Plantation, Nottoway Plantation, several other plantations; walking tour of St. Francisville; Afton Villa Gardens, Audubon State Commemorative Area; Casa de Sue Winery; Feliciana Cellars Winery; Baton Rouge; golf; Audubon Pilgrimage each March.

BUSINESS TRAVEL: Ideal for small corporate retreats.

*I*t was thickening twilight and the heavy rain had stopped, but trickles of water still ran off the Spanish moss dripping from the ancient live oaks surrounding the darkened old French-style plantation house. Suddenly an eerie, flickering light appeared inside the house. "What's you want?" a husky female voice inquired. "Dis ain't no place to be at night. Too many people died here."

This was our introduction to the Myrtles, a B&B inn reputed to be haunted by so many ghosts that it has been named America's Most Haunted House by the Smithsonian Institution and the *Wall Street Journal* as well as being featured on several television programs. (Scientists measured, among

other things, magnetic fields and temperature and pressure gradients before reaching this conclusion.) We had arrived for a ghost tour, to be followed by an overnight stay if we were brave enough.

Originally built in 1796, the house has a history of elegance and intrigue. Ten murders have occurred here, and a well on the property is said to hold the bodies of hundreds of slaves. Of the five bedrooms in the house, deaths occurred in four. The fifth was the master suite of an owner who made it only to the top of the stairs before dying of a gunshot wound.

Innocent enough looking, the 12,000-square-foot antebellum cottage (considered small in an era when houses up to 55,000 square feet were being built in the area) sits on a hill well back from the road in deep shadows created by immense magnolias and live oaks. The exterior is characterized by magnificent double dormers and lacy iron grillwork on the 120-foot-long veranda. Behind the house, a vast lawn stretches back to the gloom of a dark pond and deep woods.

Our raconteur guide took us on a tour of the darkened house by the light of one candle while recounting spine-tingling details of all the gory deaths. With quivering apprehension, we agreed to stay for the night. Once the lights were flicked on, the house was bathed in soft, friendly light as all the goblins disappeared until another night and the house was transformed into an intimate inn with elaborate plaster frieze work and faux bois as well as lovely antique furnishings and art treasures—many of French influence.

In addition to the elegant guest rooms in the main house, there is a garden cottage, which contains several more rooms and a cozy restaurant. Nothing unusual has ever been reported to have happened in the garden cottage, so if you're a little squeamish about the possibility of ghosts, perhaps you'd be more comfortable in one of those rooms. Kean's Carriage House Restaurant serves lunch and dinner Wednesday through Saturday and Sunday brunch. The cuisine is that of traditional Louisiana, with choices such as gumbo, etouffée, and wild duck.

Assuming that you've had an uneventful night, you'll awaken refreshed and ready for a breakfast of muffins, pecan spins, fresh biscuits, fresh fruit and juices, and hot beverages.

HOW TO GET THERE: On U.S. 61, 1 mile north of the intersection of U.S. 61 and LA 10.

St. Francisville Inn 🏨 ℂℂ
St. Francisville, Louisiana 70775

INNKEEPERS: Laurie and Patrick Walsh

ADDRESS/TELEPHONE: 5720 Commerce Street (mailing address: P.O. Box 1369); (225) 635-6502 or (800) 488-6502; fax (225) 635-6421

WEB SITE: wolfsinn@aol.com

E-MAIL: laurie@wolfsinn.com

ROOMS: 10; all with private bath, cable television, telephone; some with king-size beds; one with oversize whirlpool tub.

RATES: $55 to $90 double occupancy; includes full breakfast buffet, coffee, desserts, and spirits. $10 for each additional person in the room. Credit cards accepted. Ask about packages.

OPEN: Year-round.

FACILITIES AND ACTIVITIES: Antiques and coffee shops, courtyard, swimming pool. Nearby: Adjacent to Parker Memorial Park; within walking distance of historic sites, churches, and shops; convenient to hiking, cycling, golfing, bird-watching.

*L*arge, twin, steeply pitched dormers centered by a smaller dormer, all lavishly trimmed with some of the best lacy gingerbread we've ever seen, characterize the darling Gothic Revival Wolf-Schlesinger House, built in 1880 in historic downtown St. Francisville. Streamers fluttering from the narrow gingerbread-topped columns of the full-length front veranda and the rockers and an old-fashioned porch swing on the veranda make you feel welcome.

Surrounded and shaded by more-than-century-old live oak trees festooned with Spanish moss, the house contains a guest parlor and Wolf's General Store, an antiques store and coffee shop. Guest accommodations are in a two-story wing wrapped around a New Orleans–style courtyard and swimming pool.

Overnight guests share the main house with the general public who come to dine or shop there. The inn's entry hall serves as a bar well supplied with sixty-five different beers and sixty wines from all over the world.

The parlor serves as a sitting room for guests—a place where they can read, play cards, watch television, or play the baby grand piano. The veranda and courtyard are also popular with guests.

The first time we visited the inn, a small dirt courtyard in the rear of the main house separated it from the guest wing. The intervening years have obviously been good ones for the St. Francisville Inn, permitting the transformation of the courtyard with the addition of brick paving, lush landscaping, and a swimming pool. The guest chambers have been upgraded and are now furnished with a mix of antique and reproduction furniture and the added modern conveniences of cable television and telephone.

St. Francisville is a delightful, small, quiet town steeped in history and romance. Dozens of plantations and gardens open to the public ring the town.

HOW TO GET THERE: Take U.S. 61 to LA 10 and turn west. At the intersection of LA 10 and Route 3057, the inn is on your left.

Fairfield Place
Bed and Breakfast Inn
Shreveport, Louisiana 71104

INNKEEPER: Jane Lipscomb

ADDRESS/TELEPHONE: 2221 Fairfield Avenue; (318) 222–0048; fax (318) 226–0631

WEB SITE: www.fairfieldbandb.com

E-MAIL: Via Web site

ROOMS: 11, all with private bath, telephone, television, clock radio, ceiling fan, hair dryer, robes, refrigerator, cold drinks, fruit.

RATES: $112 to $250, double occupancy; includes full breakfast and afternoon tea; $14 for each additional person in the room; children OK.

OPEN: Year-round.

FACILITIES AND ACTIVITIES: Some whirlpool baths; extensive gardens and grounds. Nearby: Central business district, medical center, casinos, Louisiana Downs racetrack, Independence Stadium.

BUSINESS TRAVEL: Writing desk and telephone with dataport in guest rooms; meeting space; fax and copier available.

*W*e met Janie about fourteen years ago at her turn-of-the-twentieth-century Victorian B&B inn. She was up to her elbows in wallpaper paste—papering the outside of a claw-foot tub with Bradbury and Bradbury Victorian wallpaper to match the adjoining room. What a neat idea—we've seen it copied since, but Janie was the first. This little project is just one of the many this dynamo of artistic and business acumen dives into.

Since we first met her, Janie has acquired the house next door, another great 1890s Victorian home—this one Greek Revival—from its ninety-nine-year-old owner, who finally decided that he needed a smaller place. "The property was covered with thorn bushes—a little like Sleeping Beauty's castle."

It took four months simply to get the yard and gardens cut back and the house emptied before Janie could start the process of refurbishing and redecorating the fine old home to provide additional guest rooms as well as meeting and banquet space. Now the house and enlarged grounds are an integral part of this great property, which includes a full commercial kitchen.

Any vacationer will be enthralled by Janie's Victorian rooms and luxury suites in these two spacious, casually elegant homes in the historic Fairfield-Highland district, but she also encourages business travelers to stay by providing an elegant, relaxing alternative to standard lodging.

Unlike anonymous, standard-issue, cookie-cutter hotels where you keep to your room and reluctantly awaken in confusion about where you are, at Fairfield Place you're a valued individual. Mingle with other guests in the library, which is well stocked with books by Louisiana writers; in the richly decorated parlor with a baby grand piano; on the first- and second-story verandas; in the New Orleans–style courtyard; or in the acre and a half of terraced and walled gardens.

Sleep as if on a cloud on a hypoallergenic feather bed, then awaken eagerly, knowing that you're cared about and pampered as an individual. King- or queen-size beds—some of them romantic four-posters—European and American antiques, paintings by Louisiana artists, Bradbury and Bradbury wallpapers, and writing desks characterize the bedchambers. Modern creature comforts include telephone, television, clock radio, ceiling fan, hair dryer, thick robes, and refrigerator, as well as cold drinks, fruit, books, and magazines. Some suites boast whirlpool baths and towel warmers.

A full gourmet breakfast is served in the dining room and might include Cajun coffee, fresh fruits and juices, a breakfast casserole, muffins, and pastries.

HOW TO GET THERE: From I-20 westbound, take the Fairfield Avenue exit and turn left onto Fairfield Avenue. The inn is about 11 blocks on the left.

There is not a Fairfield Avenue exit eastbound, so from I-20 eastbound, take the Line Avenue exit, turn right onto Jordan Street, and then left onto Fairfield. The inn is about 7 blocks on the left.

Remington Suite Hotel 📱
Shreveport, Louisiana 71101

INNKEEPER: Dana McAlister

ADDRESS/TELEPHONE: 220 Travis Street; phone and fax (800) 444-6750 or (318) 425-5000

WEB SITE: remingtonsuite.com

ROOMS: 22 suites, all with king-size bed, private bath with whirlpool, wet bar, refrigerator, television, telephone, desk, robes.

RATES: $110 to $195, including continental breakfast; $199 to $250 for packages. Credit cards accepted.

OPEN: Year-round.

FACILITIES AND ACTIVITIES: Sparto's Sicilian Restaurant, indoor pool, health club. Nearby: Jogging path, restaurants, nightlife.

BUSINESS TRAVEL: Desk, telephone with dataport.

*T*he Remington has a very simple philosophy toward its guest services—you need only ask. Unprecedented attentiveness to guests along with unmatched attention to detail and extra-special upscale amenities give the intimate Remington a European ambience. A small hostelry of unusual elegance and style, the Remington provides an escape to a gentler time of old-world charm and beauty. The downtown Shreveport luxury property is larger than the typical bed-and-breakfast but offers similar ambience, personal services, and even more amenities, making the Remington a perfect retreat.

Located in a restored historic commercial building with ornate wrought-iron balconies, the exclusive B&B inn offers twenty-two spacious suites as unique and distinctive as its guests. Suites range in size from extra-large sleeping rooms to one-bedroom suites with a sitting room to one-bedroom suites with a living room and dining room. Our favorites were the bilevel suites where the living area is well separated from the bedroom, which is reached by way of a romantic spiral staircase. All with one-of-a-kind decor featuring deep rich colors and distinctive traditional furnishings, art, and appointments, the suites are similar only in their amenities. In addition to telephone and television, each suite boasts a wet bar, refrigerator, whirlpool bath, and spacious dressing room. Business travelers appreciate the large, well-lighted working desks and the dataport access for their laptops.

It is attention to detail, however, that sets the Remington apart. Fresh flowers adorn each suite. You can request luxurious robes and/or breakfast in bed. Around-the-clock concierge service is at your beck and call. Remington guests enjoy complimentary membership privileges at the prestigious University Club across the street, where you can avail yourselves of the pool and experience some of the finest dining in the city. Privileges are also extended to guests at the Cambridge Club and the Petroleum Club. Complimentary shuttle service is available to the airport and casinos.

Perfectly located a block from Shreveport's scenic riverfront, the inn is in the heart of the city's central business district, where it's an easy walk to businesses, restaurants, and nightlife. Louisiana Downs racetrack is only ten minutes away, and the casinos of Shreveport's twin Bossier City are just across the river.

HOW TO GET THERE: From I-20, take the Spring Street exit and go north to Travis Street and turn left. The inn is on the right between North Market and Spring.

Oak Alley Plantation, Restaurant and Inn
Vacherie, Louisiana 70090

INNKEEPER: Zeb Mayhew Jr.

ADDRESS/TELEPHONE: 3645 Highway 18 (Great River Road); (225) 265–2151 or (800) 44ALLEY; fax (225) 265–2626

WEB SITE: www.oakalleyplantation.com

E-MAIL: oakalleyplantation@worldnet.att.net

ROOMS: 4 cottages, 5 units; all with private bath, clock radio, ceiling fan; children welcome; no wheelchair access in the cottages, although the restaurant and the first floor of the mansion are accessible.

RATES: $95 to $125, double occupancy, including full breakfast; each additional person $15; children younger than 12 stay free. The tour of the house is an additional $10 for adults.

OPEN: Cottages open year-round, although the mansion is closed Thanksgiving, Christmas, and New Year's Days and Mardi Gras and breakfast is not served in the restaurant those days. (Continental breakfast is left in the cottages.)

FACILITIES AND ACTIVITIES: Mansion tour, extensive grounds, restaurant, gift shop. Nearby: Plantations, gardens, Baton Rouge, St. Francisville, New Orleans.

Oak Alley Plantation is known as the grande dame of Great River Road because of its spectacular ¼-mile canopy of giant 300-year-old live oak trees that create an avenue leading up to the magnificent white-columned Greek Revival mansion.

We were initially disappointed to learn that the bed-and-breakfast accommodations are not offered in the main house, but in six plain century-old Creole cottages scattered about the grounds, but we were reassured once we saw the romantic interiors. Four-poster or iron beds, other antiques, floral fabrics used for the bed coverings and window treatments, and appropriate art and

Oak Alley Plantation's Famous Pralines

3 cans evaporated milk
½ pound of butter
8 cups granulated white sugar
8 cups shelled pecans
⅓ cup vanilla extract

Combine butter, milk, and sugar in saucepan. Add vanilla extract. Cook on high heat to a rolling boil. Lower temperature to medium heat and continue to boil for 20 minutes, stirring constantly. Remove from heat. Add pecans and stir until mixture thickens. Quickly drop onto greased foil. Let cool.

accessories imbue the guest rooms with an upscale nineteenth-century flavor. Cottage Three boasts a claw-foot tub, and its bed is romantically draped with mosquito netting. Most of the cottages feature one or more bedrooms, a sitting room with a sofa bed, kitchen, a deck or screened porch, and one bathroom, so they are best shared by families or groups of friends traveling together.

A full country breakfast of Southern favorites such as beignets, grits, eggs, bacon and ham, fresh fruit, and hot beverages is served in the Oak Alley restaurant, which is also open for lunch daily. The restaurant also serves a wide selection of traditional Cajun and Creole dishes. Stop in the restaurant's gift shop for a wide variety of Louisiana and Oak Alley souvenirs, handmade collectibles, cookbooks, regional photography, and books on the architecture, history, and culture of the region.

While you're staying at Oak Alley, you'll want to take a forty-minute tour of the plantation house (additional cost), given by costumed docents. Be sure to try one of the famous mint juleps at the souvenir table at the back door of the mansion. You'll also want to take a leisurely stroll of the grounds or along the Mississippi River levee, have lunch in the Oak Alley restaurant, and browse through the gift shop, as well as relax on your deck or screened-in porch.

HOW TO GET THERE: From Baton Rouge, take I–10 east to exit 194/Lutcher/Mississippi River Bridge. Turn right on LA 641 south, which becomes County Road 3213. Continue over the Veterans Memorial Bridge (also known as the Gramercy/Wallace Bridge) and turn left onto LA 18. Go 7½ miles to Oak Alley Plantation. From New Orleans, take I–10 west to exit 194/Gramercy. Turn left on LA 641 and follow the previous directions.

Nottoway Plantation Restaurant and Inn
White Castle, Louisiana 70788

INNKEEPER: Cindy A. Hidalgo

ADDRESS/TELEPHONE: 30970 Highway 405 (Great River Road, LA 1) (mailing address: P.O. Box 160); (504) 545-2730; fax (504) 545-8632

WEB SITE: www.nottoway.com

E-MAIL: nottoway@att.net

ROOMS: 13, all with private bath, telephone, television; Bridal suite with private pool and whirlpool tub; children welcome.

RATES: $135–$250, double occupancy; includes prebreakfast wake-up call, full breakfast, fresh flowers, tour of mansion, sherry.

OPEN: Year-round except Christmas Day.

FACILITIES AND ACTIVITIES: Tour of mansion, swimming pool, restaurant serving lunch and dinner, meeting space. Nearby: Baton Rouge museums, Old and New Capitols, USS *Kidd,* casinos, 18-hole golf course, restaurants, nightlife, shops, galleries.

BUSINESS TRAVEL: 30 miles from Baton Rouge; meeting space for up to 250; food and beverage service.

*I*t rose from the fog, obscuring the tranquil surface of the Mississippi River and its banks like a mysterious castle floating on the clouds. That's how the big white mansion appeared to us the first time we saw Nottoway Plantation house from aboard the *Delta Queen,* cruising upriver from New Orleans. Little wonder that the few remaining antebellum homes along the river are dubbed "Ghosts along the Mississippi." Later, when we landed for a tour, the fog burned off and the sun came out, transforming the mansion into a gigantic wedding cake. It's no surprise that this relatively uninhabited area has taken the name White Castle from the plantation house that dominates it.

As hard as it is to believe, when this magnificent neoclassical mansion was completed by John Randolph in 1859 with modern innovations such as hot and cold running water and a gas lighting system, it wasn't the largest plantation home in the South. Soaring two-story columns across the front support vast verandas on both levels. Magnificently detailed paneling, molding, and plaster frieze work as well as original hand-painted Dresden door-knobs, marble fireplaces, and exquisite furnishings characterize the interior.

Only a few years after the mansion's completion,

the Civil War waged in the area, and the mansion might have met the same unfortunate fate as many other opulent homes of the extravagantly wealthy planter class—being burned to the ground by Union troops. Legend has it that a Union gunboat fired on the mansion, but when Mrs. Randolph appeared on the front gallery, the captain recognized her and the house where he had been a guest before the war. He came ashore and offered her protection. As a result, Nottoway is now the largest surviving plantation home in the South.

You can hardly imagine rooms more romantic than Nottoway's stunning white double parlors, so it's only natural that many weddings are held there. How ultraromantic—to be married at Nottoway and then to spend your honeymoon there, perhaps in the Bridal Suite, which features a private courtyard and a swimming pool, or in Cornelia's Room on the third floor of the mansion with sweeping views of the river.

Guest accommodations are located in the mansion and the connected annexes, which once served as children's rooms or servants' quarters, as well as in an overseer's cottage and the honeymoon cottage. Those in the main house (two on the first floor, four on the second floor, and two suites on the

Nottoway Plantation Trivia

- The mansion occupies 53,000 square feet.
- There are seventy-two rooms.
- There are 200 windows and 165 doors.
- The mansion is surrounded by twenty-two columns.
- The bell pulls to summon the servants are silver.
- A crystal chandelier is by Baccarat.
- The doorknobs and keyhole covers are hand-painted Dresden china.
- It was the first house in the area to feature hot and cold running water, gas lighting, coal-burning fireplaces, and walk-in closets.
- The house had a ten-pin bowling alley in 1859.

third floor) are the most elegant. Four rooms located in the overseer's cottage aren't quite as formal.

No matter where your bedchamber may be located, you'll be pleasantly awakened by what the staff calls a prebreakfast wake-up call consisting of hot sweet-potato muffins, coffee, and juice delivered to your room to tide you over until you're dressed and ready for breakfast in the formal dining room. The generous full breakfast consists of such items as eggs, sausage, grits, cereal, waffles, juices, fruits, and hot beverages. Other amenities include fresh flowers in all the guest accommodations and chilled champagne in the suites or a carafe of sherry in the other guest rooms.

Use the inn as a base from which to explore the many plantations in the surrounding area, or stay on the property and do little or nothing. Tour the house, of course. Spend time sitting on the verandas, watching the slow-paced river traffic glide by or reading a good book. Stroll through the acres of lawns shaded by the broad canopies of ancient oaks. Swim or sun yourself around the pool. When hunger strikes, Randolph Hall, a restaurant located on the grounds, serves Cajun and Southern cuisine for lunch and dinner.

HOW TO GET THERE: From Baton Rouge, take I–10 west to the Plaquemine exit, then take LA 1 south for 20 miles. The inn is on the left.

Select List of Other Louisiana Inns

Columns Hotel
3811 St. Charles Avenue
New Orleans, LA 70115
(504) 899-9308 or (800) 445-9308

French Quarter inn; 20 rooms; restaurant.

Prince Conti
830 Conti Street
New Orleans, LA 70112
(504) 529-4172 or (800) 366-2743

French Quarter inn; 53 rooms and 3 suites.

St. Ann/Marie Antoinette
717 Conti Street
New Orleans, LA 70130
(504) 525-2300 or (800) 537-8483

French Quarter inn; 65 rooms; pool; bar.

Mississippi

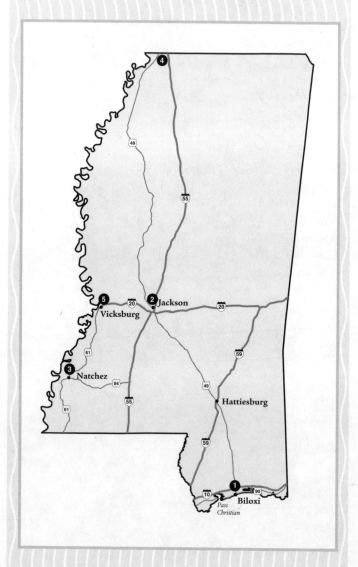

- 4
- 49
- 55
- 5
- 20
- 2 Jackson
- Vicksburg
- 20
- 59
- 61
- 3 Natchez
- 84
- 49
- 55
- Hattiesburg
- 61
- 59
- 1
- 10
- 90
- Biloxi
- Pass Christian

Mississippi

Numbers on map refer to towns numbered below.

* A Top Pick Inn

The Father Ryan House
Bed & Breakfast Inn
Biloxi, Mississippi 39530

INNKEEPER: Rosanne McKenney

ADDRESS/TELEPHONE: 1196 Beach Boulevard; (228) 435–1189 or
(800) 295–1189; fax (228) 436–3063

WEB SITE: www.frryan.com

E-MAIL: reservations@frryan.com

ROOMS: 9 in main house, 6 in cottages; all with private bath, cable television, coffeemakers, and telephone; most with whirlpool tubs. Smoking outside only.

RATES: $100 to $175, double; single $15 less; $15 for each additional guest; includes full breakfast and tea time.

OPEN: Year-round.

FACILITIES AND ACTIVITIES: Swimming pool, Gulf of Mexico ocean beach. Nearby: Restaurants, Biloxi Lighthouse, Keesler Air Force Base, Jefferson Davis home at Beauvoir, Gulf Shores National Seashore, golf courses, floating gambling casinos, art galleries and museums.

BUSINESS TRAVEL: Excellent work space and light in rooms; direct telephone lines, dataports; fax available.

> *Just a hundred feet away*
> *Seaward, flows and ebbs the tide;*
> *And the wavelets, blue and grey*
> *moan, and white sails windward glide*
> *o'er the ever restless sea.*
>
> —Father Abram Ryan, Sea Rest

*S*o Father Ryan described this place. He was the poet laureate of the Confederacy and a close friend of Jefferson Davis, president of the Confederacy. Father Ryan wrote some of his best-known poetry while he lived in this house, which was built about 1841. Legend has it that when Father Ryan was in residence, he erected a cross on the front steps to indicate that a priest lived there. When he left for the last time, the cross was blown away in a storm, but a palm seed took hold in its place. Towering over the house today and known as the Father Ryan Palm, it extends a welcome to visitors.

Standing just 20 feet from the beach, but across a busy highway, this is one of the oldest remaining structures on the Gulf Coast, and it has been faithfully restored according to information in Father Ryan's letters and other contemporary sources. Today it is a B&B inn.

To further heighten the mood, his poetry, written in calligraphy, is displayed throughout the house, as are books about him, some of his letters, and more poetry. Margaret Mitchell's *Gone With the Wind* lies open to her mention of Father Ryan's visit.

But don't suppose that the historicity of the house means it's dark and gloomy. In fact, one guest who saw it for the first time said, "How did you make it so light?"

Windows, mainly. Roseanne says that the English architect who added the second and third floors at the turn of the twentieth century "went crazy with windows," an uncommon approach at the time because homes were taxed according to the number and size of their windows. "Apparently it didn't matter," Roseanne says.

The guest rooms in the house, including the ones that once would have been Father Ryan's bedroom, study, and a room for an orphan boy he took in, are quietly elegant, almost understated, furnished with handcrafted beds and antiques dating back to the early 1800s. All the comforters and pillows are of down.

Concessions to modern travelers include private baths and bathrobes, cable television, and telephone with dataports. Most guest chambers boast whirlpool tubs. Six additional rooms are available in the historic cottages next door and behind the pool.

The inn has several appealing common areas. Upstairs, a large room that runs all the way from the north to the south side of the house overlooks the Gulf on one side and the courtyard and swimming pool on the other. The library has floor-to-ceiling shelves filled with books, including many about

Father Ryan House Bed & Breakfast Inn's Eggs Oscar

2 large croissants, split and toasted
12 asparagus spears, steamed and tender
4 artichoke hearts, quartered
½ cup fennel bulb, chopped
1 cup mushrooms, sliced
1 tablespoon fresh herbs, chopped
salt and pepper to taste
4 eggs, poached
4 thin slices Virginia ham, heated
1 cup Hollandaise and pinch saffron
1 cup white lump crabmeat
fresh tarragon leaves for garnish

Saute artichoke hearts, mushrooms, fennel, herbs, and salt and pepper in 1 tablespoon of oil or butter. Place each croissant half on a plate and arrange three asparagus spears on each croissant. Top each croissant half with one slice of ham. Divide the artichoke and mushroom mixture between the four croissants. Place one egg on each vegetable- and ham-topped croissant. Ladle saffron Hollandaise over each egg. Sprinkle the crabmeat on top and garnish with fresh tarragon. Serves four.

the South and Mississippi. Rolling ladders help you reach the high shelves. Empire furniture from the 1860s, upholstered in a light cream-colored fabric, lends dignity without being overbearing. In addition to a formal dining room, there is the Lemon Room—a bright closed-in porch with Mexican tile floors, high ceilings, and antique converted brass gaslight fixtures—where breakfast is served unless you request (free) room service.

No matter where you take your breakfast, it will be special. Elen Reeves, the chef, was trained in Denmark and brings a continental flair and expertise with herbs to the kitchen. Each breakfast includes a savory or fruit bread, fruit prepared in various ways—poached pears or yogurt-fruit soup, for instance—and a main dish that may be anything from cheese blintzes to puffy oven pancakes with fruit. That's a breakfast that gives you zing for exploring the area or going off to a day's work if you're a business traveler, but relaxing on the property is a good option, too.

HOW TO GET THERE: The inn is on Highway 90, 6 blocks west of the I-110 off ramp, 4 blocks west of the Biloxi Lighthouse, and 2 blocks east of the main Keesler Air Force Base entrance. You will receive a brochure with a map when you make a reservation.

Green Oaks B&B
Biloxi, Mississippi 39530

INNKEEPERS: Oliver and Jennifer Diaz

ADDRESS/TELEPHONE: 580 Beach Boulevard; (228) 436-6257 or (888) 436-6257; fax (228) 436-6225

WEB SITE: www.gcww.com/greenoaks

E-MAIL: greenoaks4@aol.com

ROOMS: 8; all with private bath, cable television, telephone with dataport.

RATES: $98 to $155; includes full breakfast, afternoon tea, mint juleps, and snacks; $15 for each additional person in the room.

OPEN: Year-round.

FACILITIES AND ACTIVITIES: Beach; casino shuttle stops at the door; golf packages. Nearby: Next door to the church Jefferson Davis attended; casinos, Biloxi Small Boat Harbor, casual and fine dining, shopping, museums, water sports.

BUSINESS TRAVEL: Telephone with a dataport; access to a fax machine.

Considered Biloxi's finest example of period architecture, the circa-1826 home is the oldest remaining beachfront residence and is listed on the National Register of Historic Places. Elegantly appointed with an impressive collection of fine period furnishings, including many family heirlooms, the house and historic outbuildings provide eight guest rooms and suites, each named for members of Judge Diaz's family. The family dates back to 1700, when the judge's first ancestor arrived on the Mississippi Gulf Coast with Pierre Le Moyne, Sieur d'Iberville, on his second voyage to the area.

The luxurious guest chambers in this B&B inn are well appointed with massive four-poster, full-tester, and heavily carved beds. The most popular room is the Carquot, with French doors that afford a breathtaking view of the Gulf of Mexico and provide access to the south gallery. This room boasts 14-foot-high ceilings, a spectacular mahogany full-tester bed carved by C. Lee, a bath with full-body shower, and a fireplace; but every room has its own specialty. In the main house, the Bosarge Room features a fireplace, the Ladner Room has the original chandelier and a claw-foot tub, and the Fountain Room features brick walls and an antique brass and wrought-iron bed. In the guest cottage, the Fayard Room has screened doors onto the front porch and a claw-foot tub, the Ryan Room displays hand-stenciled walls, and the Moran Room is actually a three-room suite.

Take a leisurely, romantic stroll around the two acres of landscaped grounds with twenty-eight live oaks overlooking the beach and Gulf of Mexico, or relax on the veranda with its unparalleled views.

Breakfast is an event, with gourmet selections served using china, crystal, and silver in the dining room overlooking the Gulf. There are always two to three courses featuring dishes such as Eggs Diane, Grits Jeff Davis, Cajun sausage, or, perhaps, poached eggs topped with hollandaise sauce and lump crabmeat and accompanied by steamed asparagus—all topped off with something like baked pears with caramel sauce or bananas Foster. The delicious breads are home baked. In the late afternoon, a traditional English tea is served with at least two sweet and two savory selections.

HOW TO GET THERE: Green Oaks is centrally located in Biloxi between New Orleans and Mobile. Take I-10 to I-110 South. Turn east on U.S. 90 (Beach Boulevard). The inn is located 1 mile east, between Bellman Avenue and Lee Street. Approaching from the west on Beach Boulevard, the inn is 2 miles east of the Biloxi Lighthouse.

Fairview Inn Bed and Breakfast
Jackson, Mississippi 39202

INNKEEPERS: Carol and Bill Simmons

ADDRESS/TELEPHONE: 734 Fairview Street; (601) 948-3429 or (888) 948-1908; fax (601) 948-1203

WEB SITE: www.fairviewinn.com

E-MAIL: fairview@fairviewinn.com

ROOMS: 18 rooms and suites, all with private bath, telephone, television and VCR, clock radio, hair dryer, robes; 11 with whirlpool bath; 8 with fireplace; 4 with sunroom; 1 with wheelchair access.

RATES: $115 to $290, double occupancy; includes full breakfast, snacks, and complimentary wine; $15 for additional guests in the room. Credit cards accepted. Well-supervised children welcome.

OPEN: Year-round.

FACILITIES AND ACTIVITIES: Decks, formal gardens, elevator. Nearby: Old Capitol Museum, Governor's Mansion, and New Stage Theater, the longest operating theater in the state.

BUSINESS TRAVEL: Meeting facilities in the study, which doubles as a sitting room and conference room when needed; telephone with dataport, voice mail; work desk.

*T*he first thing you'll notice as you drive up the sweeping circular drive is that the big white mansion flanked by mature magnolias and crape myrtles bears an uncanny resemblance to Mount Vernon. Owners Carol and Bill Simmons, in whose family the mansion has been since 1930, are quick to tell you, however, that the 1908 house has significant differences from the famous president's house, although the subtleties were lost on us.

Located in Old Jackson near the state capitol, both the main house and the carriage house are Colonial Revival, a style associated with formality and traditional Southern elegance. Classical detail and ordered proportions popularized by the famous designer and architect Palladio are readily apparent. The long, rectangular two-story, flat-roofed Georgian house is fronted by an immense portico supported by modified Corinthian columns.

Inside, the vast entry foyer of this B&B inn seems more like a small ballroom, with gleaming floors, crystal chandeliers, and fireplaces. The study, which is virtually unchanged since 1908, features quarter-sawn oak paneling, Tiffany lamps, a Herschede grandfather clock, an impressive collection of miniature toy soldiers, important oil paintings, and an extensive Civil War library that includes many first editions.

Guest rooms and suites are elegantly decorated with antiques and reproductions and given individual character by the use of lavish fabrics, accessories, and collectibles. In addition to all the modern conveniences, the rooms feature queen- or king-size beds as well as extra-special amenities like fine linens and upgraded toiletries. Some guest chambers boast a whirlpool tub and/or walk-in shower. The Hayloft, Tack, and Third Floor Suites offer ample sitting areas; the Executive Suite has a separate library/sitting room. The Carriage House Suite is popular with honeymooners.

Among the popular places to spend some quiet time, in addition to your room or the study, are the cheerful garden room with a piano, the porches, two decks with a hot tub, and the formal garden of box hedges and lilies.

A full Southern breakfast of bacon and eggs or French toast, grits, and biscuits is prepared to order and served at the guests' convenience in the sunny Carriage Room, which connects the main house to the carriage house.

Fairview has been named a "Top Ten Romantic Inn of 2000" by *American Historic Inns,* one of many accolades and awards it has received.

HOW TO GET THERE: From I–55 South, take exit 98A. Go west on Woodrow Wilson Drive and turn left onto North State Street. Go left at the Medical Plaza building onto Fairview. The inn is on the left. From I–55 North, take exit 96C and go west on Fortification Street to North State Street, then turn right. Turn right on Fairview.

Millsaps Buie House
Jackson, Mississippi 39202

INNKEEPERS: Judy Fenter, on-site innkeeper; Mary McMillan, Jo Love Little, and Jim Love, owners

ADDRESS/TELEPHONE: 628 North State Street; (601) 352-0221 or (800) 784-0221; fax (601) 352-0221

WEB SITE: www.millsapsbuiehouse.com

E-MAIL: mbuiehouse@aol.com

ROOMS: 10 rooms, 1 suite; all with private bath, telephone with dataport, radio, cable television; some with decorative fireplaces.

RATES: $90 to $160, single; $105 to $175, double; includes full Southern breakfast; each additional person in the room $15; children younger than age 12 considered upon special request.

OPEN: Year-round.

FACILITIES AND ACTIVITIES: Gardens. Nearby: 1½ blocks from the capitol, Old Capitol Museum, Governor's Mansion, Museum of Art, fitness center.

BUSINESS TRAVEL: Telephone with dataport; some rooms have desks.

Two of our most indelible memories of the Millsaps Buie House, a B&B inn, are of the beautiful stained-glass window on the landing between the first and second floors and the delicious pralines, which are left on your pillow when your bed is turned down at night.

Back in the 1880s when the Millsaps Buie House was built, the elite of Jackson built their mansions along State Street near the capitol. This extraordinary house with its impressive columned portico was constructed for the colorful financier and philanthropist Maj. Reuben Webster Millsaps. A founder of Millsaps College, he was also an officer in the Confederate Army. At his death the mansion passed to his nephew, Webster Millsaps Buie, whose widow lived in the house for more than fifty years. After an abortive scheme to sell the house to an oil company for use as its offices and a near-disastrous fire, three Buie heirs (sisters and a brother) converted the family home into this wonderful inn—stately and formal, yet warm and inviting. You'll have realized from this recitation that the home has remained in the same family throughout its more than century-long history—an incredible rarity in these days of far-flung families.

Created with the intent of providing a nineteenth-century urban retreat for twenty-first-century travelers, the inn features 14-foot ceilings, hand-molded frieze work, bay and stained-glass windows, highly polished newel posts and handrails, and sparkling chandeliers. Guests admire the artistry with which the foyer, library, parlor with its grand piano, and dining room are furnished. When they're feeling more casual, guests may prefer to relax on the screened porches or in the courtyard or may want to wander around the one-and-a-half-acre grounds.

Ten luxurious guest chambers and one suite are handsomely accoutered with well-chosen period pieces—including the half-tester bed of the founder himself—as well as elegant fabrics and rich colors. Rooms on the third floor have a more contemporary decor. Most sport queen- or king-size beds, several have a sleeping porch, one has a balcony, and one even boasts an observatory.

Breakfast is a very special meal when a generous buffet of casseroles, cheese grits, breakfast meats, cereals, homemade breads and pastries, fresh fruits and juices, and hot beverages are served. In the late afternoon wine and hot hors d'oeuvres are offered at social hour.

HOW TO GET THERE: From I–55, take the High Street exit. Go west to the fifth traffic light and turn right onto State Street. The inn is the fourth building on the left.

The Briars ♥
Natchez, Mississippi 39121

INNKEEPERS: Newton Wilds and R. E. Canon

ADDRESS/TELEPHONE: 31 Irving Lane (mailing address: P.O. Box 1245); (601) 446–9654 or (800) 634–1818; fax (601) 446–6037

WEB SITE: www.thebriarsinn.com

E-MAIL: thebriarsinn@bkbank.com

ROOMS: 12 rooms, 3 suites; all with private bath; some with balcony overlooking river.

RATES: $150 to $395, includes full Southern breakfast, honor bar, popcorn, tea and coffee. Can accommodate rollaway bed in some rooms for $35 extra.

OPEN: Year-round.

FACILITIES AND ACTIVITIES: Swimming pool, porches, gardens.

Nearby: Historic Natchez, Natchez-Under-the-Hill, riverboat gambling, plantation and historic town homes, casual and fine dining, shopping, special annual events, golf, tennis, biking.

BUSINESS TRAVEL: Guest rooms with writing desk and telephone with dataports.

*I*f you're a Civil War buff, you know that Jefferson Davis, only president of the Confederate States of America, was Mississippi born and bred and that he lived out his last years at Beauvoir, his stately Biloxi home on the Gulf of Mexico. You probably also know that his second wife was Varina Howell, called the Rose of Mississippi. Davis and Varina were married in front of the lovely Adam-manteled fireplace of the gracious parlor at The Briars in February 1845. Imagine their simple wedding ceremony as you stand before the very same fireplace in this house, now a B&B inn. Dream about the social occasions that must have occurred in the 48-foot-long drawing room with its twin staircases and five Palladian arches.

Perched on a promontory overlooking the Mississippi River, The Briars is an excellent example of early Southern plantation-style architecture believed to have been designed by master architect Levi Weeks of Philadelphia. Constructed with elegance and delicacy of detail and a sophisticated plan, it was erected between 1814 and 1818. One of its most outstanding features is the 80-foot-long veranda with its ten slim Doric columns, where guests can lounge on the swings and rockers while they survey the activity on the river below and watch the cars crossing the two bridges that connect Louisiana and Mississippi.

Today many of the nineteen acres that remain of the original estate are devoted to formal and informal gardens with gazebos and fountains. More than a thousand azaleas and multitudes of camellias grace the gardens. The combination of the house and grounds creates a Utopia where you can find peace and beauty.

It won't come as surprise that the fifteen spacious guest rooms and suites are so beautifully furnished with antiques and reproductions, since the owners are interior designers. Despite the Old South ambience of the bedchambers, each also offers modern conveniences such as a private bath, robes, hair dryer, and cable television. Bedding ranges from extra-long twins to queens and kings. Some rooms have direct access to the verandas and/or gas-log fireplaces.

The full Southern breakfast, which is served in the pavilion, might include any one of three entrees such as crepes but is sure to include an ample quantity of freshly baked biscuits, traditional Southern grits, breakfast meats, juices, fruits, and hot beverages.

HOW TO GET THERE: Take U.S. 64 North to Government Fleet Road (South Canal Road); immediately turn right onto Beech Street, which turns into Irving Lane. The inn is on your right.

Dunleith Plantation
Natchez, Mississippi 39120

INNKEEPER: John Holyoak

ADDRESS/TELEPHONE: 84 Homochitto Street; (601) 446-8500; for reservations (800) 433-2445

WEB SITE: www.dunleithplantation.com

ROOMS: 19, in courtyard wing and on second floor of main house; all with private bath, telephone, television, and fireplace.

RATES: $110 to $225; includes full Southern breakfast, tour of the house, and snack in room; no children under age 14.

OPEN: Year-round.

FACILITIES AND ACTIVITIES: Restaurant, pub, gardens, house tour. Nearby: Restaurants, Mississippi riverboat tours, tours of many historic homes in Natchez.

As a couple who are not very good at gardening but would like to spend much more time with plants, we found special pleasure in the grounds and gardens at Dunleith Plantation. Formal gardens are planted in colorful, low-growing flowering plants.

Dunleith is a B&B inn on forty acres of rolling pastureland, which leaves room for refreshing green space as well as for formal garden areas. Perhaps

most delightful of all, an old magnolia tree behind the house has grown so huge that park benches have been arranged under its arching branches so that you can sit in the shade and look out over the property. At night the grounds are lighted to give the feel of moonlight.

The lower floor of Dunleith, which is refurbished to the 1850 period, is open for public tours. One of the remarkable attractions is the French Zuber wallpaper in the dining room. The paper was printed before World War I from woodblocks carved in 1855 and hidden during the war in a cave in Alsace-Lorraine. If you look closely, you can see small mildew stains that developed in the cave.

The bed-and-breakfast accommodations of Dunleith are on the second floor and in a group of courtyard rooms, away from the public eye. The Castle Retreat, a restaurant and English-style pub, occupies a circa-1790 building.

Breakfast is served in what used to be the poultry house, a wonderful big room, with brick walls and polished wood floors and skylights. The country decor includes bright jars of hot peppers, and there are flowers everywhere. It is a great place to eat scrambled eggs, bacon, and sausage with cheese grits, biscuits, and pancakes.

The guest-room reflects the 1850s decor with four-poster beds, live plants, and cute little country-store baskets filled with fruit, cheese, and canned juices. The rooms are named after trees in the wing rooms and Confederate generals in the main house. Dunleith is a National Historic Landmark.

HOW TO GET THERE: Highway 81 heading south into Natchez becomes Homochitto Street. Continue about 1½ miles. The plantation is on the left. Write for a map.

Linden
Natchez, Mississippi 39120

INNKEEPER: Jeanette Feltus

ADDRESS/TELEPHONE: 1 Linden Place; (601) 445-5472 or (800) 2-LINDEN; fax (601) 442-7548

WEB SITE: www.natchezms.com/linden

ROOMS: 7 rooms, all with private bath; some with claw-foot tub. Some rooms handicapped accessible. Areas designated for smoking.

RATES: $95 to $125, single or double, including full Southern breakfast and a tour of the mansion. $35 for additional person.

OPEN: Year-round.

FACILITIES AND ACTIVITIES: 7 acres with courtyard. Nearby: Historic homes and plantations, museums; Natchez-Under-the-Hill, Natchez Trace Parkway, riverboat gambling, casual and fine dining, shopping, parks, golf, tennis, special annual events.

*L*ucky Jeanette Feltus is the sixth generation of her family to live at Linden, which dates to 1792. Most of the present manor house, however, was built between 1818 and 1849 when her ancestors bought it. Nearly all the furnishings, including Hepplewhite, Sheraton, and Chippendale pieces, are original to the house.

When we drove up the deeply shaded drive to this B&B inn set well back from the road in a parklike setting of ancient live oaks, the first thing we noticed were the unusual front verandas. A full-length, first-floor veranda is supported by numerous columns. On the second floor a smaller gallery over the entrance has four columns supporting a temple pediment. Shutters flanking all the windows give the house a more casual appearance.

A hearty breakfast, which may be served in the formal dining room or on the back gallery overlooking the courtyard, might consist of grits, sausage or other breakfast meats, a different egg dish every day, fruits, juices, and hot beverages. If you eat in the dining room, be sure to ask about the enormous lyre-shaped cypress punkah fan that hangs above the table. In the old days, it was pulled by slaves or servants to cool the diners and to keep flies off the people and food—earning it the nickname "shoo fly."

HOW TO GET THERE: Take U.S. 61/84 to Melrose Avenue; turn left on Melrose Avenue to Linden.

Monmouth Plantation
Natchez, Mississippi 39120

INNKEEPERS: Ron and Lani Riches

ADDRESS/TELEPHONE: 36 Melrose Avenue; (601) 442–5852 or (800) 828–4531; fax (601) 446–7762

WEB SITE: www.monmouthplantation.com

E-MAIL: luxury@monmouthplantation.com

ROOMS: 15, plus 16 suites, in 4 buildings, 4 cottages; all with private bath, television, telephone, hair dryers, irons and ironing boards, robes, English toiletries; some rooms with wheelchair access; 13 with whirlpool tub, fireplace.

RATES: Rooms $150 to $210; suites $195 to $380, single or double; includes full Southern breakfast, welcome basket of pralines, cold drinks, and house tour. $35 for additional adult. Children older than 14 welcome. Check Web site for packages.

OPEN: Year-round.

FACILITIES AND ACTIVITIES: 5-course prix fixe candlelight dinner daily; honor bar for guests only. Twenty-six acres suitable for walking, pond, croquet lawn. In-room massage available. Nearby: Mississippi riverboat tours, tours of many historic Natchez homes.

BUSINESS TRAVEL: Conference facilities for up to 100; desk; ideal for small retreats.

*A*t Monmouth Plantation, everything is on a grand scale—restorations, furnishings, gardens, and hospitality. In addition to operating as an inn, Monmouth is one of the mansions in Natchez open year-round for tours, so the staff includes three hostesses, all of whom can give you a mind-boggling amount of information about the history, architecture, and antiques of Monmouth.

As an overnight guest, you're apt to be more concerned with the quality of the rooms than with knowing that the house was built in 1818. But once you see that the guest rooms are as luxurious as the rest of the house you kind of get into the history and elegance and can pretend that you always live this way.

Guest chambers are found in the main house, the courtyard building, former kitchen and servant quarters, garden cottages, carriage house, plantation suites building, and Quitman's Retreat building, but you don't have to worry about getting downgraded accommodations in any of the outbuildings—all are top-notch. In fact, more suites are located in the outbuildings than in the main house, and the two most opulent are in Quitman's Retreat. No matter where it is located, every bedchamber is a different, vibrant color and has touches that set it apart from the others. Many accommodations boast fireplace, whirlpool bath, and/or private porch.

Among the standouts are the General Quitman Room in the main house, furnished with pieces that belonged to the Mexican war hero and governor

of Mississippi. Its only drawback is that it is on the public tour between 9:30 A.M. and 4:45 P.M. The two-level Lani's Suite boasts a sitting room, kitchen, and dining area with an antique spiral staircase leading up to the bedroom and bathroom with its whirlpool and separate shower. Most impressive of all, this suite has three working fireplaces—even one in the bathroom.

Early-morning coffee is served in the study, followed by a full Southern breakfast, which is a formal affair served in the dining room from 7:00 to 10:00 A.M. The charming brick patio in the rear of the mansion is the scene for afternoon hors d'oeuvres. Perhaps you'd like to order an icy cold mint julep to go with this treat, but save room for dinner.

Since our first visit, Monmouth has begun serving five-course candle-light gourmet dinners in the formal dining room, complete with the elegance of ornate silver and fresh flowers. In the Southern tradition, the food is plentiful.

If the weather is good, don't neglect the twenty-six acres of grounds and gardens, a picturesque white bridge, pebbled paths, magnolias, and moss-draped oaks—all of which make perfect places to stroll. The gazebo is a delightful place to go with a good book. Fish in one of the two ponds, explore the walking trails, or challenge each other to a game of croquet.

HOW TO GET THERE: From the 61/84 bypass just outside Natchez, turn onto Melrose Avenue and follow Melrose to where it intersects with the John A. Quitman Parkway. You will see the mansion on a small hill. Turn left onto the parkway and then immediately turn left again into the Monmouth driveway.

Bonne Terre Country Inn and Cafe
Nesbit, Mississippi 38651

INNKEEPER: Max Bonnin

ADDRESS/TELEPHONE: 4715 Church Road West; (662) 781-5100
for overnight reservations; (662) 781-5199 for dinner reservations; fax
(662) 781-5466

WEB SITE: www.bonneterre.com

E-MAIL: Max@BonneTerre.com

ROOMS: 13, plus 1 two-bedroom suite; all with private bath and telephone; most with whirlpool tub; some with fireplace. All have lake view,
soft drinks, and coffeemaker.

RATES: $150 to $235, double occupancy; Chelsea Suite $150 to $475.
Includes full breakfast, cheese or fruit tray, and sherry. Ask about corporate rates and special anniversary, weekend, and winter packages.

OPEN: Year-round except Thanksgiving, Christmas, and New Year's Day.

FACILITIES AND ACTIVITIES: Country gourmet restaurant, limo service, chapel, special-events hall, meeting room, swimming pool, in-room
massage, Bonne gifts. Nearby: Golf, horseback riding, dinner theater; 20
minutes from Memphis's Beale Street and Tunica, Mississippi casinos.

BUSINESS TRAVEL: Ideal for small meetings and retreats; complete conference facilities with food service, audiovisual equipment.

We admit it. We're terribly prejudiced when it comes to small inns
and bed-and-breakfasts. Our preference is so strong for historic
properties that we seldom like new ones. Bonne Terre is a rare
exception—and that's because of its resemblance to a historic property, its
superior setting, its fine restaurant, the quality of its amenities, and the
warm, charming owner, Max Bonnin.

Although the inn is located only twenty minutes south of Memphis, it is
secluded on one hundred acres of gently rolling farmland, pecan trees, and
lakes. As you approach the inn on a long, winding gravel road, you'll see,
carefully secluded from the highway, the three elegant classical white buildings with green roofs. Although the facility was built in 1996, you could easily believe that the gracious Greek Revival–style inn with full-length front

and back verandas supported by columns on both levels was built as a private home in 1846. The flanking structures house a popular restaurant and a special-events facility used for conferences, weddings, and the like.

Simple elegance abounds throughout the main house, the interior of which can best be described as country chic. Public and guest rooms are decorated in casually elegant style with fine French and English country antiques and fine art that Max has collected during his world travels.

Each of the thirteen enchanting guest chambers has its own personality and offers its own delights. Light and cheerful, none of the rooms is overdone and some feature wrought-iron beds, canopy beds, two-poster, or fabric headboards—all in either queen or king size. All rooms boast a feather bed, whirlpool tub, and access to a porch or balcony with serene views of the lake, pecan groves, gardens, or the swimming pool. Most have a fireplace. Located above the stables, a huge two-bedroom, two-bath suite with a living room, fireplace, and kitchen is ideal for families or two couples traveling together. Special touches such as fresh flowers and a carafe of spring water make you feel you are visiting a considerate friend.

Bonne Terre Cafe is the heart of the inn. Reminiscent of a quaint French country cafe, the restaurant is decorated in rich colors and features a double-sided fireplace, oak bar, and an open-style European kitchen. Walls of windows allow the sunshine in and permit you to enjoy the scenery.

Here the European Cordon Bleu–trained chef prepares creative dishes using organically grown vegetables and herbs from the inn's own kitchen garden. The prix fixe dinners, which are $45 for three courses or $55 for four, feature seafood, beef, or whatever happens to catch the chef's fancy. Dinner is served Monday through Thursday 6:00 to 8:30 P.M. and Friday and Saturday until 9:00 P.M. Folks will drive from Memphis for the champagne and live jazz Sunday Brunch, which is served from 11:30 A.M. to 1:30 P.M. on the first Sunday of the month (adults $22.50, children $11.00). For overnight guests, a full breakfast of an entree such as Belgian waffles or an omelette as well as yogurt, freshly baked muffins and pastries, juice, and hot beverages is served here or on the veranda of the cafe overlooking the lake each morning.

Bonne Terre offers a true getaway opportunity where you can swim in the pool, fly-fish in one of the lakes, stroll through the gardens and grounds, or simply relax in a hammock or a rocker on one of the porches.

HOW TO GET THERE: From Memphis, take I-55 to exit 287, Church Road. Go west on Church Road about 4 4/10 miles and look for the small sign on the left.

Cedar Grove Mansion Inn
Vicksburg, Mississippi 39180

INNKEEPER: Ted Mackey

ADDRESS/TELEPHONE: 2200 Oak Street; (601) 636–1000 or
(800) 862–1300; fax (601) 634–6126

WEB SITE: www.cedargroveinn.com

E-MAIL: info@cedargroveinn.com

ROOMS: 34 guest rooms, suites, and cottages; all with private bath,
cable television, movie channels, telephone, clock radio, iron and ironing board; some with patio, balcony or porch; fireplace; whirlpool tub;
coffeemaker; refrigerator; VCR; wheelchair access.

RATES: $95 to $210, double; 10 percent less for single; includes full
plantation breakfast and tour of mansion.

OPEN: Year-round.

FACILITIES AND ACTIVITIES: Full cocktail service with piano and
gourmet candlelight dining at 6:00 P.M. in Andre's Restaurant. Rooftop
garden overlooking Mississippi River; swimming pool and Jacuzzi set in
a courtyard with five acres of formal gardens, gazebos, fountains. Cedar
Grove Antiques shop, Chapel at Cedar Grove, tennis court, croquet
lawn, exercise room, bikes. Nearby: Restaurants, Mississippi riverboat
tours, historic sites in Vicksburg, casinos.

On our first visit, a Southern belle, dressed to kill in a billowing, low-
cut ballgown of an attractive pre–Civil War style, swung open the
heavy front door and invited us in. This isn't your normal everyday
greeting at Cedar Grove, mind you, but it was Pilgrimage time. At other
times of year, you'll be just as warmly welcomed inside by the current staff
(in normal dress). Voted the Best Antebellum Home in Vicksburg, this magnificent estate makes a perfect place to capture *Gone With the Wind* elegance
and romance.

The place smells like dried rose petals when you enter. Just as you start
thinking that there was a softness about the atmosphere that most antebellum
tour houses lack, you see the cannonball lodged in the parlor wall, a patch in
the door, and a ragged hole in the parlor floor that has been framed and covered with heavy glass so that you could see through to the rooms below.

What is all this?

"Union gunboat cannonball, from the Civil War," the owner said. "It came through the door and hit the parlor wall. Mrs. Klein, the owner of the house, insisted on leaving it there as a reminder after the war."

And the hole?

"War damage. After the fall of Vicksburg,

Grant slept here for three nights. He turned the servants' quarters down below into a Union hospital for his soldiers. The Kleins were in residence at the time."

The present staff's and owner's familiarity and personal fascination with the history of the house give them little stories to tell about every room of the mansion. Listening to them and knowing that the house is largely furnished with its original antiques adds a human note to the Civil War that you'll never get from reading plaques in museums or touring military memorials.

The Greek Revival home was built about 1840 by John A. Klein as a wedding present for his bride. Sure beats a set of Pyrex casseroles! The house survived the Civil War because it was used as a Union hospital and, it's rumored, because Mrs. Klein had family ties to General Sherman—a fact that caused her to be rejected by Vicksburg society during the war.

Superior guest accommodations are found in the main house, the two-story carriage house, or several humble restored cottages scattered around the five-acre grounds—some of them poolside. Each is lavishly decorated and furnished with period antiques and reproductions. Some of these furnishings are original to the house and were collected by the Kleins on their year-long European honeymoon. Romantic canopy and half-tester beds grace many guest chambers.

It's impossible to describe all thirty-four rooms and suites here, but we must mention a few of the most exceptional bedchambers—many of which are named for Civil War heroes or *Gone With the Wind* characters.

Perhaps you'd like to sleep in the very room and the very bed where General Grant spent three nights after the fall of Vicksburg. Appropriately named for him, this room features a heavily carved and opulently draped canopy bed, original rosewood and cherry antiques, and a Prudent Mallard

Chef Andre's recipe for Brandy Bread Pudding and Brandy Sauce

2 large loaves French bread (torn into 3-inch pieces), toasted

1 whole pound cake (strawberry glazed), torn into pieces

10 whole eggs

2 cans sweetened condensed milk

3 cartons hazelnut creamer

3 tablespoons nutmeg

2 tablespoons cinnamon

1 pound melted butter

2 tablespoons almond extract

Toast French bread and add strawberry-glazed pound cake. Place in baking pan (17¼-inch by 11¾-inch by 2¼ inch). Mix remaining ingredients with a large whisk. Pour over bread and cake. Cover with foil and bake 1 hour at 325 degrees. Uncover and bake 15 minutes at 350 degrees. Scoop out portions and pour hot brandy sauce over pudding. Top with chopped roasted nuts and sprinkle with powdered sugar. Garnish with a strawberry.

Chef Andre's Brandy Sauce

10 egg yolks

2 cartons whipping cream

2 bags powdered sugar

2 cups brandy

2 tablespoons almond extract

1 pound butter (melted)

Mix all ingredients well. Place sauce in a double boiler on medium heat and stir occasionally until it bubbles, then serve.

armoire bearing the master craftsman's signature mallard egg, as well as a marble bath with a whirlpool tub.

The two-story Library Suite is located in the original library, which Mr. Klein used as an office. A spiral iron staircase connects the extravagant scarlet Victorian sitting room with the bedroom. The General Lee Suite boasts king-size bed, working fireplace, entertainment center with surround sound, and private patio with a fountain. The Jefferson Davis Room sports a magnificent canopy bed with massive posts, ornately carved headboard, and fancy canopy drapings. Klein's Grand Suite, which was once the Klein children's music room, is especially spacious and well endowed with amenities including fireplace and whirlpool tub.

Bask in the luxury of the Old South and let the dedicated staff spoil you. Awaken to the sounds of Mozart and the aroma of fresh coffee, followed by a full Southern plantation breakfast. In the late afternoon or evening, relax to live piano music in the Mansion Bar, then enjoy a romantic candlelight dinner of New Orleans cuisine accompanied by fine wines in the cozy garden atmosphere of Andre's, an elegant restaurant voted the Best Restaurant in Vicksburg (additional charge). Delicacies include such mouthwatering dishes as New Orleans catfish off the grill and topped with Cajun crawfish etouffée or sushi-grade yellowfin tuna marinated in champagne with Andre's Creole seasoning, topped with crumbled hickory-smoked bacon, and served with lemon caper hollandaise sauce. Cap your meal with cappuccino and brandy bread pudding. Chef Andre's herb olive oil and cookbooks are for sale in the gift shop.

HOW TO GET THERE: From I-20, take the 1A Washington Street exit. Go north about 2 miles. Turn left onto Klein.

The Corners Bed and Breakfast Inn
Vicksburg, Mississippi 39180

INNKEEPER: Kilby Whitney

ADDRESS/TELEPHONE: 601 Klein Street; (601) 636–7421 or (800) 444–7421; fax (601) 636–7232

WEB SITE: www.thecorners.com

E-MAIL: Via Web site

ROOMS: 13, plus 2 two-bedroom suites and the two-bedroom Cottage on the Green; all with private bath, television, and telephone; some with fireplace; private porches; whirlpool tub; wet bar/kitchen. Smoking out-side only.

RATES: Double, $90 to $130, rooms; $120 to $140, suites; single, $10 less; four people in suite, $170; includes full breakfast, evening nonalcoholic beverages, and tour of house.

OPEN: Year-round.

FACILITIES AND ACTIVITIES: Formal gardens and fountains. Nearby: Restaurants, Mississippi riverboat tours, historic sites in Vicksburg, Vicksburg National Military Park.

he Corners is a champagne-and-flowers, romantic-getaway kind of place. This two-story Victorian Louisiana raised cottage–style mansion with Greek Revival and Italianate influence, along with its associated outbuildings, exudes old Southern charm and romance in all its details, inside and out.

The most distinctive feature is its veranda trimmings. Instead of round or square solid columns supporting the roof, these are flat and cut out with the shapes of hearts, spades, and triangles, forming a lacelike effect. These shapes are repeated in the spindles of the porch and stairway railings of the 70-foot veranda and were replicated for the first- and second-story verandas of the new guest house. Unique to Vicksburg, these pierced columns are known as Vicksburg Columns.

The guest rooms are furnished with canopied beds, period antiques, and individual special features to set each room apart from all the others. For instance, the Eastlake Bedroom got its name for the 1870s Eastlake queen-

size half-tester bed, dresser, and night table that together are a focal point in the room's personality. Similarly, the Library Bedroom with its cypress bookcases really was the library when the mansion was a family home. You can go on in your imagination to understand the nature of the Stained-Glass Bedroom, the Garden Rooms, the Blue Room, and so on.

Attached to the main house is the Guest Quarters, a one-story structure built in 1875 as a kitchen and servants' quarters. Today it features pine floors and fireplaces and houses two guest rooms with pencil-post beds, bathrooms with whirlpool tubs, and a veranda. The Galleries, a new two-story building, which resembles the main house but with full-length verandas on both levels, was completed in 1997 to provide additional accommodations. Each of its four extra-large rooms boasts antique beds, superior linens, intimate seating areas, and a whirlpool tub. Just across the street from the main house, with its back to the river, is the humble Cottage on the Green—a two-bedroom home with its own living room, kitchen, and dining area, making it ideal for families or two couples traveling together.

Breakfast is served by candlelight on antique porcelain and silver in the magnificent peach-and-white formal dining room. The food is extravagant.

Outside, the gallery is as good a place to catch a breeze and view the grounds today as it must have been in the 1800s. Sip morning coffee or afternoon tea in the glassed-in, wicker-filled morning room overlooking the gardens, or relax in the late afternoon with cookies and a beverage in the striking, formally furnished double parlors with their floor-to-ceiling windows, twin fireplaces, gasolier-style chandeliers, and baby grand piano. End the day by marveling at the magical sunsets over the Mississippi and Yazoo Rivers from a rocker on the front veranda.

HOW TO GET THERE: From I-20 near the state welcome center by the Mississippi River, take exit 1-A onto Washington Street. Turn left on Klein. You will receive a brochure with a map when you make reservations.

Select List of
Other Mississippi Inns

The Country Goose Inn

350 Highway 305
Olive Branch, MS 38654
(662) 895–3098 or (877) 895–3098

Lakeside cottages with picturesque surroundings; 15 rooms/5 baths; includes three meals; fishing and pedal boating.

Mockingbird Inn B&B

305 North Gloster
Tupelo, MS 38804
(662) 841–0286

1925 Arts and Crafts/Prairie–style house; 7 rooms are internationally themed; some with fireplace or whirlpool; includes full breakfast.

Anchuca

1010 First East Street
Vicksburg, MS 39180
(601) 661–0111 or (888) 686–0111

1830 Greek Revival; 6 rooms; pool; whirlpool tub; includes full breakfast.

Annabelle

501 Speed Street
Vicksburg, MS 39180
(601) 638–2000 or (800) 791–2000

1868 Victorian main house and 1881 guest house; 7 rooms; pool; includes full breakfast.

Flowerree Cottage

2309 Pearl Street
Vicksburg, MS 39180
(601) 638–2704

1860 Victorian; 8 rooms; includes full breakfast.

North Carolina

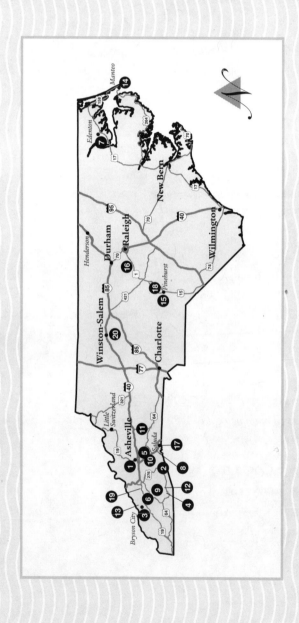

North Carolina

Numbers on map refer to towns numbered below.

*A Top Pick Inn

Albemarle Inn 💚
Asheville, North Carolina 28801

INNKEEPERS: Cathy and Larry Sklar

ADDRESS/TELEPHONE: 86 Edgemont Road; (828) 255–0027 or
(800) 621–7435; fax (828) 236–3397

WEB SITE: www.albemarleinn.com

ROOMS: 11, all with private bath, television, and telephone.
No-smoking inn.

RATES: $125 to $285 per room; includes full breakfast.

OPEN: Year-round.

FACILITIES AND ACTIVITIES: Swimming pool. Nearby: Biltmore
Estate, Blue Ridge Parkway, crafts and antiques shops, hiking, rafting,
golf; five minutes from downtown Asheville.

éla Bartók wrote his *Third Piano Concerto* while he was at Albemarle Inn. We're not suggesting that a stay here will turn you into a composer, but much about this B&B inn does call to mind musicians, artists, and literary gatherings, including the classical and contemporary music playing in the background.

This building has been restored to its early elegance and is decorated with furniture and accessories that reflect its neoclassical heritage. A couple of years ago, new innkeepers purchased the inn and upgraded the already grand property. The old oak paneling was stripped and refinished, bringing out its rich texture. The yard was completely relandscaped, new carpet was laid, and the bedding was upgraded with goose-down quilts and luxurious linens. Everything is bright and airy with a wonderful feeling of calm spaciousness.

One of the most notable features of the inn is a marvelous carved-oak staircase with a curved-frame glass window and an opposing curved balcony-like landing. It looks like a setting for the balcony scene from *Romeo and Juliet*. At least one couple has been married on that spot.

Each guest room has a special feature, such as antiques or four-poster beds or decorative brass. Bartók's Retreat, for instance, is a bright, high-ceilinged room from which you can see a bit of the Blue Ridge Mountains. It has a queen-size sleigh bed, two comfortable upholstered chairs, and floral wallpaper in greens, sand, rust, and deep red. This is one of the less expensive rooms.

At the other end of the scale, the Sunrise Suite has a 10-foot ceiling and year-round sunporch. The bedroom is dominated by a four-poster campaign bed. Dark wicker furnishes the sunporch. All the second-floor rooms are grouped around a second living room.

The innkeepers offer early-evening beverage and cheese to give guests a chance to chat with them and with one another. A particularly nice gathering spot is the sun porch. When the windows are open you can hear all kinds of birds singing—the same sound that is said to have inspired Bartók.

The Sklars are working continuously to improve the inn and their service as innkeepers. The building, listed on the National Register of Historic Places, is in Grove Park, a nice residential section of Asheville, convenient to downtown and some fine restaurants.

HOW TO GET THERE: From I–240 at Asheville, take the Charlotte Street exit. Go north on Charlotte Street about ⁹/₁₀ mile to Edgemont Road. Turn right and drive another ²/₁₀ mile. The driveway is marked with a sign.

Cedar Crest Victorian Inn Bed and Breakfast ♥
Asheville, North Carolina 28803

INNKEEPERS: Bruce and Rita Wightman

ADDRESS/TELEPHONE: 674 Biltmore Avenue; (828) 252–1389 or (800) 252-0310; fax (828) 253-7667

WEB SITE: www.cedarcrestvictorianinn.com

E-MAIL: stay@cedarcrestvictorianinn.com

ROOMS: 8, plus 1 suite and 2 suites in guest cottage; all with private bath, telephone, clock radio, iron and ironing board; cottage with service kitchen and parlor; some with wheelchair access, fireplace; one with whirlpool tub. Television on request. Rollaway bed available. Smoking in designated areas on veranda only.

RATES: $140 to $240, double; full gourmet breakfast and afternoon and evening refreshments; evening turndown service with imported sweet. Packages available.

OPEN: Year-round.

FACILITIES AND ACTIVITIES: Four acres of trees, English gardens and croquet lawn. On-site certified massage therapist. Concierge services. Nearby: Restaurants, Biltmore House, crafts and antiques shops, art galleries, boutiques, Folk Art Center, music and theater, Thomas Wolfe Memorial, golf, hiking, white-water rafting, horseback riding, trout fishing; easy access to the Blue Ridge Parkway.

BUSINESS TRAVEL: Fax and copy services available. Can accommodate small meetings.

The Wightmans view Cedar Crest as a kind of antidote to the Biltmore House, the famous mansion tourists come to Asheville to see. At the Biltmore House, everything is so massive, there are so many rooms, the furniture and art are so overwhelming, that you really can't relate to it. At Cedar Crest you see work of equal quality, purportedly done by some of the same craftsmen, in something closer to reality level.

Not that Cedar Crest is a modest little cottage. It's an 1890 Queen Anne–style Victorian mansion, so filled with splendid features that we think you'd have to stay about thirty days to see everything. The woodwork, first-generation oak and walnut, is elaborate and different in every room: heavy and masculine in the library, for instance, and delicately ornate in the dining room.

The quality of these elements is matched by other details throughout. On the main floor, four grand fireplaces with original tiles and decorative firebacks are surrounded by fluted columns, medallions, rich paneling, and beveled mirrors. Stained-glass and leaded-glass windows in the foyer and up the staircase complement hardwood floors. Period antique furnishings, Oriental rugs, lace, and richly textured window treatments enhance the ornate wall coverings.

Nearly half the bedrooms—each with a character all its own—boast a fireplace. Some of the guest chambers feature a claw-foot tub perfect for a luxurious bubble bath. The focal point of the Queen Anne room is a fascinating canopied ceiling much like those in bedrooms at the Biltmore house.

The Wightmans and their staff have created a relaxing atmosphere of warmth and comfort. Gracious hospitality, personalized service, and attention to detail are paramount. Bruce is the resident chef, turning his hobby and passion for cooking and baking into a labor of love. Rita's creative side is revealed through her efforts in the gardens and her attention to guest services. In addition, Rita is a professionally trained and certified massage therapist.

Strategically poised atop a hill overlooking what is now Biltmore Avenue, Cedar Crest catches your eye as you travel north toward downtown Asheville. Situated on four acres of trees, flowering shrubs, and gardens, Cedar Crest is an inviting oasis, a private retreat from the outside world.

HOW TO GET THERE: Take exit 50 or 50B from I–40 in Asheville. After the exit, stay in the right lane to Biltmore Avenue. The inn is 1¼ miles north of I–40.

Richmond Hill Inn
Asheville, North Carolina 28006

INNKEEPER: Susan Michel

ADDRESS/TELEPHONE: 87 Richmond Hill Drive; (828) 252-7313 or (800) 545-9238; fax (828) 252-8726

WEB SITE: www.richmondhillinn.com

E-MAIL: info@richmondhillinn.com

ROOMS: 12 in mansion, 15 garden house rooms, and 9 croquet cottages; all with private bath, telephone, and television; some with gas-log fireplace and Jacuzzi; 1 with wheelchair access. No smoking in guest rooms.

RATES: $155 to $395 for rooms, $345 to $450 for suites, double occupancy; includes full breakfast and afternoon tea. Two-night minimum on weekends.

OPEN: Year-round.

FACILITIES AND ACTIVITIES: Dinner. Beer and wine available. Library, conference facilities, croquet court, gardens, waterfalls. Nearby: Biltmore House, Folk Art Center, crafts and antiques shops, Great Smoky Mountains National Park, Blue Ridge Parkway.

This is a luxurious inn with a heroic saved-from-the-wrecking-ball story. The century-old mansion was the home of a former congressman and diplomat, Richmond Pearson, and his wife, Gabrielle. It was one of the most innovative and elegant homes of its time. But it outlasted the people who wanted to live that way and could afford it.

The building was scheduled to be torn down and then reprieved several times. Many community organizations campaigned and raised money to try to save the mansion. They also found the Michel family, who were willing to buy and restore it. It was moved, all in one piece, to its current spot on the hill.

The building was preserved where possible, and restored or re-created where necessary, with fidelity to the mansion's original state. Now listed on the National Register of Historic Places, it is considered one of the best examples of a Queen Anne–style mansion remaining. It's a "must see" if you are interested in architecture and preservation.

Because of the fine woodwork, soaring ceilings, and generously sized rooms, the mansion makes a fine inn. Some guest rooms are named for Pearson family members who once lived in them, others for important guests and, on the third floor, for Asheville-connected writers, such as Carl Sandburg. Each writer's room has a picture of the writer and a collection of his or her books.

Also re-creating the past, several hundred of Mr. Pearson's own books have been recovered and placed in the inn library along with books about North Carolina and those by North Carolina authors.

The restaurant reflects the mansion's history in being named Gabrielle's, after Mrs. Pearson. The food, however, is clearly a product of modern times. Considered American and nouvelle cuisine, it features lighter sauces and more healthful preparation than earlier haute cuisine. The crab cakes, flanked by strips of red corn tortilla chips and laced with a grilled tomato–roasted pepper sauce, are fabulous, as is the filet mignon, served with a small sweet-corn flan and whipped Yukon Gold potatoes.

HOW TO GET THERE: From I–240, take the 19/23 Weaverville exit. Continue on 19/23 and turn at exit 251 (UNC-Asheville). Turn left at the bottom of the ramp. At the first stoplight, turn left again onto Riverside Drive. Turn right on Pearson Bridge Road and cross the bridge. At the sharp curve, turn right on Richmond Hill Drive. The mansion is at the top of the hill.

The Inn at Brevard
Brevard, North Carolina 28712

INNKEEPERS: The Yager family

ADDRESS/TELEPHONE: 410 East Main Street; (828) 884–2105; fax (828) 885–7996

WEB SITE: InnatBrevard.8M.com

E-MAIL: brevardinn@citcom.net

ROOMS: 5 in main house; 9 in adjacent lodge; all with private bath. All rooms are air-conditioned and have cable television. Smoking allowed only in some lodge rooms.

RATES: $99 to $185; includes full breakfast. Extra person in double room, $10. Inquire about off-season discounts and children's rates.

OPEN: Year-round.

FACILITIES AND ACTIVITIES: Dining room. Brunch, Sunday only, 11:30 A.M. to 2:00 P.M.; dinner, Thursday and Saturday, 5:00 to 9:00 P.M. Meeting and banquet rooms. Nearby: Brevard Music Center, Pisgah National Forest, the Blue Ridge Parkway, hiking, fishing, swimming.

*I*n 1998 the Yager family took over this wonderful Greek Revival inn from its former owners, Eileen and Bertrand Bourgets. For a number of years the Bourgets had added their own personal touch to this historic mansion and its adjacent lodge, which gave the property a somewhat New England/Irish flavor.

The Yagers had a different view of the property: They restored it to its Southern roots. Carpets were taken up and the original heart-pine floors exposed and refinished. Fay Yager tells us, "We'd always heard that the original floors were badly damaged. What a wonderful surprise we had when we removed the carpeting and found the original heart pine in almost perfect condition. All it needed was a little sanding and cleaning—and a good coat of wax.

"Another wondrous surprise was when we moved into the bedrooms and discovered the fireplaces. The hearths had been covered over with plywood, flooring tile, and carpet; the actual fireplaces had been boarded over, and in some cases the mantels had been either covered over or removed and stored. We restored all of them to their original beauty—and where we did not have the original, we have found a wonderful local craftsman who has built replicas from the pieces we do have."

Paints were researched and true, bright period colors were reapplied (blues, yellows, and even bright reds). The Yagers upgraded all the furniture with antiques and period reproductions. They even found the bed that the Reconstruction governor of North Carolina slept in during his term in office.

With the dedication the Yager family has shown thus far, the inn is a jewel that will shine even more brightly than it has in the past.

In the meantime, what about the food?

Fay's breakfast features three full courses: The first is a fruit dish, coffee (or tea), and juice; the second is a hot or cold cereal course; and the final is a hot entree such as Belgian waffles with pecans and blueberries. It makes our mouths water just thinking about it. The dinner menu will also return to more traditional, fine Southern cuisine.

HOW TO GET THERE: The inn is on Route 276 in the center of town. If you take Route 64 into town, go east on Main Street.

Fryemont Inn
Bryson City, North Carolina 28713

INNKEEPERS: Sue and George Brown and Monica and George Brown Jr.

ADDRESS/TELEPHONE: : Fryemont Road (mailing address: P.O. Box 459); (828) 488-2159 or (800) 845-4879; fax (828) 488-6586

WEB SITE: www.fryemontinn.com

ROOMS: 37 in main lodge, 8 suites in 3 cottages, 1 two-bedroom cabin; all with private bath. Cabin and fireplace suites have air-conditioning, television, fireplace, wet bar or kitchen. Honeymoon suite has outdoor hot tub. No-smoking inn.

RATES: $95 to $202, double occupancy; includes breakfast and dinner. Inquire about children's rates.

OPEN: Mid-April through October. Cottage suites open year-round; no meals included in winter.

FACILITIES AND ACTIVITIES: Breakfast and dinner open to public by reservation, picnic lunches available, full bar. Swimming pool, craft-and-gift shop. Located in the Great Smoky Mountains. Nearby: Blue Ridge Parkway, rafting, horseback riding, boating, fishing, historic sites, the Cherokee Indian Reservation.

*B*eing in this inn makes you feel rustic without sacrificing any creature comforts. Just entering the lobby gives you a sense of being in a different world. It's a huge expanse of space, finished in wormy-chestnut board and batten, with a stone fireplace big enough to burn 8-foot logs. Couches and chairs are grouped for conversation in front of the fireplace and around the rest of the lobby, along with a couple of good-size tables with chairs for games or cards.

The Browns and their staff practice the kind of easy hospitality that encourages people to talk to them and to one another.

This is the kind of place that would have to have a porch with rockers for hardcore relaxing as well as for watching the view of the Smoky Mountains.

The dining room, too, is just what the location calls for, a large room with many windows and another stone fireplace.

At dinner, you could begin with soup and salad. Your choice of entrees might include fresh mountain trout, turkey with pecan dressing, and prime rib. The vegetables are fresh, served family style. It's nice to be able to order good wine to go with such a meal.

Outside, the poplar shingles of the inn make it seem to be covered in bark in such a way that the building blends into the surrounding trees and landscape as though it were itself a growing thing.

Inside and outside, everything is clean, polished, mowed, trimmed—the kind of perfectly kept place in the woods we fantasize about. The good thing is that it's you in the rocker or by the pool and somebody else out there on the property doing the work.

HOW TO GET THERE: Follow Route 74 west to Bryson City. Take exit 67. Go ³/₁₀ mile to Fryemont Road, on the right. This goes directly to the inn.

Hemlock Inn
Bryson City, North Carolina 28713

INNKEEPERS: Morris and Elaine White

ADDRESS/TELEPHONE: P.O. Box 2350, Bryson City; (828) 488–2885; fax (282) 488–8985

WEB SITE: hemlockinn.com or innbook.com/hemlock

E-MAIL: hemlock@dnet.net

ROOMS: 25 rooms and suites, 2 cottages; all with private bath; some with wheelchair access. No air-conditioning (elevation 2,300 feet).

RATES: $143 to $195; includes breakfast, dinner, and all gratuities. Additional adult $39; each child $20 (under 4 free). Inquire about long-term rates in cottages.

OPEN: Mid-April to October.

FACILITIES AND ACTIVITIES: Dining room open to public by reservation; no Sunday-evening meal; picnic lunches available on request. Shuffleboard courts, skittles, Ping-Pong, 50 acres, walking paths in the woods, wildflower tours. Located in the heart of the Great Smoky Mountains. Nearby: Rafting, fishing, hiking, birding, excursion train, Cherokee Indian Reservation..

We like everything about this place, even if it is basically just an old motel, especially the way guests are encouraged to slow down, unwind, and actively enjoy nature. The inn offers guests a calendar of bloom, compiled by the Tennessee Department of Conservation, listing the more familiar flowers you can find blooming in the Great Smoky

Mountains National Park each month from March through September. You can walk in any direction and find flowers.

The inn sits on fifty wooded acres with a couple of miles of hiking trails. Even sitting on the porch puts you in touch with the out-of-doors in a gentle way. The view of valleys and mountains is magnificent, and the lawn and landscaping complement that view while introducing enough order so that you don't feel you are roughing it.

The rooms blend into the scene, too. They're furnished with country antiques and furniture made by local craftspeople. It's all comfortable without being so overbearing as to take your attention away from the scenery and growing plants.

Now, dinner might distract you. The Whites don't think that studying wildflowers should mean you have to eat lamb's-quarters and sorrel. Substantial home-style Southern cooking in generous quantities becomes the high point of the day for many guests. The food is served on lazy Susan tables, inviting you to help yourself as often as you like.

A typical dinner includes country-fried steak, baked chicken with dressing, green beans, frosted cauliflower, apple-carrot casserole, okra fritters, and chess pie. Let's go back to that "frosted cauliflower." It's cooked with a topping of cheese, mustard, and mayonnaise that zips up the flavor and imparts a colorful gloss to the cauliflower—hence the name "frosted." The rolls are homemade, of course, as are the pumpkin and apple chips to spread on them. These "chips" also need explanation. They're pieces of fruit in a thick syrup, like preserves, and so many guests have become addicted that the Whites now offer jars of pumpkin and apple chips for sale.

HOW TO GET THERE: The inn is just east of Bryson City, about a mile off Highway 19 on top of a small mountain. The turn is marked by a HEMLOCK INN sign. When you make reservations, you will receive a highlighted map with full directions from all interstate highways in whatever direction you will be traveling.

Nantahala Village
Bryson City, North Carolina 28713

INNKEEPERS: John Burton and Jan Letendre
ADDRESS/TELEPHONE: 9400 Highway 19 West; (828) 488–2826 or (800) 438–1507; fax (828) 488–9634

WEB SITE: www.nvnc.com

E-MAIL: nvinfo@nvnc.com

ROOMS: 11, in main lodge; all with private bath and television; 50 cabins, cottages, and privately owned homes; all with private bath; some with television, fireplace, whirlpool tub, coffeemaker, kitchen. No smoking in public rooms.

RATES: $60 to $320, single or double; $10 each extra person in room over regular number, up to maximum allowed. Rates vary seasonally. Meals extra. MAP packages available. Children under 13 free. Some handicapped accessible rooms. Lodge rooms are non-smoking.

OPEN: March to December.

FACILITIES AND ACTIVITIES: Restaurant open to guests and public three meals a day; weekend brunch. Brown bagging permitted. Swimming pool, tennis courts, volleyball court, Ping-Pong, horseshoes, hiking trails, horseback riding. Nearby: Great Smoky Mountains National Park, rafting, fishing, bicycling, Great Smoky Mountain Railroad, Cherokee Indian Reservation.

*N*antahala Village has been a special place over many years. The bad news is that the old lodge burned down in 1997. The good news is that a new lodge building opened in mid-1998 and is better than ever. The architecture is classic, the number of rooms has been reduced to eleven, the amenities upgraded, there are now six meeting rooms, and the view from the restaurant is still spectacular.

The Village covers 200 mountain acres, so the place lends itself to outdoor recreation, but the rebuilt stone lodge is a cozy place to relax inside, too. The rooms are spacious, furnished in country-style furniture. The beds are good. The showers are hot. We've stayed in some of the cabins, when we were traveling with friends, and we found each experience there just right, too. Innkeepers John Burton and Jan Letendre take care to book guests into cabins that fit their situations—no cliff-edge cabins for people with little kids, a romantic cabin well away from everyone else for honeymooners, and so on.

The food here has always been good in the almost-Thanksgiving-dinner style, and still is, but you now have choices of vegetarian entrees and other lighter food as well. In addition to country ham, trout, and rib eye, for instance, you could try Wild Forest Pasta, with a cheesy sauce of herbs and vegetables. Spinach lasagna and mushroom-cheese pie are other new favorites. A children's menu is offered at each meal so that you can order the kinds of things kids like in quantities appropriate to their appetites. The view of the mountains from the dining room is so breathtaking, we like to take a long time to eat.

Nantahala Village gets better and better. That's good news for all of us who love the mountains and the Nantahala Gorge.

HOW TO GET THERE: The inn is 9 miles southwest of Bryson City on Highway 19.

High Hampton Inn and Country Club 🫀 👪
Cashiers, North Carolina 28717

INNKEEPERS: W. D., Will, and Becky McKee

ADDRESS/TELEPHONE: P.O. Box 338; (828) 743-2411 or (800) 334-2551; fax (828) 743-5991

WEB SITE: www.highhamptoninn.com

E-MAIL: Information@HighHamptonInn.com or Reservations@HighHamptonInn.com

ROOMS: 117 rooms and cottages; all with private bath; some with fireplace.

RATES: $86 to $114 for rooms in the inn per person, double occupancy, depending on the season and whether midweek or weekend; $60 to $79 for an additional person in the room; $53 for a child under 6 in the room with two adults. Ask about rates for the colony homes, which are rented by the week but can also be rented for less than a week with a three-night minimum. All include full American plan (three meals daily), afternoon tea, many of the sports and recreation facilities; alcoholic beverages are extra; five-day/four-night Thanksgiving package $149 per person, double occupancy; golf and tennis packages.

OPEN: Closed November through mid-April, with the exception of Thanksgiving weekend.

FACILITIES AND ACTIVITIES: Restaurant, tavern, cafe, gift shop, tennis and golf pro shops, exercise room, pool table, Ping-Pong, playground; lake, exercise room, fishing, swimming, boating; eighteen-hole golf course, six clay tennis courts; hiking trails, fitness trail, mountain biking, summer children's program, bird walks; bridge lessons and tournaments, golf schools and tournaments, wildflower workshops, watercolor and other art workshops, literary conference, Teddy Bear Picnic.

BUSINESS TRAVEL: Meeting rooms; ideal place for executive retreats.

*W*e'd been hearing about High Hampton for years from two couples who traditionally visited the mountain inn and resort for the annual Thanksgiving house party. They continually raved about the ambience and the food, so finally we simply had to check it out for ourselves. Much to our delight we learned that the inn is everything they said and much more. We immediately felt at home in the rustic, wood-paneled inn, where the ambience is casual. We instantly knew that although there was plenty to do, we could engage in our favorite vacation activity—doing nothing.

High Hampton is a true mountain getaway, located as it is in the stunning Blue Ridge Mountains of western North Carolina 50 miles from Asheville and 70 miles from Greenville, South Carolina. No superhighways penetrate this remote area, only winding two-lane roads with a waterfall, mountain peak, deep valley, or other spectacular sight around every turn.

The rustic architecture of the wood-frame inn and guest cottages blend with the natural beauty of the surroundings. We particularly loved the great stone four-sided fireplace in the lobby that folks gather around in cool weather. The simple, basic public and guest rooms are all furnished with comfortable, mountain-crafted furniture. Very little changes here except the seasons.

Cozy guest rooms, which are paneled with natural woods from the estate that are applied in a board-and-batten pattern, have rustic furnishings, simple bedspreads, and a private bath. Bedding ranges from twins to kings. There are no telephones or televisions (oh, happy day)—you'll find those in the lobby if you can't live without them. Most people come to High Hampton for the serenity, the unparalleled scenery, the good food, and the other guests, anyway.

If you need more room to spread out, there are suites as well as colony homes with varying floor plans. The Honeymoon Cottage is about as picturesque as you can get. Located on the lake shore and with its own little dock, it is a log cabin with a wraparound deck, a fireplace, and a waterwheel. The privately owned colony homes feature a great room, fireplace, fully-equipped kitchen, two to four bedrooms with private baths, television and VCR, telephone, and top-of-the-line furnishings. Although these are ideal for families or groups traveling together, we think you're missing a lot of what High Hampton is all about if you don't stay in the inn itself.

Dining at High Hampton is an epicurean experience. First of all, the rustic dining room has two walls of windows so that you can enjoy the majestic scenery while you dine. All meals are served buffet style, and dinner might include fried chicken, fresh local trout, or prime rib accompanied by delicious soups, salad, fresh vegetables, freshly baked bread, and tempting desserts. Guests are assigned their own table and their own wait staff for the duration of their stay. About the only concession to the outside world of rules is that coats and ties are required for gentlemen for the evening meal—a relic of the past we cherish.

Another culinary tradition at High Hampton is Afternoon Tea, a holdover from a slower-paced era when people made time for leisure and conversation. Today's guests find this afternoon break an excellent opportunity to get to know one another. Don't fill up so much that you spoil your dinner, though. Music and dancing are there for your enjoyment in the Rock Mountain Tavern, and other evening activities and entertainment are posted on the bulletin board.

Just so you'll know: High Hampton does not add a service charge to your bill, and it is not necessary to tip. For those who can't be parted from their pets, there are kennels.

HOW TO GET THERE: High Hampton is located near the intersection of U.S. 64 and NC 107 in Cashiers.

Dogwood Inn ¢¢¢

Chimney Rock, North Carolina 28720

INNKEEPERS: Marsha Reynolds and Robert Brooks

ADDRESS/TELEPHONE: U.S. 64/74A (mailing address: P.O. Box 159);
(828) 625-4403 or (800) 992-5557; fax (828) 625-8825

WEB SITE: www.thedogwoodinn.com

ROOMS: 11 rooms, 7 with private bath, 4 with shared bath; 2 with
whirlpool tub, 1 with gas-log fireplace; all with ceiling fan, clock radio; 1
with television; children 12 and older welcome; no wheelchair access.

RATES: $94 for shared bath, $99 to $115 for private bath, $129 for
whirlpool rooms, double occupancy; includes full breakfast. Many special packages; weekends require a two-night minimum stay.

OPEN: Closed January and February.

FACILITIES AND ACTIVITIES: Two sitting rooms, gift shop, patio,
porches. Nearby: Village of Chimney Rock, shops, restaurants, Chimney
Rock Park, Lake Lure, water sports, hiking, white-water rafting, golf,
horseback riding, Asheville, Biltmore Estate.

*A*n inn has stood on this spot on the banks of the Rocky Broad
River and in the shadow of spectacular Chimney Rock for
more than one hundred years. In the days before automobiles,
a rough road known as the Hickory Nut Gap Turnpike wound through the
area, and the Logan Inn offered overnight accommodations for guests traveling through by horse and buggy or stagecoach. The Logan family operated
the inn—known for its fine food and good times—through thick and thin for
three generations. Challenges along the way were the flood of 1916 and the
fire of 1930, which raged through the village, demolishing nine buildings
including the inn. Undaunted, the Logans rebuilt with the pleasant, simple,
white two-story structure that is now known as the Dogwood Inn. Today it
is operated by Marsha Reynolds and Robert Brooks.

We're talking location, convenience, and casual comfort here. From riverside rooms, you can hear the gurgling of the rushing river and gaze in awe at
the gargantuan rock formation that gave the village its name. (Log onto the
inn's Web site to hear the river and birds chirping.) Streetside rooms have a
view of the village. Four porches and a lovely yard provide many options for
enjoying the river and mountain view. The downstairs level provides a comfortable den and a large living/reading/dining room.

Eleven cozy guest rooms, ten of which are upstairs and one of which is on the river level, may be a little tight on space but do provide comfortable bedding and a small seating area. Two special rooms boast whirlpool tubs; one also features a fireplace.

Awaken in the morning to a special blend of coffee served every morning in the upstairs hall, followed by breakfast served in the dining room or alfresco on the porch. Guests can choose from a European buffet or the chef's special of the day.

Located in the heart of the hamlet, the B&B is within easy walking distance of restaurants and crafts and antiques shops. A short drive takes you part of the way up the mountain to Chimney Rock Park, where part of *Last of the Mohicans* was filmed. Be prepared for some serious climbing the rest of the way, but you'll be rewarded with spectacular views of the village, valley, and Lake Lure.

HOW TO GET THERE: From 1-40 or the Blue Ridge Parkway, take U.S. 74 southeast. It goes right through Chimney Rock Village. The B&B is on the right. From I-26, take U.S. 64 northeast until it dead-ends into U.S. 74 at the village and turn right. The B&B is on the right.

Jarrett House ¢¢¢
Dillsboro, North Carolina 28725

INNKEEPERS: Jim and Jean Hartbarger

ADDRESS/TELEPHONE: 100 Haywood Street (mailing address: P.O. Box 219); (828) 586-0265 or (800) 972-5623; fax (828) 586-6251

WEB SITE: www.jarretthouse.com

ROOMS: 18, all with private bath; some with wheelchair access. No smoking inn.

RATES: $80 per person, single or double; $5.00 each additional person; full breakfast included in room rate. No credit cards.

OPEN: April to October.

FACILITIES AND ACTIVITIES: Lunch, dinner; dining room with wheelchair access, open to public; brown bagging permitted.

arrett House is famous for its food, so we'll tell you about that first. It's been a matter of pride since the inn began business back in the 1800s that the table be so generous that no one should ever have to ask for seconds.

For lunch try the country ham or fried chicken. That is the only choice except for a beverage. Everything else comes automatically—green beans, slaw, pickled beets with onion, candied apples, browned potatoes, and a seemingly endless supply of the lightest little biscuits you've ever tasted. A squeeze bottle on the table is filled with honey for the biscuits.

After all that, you'll wish you could order a cot to take a nap. And that's just lunch. After a big dinner here, a hospital bed may be called for.

But after-meal dozing is what the rockers on the porch are for.

For serious sleeping, the guest rooms, furnished in oak, walnut, and cherry antiques, are nice. Everything is squeaky clean, a feeling enhanced by the white chenille bedspreads. Most of the rooms have claw-foot bathtubs.

Downstairs, the Victorian parlor is almost eerie in the feeling it gives you that any second the old inhabitants will come in and sit down. In one corner, an old Bacon & Ravern piano that belonged to Jim's grandmother is partly covered by a lovely folded lace tablecloth. On the wall is a framed hanging of the Lord's Prayer that she crocheted when she was ninety-two years old.

The sense of family pervades this inn in another manner, too. Jim and Jean's sons, Scott and Buzz, and their wives, Mary and Sharon, are all involved in its operation.

HOW TO GET THERE: Dillsboro is 47 miles west of Asheville. Routes 19A/441 and 23/19A form an intersection in town. The inn is on the corner at the intersection.

The Lords Proprietors' Inn
Edenton, North Carolina 27932

INNKEEPERS: Arch and Jane Edwards

ADDRESS/TELEPHONE: 300 North Broad Street; (252) 482-3641 or (800) 348-8933; fax (252) 482-2432

WEB SITE: www.edentoninn.com

E-MAIL: stay@edentoninn.com

ROOMS: 16 rooms and 2 luxury suites; all with private bath, television, VCR, and telephone. Suites have a whirlpool tub, fireplace, king-size bed, wet bar, and robes. No-smoking inn.

RATES: $155 to $225, including a full breakfast. Dinner served Tuesday through Saturday for $35 per person, including gratuity. Credit cards accepted.

FACILITIES AND ACTIVITIES: Restaurant, gift shop. Nearby: Restaurants, waterfront parks, guided walking tours of Edenton Historic District, Hope Plantation tours, Somerset Place tours, tennis, golf, biking, sailing.

BUSINESS TRAVEL: Telephone and good work space in room; fax available, meeting space.

*T*his inn has earned a reputation as one of the most elegant and gracious inns in the state. Three separate restored buildings—the White-Bond House, the Satterfield House, and the Pack House—in the historic district cluster around a lawn and gardens; these buildings house the guest rooms, three big parlors, and a library. Breakfast and dinner are served at the Whedbee House, set on a brick patio surrounded by dogwoods in the center of the complex. The Pack House was originally a tobacco barn that was sawed in half and brought to the grounds in two pieces. Its conversion created lodging with huge amounts of open space, vast floors, and soaring ceilings. The guest rooms open onto a balcony that runs around the inside of the building and overlooks the common rooms.

Dinner at the inn, served only to guests, gets raves. Entrees, which change daily, range from roasted rabbit and pork with a porcini mushroom sauce to striped bass with a pistachio vinaigrette.

Edenton, located on the Albemarle Sound, boasts a lot of history. Settled in 1685 and incorporated in 1722 as the first capital of the province of North Carolina, the town has kept alive the memories of its early leaders, men who signed the Declaration of Independence, supplied Washington's army in defiance of British blockades, and convinced the people of North Carolina to ratify the new United States Constitution.

Many of the people in the community are direct descendants of those early leaders. Those descendants and others who care have turned virtually the entire community into a project of historic preservation.

Arch and Jane Edwards have been deeply involved in the community and value their inn's place in it. Their hospitality extends to inviting guests to use their residential swimming pool and to tour their private home, Mount Auburn, an authentically restored waterfront plantation house of the 1800s.

HOW TO GET THERE: Edenton is 90 miles east of I-95 at the junction of Highways 17 and 32. Broad Street runs through the center of town.

Highland Lake Inn: A Country Retreat
Flat Rock, North Carolina 28731

INNKEEPERS: The Grup family

ADDRESS/TELEPHONE: Highland Lake Drive (mailing address: P.O. Box 1026); (828) 693-6812 or (800) 762-1376; fax (828) 696-8951

WEB SITE: www.hlinn.com

E-MAIL: dgrup@hlinn.com

ROOMS: 20 in lodge, 16 in inn, 10 cabins, 6 cottages; all with private bath, telephone, television, dataport, coffeemaker, iron and ironing board; some with fireplace, whirlpool, wheelchair access, and facilities for handicapped. No-smoking inn.

RATES: $89 to $215, double, for rooms in cabins, lodge, and inn; single $10 less; includes breakfast, innkeepers social, sports equipment, turndown service. Inquire about cottage rates.

OPEN: Year-round.

FACILITIES AND ACTIVITIES: Restaurant; Olympic-size pool, lake, canoes, tennis, fishing, volleyball; one hundred acres of walking trails.

BUSINESS TRAVEL: Telephone and excellent work space in cabins; conference facilities.

Regardless of what we tell you about Highland Lake Inn, you'll find something more when you get there. This place, which in earlier years variously functioned as a club, a boys' school, and a camp, has almost as many personalities as Sibyl. It's been an inn and conference center since 1985, a place that delights all who experience it, but somehow it has remained a secret from most of us. Perhaps the most fascinating thing about it is that it's a self-sufficient compound. The restaurant serves vegetables and herbs organically grown on the property; bakers make bread from Arrowhead Mills' organically grown grains, which are stone-ground in the inn's kitchen; eggs come from free-range chickens. If you stay in a cabin, you'll probably burn wood that was cut on the property in the fireplace.

The significance of all this to you, even if you don't care about such things in general, is threefold: First, the food has taste, texture, and color. If you are one of those who complains that tomatoes don't taste like tomatoes anymore, wait until you eat here! When you taste an egg with a brilliant bright-yellow yolk produced by a free-range chicken, you'll be angry at the tastelessness mass-produced eggs force upon us.

Second, you can bring kids here to learn how to take an egg out of a chicken nest; watch goats being milked; see vegetables growing in family-size gardens; and roam freely through lawns, and fields, and woods.

Finally, this place is pretty, comfortable, and "far from the madding crowd," with lots of outdoor things to do, pleasant places for doing nothing at all, and, of course, that fabulous food.

So, we are discovering Highland Lake. Who knows what will have been added when you get here? Wood-fired bake ovens? More fruit and vegetable crops? Larger greenhouses?

Whatever. It will be wonderful.

HOW TO GET THERE: From I-26, take exit 22 and go west on Upward Road, which becomes Highland Lake Road at U.S. Highway 176. The entrance is at the waterfall; follow signs up the driveway to the office.

The Woodfield Inn 💙
Flat Rock, North Carolina 28731

INNKEEPERS: Rhonda and Michael Horton

ADDRESS/TELEPHONE: U.S. 25 South (mailing address: P.O. Box 98); (828) 693–6016 or (800) 533–6016; fax (828) 693–0437

WEB SITE: www.woodfieldinn.com

E-MAIL: wood1@IOA.com

ROOMS: 18 rooms; all with private bath and king- or queen-size bed, iron and ironing board, ceiling fan, private veranda; some with fireplace, whirlpool, and/or television/VCR; no telephones. No-smoking inn.

RATES: $119 to $189, including breakfast; weekend package available for the annual Civil War reenactment includes two breakfasts, two dinners, tickets for both days, and tickets to the Southern Jubilee Ball.

OPEN: Year-round.

FACILITIES AND ACTIVITIES: Restaurant, verandas, patio, gift shop, walking trails, corporate retreats, weddings and receptions, special events. Nearby: Flat Rock Playhouse, Carl Sandburg Historic Site, antiques and crafts shopping, casual and fine dining, hiking, golf.

BUSINESS TRAVEL: Meeting space, secretarial assistance and audiovisual equipment for meetings; pavilion and gazebo for special functions.

*S*teeped in history and romance, the inviting three-story inn sits on twenty-eight acres well back from the road on a rise at the top of a circular drive. Its most distinguishing feature is its double tier of verandas with their unusual double-X railings and deeply curved brackets topping the second-story columns. Inside, high ceilings, hardwood floors, and simple moldings characterize the unpretentious yet appealing rooms. Victorian antiques and curios adorn both public and guest chambers. Be sure to check out the huge hand-carved ebony chest large enough to hide an elephant and ask about the secret room where Confederate soldiers hid not only gold and silver but also the ladies of the house from Union troops, renegades, and scallywags from remote mountain coves. When the weather doesn't permit socializing out on the verandas, diners and guests alike gather around the fireplace in the graceful formal parlor, which is warmly furnished with Victorian-era antiques and accented with rich colors and interesting accessories as well as games, books, and magazines.

Upstairs, eighteen restful guest bedchambers all offer private baths. Many of them also boast gas-log fireplaces and French doors opening onto the veranda with majestic vistas in the distance. Two very special rooms sport whirlpool tubs. Different style beds from four-posters to sleigh beds as well

Flat Rock Rockers

One of the previous owners of The Woodfield Inn was Squire Henry T. Farmer of the prominent Charleston family who made Flat Rock a popular summer destination for society's elite. During his tenure the inn was known as the Farmer Hotel, and even today the restaurant is called Squire's in his honor.

Something that annoyed Squire Farmer immensely was that no matter what kind of rockers he bought for the verandas, they creaked and crept across the floor when rocked. He put his brain and talents to work and developed a black-walnut rocker that didn't creep. These rockers were so well liked by visitors to the inn that they wanted to buy them, so he opened a furniture factory nearby to produce them. Unfortunately, the factory was forced to close down during the Civil War, and his exact design has never been duplicated. Fortunately for all of us, two of those very original rockers survive and are actually in use on the veranda. (We can't believe they're not in a museum.) Try one out for yourself.

as carefully chosen bed coverings and window treatments give every guest room distinct personality. Not at all overdone, the simple rooms are painted in warm, deep colors and adorned with just enough artwork and accessories to make them interesting without being overpowering.

Breakfast is a substantial affair that begins with a generous bread basket, juice, and hot beverages. Don't fill up too much, though, because you'll soon be treated to a hot entree ranging from scrambled eggs to French toast to waffles and breakfast meats accompanied by such hearty side dishes as grits and/or hash browns.

Ample country-size portions are served to guests and the public for dinner and Sunday brunch at Squire's restaurant. Three dining rooms provide enough space for a crowd but still offer window tables and little out-of-the-way nooks intimate enough for a romantic meal à deux. Antique coverlets adorn the walls, and the cozy fireplace blazes in cool weather. Walls of windows in the Garden Dining Room let the outdoors in—a particularly pleasant state of affairs in the spring and fall when the grounds blaze with color.

Dinner entrees might feature prime beef, North Carolina trout, pork chops, or tenderloin medallions accompanied by a bread basket, salad, and

fresh vegetables. Wild turkey and swordfish make an appearance in season. A groaning-board Sunday brunch features eggs Benedict, other egg dishes, French toast, waffles, bacon, sausage, pork chops, breads, vegetables, and cobblers.

Begin or end any meal with a Woodfield Inn tradition: Lemon Juleps, a lemon and whiskey drink with a twist of lemon peel instead of mint, on the veranda.

HOW TO GET THERE: The Woodfield Inn is located on U.S. 25, 2½ miles from Hendersonville. From I-26, take U.S. 64 west to Hendersonville, then turn south on U.S. 25. Pass through the town of Flat Rock. The inn is on the right just past the Carl Sandburg Historic Site.

Innisfree Victorian Inn
Glenville, North Carolina 28736

INNKEEPER: Henry Hoche

ADDRESS/TELEPHONE: Highway 107 North (mailing address: P.O. Box 469); (828) 743–2946

WEB SITE: www.innisfreeinn.com

ROOMS: 10 rooms and suites, all with private bath, clock radio, ceiling fan; some with fireplace or woodstove, whirlpool tub, telephone, television with VCR, refrigerator.

RATES: Range from $150 to $290, varying by season and day of the week; based on single or double occupancy; includes candle-light breakfast in the tower for inn guests or breakfast delivered to the suite for Garden House guests, afternoon hospitality hour from 5:30 to 6:30 P.M., Irish coffee by the fireplace in the evening, and Godiva chocolates; weekends require a 2-night minimum, holidays a 3-night minimum; wedding, honeymoon, and anniversary packages. Only the Garden House is suitable for children.

OPEN: Year-round.

FACILITIES AND ACTIVITIES: Gardens, verandas, walking trails, hammock, gazebo, private beach, games, small gift shop. Nearby: Water sports, boat rentals, fishing, tennis, golf, hiking, snow skiing, antiques and crafts shopping, restaurants.

*W*e're crazy about Christmas, so you can just imagine how enchanted we were to see the lavish Victorian decorations at Innisfree. Our first glimpse was of what seemed like miles of garlands draped around two stories of wraparound verandas and decks. Inside, a magnificent Christmas tree reached to the cathedral ceiling.

Even if you're not lucky enough to visit Innisfree at Christmastime, there are plenty of Victorian furnishings and accessories to admire. First, the stately house itself. Although it was built in 1989, it has many of the Victorian characteristics you'd expect—gables, verandas, gingerbread, and, the most obvious, a three-story turret. Perched on a hillside on twelve acres, the house boasts walls of windows overlooking Lake Glenville—the highest lake east of the Rockies—with the Blue Ridge Mountains providing a backdrop.

The cathedral ceiling in the great room simulates the high ceilings of yore, and the marble mantelpiece is just as grand as any you'd see in a century-old house. Exuberantly furnished, the great room, breakfast room, and guest rooms feature antiques and reproductions, Oriental carpets, and carefully chosen accessories from years of world travel. Under the eaves is an informal observatory/TV/game room equipped with binoculars. Guest chambers are divided between the main house and a smaller garden house.

Every guest room or suite has its own charms. In the main house, rooms are named for Queen Victoria and Prince Albert as well as the English cities of Cambridge, Canterbury, and Windsor. The Queen Victoria Suite, the grandest of them all, boasts a tray ceiling; bay window; massive, ornate canopy bed; whirlpool bath; and even a bidet. The Windsor Room has a fireplace and an Italian lavatory with hand-painted blue irises and gilded dolphin faucets. Exotic Chinese headboards are the focal point in the Prince Albert Suite and Canterbury Room. The Cambridge Room features a private porch and separate entrance.

The Garden House, a small Dutch Colonial–style house with its own turret, located down the hill from the main house, contains five suites named for English authors. Offering more privacy than the big house, these suites boast a fireplace, wet bar, refrigerator, telephone, and a fireplace—some of them double-sided so that you can enjoy the fire in your bedroom and, the height of luxury, in your bathroom. Several offer garden tubs for two with spectacular views out the window. Because the tower dining area in the main house won't accommodate more guests than those staying in the main house, breakfast and evening liqueurs are brought to the Garden House Suites.

Open to its rafters and surrounded with stained-glass windows, the tur-

ret of the main house is the striking setting for the ample breakfast of egg dishes, breakfast meats, juices, fruits, special breads, and hot beverages. You'll feel like royalty feasting by candlelight under the ornate chandelier. Later, whether you've had a strenuous day hiking, a leisurely day shopping for mountain crafts, or a do-nothing day with a good book, you'll enjoy gathering with your fellow guests for afternoon refreshments on the veranda in good weather or around a crackling fire in the great room in inclement weather. After you return from dinner, Irish coffee and hot chocolate are waiting, and you'll find a Godiva chocolate on your pillow at bedtime.

HOW TO GET THERE: From U.S. 64 in Cashiers, turn north on NC 107 and go 6 miles. Watch for the signs to the inn on the left.

The Claddagh Inn
Hendersonville, North Carolina 28792

INNKEEPERS: Geraldine and August Emanuele

ADDRESS/TELEPHONE: 755 North Main Street; (828) 697–7778 or (800) 225–4700; fax (828) 697–8664

WEB SITE: www.CladdaghInn.com

E-MAIL: Innkeepers@CladdaghInn.com

ROOMS: 16 rooms, including a 2-bedroom, 2-bath suite; all with private bath, telephone, television, clock; children welcome; no wheelchair access. Smoking outside only.

RATES: $99 to $155, double occupancy; includes full breakfast. Additional person $20; children under 10 free in the room with parents. Credit cards accepted.

OPEN: Year-round.

FACILITIES AND ACTIVITIES: Large wraparound veranda, small lawn and garden. Nearby: Within a block of a public park with tennis courts and miniature golf; walking distance of antiques shops, boutiques, and restaurants; easy drive to the Village of Flat Rock, Carl Sandburg National Historic Site, Flat Rock Playhouse, Blue Ridge Parkway, Biltmore Estate, Chimney Rock Park, water sports on Lake Lure, hiking, fishing.

*A*s you might guess, the ambience here is Irish. The Emanueles aren't Irish themselves; it was a former owner who gave the inn its name and personality, but Gerri and Augie are only too happy to continue the tradition. They had stained-glass windows depicting Irish symbols created for the transoms over the doors to several of the guest rooms. Other touches of whimsy we enjoyed are the fish tank incorporated into the registration counter and an old carousel elephant in the second-floor hall.

The cheerful yellow three-story late-nineteenth-century house, trimmed in green and white, has a welcoming wraparound veranda. Although it was built in 1888 as a single-family home for W. A. Smith, Hendersonville's first mayor, it became the Charleston Boarding House in 1906 to house residents from the Low Country who escaped to the high lands in the summer for relief from coastal heat and humidity. The stately house has served some type of hospitality function ever since. It became the city's first bed-and-breakfast in 1985.

Inside are formal and informal parlors, a large dining room, numerous sitting nooks, and sixteen guest rooms ranging in size from a small room perfect for a business person traveling alone to family rooms with several beds and a two-bedroom, two-bath suite. Several rooms are on the first floor, so although the inn isn't technically wheelchair accessible, it is user friendly for those who have trouble with stairs. Each room has its own distinct personality and is furnished in a mixture of antiques and reproductions.

The food is Gerri's favorite part of the whole project. She and Augie come from large families and often entertained hordes on holidays, so cooking for large numbers of people doesn't faze her at all. Early risers or those who desire only a light breakfast can enjoy the buffet of fresh fruit, yogurt, granola, and breads. Eggs, a breakfast meat, and grits are on the menu every day as well as a specialty item such as pancakes or rum-raisin French toast with raisin-cinnamon sauce.

HOW TO GET THERE: From I-26, take U.S. 64 into Hendersonville. Turn right on U.S. 25. The inn is almost immediately on the left.

The Waverly Inn
Hendersonville, North Carolina 28792

INNKEEPERS: John and Diane Sheiry, Darla Olmstead

ADDRESS/TELEPHONE: 783 North Main Street; (828) 693–9193 or
(800) 537–8195; fax (828) 692–1010

WEB SITE: www.waverlyinn.com

E-MAIL: waverlyinn@IOA.com

ROOMS: 13, plus 1 two-room suite; all with private bath, cable TV, and
telephone with dataport; some with VCR. No smoking indoors.

RATES: $109 to $169, double; $90 to $100, single; $175 to $225, suite;
includes full breakfast and evening social hour.

OPEN: Year-round.

FACILITIES AND ACTIVITIES: Nearby: Restaurants, hiking, tennis,
miniature golf, antiques and crafts shops; easy drive to Biltmore Estate,
Carl Sandburg home, Flat Rock Playhouse, DuPont State Forest.

BUSINESS TRAVEL: Telephone with dataport in each guest room; fax for
guest use; printer and paper available.

The Waverly opened its doors in 1898 and has never been closed
since. Many of the guests come back year after year to this B&B
inn to cool off. Hendersonville is a mountain town where people
have gone for years to escape the summer heat. Even on the hottest days you
can expect to sleep under blankets at night. But don't worry about unexpected heat waves. All rooms are air-conditioned just in case.

John and Diane Sheiry each have more than twenty years' experience in
the hotel business. They chose Hendersonville and The Waverly because they
wanted to get out of the fast-
track life that kept John traveling most of the time and
made it hard for them to nur-
ture family life. It's not that
they work less as keepers of a
small inn but that now they
can work together, at home.
In recent years they have contributed a high level of
innkeeping professionalism
to the area.

Diane's sister, Darla, as third innkeeper, adds another family dimension to the mix.

Their values line up beautifully with the family orientation that has traditionally been typical of The Waverly, but there is growth here, too. These days, The Waverly attracts guests in addition to those escaping the heat: overnight travelers looking for a place more interesting than a motel and vacationers looking for lodging with a personal feel. The result is a fascinating combination. You can see it on the porch—young travelers, middle-aged couples, retired people, and families with children, not just occupying rockers side by side, but talking and actually listening to one another.

It's a good setup for socializing. In addition to using the porch, guests can gather in the library or in the Victorian parlor, where a fireplace is the focal point on nippy evenings. There are sitting rooms on all three floors.

John and Diane have renovated extensively and have furnished the place with the kind of turn-of-the-twentieth-century blend you'd have expected to find originally in such a home.

Two additions to the inn's activities, Murder Mystery weekends and Wine Lovers' weekends, each offered twice a year, are turning out to be a lot of fun for guests and for John and Diane. On weekends when these are scheduled, the inn accepts reservations only for people planning to participate, so you don't have to worry about arriving and finding yourself in the middle of *Murder, She Wrote* if that's not what you had in mind.

For the mystery weekends, the actors check in the same as any other guests, so you really have no idea who is a player and who is not until the whole thing is over. The wine weekends include a French meal and an Italian dinner, preceded by a tasting and discussion of five French or Italian wines and served with three more. Diane says that after either kind of weekend guests inevitably go home feeling they've made some new friends.

The Waverly Inn is listed on the National Register of Historic Places and is the oldest inn in Hendersonville.

HOW TO GET THERE: From I-26 take exit 18B, go west on Route 64 for 2 miles, then right on Main Street. The inn is 1 block up on the left.

Lake Lure Inn 🖼️ 💿

Lake Lure, North Carolina 28746

INNKEEPERS: Jim and Mary Hinkle

ADDRESS/TELEPHONE: P.O. Box 10; (828) 625-2525;
fax (828) 625-9655

WEB SITE: www.lakelureinn.com

E-MAIL: Jimmys@blueridge.net

ROOMS: 50 rooms, all with private bath, desk with telephone, television,
ceiling fan; smoking and non-smoking rooms available.

RATES: $89 to $119, double occupancy; includes continental breakfast.
Some handicapped-accessible rooms. Credit cards accepted. Packages
available. Children welcome.

OPEN: Year-round.

FACILITIES AND ACTIVITIES: Restaurant, informal dining porch,
Moosehead Lounge, pool, exercise room, elevator, Lake Lure, water
sports. Nearby: Casual and fine dining, antiques and crafts shops, Bat
Cave, Chimney Rock Park, The Bottomless Pools, hiking, golf, boating,
tennis, horseback riding, boat tours of Lake Lure, Biltmore House,
Blueridge Parkway, Asheville.

BUSINESS TRAVEL: 25 miles from Asheville; adjacent conference center
will accommodate up to 200; several conference rooms, audiovisual
equipment.

When it opened in 1927, the pleasant, three-story stucco
Mediterranean-style hotel was called "the little Waldorf of the
South," and it attracted such distinguished visitors as Calvin
Coolidge, F. Scott Fitzgerald, Franklin D. Roosevelt, and Emily Post. During
World War II it served as a place of rest and relaxation for Air Force officers.
In more recent years, movie stars Patrick Swayze and Jennifer Grey stayed
here during the filming of *Dirty Dancing*. Located across the road from a
quiet cove on Lake Lure, which *National Geographic* has called the most beautiful man-made lake in the country, the small hotel is backed by rocky
escarpments and tree-covered mountains. With its historic building and
long tradition of Southern hospitality, the inn is a member of the National
Trust for Historic Preservation's Historic Hotels of America.

More standard than you'd expect from all these accolades, the inn is a
comfortable place to stay with a family. Upgraded rooms feature period
reproduction furniture; the rest are furnished with standard motel/hotel

issue, but all have spectacular views of the lake or the mountains and the usual hotel amenities.

Public areas include the long columned lobby with comfortable seating areas—which doubles as a special-events function area—a formal restaurant, informal restaurant, cozy bar, two terraces, and a swimming pool.

A complimentary continental breakfast of pastries, hot and cold cereals, fresh fruits and juices, and hot beverages is served each morning on the sunporch or in the informal restaurant. White linen service for dinner and Sunday brunch are offered in the handsome Tanner Dining Room. The varied menu features steak, chicken, and seafood dishes. You can choose from such specialties as smoked trout and crab cakes, old-fashioned venison stew, chicken with dumplings, linguine and shrimp, or roast duck, then finish off with desserts such as bread and raisin pudding with rum sauce or Lake Lure Mud Pie. The lavish Sunday brunch is extremely popular with residents as well as visitors.

Dominating the very small and cozy Moosehead Lounge is, of course, a gigantic moose head as well as an ornately carved and mirrored bar back. Seating is at the bar and several high tables.

The inn is conveniently located across the street from the town beach and features a boardwalk to the town park and marina, which is equipped with picnic tables and is the departure point for boat tours of the lake. Interesting shops are nearby.

HOW TO GET THERE: The inn is located on U.S. 64/74 southeast of Asheville. You can take scenic U.S. 74 from Asheville or come south on I–26 to exit 18A and turn east on U.S. 64. From the south, take U.S. 108 to U.S. 9 and turn north to Lake Lure.

The Lodge on Lake Lure ♥
Lake Lure, North Carolina 28746

INNKEEPER: Gisela Hopke

ADDRESS/TELEPHONE: 361 Charlotte Drive (mailing address: Route One, Box 519A); (828) 625-2789 or (800) 733-2785; fax (828) 625-2421

WEB SITE: www.lodgeonlakelure.com

E-MAIL: Info@lodgeonlakelure.com

ROOMS: 12, all with private bath; 1 with deck and fireplace.

RATES: $139 to $169, single or double; includes full gourmet breakfast and evening sunset cruise with cocktails and hors d'oeuvres. Inquire about discounts for midweek or weeklong stays; $15 for additional person; 2-night minimum on weekends, 3-night minimum on holidays; high season is April through November. Ask about special packages, including admission to several nearby attractions.

OPEN: Year-round.

FACILITIES AND ACTIVITIES: Lakefront, fishing, 3 canoes, boathouse and boat rentals. Nearby: Restaurants, 2 golf courses, hiking, tubing, tennis, horseback riding, indoor and outdoor swimming pools, antiques and crafts shops, Chimney Rock Park, Biltmore Estate.

"Our guests love our guests," the former owner told us in summing up this B&B inn's ambience. We certainly hit it off with several couples we met there. It was December and there was a nip to the air, so in the evening we all settled in by one of the fireplaces and got to know one another over several bottles of Biltmore Estate wine we'd each bought that day.

It's a matter of kindred spirits. People who are attracted to a very casual atmosphere—with overstuffed chairs pulled around a fireplace, rooms with wormy-chestnut walls, rustic pieces paired with fine art and antiques from around the world, displays of family photos and collectibles, breakfasts ranging from banana-buckwheat pancakes to eggs Benedict, outdoor activities, and a view to die for—are bound to like one another. If this describes you, we guarantee that this is the place for you.

Summer evenings at 5:00 P.M. cocktail time, a staff member gets out the inn's pontoon party barge to take whoever wants to take a tour of the lake, followed on their return by a glass (or two) of wine and some hors d'oeuvres. In the sunny breakfast room, the hanging rack of personalized mugs belonging to frequent guests attests that The Lodge on Lake Lure does everything right.

The lodge is built in European hunting-lodge style that sort of nestles into the steep lakeside without calling attention to itself. Inside, the high vaulted ceilings, hand-hewn beams, and the huge 20-foot-tall stone fireplaces (one with a large gristmill stone imbedded in it) in the two public lounges make you think of one of the national park lodges built during the Depression, just not quite as imposing. The key is really the view from the long row of windows in the sunporch/breakfast room, from many of the guest rooms, and from the great lower level open-air stone veranda that all overlook the deep blue of a crystal-clear mountain lake that *National Geographic* has dubbed the most beautiful man-made lake in this country and one of the top ten in the world, surrounded by steep hillsides of the Blue Ridge Mountains covered with a forest of pines and hardwoods and all capped with a clear sky dotted with puffy clouds.

The inn has capitalized on this wonderful gift of nature by taking advantage of the outdoor possibilities. The covered patio is filled with rockers, hammocks, and other comfortable places to relax. From here a terraced path leads down the steep hillside to the water. Halfway down a deck with bench seating is another place to while away some time. At the water's edge, the boathouse is headquarters for swimming, fishing, and boating (there are three canoes, a paddle boat, and a sea cycle). Its rooftop deck provides yet another perfect spot to sit and enjoy the serenity and beauty that surround you.

Back inside, in addition to the great room with its grand piano, there's a more cozy library, with a woodstove insert in its stone fireplace; a television and VCR; and mounds of books, magazines, and games. The enclosed sunporch creates a light, airy scene for breakfast.

Cozy, comfortable guest rooms, most of which are in the main lodge, boast wormy-chestnut walls and furnishings with country charm—quilts; down comforters; simple locally produced beds, night tables, and dressers; and some four-poster or canopy beds. Private baths have been cleverly tucked wherever they'll fit (one is across the hall). Two rooms boast garden tubs. The extra-large Veranda Suite features a canopy bed, fireplace, and garden tub. Next door, a modern house called Shared Dreams offers four accommodations. The rooms can be rented individually, or a family or group can take the whole house, which also has a living room and kitchen.

In our humble opinion, The Lodge on Lake Lure is a little piece of heaven.

HOW TO GET THERE: From I-26, take Highway 64/74 to Lake Lure. The lodge is on Charlotte Drive, just off Highway 64/74. Turn at the Lake Lure fire station opposite the golf course. Ask for a map when you make reservations.

Greystone Inn 💟
Lake Toxaway, North Carolina 28747

OWNERS: Tim and Bobo Lovelace

ADDRESS/TELEPHONE: Greystone Lane; (828) 966-4700 or (800) 824-5766; fax (828) 862-5689

WEB SITE: www.greystoneinn.com

E-MAIL: greystone@citcom.net

ROOMS: 33, all with private bath, Jacuzzi, television, and telephone; some with fireplace and private balcony. One room handicapped accessible.

RATES: $295 to $600 per couple; single $40 less; includes breakfast and dinner, afternoon tea and cakes, hors d'oeuvres, and all recreational activities except golf fees (greens fees waived on weekends during the shoulder season). Inquire about children's rates. Off-season rates and several packages are available.

OPEN: Year-round.

FACILITIES AND ACTIVITIES: Library-lounge with full bar service. Lake for swimming, boating, waterskiing, and fishing; heated swimming pool, golf course, tennis courts, croquet, horseshoes, lawn games, use of boats, spa. Nearby: Hiking, scenic drives, antiques and resort shops.

BUSINESS TRAVEL: Meeting space for up to 30; can handle groups up to 60.

Ringed by an exclusive resort community, placid Lake Toxaway sits among several thousand acres of heavily wooded highlands. Driving past beautiful lakeshore homes and a golf club, tennis courts, and swimming pool, we followed the road for quite some way before we ultimately came to the centerpiece of the community—the historic Swiss revival–style, four-star Greystone Inn and its additions perched on a promontory peninsula overlooking the lake. In addition to the mansion, there are several two-story almost motel-like buildings—although they do blend in architecturally with the historic house—that contain upscale rooms and suites and another structure that houses the Lakeside Dining Room, which offers a panorama of the lake.

Enter the inn through the enclosed sunporch, the location of a delightful afternoon tea. Just beyond the sunporch is the first of two handsomely paneled lounges, where you check in, and a small gift shop. Behind the first lounge is a second one, which serves as a library and a cozy bar. In winter, fires blaze in both lounges. In good weather guests throw open the sets of French doors in the library and step out onto the stone terrace.

Early in the twentieth century the Greystone was built as the private mansion of Lucy Moltz. When she first decided that she wanted to build a summer place in the woods beside Lake Toxaway, her husband, apparently a practical man, suggested that she camp out there for a while first to see if she really liked it. This she did—in a tent with hardwood floors staffed with eleven servants. After a successful season of "roughing it," she had the 16,000-square-foot mansion called Hillmont built.

Every room in the inn has a magnificent view of the lake or grounds and is furnished in antiques and period reproductions similar to the furniture Mrs. Moltz had. The television sets are hidden in armoires. The rooms are named after the wealthy and famous people who used to visit Lake Toxaway: Vanderbilt, Rockefeller, Wanamaker.

Although we're partial to the quaint charm and eccentricities of the sumptuous rooms in the mansion, those in the Hillmont and Lakeside Suites buildings have their own considerable appeal. They're very spacious and contain a large seating area or separate sitting room, as well as a fireplace, whirlpool tub, ceiling fan, and private porch—some of them screened.

Guests dine in the Lakeside Dining Room, where every table has a great view of the water and the cuisine is gourmet. Breakfast and dinner are included in the nightly rate. Lunch is available at the golf club for an additional cost. During the peak season, jackets are required for gentlemen.

Pampering is what a stay at the Greystone Inn is all about, and you can take that concept to new heights. Services at the Spa at the Greystone Inn are guaranteed to reduce tension and increase your sense of well-being. Half-

and full-day packages as well as a la carte services include body care, skin care, massage therapy, and hair and nail care. Soft music and gentle touch can be followed by a cleansing session in the sauna.

But as lovely as everything is inside the inn, the outdoor activities thrilled us more. In good weather, Tim is available to lead hikes along Horse Pasture River past three magnificent waterfalls. During the warmer months, he takes guests out on the lake on the party boat to watch the sunset. What could be more romantic than a champagne cruise before dinner?

HOW TO GET THERE: The inn is in western North Carolina, 50 miles south of Asheville. It is off U.S. 64, 10 miles east of Cashiers and 17 miles west of Brevard. Turn into the Lake Toxaway entrance. It is clearly marked. Follow the signs 4 miles to the inn. Because you are driving steep, winding roads, it will feel longer, but keep going.

Cataloochee Ranch 🏠
Maggie Valley, North Carolina 28751

INNKEEPERS: Alex and Ashli Aumen

ADDRESS/TELEPHONE: 119 Ranch Drive; (828) 926–1401 or (800) 868–1401; fax (828) 926–9249

WEB SITE: www.cataloochee-ranch.com

E-MAIL: info@cataloochee-ranch.com

ROOMS: 6; plus 6 suites, 12 cabins, 1 house; all with private bath; some with fireplace, whirlpool bath, and/or kitchen.

RATES: $145 to $185 for rooms in the ranch house, $165 to $210 for Silverbell Lodge suites, $195 to $275 for individual cabins; double occupancy; includes breakfast and dinner. Rates for four in a Silverbell Lodge suite are $335 to $355; $50 for each additional child younger than 12 and $60 for an additional guest older than 12; rates for 4 in a cabin are $360 to $385; $50 for a child younger than 12, $60 for a guest older than 12.

OPEN: April 1 through November 30 and December 26 to January 3.

FACILITIES AND ACTIVITIES: Pond, pool, horseback riding, tennis court, children's playground, ranch activities. Nearby: White-water rafting, golf courses, Appalachian Trail, Great Smoky Mountains National Park, Cherokee Indian Reservation, Ghost Town in the Sky, Tweetsie Railroad, Cataloochee Ski Area.

Meeting space will accommodate up to 50; ideal for executive retreats.

*I*t doesn't get much better than this, we thought—sitting astride a horse surveying more than a thousand acres of mountaintop ranch with vistas of the Great Smoky and Blue Ridge Mountains in the distance and the town of Maggie Valley below. *Cataloochee* is believed to be the Cherokee word for "wave upon wave," and this is just what we saw from the Cataloochee Ranch—wave upon wave of mountain peaks. We quickly realized that anyone who loves the active outdoor life will revel in the exciting activities at the Cataloochee Ranch. And best yet, we didn't have to sleep on the ground or do our own cooking over a campfire. We found plenty of creature comforts.

In the olden days before everyone's life was so dominated by television, movies, video games, and the Internet, there was good, clean family fun of quite another sort, and you can discover or rediscover it at the ranch. In addition to swimming, fishing, horseback riding, and hiking, guests at the ranch join in storytelling, clogging, square dancing, lawn games, hayrides, bonfires, and marshmallow roasts. There's a tennis court as well and three entrances directly into the Great Smoky Mountains National Park.

The ranch with overnight lodging, which has evolved into a resort, was founded in 1933. When the first location was absorbed by the newly created Great Smoky Mountains National Park, the ranch was moved to the lofty 5,000-foot peaks of Fie Top Mountain in 1938. The property's sturdy stone-and-log cattle barn became the main ranch house, and several original cabins continue to provide comfortable accommodations. To these have been added several more cabins and the Silverbell Lodge, which contains six suites.

We particularly liked the suites in the Silverbell Lodge. We thought the cathedral ceiling and fireplace in the living room and the loft bedroom were just right. The cabins are appealing, too. All of them have a fireplace, refrigerator, coffeemaker, and radio. Four of them boast a whirlpool, wet bar, and private deck. Several of the suites and cabins have an additional one or more bedrooms, which make them perfect for families or friends.

Although there are so many activities to tempt you away to the far reaches of the ranch, the good home cooking served family style in the ranch house dining room may make you want to stay close by. The modified American plan provides you with breakfast and dinner daily. Lunch and box lunches are available at an additional charge. Fresh mountain-grown products are used to create the rib-sticking meals, and the breads, jellies, and preserves are homemade. Entrees might feature rainbow trout or wild game in season. Frequent outdoor barbecues or "steak outs" are a big hit with all ages.

There's so much to experience at the ranch, you couldn't possibly get the full benefit of a ranch vacation in a short stay, so one-night visits aren't encouraged. In fact, we recommend that you plan on at least a week to unwind from the stresses of your everyday life.

HOW TO GET THERE: At the west end of Maggie Valley, look for the CAT-ALOOCHEE RANCH sign at the Ghost Town in the Sky attraction. The ranch is located 3 miles up the paved Fie Top Road.

The Tranquil House Inn
Manteo, North Carolina 27954

INNKEEPERS: Don and Lauri Just

ADDRESS/TELEPHONE: Queen Elizabeth Street (mailing address: P.O. Box 2045); (252) 473-1404 or (800) 458-7069; fax (252) 473-1526

WEB SITE: www.tranquilinn.com

E-MAIL: djust1587@aol.com

ROOMS: 25, all with private bath, television, and telephone; some with wheelchair access. No-smoking rooms available.

RATES: $89 to $189, single or double, seasonal; includes continental breakfast buffet each morning and wine and cheese at check-in. No charge for 1 or 2 children under 16 in the same room as adult.

OPEN: Year-round.

FACILITIES AND ACTIVITIES: Restaurant on premises open for dinner; touring bikes. Nearby: Walk to restaurants and shops; Fort Raleigh National Historic Site, Elizabeth II State Historic Site, Elizabethan Gardens, North Carolina Aquarium, all kinds of fishing.

*T*he Tranquil House Inn is strikingly attractive, inside and out. The building is a reproduction of a typical century-old Outer Banks inn. The interior, done in cypress, furnished with light pine furniture and decorated with Oriental rugs, seems as bright and sunny as the docks outside. Stained-glass windows and handmade comforters in the guest rooms whisper luxury. Perhaps because of its location right on Shallowbag Bay, a sense of quiet permeates the place, even though it is close to Manteo's tourist activities.

And, nice as it is, you probably won't spend many daylight hours in the inn because there is so much to do in and around Manteo. The Manteo Walking Tour takes a couple of hours and instructs you in much of the area's early history, including the mystery of the colony set up by Sir Walter Raleigh that disappeared sometime between 1587 and 1591, while its leader was away procuring supplies.

People fish and crab right from the docks here, and the inn has bikes if you want to pedal around the rest of the town.

One of the town's "must see" attractions is one of the very first Christmas shops in the United States, which has been around for a long time. Over the years, this wonderful shop has not lost its magic.

When you need to sit down for a while, one of the most popular spots at the inn is on the second-floor deck, from which you can watch boats maneuvering in and out of their slips in the marina.

At dinnertime, the inn's restaurant, 1587, offers a variety of gourmet entrees, including such unusual dishes as seared salmon and puff pastry tower with flash-sautéed leeks, fried spinach, and lemon-artichoke beurre blanc. It also has an above-average wine list.

HOW TO GET THERE: Take Highway 64 from the west or Highway 158 from the north. Follow the signs for the Elizabeth II State Historic Site. You'll see the inn on the Manteo waterfront. Sir Walter Raleigh Street leads directly to the inn.

Pine Crest Inn
Pinehurst, North Carolina 28374

INNKEEPER: Peter Barrett

ADDRESS/TELEPHONE: 50 Dogwood Road; (910) 295–6121 or (800) 371–2545; fax (910) 295–4880

WEB SITE: www.pinecrestinnpinehurst.com

E-MAIL: frondesk@pinecrestinnpinehurst.com

ROOMS: 40; all with private bath, cable television, and telephone. Some handicapped-accessible rooms.

RATES: $59 to $88 per person, double occupancy, depending on season; single, $20 to $50 more; includes breakfast and dinner. Corner rooms $10 extra. Inquire about package rates including greens fees. Credit cards accepted. Children welcome.

OPEN: Year-round.

FACILITIES AND ACTIVITIES: Breakfast and dinner open to the public; bar. Access to Pinehurst Country Club golf course and 35 other area courses. Nearby: Tennis, horseback riding, skeet shooting; fishing, sailing, and swimming on Pinehurst Lake.

*Y*ou'll always find something going on at Pine Crest Inn. Most people come for the golf. Visitors at the inn are afforded access to the Pinehurst Country Club golf course and thirty-five other area courses; the inn is happy to set up times for you. Pinehurst is famous for the number and quality of its golf courses. But golf is by no means the only attraction at the inn.

The dining room is famous. Executive Chef Carl Jackson has been here more than sixty years; his assistant and nephew, Chef Peter Jackson, has been here about thirty years. Local folks as well as inn guests fill up the dining room regularly. The menu changes every day. It features everything from spaghetti to roast leg of spring lamb and homemade soups, breads, and desserts. The Happy Heart Dinner, a low-fat, low-cholesterol offering, is available each day. As for desserts, we find the Château Margaux Sundae elegant and appropriate to our growing interest in lower-fat diets. It's made of orange sherbet, orange slices, and Château LaSalle wine.

The inn has piano-bar music for dancing in the lounge. Sports talk in the bar is by no means limited to golf, popular as it is. The area also has good tennis and many horse farms.

For all its activity, the inn is definitely a family affair, the kind of place that includes the names and pictures of all the staff and many guests in its advertising. The easy hospitality makes you feel as though you've known everyone here forever.

HOW TO GET THERE: U.S. 1 and 15–501 go directly into Pinehurst. When you get into the town, follow the TO VILLAGE SHOPS signs to the market square. The inn is on Dogwood Road, 1 block from the center of the village.

The Fearrington House 💚
Pittsboro, North Carolina 27312

INNKEEPER: Richard M. Delany

ADDRESS/TELEPHONE: 2000 Fearrington Village Center;
(919) 542–2121 or (800) 733–2785; fax (919) 542–4202

WEB SITE: www.fearrington.com

E-MAIL: fhouse@fearrington.com

ROOMS: 31, all with private bath, cable television, telephone, hair dryer, iron and ironing board; some with wheelchair access. No-smoking inn.

RATES: $175 to $350 per room; includes full breakfast, afternoon tea.

OPEN: Year-round.

FACILITIES AND ACTIVITIES: Fearrington House Restaurant, with wheelchair access, open to guests and public Tuesday through Saturday, 6:00 to 9:00 P.M., and Sunday, 6:00 to 8:00 P.M. The Fearrington Market Cafe is open Monday through Friday for lunch and dinner 9:00 A.M. to 7:00 P.M., Saturday and Sunday 9:00 A.M. to 6:00 P.M. Galloways Bar, shops, swim and croquet club.

BUSINESS TRAVEL: Meeting space to accommodate up to 200; computer-friendly telephones; fax and copy service.

"It's not so much where you go, but how you're treated that's hospitality" is founder R. B. Fitch's Fearrington Formula, which has earned The Fearrington House international renown as well as the coveted five-diamond rating for both its accommodations and its restau-

rant—the only establishment in North Carolina to do so. Who wouldn't like to investigate this extraordinary inn to see what it's all about? In this particular case, however, we decided to visit because R. B.'s special approach to development piqued our curiosity.

We'd been told that The Fearrington House isn't just a fabulous inn but a complete concept—but that's pretty nebulous. Right up until the very moment we arrived, we were still more than a little hazy about how an award-winning inn and restaurant, combined with a village of shops and services, residential neighborhoods, gardens and common spaces—all newly created from scratch out of farm land while leaving some of the fields and buildings intact—fit together as a whole.

Our first hint that we were on to something unique was when we came to the field of Belties (a rare breed of Scottish Belted Galloway cattle that are black at both ends with a wide white band around the middle) at the entrance to the planned community. We registered the signature silo, a former barn—now a special events facility—the graceful 1927 white-columned colonial-style home that now houses the restaurant, and numerous small many-gabled buildings scattered about a square with tasteful new neighborhoods stretching out beyond. As we drove up a flower-lined lane, so clever is the design that we weren't sure which was the inn—nothing looked big enough.

As it turned out, we were right to wonder. The inn rooms are scattered in multiple buildings in two areas. The original section, located behind the restaurant and wrapped around several courtyards, is contained in little houselike buildings with gabled roofs. Newly added rooms are connected to some of the businesses.

We knew we were in for an exceptional level of service when several blazer-clad staff members rushed out to unload our bags and escort us to registration, then whisked us to our magnificent accommodations across the square—an oversized room with subdued colors, a king-size bed, English-pine antiques, original art, a cozy little sitting area in a window alcove, an extensive entertainment system, and a huge bathroom with every amenity we could think of. In all, this was a room fit for royalty, and it wasn't even one of the most deluxe rooms; some feature separate sitting area, fireplace, and/or whirlpool bath.

Fearrington Village

The twenty-year-old brainchild of R. B. and the late Jenny Fitch, the planned community is the result of their quest to build a low-key, high-style lifestyle for themselves and others when they bought the dairy farm that had been in the Fearrington family for almost 200 years. They combined all the elements they liked about places they'd traveled, particularly European villages, and strove to balance private space and common space, building structures and open land. What they created is a real village where people live and play, where shops and service businesses provide what residents and visitors need, and where guests can come to stay and play. These disparate elements blend into a coherent whole that could well be copied by developers and town planners nationwide.

Many of the original farm buildings have found new life as integral parts of the town. The former granary is home to the Market, which features a Mediterranean bistrolike cafe. Dovecote: A Home and Garden Shop, located in the old milking barn, is the starting point for formal garden tours with the director of landscape design. The Potting Shed, located in the old corn crib, sells more than 200 species of plants propagated from Fearrington's gardens.

In new buildings, McIntyre's Fine Books and Bookends is as comfortable as your own living room, but with enough books to keep you busy for life. The Cottage Shop sells fine linens and accents. Other shops purvey jewelry, pottery, and other specialties. A bank, travel agency, and beauty shop are on-site, too.

Another of the passions of the multitalented Jenny Fitch was gardening, and she developed the formal and informal gardens at Fearrington. Take a stroll or several around the knot, rose, perennial, and herb gardens.

Once they'd established a town, the Fitches started the restaurant. Jenny, who studied French cooking for seven years, was the first executive chef. The next best thing to eating at the Fearrington House is buying a copy of Jenny's *The Fearrington House Cookbook: A Celebration of Food, Flowers, and Herbs*.

The Fitches put their creative talents to work developing an inn that would meet their personal ideas of a luxurious getaway. Central to their philosophy is the Fearrington Formula: providing highly attentive, yet unobtrusive service. Although Jenny is gone, we wonder what R. B. will do next.

If the good weather and our curiosity about the hamlet, the spectacular gardens, the fascinating shops, and divine eateries hadn't begged us to come out to explore, we could cheerfully have stayed cocooned in our room for the duration.

We headed back to the village center (a walk of less than half a block) to investigate. Explorations work up an appetite, so we stopped in the cozy Garden Room for a substantial afternoon tea of iced and hot English teas, cookies, tea cakes, scones, and cheese and crackers to tide us over until dinner.

Sophisticated regional cuisine prepared according to classical techniques blends Southern basics with haute cuisine. Today's chefs prepare staples such as grits or fried green tomatoes and exotic fare such as ostrich or antelope carpaccio for a prix fixe four-course dinner Tuesday through Sunday. Impeccable service and a comfortable and upscale atmosphere (jacket and tie for gentlemen are recommended) combine to make a perfect evening.

A hearty breakfast is served to guests on one of the restaurant's glassed-in porches. The mornings we were there, the choices included freshly squeezed juice, warm muffins and just-baked breads, yogurt, granola, fresh fruit, eggs to order, fried cheese grits, French toast with cinnamon syrup, and hickory-smoked bacon. If you're hungry at midday, grab a quick lunch at the deli or the Market Cafe. And don't forget about the afternoon tea.

We loved wandering through the gardens—drinking in both the sights and smells. If we had had more time, we could have used the sports facilities in the residential area: the swim and croquet club and the hiking and biking trails.

One last suggestion: If you're departing on a Tuesday afternoon, take home some produce, fresh baked goods, flowers, or local cheeses from the Fearrington Farmers' Market—an informal gathering of local producers.

HOW TO GET THERE: Fearrington is 8 miles south of Chapel Hill on U.S. 15/501 toward Pittsboro.

The Orchard Inn 💙
Saluda, North Carolina 28773

INNKEEPERS: Kathy and Bob Thompson

ADDRESS/TELEPHONE: Route 176 (mailing address: P.O. Box 128); (828) 749-5471 or (800) 581-3800; fax (828) 749-9805

WEB SITE: www.orchardinn.com

E-MAIL: orchard@saluda.tds.net

ROOMS: 9 in main house, plus 4 cottage suites; all with private bath; some with fireplace and whirlpool tub. No-smoking inn.

RATES: $119 to $245, single or double; includes full breakfast.

2-night minimum stay for advance reservations on weekends. Inquire about special conference rates. Credit cards accepted. Children older than 12 are comfortable at the inn.

OPEN: Year-round.

FACILITIES AND ACTIVITIES: Dinner Tuesday through Saturday, open to public by reservation; full wine and beer service. Conference room, gift shop, library, horseshoes, nature trail, hiking, birding. Nearby: Antiques and crafts shops, Biltmore Estate, Carl Sandburg home.

This place simply overwhelmed me. It sits on eighteen wooded acres at the top of the Saluda rise, at an elevation of 2,500 feet. All you can see in any direction are treetops and mountains. It is unbelievably quiet.

As you enter the inn from the front porch, you step into a huge living room where beautifully arranged plants, paintings, antiques, and books all invite your attention. Guest rooms are also decorated in an upscale country style.

In the small cottages, the atmosphere is romantic, with whirlpool tubs, fireplaces, wormy-chestnut paneling, and twig furniture.

For many years this well-established inn has attracted guests from all over with gourmet cooking and easy hospitality. Kathy and Bob Thompson, who enjoyed the inn as guests for ten years prior to becoming innkeepers, have come to this place full of good humor, energy, and ideas. They have certainly kept the inn's old following and are building their own coterie of new and repeat guests.

The food is still a draw, too. Award-winning chef Sallie Corley brings her native South Carolina talent for traditional dishes such as mountain trout, Low Country filet, and pan-seared quail.

For a romantic evening, dine on the glassed-in porch that overlooks the Warrior Mountain Range. As the day fades and candles are lit, classical music chases back the shadows, and from the nearby kitchen come the aromas of garlic, wine, and grilled meats.

HOW TO GET THERE: The Orchard Inn is in western North Carolina, on Highway 176 between Saluda and Tryon. From I–26 north of Hendersonville, take exit 28 and follow the connector road (West Ozone Drive) to Route 176. Turn left on 176, and drive ½ mile. The inn is on your right.

Pine Needles Lodge and Golf Club
Southern Pines, North Carolina 28388

INNKEEPER: Peggy Kirk Bell

ADDRESS/TELEPHONE: 1005 Midland Road (mailing address: P.O. Box 88); (910) 692-7111 or (800) 747-7272; fax (910) 693-4324

WEB SITE: www.pineneedles-midpines.com

E-MAIL: info@rossresorts.com

ROOMS: 11 rustic lodges contain a total of 72 rooms, all with private bath, television, telephone, coffeemaker, safe, voice mail, hair dryer, balcony.

RATES: $100 to $140 per person, double occupancy; includes 3 meals daily. Discounts are available for weekday stays and groups. Credit cards accepted.

OPEN: Year-round.

FACILITIES AND ACTIVITIES: All of the chalet-style lodges are connected to the clubhouse, which contains a full-service dining room, lounge, and golf shop. Pine Needles Donald Ross–designed golf course. Meeting and conference facilities, swimming pool, lighted grass tennis courts, extensive practice facilities. Located in the sandhills of North Carolina, known for many golf courses and horse farms.

*S*omething new is always going on at Pine Needles, so whatever is written now, you can bet there will be more by the time you read this. A new lodge with eight bedrooms was completed in May 2001. It's not so long ago that the lobby and rooms were redecorated, so here's what you'll almost certainly find there: In the main lobby, a dark green carpet bordered in red and white dramatically sets off light country pine furniture and drapes and upholstery done in tweeds and a burgundy, green, and tan plaid known as Pine Needles Plaid. The plaid is used throughout Pine Needles, even on brochures.

The room has a vaulted ceiling and a raised-hearth fireplace in the brick wall along the far end. In the spring and summer, vases of flowers decorate the massive oak mantel.

The Bells built the inn mainly so that Peggy would have a place to teach golf. Certainly golf is the main attraction for most people who stay here.

Guests especially like knowing that the course will never be crowded, because play is restricted to guests of the inn, if the inn is full, or will include outside players to a maximum of 140 players in off-seasons. Pine Needles has added many golf learning centers, concentrated three- and four-day schools that take as many as sixteen people, intended for the intense golfer who wants a precise school to develop specific skills. It would be a good idea to write or call for more information, because schedules will certainly change often.

We don't golf, but we could still stay all but forever and have a good time. The other facilities are first-class, especially the large heated swimming pool. The food is good; the wine list is above average. The area is secluded and usually quiet. (Peggy and members of the family teach an amazing number of "Golfari" sessions, basically golf workshops, for groups ranging from all women to young people. If you want a quiet escape, it is important to make sure your visit doesn't overlap with a Golfari.)

Although Pine Needles has several different kinds of guest rooms, we think you can get an accurate picture of the new look if you know that many rooms have brass headboards but are still comfortable enough that you feel free to kick off your shoes and sprawl. The Pine Needles expression for it is "casual elegance."

During the off-season the inn offers a B&B package, but in the main season golf takes precedence.

HOW TO GET THERE: Pine Needles is ¼ mile off U.S. Highway 1 on NC Route 2 between Pinehurst and Southern Pines.

Grandview Lodge
Waynesville, North Carolina 28786

INNKEEPERS: Stan and Linda Arnold

ADDRESS/TELEPHONE: 466 Lickstone Road; (828) 456-5212 or (800) 255-7826; fax (828) 452-5432

WEB SITE: www.grandviewlodgenc.com

E-MAIL: innkeeper@grandviewlodgenc.com

ROOMS: 9 in main lodge and attached porch, plus 2 two-room apartments; all with private bath; 2 beds, one of which is a king or queen; and television. Guest rooms, living and dining rooms air-conditioned. No-smoking inn.

RATES: $110 to $120, double occupancy; $85, single; includes breakfast and dinner. Inquire about rates for children and apartments. Minimum stay of 2 nights high season and holidays. Credit cards accepted.

OPEN: Year-round.

FACILITIES AND ACTIVITIES: Lunch by special arrangement, dinner open to public by reservation, brown bagging permitted. Library, game room, shuffleboard courts. Nearby: Golf at Waynesville and Laurel Ridge country clubs, tennis, outlet shopping, easy access to Blue Ridge Parkway, and many historic sites.

*S*tan and Linda Arnold run Grandview Lodge much as it has been operated for the past fifty-plus years. It's furnished with what Stan calls "the kind of antiques you're not afraid to sit on, but definitely not rustic. More like Grandmother's house." They've arranged two separate groupings of furniture in the living room, one for watching television and one for conversation and maybe (Stan hopes) bridge games.

Just as Stan says the furniture's not rustic, Linda says the cooking's not Southern in the old sense. She cooks with herbs from her garden, fresh garden vegetables that a neighbor brings pot-ready, fresh local fruits, and whole-grain flours. But you're not getting into health-nut meals—unless you consider barbecued beef ribs, corn pudding, and homemade ice cream hair-

shirt. Linda also makes her Chocoholic Tart that has in it two kinds of chocolate plus chocolate liqueur. Dinner is not served Sunday night.

Grandview now offers one thing we're relatively sure you can't find at any other inn in the South—an innkeeper who speaks Polish, Russian, German, and Hebrew. It sounds like a talent Stan might not get to use often in Waynesville, but the area is increasingly becoming known for its international folk-dance festivals, and in past seasons, dancers from eleven foreign countries came. Stan had a ball!

HOW TO GET THERE: From I-40, take U.S. 23-74 to exit 98 (West Waynesville). Turn east (follow the WAYNESVILLE signs). Turn left at the first traffic light onto South Main Street. At the second traffic light, turn right onto Allens Creek Road. Go exactly 1 mile. Turn left at the GRANDVIEW LODGE sign onto Lickstone Road and continue ⁴/₁₀ mile up a winding road to the lodge driveway on your right. Stan and Linda will send a map when you make reservations.

The Old Stone Inn
Waynesville, North Carolina 28786

INNKEEPERS: Cindy and Robert Zinser

ADDRESS/TELEPHONE: 109 Dolan Road; (828) 456-3333 or (800) 432-8499

WEB SITE: www.oldstoneinn.com

ROOMS: 18 rooms and 4 suites in 7 separate buildings; all with private bath and television.

RATES: $104 to $164, double; single, $15 less; includes full breakfast. Not appropriate for children. Credit cards accepted.

OPEN: Closed January 1 to Good Friday.

FACILITIES AND ACTIVITIES: Restaurant; wine and beer available. Game room with television and piano, Wendell's Attic reading lounge; robes in cottages and Chestnut Rooms. Nearby: Walking distance to Waynesville shops; short drive to hiking, biking, tubing, white-water rafting, trout fishing, rockhounding, horseback riding; golf at five local courses; crafts museums and shops; Great Smoky Mountain Railway; 30-minute drive to Cherokee or Asheville. Inquire about special mountain activity package.

This rustic inn, which used to be known as Heath Lodge, sits under huge oak trees, surrounded by dogwoods, rhododendrons, and mountain laurels, at an elevation of about 3,200 feet, in the Smokies. In summer, the foliage shuts out the hot sun and almost all sounds of civilization. You feel isolated in the woods.

But you're not. A quick walk down the hill takes you into Waynesville, a community full of interesting crafts and art shops, a great Mast Farm store, and lots of interesting nooks and crannies. Even a bookstore.

At one time the inn's dining room served a one-price, no selection, family-style meal, but service is now from a menu. The food itself is still Southern regional, pretty much the same cuisine, only now you have more choices, with seatings at 6:00 and 8:00 P.M. as well as appetizers and wine in a guest lounge off the dining room from 4:00 to 8:00 P.M. This means you can have anything from a full-course meal in the dining room, with entrees such as marinated lamb chops or a tart of smoked gouda with wild mushrooms, to a light-bite sitting on the sofa beside the fire.

If you've been here before, you'll be surprised when you see the revamped guest lounge and dining room. The dining room has been made smaller and more intimate, seating about thirty-six people at small tables for two and four. In the new guest lounge, you'll find several seating groups of sofas and chairs, with rockers in front of the fire and lots of books, games, and puzzles. The space is comfortable, with stone walls, log ceiling, quilts, and fireplace working together to create a mountain atmosphere.

Both rooms are in a stone and log building with a huge fireplace, hardwood floor, and exposed beams. For more quiet moments, guests like the second-floor lounge; this is where we go to read.

The shady site, rustic buildings, comfortable rooms, and pleasantly served food (with wine or beer, a triumph in much of North Carolina) make this a great rejuvenating spot.

HOW TO GET THERE: From Highway 23, exit onto 276 south and continue to Dellwood Road, the second stoplight. Turn right and go 4/10 mile to Love Lane, turn right, and drive uphill to Dolan Road. Turn left; the lodge is on your left.

The Swag
Waynesville, North Carolina 28786

INNKEEPER: Deener Matthews

ADDRESS/TELEPHONE: 2300 Swag Road (mailing address: Route 2, Box 280A); (828) 926-0430 or (800) 789-7672; fax (828) 926-2036

WEB SITE: www.theswag.com

E-MAIL: dianem@theswag.com

ROOMS: 16 rooms, plus 3 cabins; all with private bath, feather bed, small refrigerator, robes, CD player, coffeemaker, coffee grinder with beans; 9 with fireplace or woodstove; some with whirlpool or steam shower; 2 with wheelchair access. No-smoking inn.

RATES: $265 to $515 weekdays, $325 to $580 weekends, single or double, includes 3 meals daily, tea-time cookies, and an hour of hors d'oeuvres. Extra person in room $80 to $130. Children especially welcome. Two-night minimum stay. Corporate packages and group rates. Credit cards accepted.

OPEN: May through November (closed weekend before Thanksgiving).

FACILITIES AND ACTIVITIES: Restaurant, brown bagging permitted. Gift shop, library of books and videos, racquetball court, sauna, croquet, badminton, pond, 3 miles of hiking trails with marked plants and trees on Swag property, special-interest events, entrance to hiking trails in Great Smoky Mountains National Park. Nearby: Asheville and Biltmore Estate, Maggie Valley.

BUSINESS TRAVEL: Meeting space and the isolated location are ideal for small meetings and retreats.

The Swag is a collection of pioneer buildings that, back in the early 1970s, were hauled up the mountain, where they were grouped about vast, grassy grounds right at the edge of the Great Smoky Mountains National Park. The vista from this 250-acre privately owned mountaintop is more than 50 miles.

Everything is set up to make the most of the views and the outdoors: big windows and porches, rockers and hammocks, picnic nooks, a path, and several overlooks. We dropped into a pair of Adirondack chairs arranged along the brow of the mountain to contemplate the view, and we were mesmerized. You will be, too.

Inside, the public and guest rooms vary in detail but have in common rough wood walls, exposed beams, and wood floors. The rustic ambience contrasts with such luxuries as coffee grinders and coffeemakers, hair dryers, terry-cloth robes, and handmade rugs. From many of the rooms you have a view of the mountains from your windows or your private porch.

Accommodations are also offered in several cabins, including Chestnut Lodge. Recently this lodge was gutted so that its three guest rooms could be converted to two "super" rooms. Each of these new-and-improved accommodations now boasts a sleeping loft with a sofa, reading lamps, and a view as well as two bathrooms, one of which sports a whirlpool and separate steam shower and the other of which has a skylight shower. The lodge's common living room, which is often used for lectures in the special-events series, has a new library loft with a Putnam rolling ladder to reach the high shelves.

You find more contrasts in the dining room. The room itself is rustic, with more wood walls and floors, plus tables that were handmade by a Tennessee furniture maker. Yet the service is professional. The food is sophisticated enough to include shredded jicama in a salad and simple enough to offer fresh trout without unnecessary extra trappings.

The library is filled with books stashed in old, stacked wooden crates, organized by category, and has an honor borrowing system. The collection ranges from local history to philosophy, with lots of mysteries, science fiction, and nature books as well. The inn also has a theological library.

What will come as a complete surprise to you is that deep in the bowels of the inn, burrowed into the mountain, is a racquetball court. So those Type-A personalities, to whom a stiff competition of some sort is their only idea of relaxation, won't have to worry about being bored. And when they're finished torturing their bodies, they can sweat off some more calories in the sauna.

You could drive down the mountain to any number of tourist attractions in the area—but it seems to us that once you get up to the top of this mountain, walk in the woods, and look down on range after range of mountains following one another into the clouds, you've got all the entertainment you could possibly need.

HOW TO GET THERE: From I–40, take exit 20. Go south on Route 276 for 2⁸/₁₀ miles, turn right on Hemphill Road, and drive about 4 miles to the private road that winds up the mountain to the inn. The road is narrow and rough; it's only a few miles long but will feel much longer.

Brookstown Inn
Winston-Salem, North Carolina 27101

INNKEEPER: Gary Colbert

ADDRESS/TELEPHONE: 200 Brookstown Avenue; (336) 725–1120;
reservations (800) 845–4262; fax (336) 773–0147

WEB SITE: www.Brookstowninn.com

E-MAIL: Brookstowninn@aol.com

ROOMS: 71; all with private bath, television, electronic lock system;
some with wet bar, garden tub, and private sitting room; some with
wheelchair access. Two rooms equipped for the handicapped.

RATES: $100 to $150; includes European-style breakfast and evening
wine and cheese party, cookies and milk at 8:00 P.M., turndown service,
morning newspaper. Children under 12, free; 12 and older, $20. Credit
cards accepted.

OPEN: Year-round.

FACILITIES AND ACTIVITIES: State-of-the-art exercise facility. Nearby:
Restaurants, Old Salem, local colleges, galleries, museums.

BUSINESS TRAVEL: Located 3 blocks from business district. Meeting
facilities, reception space, photocopier, fax available; dataports.

As a B&B inn, this old building is in its fourth incarnation. It was
built in 1837 by the Moravians to be a cotton mill. Then it
became a flour mill and later a storage building for a moving
company. The mill was restored as an inn and a complex of specialty shops
and restaurants in 1984. It's listed on the National Register of Historic Places.

As often happens in building within an existing large structure, the new
spaces are larger than average, with spectacularly high ceilings, surprising

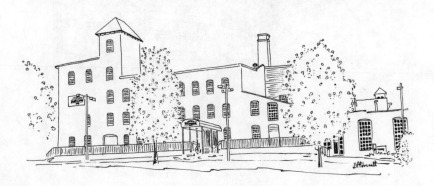

twists and turns, nooks and crannies, and a wealth of visual interest in exposed beams, old brick, and historic artifacts.

More specifically: On the fourth floor, in what originally was a dormitory for girls who worked in the cotton mill, renovators found and have preserved behind glass a plaster wall full of graffiti. The old factory boiler visually dominates Darryl's Restaurant. In guest rooms, architectural features of the original building, such as brick buttresses, unusual roof slopes, and interesting spaces, have been incorporated into the design of the room.

The decor throughout the inn is Early American, appropriate to the building and its Old Salem connection, without being oppressive. Quilts decorate lobby walls; country touches like hand-woven baskets, pieces of pewter, and silk flowers are scattered throughout the public areas. The huge open spaces keep it from feeling at all cluttered. In the guest rooms, furnishings are reproductions appropriate for the period set off with Wedgwood-blue stenciling around the windows. The poster beds are covered with handmade quilts.

In the breakfast room, which has brick floors and comfortable club chairs around the tables, your European-style breakfast is served each morning.

The old Moravians were famous for their hospitality. Brookstown Inn is doing a remarkably good job communicating that spirit at the same time it offers the modern creature comforts you expect from a first-class hostelry.

HOW TO GET THERE: Coming from the west on I-40 Business, take the Cherry Street exit. Turn right when you come to the light at the top of the ramp, onto Marshall Street. Follow the inn signs, turning left onto Brookstown Avenue. The inn is on the right. Coming from the east on I-40 Business, take the Cherry Street exit. As you come to the light coming off the ramp, turn left onto First Street. Go 1 block and turn left on Marshall. Follow the inn signs, turning left on Brookstown.

Select List of
Other North Carolina Inns

Haywood Park Hotel
1 Battery Park
Asheville, NC 28801
(828) 252-2522 or (800) 228-2522

Historic commercial building downtown, 33 suites, some with whirlpool; restaurants, bars, shops.

Balsam Mountain Inn
Seven Springs Drive off US 23/74
Balsam, NC 28707
(828) 456-9498 or (800) 224-9498

1908 neoclassical Victorian inn on twenty-six acres; 50 rooms; 100-foot-long porches; restaurant.

Ellerbe Springs Inn
2527 North U.S. 220
Ellerbe, NC 28338
(910) 652-5600 or (800) 248-6467

1857 inn and guest house; 16 rooms, some with gas-log fireplace; Murder Mystery Weekends monthly; restaurant, full breakfast, other refreshments.

Rubin Osceola Lake

P.O. Box 2258
Hendersonville, NC 28793
(828) 692-2544

Rustic lodge built in 1902; 80 rooms; restaurant; continental breakfast buffet, evening tea and coffee.

First Colony Inn

Milepost 16
Nags Head, NC 27959
(252) 441-2343 or (800) 368-9390

Beach inn with wraparound porches; 26 rooms; breakfast buffet, afternoon tea.

Snowbird Mountain Lodge

276 Santeetlah Road
Robbinsville, NC 28771
(800) 941-9290

1940s stone and chestnut lodge; 22 rooms; full American plan.

South Carolina

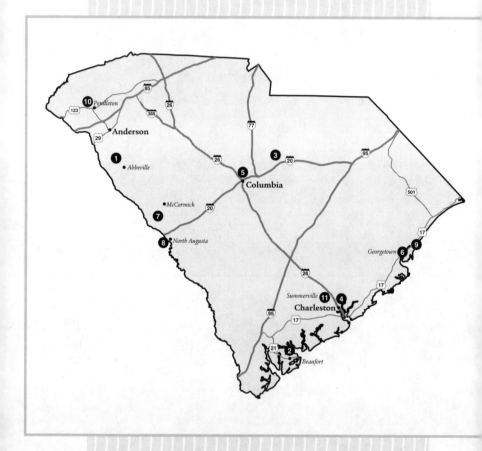

South Carolina

Numbers on map refer to towns numbered below.

* A Top Pick Inn

Belmont Inn ♥ ©©

Abbeville, South Carolina 29620

INNKEEPERS: Alan and Audrey Peterson

ADDRESS/TELEPHONE: 104 East Pickens Street; (864) 459–9625 or
(877) 459–8118; fax (864) 459–9625.

WEB SITE: BelmontInn.net

E-MAIL: BelmontInn@wctel.net

ROOMS: 25 rooms and suites, all with private bath, cable television, telephone, clock radio, coffeemaker. No-smoking inn.

RATES: $54 to $79, double occupancy, nonplay weekends; $74 to $99
play weekends; includes continental breakfast. Golf packages. Credit
cards accepted.

OPEN: Year-round.

FACILITIES AND ACTIVITIES: Restaurant, lounge, porches, meeting
rooms, banquet facilities. Nearby: Abbeville Opera House, Burt-Stark
House, Abbeville County Museum, Trinity Episcopal Church, Park Seed,
Emerald Farms, Old 96 District, Erskine College, Richard B. Russell
Lake; water sports, tennis, golf.

BUSINESS TRAVEL: Meeting rooms and banquet facilities.

We love quaint, sleepy little Abbeville, which is primarily grouped
around a delightful town square. This hamlet has two claims to
fame. First, it bills itself as the Birthplace and Deathbed of the
Confederacy because the secession papers were first read in Abbeville in 1860
and the rebel cause died when the War Council formally disbanded here in
1865 during its flight from Richmond. Abbeville's 1908 Opera House, which
brought a steady stream of performers to tread its boards, from vaudevillians
such as Fanny Brice and Jimmy Durante to serious thespians, still attracts visitors to Abbeville with an impressive summer and winter season of theatricals.

Visiting stars and the fans who came to see them stayed in the sturdy
brick hotel just across the street from the Opera House. Built in 1903 and
originally called the Eureka, but now known as the Belmont Inn, it also
catered to railroad and textile executives and remained in business long after
the Opera House itself closed. Although the inn sat empty from 1972 to
1982, it was fully restored and reopened in 1984. Listed on the National Register of Historic Places, the intimate inn continues to offer delightful accommodations. The charm of the early twentieth century is reflected in the large

rooms, high ceilings, fireplaces, and the sweeping veranda. We were delighted with its understated ambience when we stayed there one summer weekend.

Our light, airy room was simply and tastefully furnished with antiques and period reproductions. Its best feature, however, was its private veranda—the only one in the inn. We enjoyed a queen-size bed (other rooms offer kings or twins). Armoires were a matter of course here long before they became a popular way for most modern hotels to hide televisions and other amenities, simply because these rooms weren't built with closets. Although we had cable television, we never turned it on.

The inn's restaurant is the scene of an extensive twenty-item continental breakfast of fruits, juices, waffles, several kinds of muffins and Danishes, and hot beverages. The restaurant is also open to the public for dinner and Sunday brunch. Dinner, which innkeeper Alan Peterson describes as Southern fine dining, features such popular favorites as shrimp and grits with vegetables, sweet potato biscuits, and brandied peaches. At Sunday brunch, in addition to all the usual brunch items, there's a carving station and sometimes an omelette station. Folks look forward to the live entertainment at the Jazz Brunch held the last Sunday of every month.

For anyone who has ever been to the Belmont, the old lobby with its four fireplaces on the first floor has been converted to special function space, and the new lobby is on the lower level with the aptly named Curtain Call Lounge, the perfect place for a drink before or after the show or during intermission. Be sure to look at the pictures showing the stages of the renovation, which are displayed near the bar.

Since the weather was pleasant while we were there, we took our after-breakfast tea and coffee out to the porch, as did some of our fellow guests—giving us all an opportunity to get to know one another and to trade suggestions about sight-seeing and shopping. Abbeville is filled with delightful antiques shops and boutiques.

Weekend theater packages include wine and cheese before the show, dinner, theater tickets, coffee and dessert afterwards, breakfast the next morning, and admission to the historic Burt-Stark House—all for $169, quite a good deal.

HOW TO GET THERE: From I-85, take the U.S. 76 exit and go south. Follow SC 28 south to Abbeville. At the square, turn left onto Pickens Street. The inn is on your left.

Abbeville Opera House

From Reconstruction to well into the 1920s, traveling troops of actors, musicians, and vaudevillians passed through Abbeville, where the citizens had an insatiable thirst for entertainment. The town's location on the rail line between New York and Atlanta made it a natural stopover. Many a one-night-stand production was performed in the town square alfresco or in a tent. Then the citizens got the bright idea of combining the need for a municipal office building with the desire for an opera house. The result, completed in 1908, is the handsome brick building that provides space for both.

The building's modest two-story facade fronts on the square and doesn't prepare you for the spacious interior. Because the lot slopes down in the back, the performance space is actually six stories tall and qualifies as an opera house because the stage area exceeds the seating area. The small but elegant theater provides seating for 350 on the main floor, a balcony, and four impressive boxes.

An orchestra pit is recessed under the stage. Backstage, three floors of dressing rooms have a hallway window onto the stage so that the performers could follow the action and not miss a cue. The back wall of the building stands more than 100 feet tall. Built four bricks thick without restraining rods, it is believed to be one of the tallest freestanding brick walls in the western hemisphere.

Sets were changed with a rope-pulled system of counterweights balanced by sandbags on hemp ropes—hence the name "hemp house." This system is still in place. Abbeville's Opera House is the only remaining hemp house in South Carolina.

Between 1908 and 1930, the theater provided melodrama, minstrels, Shakespeare, and opera. The first production was *The Great Divide,* which was followed later that year by *The Clansman,* played with a troop of cavalry horses on stage. Beginning in 1920, silent movies came to the theater with musicians and full sound effects, but the advent of talkies spelled decline for all live entertainment. As fewer and fewer traveling shows passed through town, Abbeville's influence as a cultural center faded. The Opera House remained a movie theater until the 1950s, when its doors were closed. In the late 1960s the Abbeville Community Theater formed, and through a community-wide effort the Opera House was restored and reopened to theater once again. Today the community theater offers thirty-six weeks of live theater annually.

The Rhett House Inn
Beaufort, South Carolina 29902

INNKEEPERS: Marianne and Steve Harrison; general manager, Stephanie Fairbanks

ADDRESS/TELEPHONE: 1009 Craven Street; (843) 524–9030 or (888) 480–9530; fax (843) 524–1310

WEB SITE: www.rhetthouseinn.com

E-MAIL: rhetthse@hargray.com

ROOMS: 17, all with private bath, telephone, CD player, television; 9 with fireplace; 8 with whirlpool tub; 1 handicapped accessible.

RATES: $150 to $300, double or single (inquire for details); includes full breakfast and homemade desserts after dinner. Children age 5 and older are welcome. Packages are available year-round. Credit cards accepted. No smoking indoors.

OPEN: Year-round.

FACILITIES AND ACTIVITIES: Bicycles. Nearby: Beach, golf, swimming, tennis, walking and carriage tours of historic sites in Beaufort, 1-hour drive to Charleston or Savannah.

BUSINESS TRAVEL: Located 1 hour from Charleston or Savannah. Telephone in room, fax available, conference facilities, 24-hour desk.

*B*eaufort does something to people. Lured by tourist literature laced with phrases like "picturesque old port town" and "nestled along the Intracoastal" and "quaint historic community," people come to visit this place that time is supposed to have skipped over. And sure enough, it has.

Except for telling you that the only reason Sherman didn't burn Beaufort is because it was under Union occupation at the time, nobody gets very worked up over anything. Breezes really do "waft." The streets really are "tree-lined." Folks really do "stroll."

Nestled amid this idyllic setting, the 1820 Rhett House Inn has wraparound verandas with classic columns and porticos and beautifully curved entry stairs. Live oaks swathed in Spanish moss shade the house. The white exterior almost sparkles. The scene cries out to be a movie set for a Southern romance with violins playing in the background.

Across the street is an 1850s cottage, which has been restored as seven new luxury rooms, each complete with a small refrigerator, minibar, coffeemaker, whirlpool tub, and fireplace.

All rooms are furnished with antiques, but everything has been chosen to keep the rooms light and bright, avoiding the slightly gloomy look we sometimes associate with antiques.

The room we stayed in was huge. It opened onto the courtyard garden, so that we could hear the fountain all night. The fireplace had a raised brick hearth. The drapes, rugs, and furniture were done in a country motif with blue-and-white gingham and ticking.

It seemed like a good idea just to stay there with the door open to the courtyard and spend the morning reading, but we didn't want to miss breakfast.

We sat around the dining room table, digging into bowls of huge strawberries and plates of tiny poppy-seed muffins with unromantic vigor and a most un-Southern display of energy.

After breakfast, check out one of our favorite places, Hunting Island State Park, a 5,000-acre park just 16 miles from downtown Beaufort, with several miles of perfect swimming beaches that are also uncommonly good for shelling.

For information about other area attractions, contact the chamber of commerce, which provides more information than you can possibly use about Beaufort and the area, and it offers a nice brochure for a self-guided tour of historic sites.

This inn has been enjoying a lot of publicity and the presence of some celebrity guests, including Ben Affleck, Sandra Bullock, and Gwyneth Paltrow. (Not at the same time, understand.)

HOW TO GET THERE: From I–95, take exit 33 to Beaufort. From Savannah, follow the signs to Hilton Head Island and then to Beaufort. The inn is 1 block from the Intracoastal Waterway at the corner of Craven and Newcastle Streets. Ask for a map when you make reservations.

Greenleaf Inn of Camden
Camden, South Carolina 29020

INNKEEPERS: The Catania family

ADDRESS/TELEPHONE: 1308 North Broad Street; (803) 425–1806
or (800) 437–5874; fax (803) 425-5853

WEB SITE: www.greenleafinncamden.com

E-MAIL: glicamden@aol.com

ROOMS: 12; all with private bath, telephone, clock radio, cable television, iron and ironing board, hair dryer, dataport; some with decorative
fireplaces; children welcome. No pets.

RATES: $89 to $109; includes continental breakfast. Credit cards
accepted. Smoking and non-smoking rooms.

OPEN: Year-round except Christmas Eve and Christmas Day.

FACILITIES AND ACTIVITIES: Restaurant and bar. Nearby: National
Register of Historic Places historic district, Historic Camden Revolutionary War Site, Camden Archives and Museum, Bonds Conway House,
Hobkirk Hill Battle Site, Springdale Race Course, Lake Wateree, Battle
of Camden site, Historic Boykin, Battle of Boykin's Mill site, golf, tennis, fishing, boating.

BUSINESS TRAVEL: Telephone with dataport.

We were visiting Camden because Carol's mother's family lived
there before the Revolutionary War until the 1830s, when they
migrated to Alabama, and Carol wanted to use the Camden
Archives for genealogical research. Whether you're visiting this lovely Southern town for its rich Revolutionary War history, your own genealogical
research, or to watch the world-renowned steeplechases at Springdale Race
Course, a good base of operations is the Greenleaf Inn of Camden.

Located on a shady tree-lined street of impressive historic homes just a
couple of blocks from the main downtown business district, the inn offers
elegant and comfortable accommodations in two adjacent houses. By far the
fancier of the two, the imposing McLean House—built in 1890—houses several elegant upstairs guest rooms and the locally popular Avanti's Restaurant
and pub downstairs. High ceilings, tall windows with dramatic window
treatments, antiques, rich fabrics, and decorative fireplaces characterize the
spacious bedchambers. Next door, the Reynolds House, circa 1805, is much
more basic, as befits a home of its venerable age. Rooms are smaller and the
ceilings lower.

Under new ownership since September 2000, all the inn's public and guest rooms are getting a face-lift.

Camden is a delightful small town with more than 250 years of history: from the Revolutionary War through the antebellum South and the Civil War through the turn-of-the-twentieth-century era when the town became a winter playground for wealthy Northerners and their horses. Its present claim to fame is steeplechasing at the spring Carolina Cup and the fall Marion DuPont Scott Colonial Cup.

HOW TO GET THERE: From I-20, take the U.S. 521 exit north. The inn is 1½ miles past the intersection of U.S. 521 and U.S. 1.

Anchorage Inn
Charleston, South Carolina 29401

INNKEEPER: Barry Hutto

ADDRESS/TELEPHONE: 26 Vendue Range; (843) 723-8300 or (800) 421-2952; fax (843) 723-9543

WEB SITE: www.anchoragencharleston.com

ROOMS: 17, plus 2 suites; all with private bath; some with whirlpool tub, telephone, dataport, and television.

RATES: $95, single or double, $225, suites, includes deluxe continental breakfast buffet, turndown service, afternoon wine and cheese, evening sherry. Inquire about off-season rates.

OPEN: Year-round.

FACILITIES AND ACTIVITIES: Nearby: Across from Waterfront Park; walking distance to restaurants, Dock Street Theatre, Footlight Players Theatre, and the Old City Market; carriage tours.

BUSINESS TRAVEL: Located minutes from business district. Computer and modem setup, good work space, and telephone with dataport in room; fax available.

*A*nchorage means "safe harbor." The woman, a local historian, who opened this B&B inn in 1991 chose the name because it seemed to fit the location of the inn and the history of the building. The redbrick, two-story structure was built about 1840 as a warehouse in what used to be a commercial shipping district of the city. The shipping is long gone, of course, but people stay here because they've heard it's not only a safe harbor but also a comfortable one, noted especially for providing extra services that don't show up in any brochure. More about that in a minute.

The inn has a British feel, which many people find a pleasant change from the almost overwhelming Civil War emphasis of Charleston. Charleston was an important settlement for British colonists, so the taste of an Anglophile makes sense here.

When you come into the foyer, which is open to the second-story roof and skylights, you see the exposed post-and-beam construction of the original building. Farther back, an English library with dark wood beams and paneling and big stuffed chairs arranged near the fireplace remind you of the pubs you'd visit on a trip through the British countryside.

The guest rooms have seventeenth century–style bedsteads and straight, paneled tapestry drapes. The Berber carpet suggests the sisal matting of the seventeenth-century floor coverings. But the conveniences are entirely of this century, with everything from hair dryers in the bathroom to spaces where you can hook up your computer and modem if you just can't stop working, even in a safe harbor.

That brings us to the highly personal service. The young, obliging staff are visibly proud of working in the inn. Moreover, they are local and pride themselves on providing both local information and all the service you need.

HOW TO GET THERE: From I–26, take the East Bay Street exit to the heart of the city. Turn left on Vendue Range; the inn is in the middle of the block on the left.

Ansonborough Inn ♥

Charleston, South Carolina 29401

INNKEEPER: Allison Fennell

ADDRESS/TELEPHONE: 21 Hasell Street; (843) 723–1655 or
(800) 522–2073; fax (843) 577–6888

WEB SITE: www.ansonboroughinn.com

E-MAIL: info@ansonboroughinn.com

ROOMS: 37 suites; all with private bath, telephone, cable television,
clock radio, ceiling fan, sofa sleeper, iron and ironing board, hair dryer,
voice mail, dataport, Internet access, safe, kitchenette with minirefrigerator and microwave. Five have a fireplace. No-smoking inn.

RATES: Spring and fall, $149 to $259, double; summer and winter,
$109 to $229, double; includes continental breakfast, afternoon wine
and cheese, newspaper, hot and cold beverages, afternoon cookies. $10
for each extra adult in suite. Children 12 and under free. Inquire about
discounts. Credit cards accepted.

OPEN: Year-round.

FACILITIES AND ACTIVITIES: English-style pub, rooftop terrace; free
off-street parking. In heart of waterfront historic district. Nearby: Historic sites, restaurants, shuttle transportation to visitors center. Walking
distance to antiques shops and downtown Charleston.

BUSINESS TRAVEL: Located minutes from business district. Telephone,
computer and modem setup, excellent work area in room; fax, copy
service available; meeting room.

*L*ike so many Charleston inns, this B&B inn had a different function
in its earlier time. It was a three-story stationer's warehouse built
about 1900. The building's renovation not only kept the heart-of-
pine beams and locally fired red brick, which are typical of the period, but
actually emphasized them. The lobby soars three stories high, with skylights; the original huge, rough beams are fully visible, an important part of
the decor.

The original plan to use the renovated building as a condo complex did-
n't work out, which probably was bad news for some investors; but it's great
for inn guests now, because the rooms, which are really suites, are huge. At
least one wall in each features the exposed old brick. The ceilings are about
20 feet high. Because all the rooms were fit into an existing shell, no two

rooms are exactly the same shape or size. Nothing is exactly predictable. The resulting little quirks, nooks, lofts, and alcoves add a lot of interest.

The living rooms are furnished in period reproductions with comfortable chairs and sleeper sofas to accommodate extra people. Kitchenettes make snacking and light meals possible—a good way to save your calories and your dollars for some sumptuous dinners in Charleston's excellent restaurants.

Clearly this isn't the kind of place where everyone sits around the breakfast table comparing notes about dinner the night before, but the continental breakfast (with sweet breads baked at a plantation in Walterboro) and the evening wine and cheese are set up in the lobby so that guests can sit in conversational clusters. If someone on the staff thinks that you may have something in common with another guest, he or she will take the trouble to introduce you. Indeed, the staff here is personable and helpful—attitudes you don't always encounter in Charleston hostelries.

HOW TO GET THERE: From I-26 East, take the Meeting Street/Visitor Center exit. Go 1^2/$_{10}$ miles to Hasell Street. Turn left and go through the next traffic signal. From Route 17 South, take the East Bay Street exit, go 1^3/$_{10}$ miles to Hasell, and turn left. From Route 17 North, after crossing the Ashley River, exit to the right and go through the first traffic signal onto Calhoun Street. Drive 1^4/$_{10}$ miles to East Bay Street, turn right, and go to the second traffic signal (Hasell Street) and turn left. The inn is on your right.

The Battery Carriage House Inn
Charleston, South Carolina 29401

INNKEEPER: Katharine Hastie

ADDRESS/TELEPHONE: 20 South Battery; (843) 727-3100 or
(800) 775-5575; fax (843) 727-3130

WEB SITE: www.batterycarriagehouse.com

E-MAIL: bch@mymailstation.com

ROOMS: 11, plus 1 suite; all with private bath, either a steam bath or whirlpool, robes, private entrance, cable television, and telephone. Not handicapped accessible. No children under 12. No-smoking inn.

RATES: $99 to $269, single or double; includes continental breakfast, beverages, and turndown service. Two-night minimum stay on weekends. Credit cards accepted. AAA discount.

OPEN: Year-round.

FACILITIES AND ACTIVITIES:
On the Battery. Nearby: Walking
distance to restaurants, houses,
museums, and city marina; short
drive to shopping on Broad and
King Streets, the Old Exchange
Building and Dungeon, and theaters on Queen and Church
Streets.

BUSINESS TRAVEL: Located minutes from business district.
Direct-dial telephone with
answering machine; concierge service for tours and restaurants; fax and
copy service available.

rom the front door of the Battery Carriage House you see White
Point Gardens, the Battery, and Fort Sumter in Charleston Harbor, where the Civil War began.

Built in 1843, this landmark antebellum house was home to ancestors of
the current owners, Kat and Drayton Hastie. Photographers from all over the
world have shot this house, and film directors have used it as the setting for
such films as *North and South* and *Queen.*

As a guest here, you stay in the large carriage house behind the main
house, where the garden separates you from street noise. Several of the
rooms have four-poster canopy beds and are decorated with local artists'
watercolor paintings. The suite is particularly peaceful, with a cream carpet
over parquet floors and bare brick walls.

In the parlor, a gaming table is outfitted for checkers, chess, and
backgammon, and you'll find a separate bridge table. In the afternoon, this
is a nice place to drink wine and discuss dinner plans. Or you can move out
into the gardens or the Lady Bankshire Rose Arbor.

Another special place sets this inn apart. On the ground level, underneath
the front porch, you can sit in wicker chairs hidden from the street by a
wrought-iron fence, pillars, and plantings. From here you see the White
Point Gardens and the harbor and catch a cool, steady breeze in the shade.

Speaking of cool breezes, the inn is said to be inhabited by two ghosts.
One is a man's torso, the other a friendly (and certainly more useful) full-
figured male. They hang around Rooms 8 and 10. No extra charge.

HOW TO GET THERE: From I–26, take the Meeting Street exit where I–26
ends. Follow Meeting to Battery, and make a right. From U.S. 17 North, cross
the Ashley River Bridge and bear right onto Lockwood Boulevard. Keep mak-

ing every possible right until you are on Murray Boulevard. Then make a left on King Street. Turn right onto South Battery. From U.S. Highway 17 south, take East Bay or King Street exit and follow the street to the Battery. The inn is at 20 South Battery.

Elliott House Inn
Charleston, South Carolina 29401

INNKEEPERS: Al and Mavis Boerman

ADDRESS/TELEPHONE: 78 Queen Street; (843) 723–1855 or (800) 729–1855; fax (843) 722–1567

WEB SITE: www.elliotthouseinn.com

ROOMS: 26, all with private bath, telephone (some with dataports), and television; some handicapped accessible. No-smoking inn.

RATES: $94 to $160, single or double; includes continental breakfast served in guest room with local newspaper, wine and cheese reception, turndown service with chocolates. Off-season rates $75 to $105.

OPEN: Year-round.

FACILITIES AND ACTIVITIES: Large whirlpool in courtyard, bicycles. Nearby: Walking distance to restaurants, historic sites, tourist attractions, and antiques shops.

BUSINESS TRAVEL: Located 5 minutes from commercial district. Telephone in room, corporate rates.

*B*usiness people who spend a lot of time in Charleston (poor babies!) say this is one of their favorite B&B inns, because the people on staff are "so sweet" and the rooms are so comfortable.

The building is a renovated three-story frame house built about 1865, expanded with a newer section. The rooms are furnished in period reproductions, with such modern amenities as color televisions hidden

away in walnut armoires. Oriental rugs cover good wood floors, and Oriental-patterned wallpaper carries through the theme.

If you stand back and inspect the entire building, you'll notice that the second- and third-floor balconies slope noticeably toward the ground. Seems that the earthquake of 1886 knocked things a bit wopperjawed. Everything is structurally sound, but the result of the quake is evident in the slant of those balconies, a touch that appeals to people associated with the place who enjoy its uniqueness.

Elliott House is ideally situated if you're planning to spend some time walking through the historic streets of Charleston. It is in the heart of downtown Charleston, a block from the antiques district in one direction, a block from famous historic sites in the other.

At the end of a day of sight-seeing or business, when it's nice enough to be outside, you'll enjoy the courtyard. Designed around the whirlpool, it includes fountains and shady sitting areas and gleams with flowering plants most of the year. What a place to enjoy a glass of wine!

It would be a mistake to relax with your wine so much that you miss dinner, however, because the inn is right next to 82 Queen, one of Charleston's better restaurants, with an exotic menu.

HOW TO GET THERE: Take the Meeting Street exit from I-26; go south on Meeting to Queen and right onto Queen. The inn is in the first block.

Fulton Lane Inn
Charleston, South Carolina 29401

INNKEEPER: Michelle Woodhull

ADDRESS/TELEPHONE: 202 King Street; (843) 720-2600 or
(800) 720-2688; fax (843) 720-2940

WEB SITE: www.charminginns.com

E-MAIL: fli@charminginns.com

ROOMS: 27, all with private bath, minirefrigerator, and cable television; some with fireplace, whirlpool tub. Two fully equipped wheelchair accessible rooms. No-smoking inn.

RATES: Low season, $115 to $295; high season, $135 to $295; includes continental breakfast and afternoon sherry. Discover Charleston package seasonally $295 to $395. $20 each additional person. Children under 12 years old free. Credit cards accepted. AAA and AARP discounts.

OPEN: Year-round.

FACILITIES AND ACTIVITIES: Located in the heart of the antiques district. Nearby: Shopping at the Old City Market and The Shops at Charleston Place, restaurants, museum homes and other historic sites, carriage tours, walking tours.

After Hurricane Hugo in 1989, all the king's horses and all the king's men couldn't put the building at King Street and Fulton Lane back together again. The building's history probably contributed to its demise: The two-story structure is thought to have been built in haste for the World Expo in 1912.

What rose from the ashes is a building so sympathetic to its surroundings that it looks just right with its centuries-old neighbors. This was particularly important because two attached buildings, 202 and 208 King Street, were part of the project. In keeping with the King Street tradition of shops on the ground floor and sleeping quarters above, Golden and Associates Antiques and A'Riga IV Antiques, longtime tenants evicted by the storm, have reopened at street level, off of the Fulton Lane Inn lobby. Guest rooms are on the second and third floors of the three buildings.

The new building, modeled after the demolished structure, incorporates the lines and even some of the decorative tin salvaged from the old building by The Historic Charleston Foundation. The inn's owner asked for an interior with a cool, but sexy feel. That it is. The sherbet-green halls, with glossy white wainscoting, and the guest rooms, with chenille bedspreads, wicker lampshades, and floor-to-ceiling windows that catch a steady breeze from the nearby harbor, make this quiet, private place special.

The inn provides an Old Charleston atmosphere with all the modern amenities, including stocked refrigerators, kitchens in the suites, and some baths with whirlpools. From many of the rooms you can see the infamous Fulton Alley. Today it's part of the fashionable downtown business district and the location for the elegant Fulton V restaurant and Historic Charleston Foundation offices. But way back when, the very building occupied by the venerable foundation was one of the city's most notorious brothels. Now *that's* what we call "living history."

HOW TO GET THERE: The inn is ½ block south of the intersection of King and Market Streets.

The John Rutledge House Inn
Charleston, South Carolina 29401

INNKEEPER: Linda Bishop; Richard T. Widman, owner

ADDRESS/TELEPHONE: 116 Broad Street; (843) 723–7999 or (800) 476–9741; fax (843) 720–2615

WEB SITE: www.charminginns.com

E-MAIL: jrh@charminginns.com

ROOMS: 19 in the main house and 2 carriage houses; all with private bath, cable television, telephone, and minirefrigerator; some with Jacuzzi and/or fireplace; some with wheelchair access. No-smoking rooms available.

RATES: $165 to $375 low season, $235 to $375 high season; includes continental breakfast, manager's tea, wine, and brandy; evening turndown. Extra person in room $20. Children under 12 free. Discover Charleston Package available seasonally $345 to $465. Credit cards accepted.

OPEN: Year-round.

FACILITIES AND ACTIVITIES: Courtyard, verandas. Nearby: Restaurants, walking distance to historic sites of Historic Charleston; theaters, shops, Charleston's slave market, historic tours.

This B&B inn has taken connoisseurs of inns by storm, not only for its historic value and its elegance, but also for its vitality. In Charleston, some established inns seem to have reached the point of polite indifference. When you talk to people at this one, their pride in the place and their concern for guests are refreshing.

When you meet the innkeeper, Linda Bishop, you get a good idea of what the truly skillful Southern hostess of antebellum times must have been like.

Linda translates that graciousness and skill into contemporary situations. She speaks knowledgeably about the city and this inn without ever boring you and without ever losing sight of the reasons you are visiting. Most important, she sees to it that whatever should happen does, and she makes it look effortless. She fits perfectly into a building of this elegance and historic importance.

First, the history: John Rutledge, signer of the U.S. Constitution, lived here. The house was built in 1763 and is one of only fifteen homes of signers of the Constitution standing today. Also, much of the history of South Carolina was made during meetings in the ballroom and library.

As for the elegance, original plaster moldings and intricate ironwork have been restored, as have twelve marble mantels carved in Italy. Bordered parquet floors simply take your breath away, as does the expanse of the ballroom where, from 4:30 to 6:00 P.M., guests are invited to mingle and share complimentary refreshments.

The guest rooms are furnished in a mixture of antiques and period reproductions, with warm, cheerful colors—rose, peach, deep green, and ivory. Rooms in the carriage house are smaller and simpler than those in the main house, but they are still luxurious.

Breakfast has become an elaborate affair here, with some of the offerings directly related to the history of the house. For instance, the house specialty is biscuits with hot sherried fruit, because John Rutledge loved sherry. If you want a bigger breakfast, you can order from a printed menu that is hung on your doorknob each evening. The choices range from the biscuit with sherried fruit to such Southern favorites as grits or poached eggs with shrimp and hollandaise sauce. Health-conscious choices have also been included. The continental breakfast items are complimentary; the charge for the more elaborate entrees is marked on the menu. You also choose what time you'd like your breakfast to be delivered and where—in your room or in the courtyard.

HOW TO GET THERE: The inn is near the corner of King and Broad Streets. Ask for a map when you make a reservation.

Kings Courtyard Inn
Charleston, South Carolina 29401

INNKEEPER: Michelle Woodhull; Richard Widman, owner

ADDRESS/TELEPHONE: 198 King Street; (843) 723–7000 or
(800) 845–6119; fax (843) 720–2608

WEB SITE: www.charminginns.com

E-MAIL: kci@charminginns.com

ROOMS: 41 rooms and suites; all with private bath, cable television,
minirefrigerator, and telephone; some with fireplace and/or whirlpool
tub; some with wheelchair access. Nonsmoking rooms available.

RATES: $110 to $260 low season, $165 to $260 high season; includes
continental breakfast, complimentary wine and sherry on arrival,
evening brandy and chocolates, morning newspaper. Extra person in
room $20. Children under 12 free. Credit cards accepted. Discover
Charleston package available seasonally $285 to $340.

OPEN: Year-round.

FACILITIES AND ACTIVITIES: Bar service in courtyards all afternoons
but Sunday; whirlpool tub. Nearby: Restaurants, historic sites and tours,
tourist attractions, antiques shops.

The B&B inn is a three-story 1853 building designed in the Greek
Revival style. The building is one of historic King Street's largest
and oldest structures and has had many usages in its almost 150
years of existence: high-quality shops and private residences, and at one time
the upper floors were used as an inn catering to plantation owners, travelers
with shipping interests, and merchant guests.

We are endlessly fascinated by the old-city way of creating little areas of
calm and quiet away from the streets with courtyards. It's done well here,
with two brick courtyards filled with tropical plants and geraniums and
accented with fountains: One has a large whirlpool tub, and the other provides lots of shady spots for enjoying a cocktail.

The rooms are decorated individually and furnished with period reproductions. Some have canopied beds; some have fireplaces. They feel quiet,
cool, and restful after you've been out pounding the Charleston sidewalks
for a day.

The same tranquil feeling prevails in the lobby, where the fireplace and
Audubon prints could as easily be part of a family living room as an inn.
The desk of the concierge is here, too, with some very pleasant people to

help with tours, transportation, and advice. We were impressed with the friendliness of the staff.

HOW TO GET THERE: King Street parallels Meeting Street. From King Street, turn left on Market Street or Horlbeck Alley to park in the city parking lot behind the inn.

The Lodge Alley Inn
Charleston, South Carolina 29401

INNKEEPER: A Bluegreen Resort

ADDRESS/TELEPHONE: 195 East Bay Street; in South Carolina, (843) 722-1611 or (800) 845-1004; fax (843) 722-7497

WEB SITE: www.lodgeallyinn.com

ROOMS: 34, plus 62 suites; all with private bath, television, VCR, and telephone; some with wheelchair access; some suites with whirlpool tub, private courtyard entraces.

RATES: $160 to $360, single or double; including continental breakfast, cookies, sherry, turndown services. Credit cards accepted. No personal checks.

OPEN: Year-round.

FACILITIES AND ACTIVITIES: Restaurant open for breakfast, dinner; lounge open to public and guests. Located on a restored alley in the heart of Historic Charleston, within walking distance of most historic sites. Nearby: Carriage tours, Waterfront Park.

BUSINESS TRAVEL: Located five minutes from the business district.

Telephone with voice mail and modem hookup in all accommodations; good work surface in suites; fax, copy service available; corporate rates.

his is one of those saved-from-the-wrecking-ball stories. The whole alley of old warehouses was supposed to have been wiped out in 1973 to make way for condominiums, but the Save Charleston Foundation and some enterprising developers got into the act, saved the alley, and restored the buildings.

There's a lot of elegance in Charleston's history, which is reflected in the inn. When you arrive, you walk under a canopy, and a uniformed valet comes to park your car.

A bellman, also in uniform, helped us get our bags to our room, making sure that we noticed the neatly hidden minirefrigerator, the gas-log fireplace, and the eighteenth-century furniture reproductions. We were fascinated by one wall of the room: It still had the original brick and a huge exposed beam left from the old warehouse. The wide floor planks had the kinds of nicks and dark spots you'd expect to find in a warehouse. The floors were finished to a high gloss and partly covered with Oriental rugs. From our window, we could see the steeples of some of Charleston's famous old churches.

The Lodge Alley Inn has gradually been renovating the other old warehouses around it to create an interesting variety of rooms and suites, many especially suited to small groups and business meetings. The rooms in one area have a less formal, Country French decor and are very spacious. Some have a second-level loft for bedroom and bath, with dining, living, and kitchen space below. If you have special requirements, mention them when you call for reservations. Even if you end up with a kitchen, though, you should give the restaurant a try.

At one time the restaurant served with formality, but now the mode is casual courtyard dining, under umbrellas at wrought-iron tables in spring and fall. The restaurant has the only grand rotisserie in town, from which such delicacies as Chateaubriand and rack of lamb are served. You often dine to the music of a jazz band if you eat outside in spring or fall. The rest of the time, of course, there's ample seating indoors.

HOW TO GET THERE: I–26 and U.S. 17 are the major routes into Charleston. From either, turn right just before the Cooper River Bridge onto East Bay Street. Go 2 miles. The inn is on the right.

Maison Du Pré
Charleston, South Carolina 29401

INNKEEPER: Mark Mulholland, manager

ADDRESS/TELEPHONE: 317 East Bay Street; (843) 723–8691 or (800) 844–INNS; fax (843) 723–3722

WEB SITE: www.maisondupre.com

ROOMS: 15, including 3 suites; all with private bath, television, telephone, clock radio. No-smoking inn.

RATES: $98 to $215, single or double; includes continental breakfast and afternoon "Low Country tea." Inquire about off-season rates and packages. Credit cards accepted.

OPEN: Year-round.

FACILITIES AND ACTIVITIES: Patios and landscaped gardens; facilities for small meetings, parties, weddings. Located in historic district of Charleston, next to the Gaillard Auditorium. Nearby: Restaurants, historic sites and tours, antiques shops.

*M*aison Du Pré, dating back to 1804, comprises five buildings— three restored single houses and two carriage houses—surrounding a brick courtyard full of flowers, fountains, and an old well. Most innkeepers like to say that each room of their inn is different. When you consider all the nooks and crannies and assorted shapes and sizes inevitable in a collection of five old buildings, you can see that at Maison Du Pré that boast would almost inevitably have to be true.

There's a morning room, an evening room, an upstairs drawing room fitted out with a grand piano, a space for meetings and formal dining, and, of course, the fifteen guest rooms variously furnished with period furniture, antiques, and Oriental rugs. The most memorable is undoubtedly the honeymoon suite, which has an old claw-foot bathtub (and a separate shower in case your love of history doesn't extend to bathing) and a fireplace. You get a chilled bottle of champagne when you rent this suite. The unusually nice courtyard and gardens unify all buildings and rooms and provide a pleasant common area in good weather.

HOW TO GET THERE: The inn is between George Street and Laurens Street on East Bay.

Meeting Street Inn
Charleston, South Carolina 29401

INNKEEPER: Allen Johnson

ADDRESS/TELEPHONE: 173 Meeting Street; (843) 723-1882 or (800) 842-8022; fax (843) 577-0851

WEB SITE: www.meetingstreetinn.net

E-MAIL: meetingstreet@cchat.com

ROOMS: 56 rooms, all with private bath, television, telephone, piazza.

RATES: $99 to $220; includes continental breakfast, afternoon refreshments, turndown service.

OPEN: Year-round.

FACILITIES AND ACTIVITIES: Garden courtyard, oversized Jacuzzi. Located in historic district of Charleston. Nearby: Waterfront Park, museums, historic houses and buildings, restaurants, boutiques, antiques shops.

BUSINESS TRAVEL: Elegant boardroom can accommodate up to 12.

So perfectly does this 1870s edifice work as an inn, we would never have guessed that it has such a checkered past—serving variously as a saloon, restaurant, wholesale wine and beer dealership, brewing and ice company, club and restaurant, antiques shop, auto parts distributorship, dental equipment sales office, liquor store, and bicycle rentals storefront. The venerable building has been an inn only since 1981.

Despite its history of commercial use, the building is in the style of a Charleston single house and provides distinctive lodging in fifty-six guest rooms that open onto the lush garden courtyard. Each lavishly decorated guest chamber features high ceilings and antique reproduction furnishings, including canopy beds and ornate four-poster rice beds (so called because the carving on the bed posts represents rice plants). Period reproduction wallpapers either complement or match the bed coverings. Other furnishings and accessories are carefully chosen to create an Old Charleston ambience and a unique personality for each room. Some rooms boast a decorative fireplace and/or whirlpool bath; all make such concessions to the twenty-first century as modern private bath, television, and telephone.

Each day begins with a continental breakfast of fresh fruit and juice, bagels, ham biscuits, Danishes, muffins, hot beverages, and a newspaper and ends with a chocolate on your pillow. In between you might want to unwind in the oversized courtyard hot tub, linger over complimentary afternoon refreshments of wine and hors d'oeuvres, or imbibe your favorite libation from the lobby bar. The friendly staff is always ready to help you with sightseeing suggestions or reservations.

Bustling Meeting Street, the heart of the historic district, and the ever-popular City Market are right at your doorstep, as are Charleston's renowned restaurants, boutiques, and antiques shops.

HOW TO GET THERE: From I-26, take the Meeting Street/Visitors Center exit and continue following Meeting Street into the historic district. The inn will be on your right; parking is in the rear.

Middleton Inn at Middleton Place
Charleston, South Carolina 29414

INNKEEPER: Mary Stowe

ADDRESS/TELEPHONE: 4920 Ashley River Road; (843) 556-0500 or (800) 543-4774; fax: (843) 556-5673

WEB SITE: www.middletonplace.org

E-MAIL: info@middletonplace.org

ROOMS: 55 rooms, all with private bath, telephone, television, wood-burning fireplace, views of Ashley River, coffeemaker, refrigerator, iron and ironing board, hair dryer, dataport, voice mail.

RATES: $129 to $179 ($350 for the River Room), including evening hors d'oeuvres and access to Middleton Place Gardens, House Museum, and

Stableyards. Packages are available. Credit cards accepted.

OPEN: Year-round.

FACILITIES AND ACTIVITIES: Breakfast is available at the Middleton Inn. Lunch and dinner are available at the Middleton Place Restaurant. Guided tours of the Ashley River and Cypress Swamp, guided nature hikes through the surrounding woodlands and the eighteenth-century rice fields, horseback riding. Outdoor swimming pool. Middleton Place self-guided tours of the gardens, tours of the House Museum, carriage rides. Nearby: Historic Charleston, plantations, gardens, beaches, restaurants, shopping, water sports.

BUSINESS TRAVEL: Ideal for small meetings and retreats; conference center, team building and challenge course activities; dataport, copy, and fax service available.

"What were they thinking?" we both gasped in complete shock when we pulled out of the heavy woods into the clearing and saw the starkly ultramodern building that is the Middleton Inn. First of all, we expected just about everything in Charleston to be historic or at least *look* historic. Second, this inn is on the property of Middleton Place, a famous eighteenth-century plantation with world-renowned gardens—the oldest landscaped gardens in America.

Well, our reaction just goes to show how little *we* know. When it was completed in 1987, the design won the highest national honor of the American Institute of Architects. Concrete, walls of glass, and sharp angles distinguish the exterior. The interior and furnishings are also contemporary. If modern design is OK with you, read on; this inn has much to recommend it.

Located on a bluff above the Ashley River just 14 miles from Charleston, the inn offers a wealth of activities. You'll have free daylight access to the famous gardens, the stable yards where artisans often work, and the plantation restaurant and gift shop, and you can tour the museum house. Recreational activities include a swimming pool, guided horseback rides, kayak tours, and nature hikes. Carriage rides are available from the inn to Middleton Place, and there are also carriage tours of the plantation.

Middleton Place rose to prominence as a rice plantation in the 1700s. Flooded rice fields that border the river are maintained to attract migrating and resident waterfowl and other wetland inhabitants. Solitary tours or those taken with an experienced naturalist may be rewarded with sightings of otters, wood ducks, deer, egrets, herons, and, fall through spring, a pair of nesting bald eagles. You can explore miles of bicycle and nature trails. During the winter you can propel a flat-bottomed keowee (a kind of kayak) through rice fields and canals. Bicycles, kayaks, and tandems are available to rent.

Decorated with understatement, the interior of the inn displays sleek, clean lines and earth tones. Prodigious use of natural wood paneling provides warmth. Each guest room showcases cypress wall paneling, hand-crafted furniture, and floor-to-ceiling windows. A definite plus—every room boasts a wood-burning fireplace. Large European-style bathrooms feature marble floors, oversized tile tubs, and lots of natural light coming through privacy-ensuring glass-block walls.

When it comes to meals, Middleton Inn offers breakfast in the dining room daily. For lunch, try the Middleton Place Restaurant, located in an old outbuilding on the grounds of the plantation. Try the Low Country specialties such as hoppin' John, ham biscuits, okra gumbo, she-crab soup, collard greens, and Huguenot torte. Middleton Place Restaurant serves sophisticated entrees such as pan-fried quail, beef, or chicken nightly. Reservations are recommended for dinner.

Neighbors of the Middleton Inn on the Ashley River Road are Magnolia Plantation and Gardens, Audubon Swamp Gardens, and the National Trust for Historic Preservation's Drayton Hall. Charleston is only minutes away.

HOW TO GET THERE: From I-26, exit at 199A and go through Summerville. Turn left onto SC 165, then left onto the Ashley River Road (SC 61 South). The inn is 5 miles ahead on the left—½ mile past the entrance to Middleton Place.

Planters Inn
Charleston, South Carolina 29401

INNKEEPER: Larry Spelts

ADDRESS/TELEPHONE: 112 North Market Street; (843) 722–2345 or (800) 845–7082; fax (843) 577–2125

WEB SITE: www.plantersinn.com

E-MAIL: reservations@plantersinn.com

ROOMS: 56, plus 6 suites with separate sitting rooms; all with private bath, television, and telephone; some with fireplace or whirlpool tub. No-smoking rooms; the inn is handicapped accessible.

RATES: $175 to $300, single or double; $300 to $500, suites; includes coffee and tea in the lobby parlor, newspaper, turndown service with chocolates.

OPEN: Year-round.

FACILITIES AND ACTIVITIES: Restaurant, large interior courtyard garden with fountains, valet parking. Located adjacent to City Market. Nearby: Tours; walk to historic sites, shopping on King Street and in the Shops at Charleston Place.

A Charleston native remembers the Old City Market this way. "It was the kind of place where for less than $10 and in less than half an hour, you could get a bowl of chili, a tattoo, and a social disease."

The market is still the center of action, especially for tourists, but it has changed. Over the years the city has put money and muscle into revitalizing neglected parts of downtown, including the corner of Market and East Bay Streets, the very intersection where you now find Planters Inn. Today the market bulges with arts, crafts, interesting shops, street vendors, carriage tours, and, of course, tourists.

Inside the inn you can't hear the commotion of the busy market. And the single most distinctive feature about the guest rooms is their sheer size. Even in fine older homes you don't often see bedrooms this large. These are furnished with Baker reproduction four-poster beds. Armoires hide the television and drawers. Settees, chairs, and a coffee table create a separate sitting area in each room.

Prints of horses in the quiet, tan hallways carry the British-born planter's theme from the rooms to the front parlor, where tea is served in the afternoons. You'll notice a number of Audubon prints in this room and the foyer. The artist, who spent much of his time living and working in Charleston, was—and, indeed, still is—much revered in these parts.

The inn's restaurant, Peninsula Grill, opened to rave national reviews in 1997. The dining room is a tasteful fusion of traditional Charleston style with contemporary embellishments. The interior decor coupled with views of lush gardens outside create an elegant yet relaxed setting for exquisitely prepared and presented local cuisine.

In January 1999 the inn became a member of Relais & Chateaux, which is renowned for wonderful standards of service. Over the years we've watched the property grow and improve from a simply good property to the really fine one it is today.

This is a quiet, well-run inn sheltering you right in the middle of an area that produces all the excitement you can stand—even without the chili, the tattoo, and the disease.

HOW TO GET THERE: From I-26, take the East Bay Street exit downtown, turn left on South Market Street, and take the next left on Church Street. Go left again onto North Market Street. (You must make this U-turn because North and South Market Streets are both one-way.) The inn will be on your right at the Meeting Street intersection.

Two Meeting Street Inn ♥
Charleston, South Carolina 29401

INNKEEPERS: Pete and Jean Spell

ADDRESS/TELEPHONE: 2 Meeting Street; (843) 723–7322

WEB SITE: www.twomeetingstreet.com

ROOMS: 9, all with private bath, television, iron and ironing board, hair dryer, ceiling fan, clock radio, queen poster bed. Not handicapped accessible. No-smoking inn.

RATES: $165 to $295, single or double; includes continental breakfast. Minimum 2-day stay requested on weekends. No credit cards. Children over 12 welcome.

OPEN: Year-round.

FACILITIES AND ACTIVITIES: High tea each afternoon. Nearby: Restaurants, walk to most historic sites in Charleston.

On a scale of one to ten for elegance, Two Meeting Street Inn is at least a twelve. Incredible. It's a renovated 1892 Queen Anne mansion filled with family antiques, Oriental rugs, lamps, silver, and crystal. The Tiffany stained-glass windows and carved-oak paneling are simply breathtaking.

The guest rooms in this B&B inn are similarly luxurious, with four-poster and canopied beds and period museum-quality furniture.

We don't want to give you the impression that the inn feels like a touch-me-not museum. It's livable. There is a small kitchen on each floor, for cooling wine and making coffee and snacks.

And staying at the inn is fun. From the piazzas, you can see everything that goes on in Battery Park. In the early evening, guests often gather on the porch for sherry or a cocktail and conversation and to watch the action in the park: kids, couples, carriages. Weddings are the best fun. As one guest said, "We sit and gawk."

The exterior of the inn, with its sweeping piazzas and gleaming white paint, is one of the most photographed and sketched and painted buildings in Charleston. You often see artists in Battery Park, facing the inn, deeply absorbed in trying to capture its splendor on paper or film. Not surprisingly,

the inn has also been discovered by the television travel programs.

HOW TO GET THERE: From I-26 or U.S. 17, take the Meeting Street exit and stay on it until you come to the Battery, at the end of the street. The inn is at the corner of South Battery and Meeting.

Vendue Inn
Charleston, South Carolina 29401

INNKEEPER: Linda Edmison

ADDRESS/TELEPHONE: 19 Vendue Range; (843) 577-7970 or (800) 845-7900; fax (843) 577-2913

WEB SITE: www.vendueinn.com

E-MAIL: vendueinnresv@aol.com

ROOMS: 65, all with private bath, television, and telephone; some with whirlpool; some with gas fireplace, sitting area, canopy or sleigh bed; some handicapped accessible. Most non-smoking.

RATES: $135 to $175 standard, $229 to $305 suites; includes Southern breakfast buffet, wine and cheese, turndown service, after-dinner cordials, nightly milk and cookies. Packages available. Rates lowest between

July 1 and September 14. Credit cards accepted. Children welcome.

OPEN: Year-round.

FACILITIES AND ACTIVITIES: Fine and casual dining for guests and the public by reservation Monday through Saturday, bar service with dinners in dining room, dinner and cocktails overlooking courtyard at Harbor on Rooftop. Nearby: Historic sites and tourist attractions of Charleston, antiques shops.

BUSINESS TRAVEL: Two-line telephone with dataport in room, fax and copy machine available. Three meeting rooms. Catering and private parties. Concierge and meeting planner on-site.

*Y*ears ago, on our first trip to Charleston we stayed at the Vendue, and we've kept up with its growth and changes ever since. We walked in about 5:00 P.M. to find guests sipping wine in the sunken indoor courtyard. Sometimes we'd rather enjoy a cocktail up on the roof garden, from where you can see Patriot's Point and Fort Sumter and enjoy the coolest breeze around.

The inn is in the French merchant district, created in what was once an old warehouse. At various points throughout the inn, you can still see the old beams and old pine floors burnished to a rich glow.

The guest rooms vary in size and style. They may have canopied or sleigh beds, with Oriental rugs and eighteenth-century reproduction furniture. Some suites have sitting rooms with fireplaces, whirlpool tubs in the bathrooms, and wet bars. Junior suites are done in a French style consistent with the inn's location in the French Quarter of Charleston. These have marble baths with whirlpools, marble fireplaces, and luxurious sitting rooms.

The inn's restaurant, called The Library at Vendue, is decorated in a bright, eclectic style, with lots of leather-bound books tucked into niches around the restaurant. The cuisine is continental with Southern overtones. Not surprisingly for Charleston, the seafood dishes are outstanding. Other specialties include lamb, beef, and duck. (You can have cocktails and hors d'oeuvres on the rooftop before dinner if you like.)

For intimate dinners or private parties, you may request a separate dining room.

HOW TO GET THERE: Take I-26 to the last exit (Meeting Street), go 8 blocks to Market Street, turn right, go 2 blocks on East Bay and take a left on Vendue Range.

Victoria House Inn
Charleston,
South Carolina 29401

INNKEEPERS: Rick Widman, owner; Michelle Woodhull, manager

ADDRESS/TELEPHONE: 208 King Street; (843) 720-2944 or (800) 933-5464; fax (843) 720-2930

WEB SITE: www.charminginns.com

E-MAIL: vhi@charminginns.com

ROOMS: 18; all with private bath, minirefrigerator, cable television, and telephone; some with fireplace or whirlpool. No-smoking rooms available. Limited wheelchair access.

RATES: $125 to $255 low season, $185 to $255 high season; includes continental breakfast and afternoon wine and sherry; turndown service. Discover Charleston package available seasonally, $295 to $345. Extra person $20; children under 12 years old free. Credit cards accepted.

OPEN: Year-round.

FACILITIES AND ACTIVITIES: Located in the heart of Charleston. Nearby: Walking distance to restaurants, antiques shops, historic sites. Plantations and beaches nearby.

*L*ocation, location, and location. The Victoria House Inn is on King Street, the Rodeo Drive of Charleston for more than 200 years. The area has more antiques shops, boutiques, fine restaurants, and music clubs than you could do justice to in a month's time. Staying here provides just the right balance for folks who want to be in the thick of things but also need a little rest and relaxation.

You enter the lobby of this B&B inn off an alley on King Street. In keeping with the building's Romanesque style, popular in the 1880s, the lobby is decorated with antiques and period reproductions such as the late-Victorian sofa and the gold-painted Eastlake mirror. An interior designer complemented the furnishings with sheer lace panels and terra-cotta and gold tasselled silk damask valances for the floor-to-ceiling windows. The glossy white wainscoting is accentuated by dark green striped wallpaper above—the stripes make the 12-foot-high ceilings seem even higher.

You might fall in love with the suite that has a bay window with a table and armchairs overlooking King Street. From this spot, you can watch the morning get going while you're having your first cup of coffee and enjoying the morning paper.

There's a nifty quirk in the inn, too. The handles on the water faucets in the baths turn backwards—by design—from the way American-made handles turn. They give the inn a European flair!

HOW TO GET THERE: The Victoria House is on King Street just south of the Market Street intersection.

Claussen's Inn at Five Points
Columbia, South Carolina 29205

INNKEEPER: Ron Jones

ADDRESS/TELEPHONE: 2003 Greene Street; (803) 765–0440 or (800) 622–3382; fax (803) 799–7924

WEB SITE: www.columbiasc.com/claussensinn

ROOMS: 21, plus 8 suites, some bilevel; all with private bath, telephone, clock radio, television, desk, ceiling fan, and/or private balcony; some wheelchair accessible.

RATES: $110 to $128 for rooms, $125 to $140 for suites; includes continental breakfast, sodas, fruit, wine, turndown service; extra person $15; children younger than 12 years old are free in the parents' room.

OPEN: Year-round.

FACILITIES AND ACTIVITIES: Courtyard lobby with skylights, fountain, hot tub. Nearby: University of South Carolina, museums, galleries, shops.

As soon as we learned that this B&B inn was located in a building constructed in 1928 as Claussen's Bakery, we were intrigued and had to check it out. Once we did, we were sorry we couldn't stay longer. Situated on a tree-shaded street in the Five Points district conveniently near the campus of the University of South Carolina, the neighborhood in which the inn is located has a quiet residential feel with sidewalk cafes, small shops, and good restaurants only steps away.

Warm brown-toned bricks concealed the many delights in store once we got inside. A courtyardlike area with lush plantings, terra-cotta tile floors, a fountain, and groupings of indoor/outdoor furniture are all under the cover of a huge skylight, which gave us the impression of being outside. What a treat this must be on days when the weather is less than ideal. A continental breakfast of juice, hot beverages, and muffins and croissants is served here each morning, and a complimentary bar with sodas, wines, brandy, sherry, and fresh fruit is available all day. The courtyard makes an ideal place to relax with one of the inn's magazines or newspapers or to gather with friends or business associates for some quiet conversation. Many other original architectural features have been preserved throughout the building.

Spacious, well-appointed guest rooms are a giant step above cookie-cutter motel/hotel rooms, although they aren't as distinctive and individual as you might find in a great bed-and-breakfast. Traditional furnishings are period reproductions and overstuffed upholstered pieces. Many beds are romantic four-posters or iron and brass. Ample storage and closet space as well as generous amenities contribute to the modern creature comforts. We particularly liked the bilevel suites, with a sitting room and bathroom on the first level and a loft bedroom and bath on the second level.

The inn's location near the University of South Carolina makes it an ideal place to stay for parents and those doing business with the college. Tourists to Columbia will love trendy Five Points. We'd definitely stay here on a future trip to Columbia.

HOW TO GET THERE: Take I-126 into town, where it turns into U.S. 76. Follow U.S. 76 to Harden Street and turn right. Follow Harden to Greene Street and turn right. The inn is in the first block on your right.

1790 House
Bed and Breakfast Inn ♥
Georgetown, South Carolina 29440

INNKEEPER: Patricia and John Wiley

ADDRESS/TELEPHONE: 630 Highmarket Street; (843) 546–4821 or
(800) 890–7432

WEB SITE: www.1790house.com

E-MAIL: jwiley1212@cs.com

ROOMS: 6, all with private bath and sitting area, telephone, clock
radio; some with decorative or gas-log fireplace, ceiling fan, wheelchair
access; ask about children.

RATES: $95 to $135, double occupancy; includes full breakfast and
evening refreshments. Ask about special packages.

OPEN: Year-round.

FACILITIES AND ACTIVITIES: Formal parlor, dining room, informal
keeping room, veranda, gardens, gazebo, tearoom, and gift shop.
Nearby: Historic district; museums, house museums, historic
churches; shops, restaurants; plantations; boat, tram, and horse-and-
carriage tours; biking, fishing, golf.

BUSINESS TRAVEL: Telephone jack to download computer; corporate
discounts.

*T*he first thing that caught our eye was the gracious double stairway
leading from the street up to the full-length veranda of this
imposing three-story home. It's no wonder that staircases such as
these are known as "welcoming arms." We weren't disappointed; the Wileys'
welcome and hospitality were just as warm as we'd hoped.

The 1790 House is a meticulously restored West Indies–style Colonial
house named after the year it was built by the Allstons, one of the most
prominent families in South Carolina history. An attractive frame house,
with its hipped roof and five hip-roofed dormers, it has a foundation laid in
English bond brick except for the porch foundation, which is Bermuda coral.
These large pieces of coral were used as ballast in early cargo ships coming
from the British West Indies to Georgetown and then appropriated for
building material.

Hardwood floors, 11-foot-high ceilings, elegant detailed cornices, original chair rail, wainscoting, fluted mantels, and hand-carved dental molding characterize the generously proportioned public rooms and guest chambers. Whether you want to socialize with other guests and your hosts or spend some time alone, there are numerous attractive, tastefully decorated places to indulge your desires. Curling up by the fire in the formal parlor is a popular thing to do on chilly evenings. A television, VCR, books, games, and refreshments in a guest refrigerator draw guests to the keeping room, which was created by enclosing a veranda. While you're relaxing there, take note of the unusual ceiling plaster. In nice weather, rocking chairs and wicker furniture beckon you to the veranda, where you can survey the handsome historic district. Brick paths meander through the formal gardens; here you can sit on a stone bench to watch the birds or relax in the gazebo.

You'll get a wonderful night's sleep in one of the spacious guest rooms in the main house or in the cottage. A gracious guest room located on the first floor in the old library sports lovely built-in bookcases and a Victorian-era queen-size iron and brass bed, but the best feature is the gas-log fireplace. Created from old servants' quarters, Captain Quarters has a wood-beam ceiling, a comfortable sitting area with a television, and a game table and chairs. A twin-size sleigh bed in addition to the king-size pencil-post bed makes the Indigo Room ideal for those traveling with an additional person. A fireplace and a desk complete the picture. Romance abounds in the Rice Planters Room, which is dominated by a queen-size rice-carved canopy bed and a fireplace. Tucked up under the eaves, the Prince George Suite features an antique iron-and-brass bed, a separate sitting room with an additional daybed, and a bathroom with a square-foot tub. A whirlpool tub is just one of the attractions at the Dependency Cottage, which boasts a patio overlooking the garden and a separate sitting room.

Taking tea is quintessentially English—a social event and a culinary delight. The Wileys operate the Angel's Touch Tea Room, where a proper English tea is served to the public at 12:30 P.M. and 2:30 P.M. Tuesday, Thursday, and Saturday. Reservations are required. Handmade tea cozies, Christmas ornaments, angels, note cards, and jewelry pouches are among the gifts sold in the tearoom's gift shop.

HOW TO GET THERE: From Myrtle Beach, take U.S. 17 south to Georgetown, cross over the bridge, and go about ¼ mile to St. James Street and turn left. Go 2 blocks to Highmarket Street and turn right. The B&B is ahead 3 blocks, at the corner of Highmarket and Screven. From Charleston, take U.S. 17 north to Georgetown, cross over the bridge, and go to the third traffic light. Turn right on Highmarket and go 7 blocks to the B&B. From I-95, exit at

Manning and take U.S. 521 into Georgetown where it becomes Highmarket Street. Continue to number 630.

Fannie Kate's Inn, Restaurant & Pub ⊄⊄

McCormick, South Carolina 29835

INNKEEPER: Lee and Jerry Lapp

ADDRESS/TELEPHONE: 127 South Main Street (mailing address: P.O. Box 899); (864) 465–0061 or (800) 965–0061; fax (803) 465–3238

WEB SITE: www.fanniekates.com

E-MAIL: fanniekates@wctel.net

ROOMS: 8, all with private bath, ceiling fan, window air conditioner, telephone; 3 with gas-log fireplace; 1 with sofabed; 1 with small refrigerator; 1 with wheelchair access; all with access to porches and grounds. Children welcome; dogs under 15 pounds allowed. Upstairs porch for smoking.

RATES: $70 to $85, double; includes full breakfast and evening beverage. Additional person $10; AAA and military discounts. Credit cards accepted.

OPEN: Year-round.

FACILITIES AND ACTIVITIES: Restaurant, pub, porches, patio, deck. Nearby: Theatrical performances and art exhibits at the McCormick Arts Council at the Kenturah, old-fashioned soda fountain, antiques shops, Sumter National Forest, Clarks Hill Lake/Lake Thurmond, hiking, biking, water sports, four golf courses, skeet shooting.

*I*n the booming railroad days at the end of the nineteenth century, McCormick supported several hotels, one of which was the McCormick Temperance Hotel. Built in 1882, the hotel provided safe lodgings for railroad passengers as well as "sample rooms"—places designated for drummers (traveling salesmen) to display their wares to local shopkeepers. In 1905 Mrs. J. M. Marsh bought the hotel. All her children, including seven-year-old Fannie Kate, assisted her with her duties at the hotel. Years later, when Mrs. Marsh died, an adult Fannie Kate took over the opera-

tion of the hotel and continued to run it in the family tradition. Locals began to refer to the hotel affectionately as "Fannie Kate's." Time passed and Fannie Kate passed, and the hotel fell into disrepair. In 1995 the hotel was completely renovated to add the guest rooms and private
baths. In a stroke of luck, much of Fannie Kate's furniture remained and has been refurbished to give the hotel the ambience it had during its heydey—with lots of modern conveniences added, of course.

Cozy rooms are simply furnished and accessorized with quilts and other country accents. Hardwood floors, high ceilings, and tall windows create a light, airy look. Soft colors, ceiling fans, and 1930s iron beds original to the hotel complete the comfy, country ambience. Guests enjoy a full hot breakfast each morning with some of the best pancakes and coffee around. The restaurant is open Monday through Saturday for breakfast, lunch, and dinner and features the soft glow of gaslights during the evening meal. The ambience is further enhanced by fireplaces in each of the dining rooms. The menu offers diners a variety of dishes from seafood to spaghetti and has something for everyone's taste.

The newest addition since we visited is the Pub, open Monday through Saturday. Located below street level, it opens out onto the patio and a new large deck for alfresco drinks and dining. Often customers come to relax, listen to music, play cards, and at times dance to live entertainment.

Guests also like to gather and relax in the upstairs parlor, where there's a gas-log fireplace, comfy seating, and a television. When the weather's good, a common sight in McCormick is folks sitting on one of the rockers on the porch of Fannie Kate's chatting and having a cool drink. There's no better or more peaceful place from which to watch the slow-paced world of McCormick through a screen of oaks and azaleas.

HOW TO GET THERE: From I-85, take SC 187 to SC 81 into the center of McCormick. From I-20, take SC 28 to U.S. 221 into McCormick. From I-26 in Columbia, take I-26 in Columbia, take I-126 west to U.S. 378 and follow it west into McCormick.

Rosemary Hall
and Lookaway Hall 💙
North Augusta, South Carolina 29841

INNKEEPER: Geneva Robinson

ADDRESS/TELEPHONE: 804 Carolina Avenue; (803) 278–6222 or
(800) 531–5578; fax: (803) 278–4877

ROOMS: 23 rooms, all with private bath, robes, hair dryer, cable
television, direct-dial telephone with dataport, clock radio; some
with sitting room, porch, whirlpool; some wheelchair accessible;
not suitable for children.

RATES: $89 to $195 single or double occupancy; includes breakfast,
afternoon refreshments, evening hor d'oeuvres at the cocktail hour,
turndown service; High Tea served once a month.

OPEN: Year-round.

FACILITIES AND ACTIVITIES: Parlors, verandas, beautifully landscaped grounds, courtyard, sunken garden, 24-hour concierge. Nearby:
Historic district; across the river from Augusta, Georgia; museums, art
galleries, golf courses.

BUSINESS TRAVEL: Telephone with dataport; meeting space for up
to 125; fax and copy service available.

wo of the best places to stay in Augusta, Georgia, aren't in Georgia
at all but across the river in North Augusta, South Carolina. The
epitome of Old South elegance and old-world luxury, these two
extraordinary sister Greek Revival mansions located across the street from
each other were built at the turn of the twentieth century by wealthy brothers
James and Walter Jackson high on a hill above the Savannah River, where they
could gaze across to Augusta, Georgia, without any other structures imped-
ing their view. Today they operate as an exceptional four-diamond B&B inn in
the European tradition, and, despite the intervention of a century, we sat in
rockers on the majestic many-columned verandas and enjoyed a similar vista.

Inside the towering foyer in Rosemary Hall, we could just imagine a determined Rhett Butler carrying a protesting Scarlett up the breathtaking grand
staircase. Framed by two majestic fluted pillars at the bottom and two ornate

converted gas lamps, a stained-glass window, and a portrait at the landing, the staircase then splits and continues its course to the second floor. Throughout the houses, extraordinary original curly-pine paneling, woodwork, light fixtures, door fixtures, and tile surrounding the fireplaces reveal the immense wealth these brothers enjoyed. Public parlors and dining rooms are elegantly furnished with original antiques, period reproductions, impressive artwork, and Oriental carpets.

Between the two mansions and a new addition built onto Lookaway Hall are twenty-three spacious guest chambers—eight at Rosemary, five at Lookaway, and ten in the addition. Rooms in the main houses benefit from high ceilings and tall windows. Carefully chosen antiques and reproductions as well as lavish fabrics give each room its own seductions that allow you to escape to another time. Every bedchamber has a private bath and all the modern conveniences; some boast a secluded sitting area, private veranda, and whirlpool tub to promote relaxation.

With the staff's commitment to traditional European service, guests are treated to a complimentary full breakfast, afternoon tea and cookies, and evening hors d'oeuvres. A more extensive, traditional English High Tea is offered once a month, and cocktails are available at a nominal charge.

Recapture the romance and charm of a bygone era by lounging in the elegant parlors or on the verandas or strolling through the well-manicured grounds.

HOW TO GET THERE: From I-20 west, as soon as you cross the Savannah River, take exit 1 and go 2⁶⁄₁₀ miles south on Martintown Road. Just before the third traffic light, turn right onto Carolina Avenue. Rosemary Hall, where you will check in, is ½ mile down the hill on the right.

Sea View Inn
Pawleys Island, South Carolina 29585

INNKEEPER: Page Oberlin

ADDRESS/TELEPHONE: Box 210; (843) 237-4253; fax (843) 237-7909

WEB SITE: www.virtualcity.com

ROOMS: 20, all with private half-bath (showers at ends of halls), some with air-conditioning.

RATES: $95 to $120, single; $70 to $98 per person, double occupancy; includes three meals a day. Weekly: $650 to $795, single; $460 to $630 per person, double occupancy; includes 3 meals a day. Minimum 2-night stay. Priority given to stays of a week or longer. Inquire about spring watercolor weeks and fitness weeks. No credit cards.

OPEN: Last week of April through October.

FACILITIES AND ACTIVITIES: Beachfront and umbrellas; crab dock in salt marsh. Nearby: Boating, fishing, naturalist's studies in the salt marsh and surrounding area.

*P*awleys Island is a small sea island, 4 miles long and one house wide, where the people are proud to say that nothing changes and nobody hurries. You won't find any commercial activity here, just what Page likes to call "barefoot freedom at its best."

Guest rooms are simple and comfortable. The living room has a brick fireplace, grass mats on the floor, and couches and chairs upholstered in pastel colors. There are good books everywhere.

Many watercolors, mostly beach and water scenes, hang on the walls. They are the work of artists who take the weeklong watercolor workshop held at the inn early each spring. Some of the pictures are for sale.

The beach is the kind of soft white sand that seems to beg to be pictured on canvas or watercolor paper.

You can hear and see the ocean from practically every point in the inn, including the dining room. Meals served here emphasize Low Country foods such as gumbos and black-eyed peas with corn bread, and seafood in some form each day. The desserts range from a creamy chocolate pie to a light and fluffy peanut butter pie.

If you're here for the early spring wellness week, when people come to shake off winter lethargy with yoga, daily massage, and exercise, the meals feature vegetarian entrees, seafood, and whole grains. Then in the fall, there's a nature week featuring bird talks, shelling, beach walks, canoe trips, and other outdoor activities.

During the rest of the season, sunning, swimming, and shelling take up guests' time. Toward the end of the day, they sometimes gather on the porch facing the marsh for an afternoon cocktail. Even if no other people show up, you're not exactly alone on the porch. You can talk to the green parrot in the big white cage. We don't know his name. He wouldn't tell us.

HOW TO GET THERE: From Route 17 northbound, turn at the PAWLEYS ISLAND sign onto the connector road. In less than a mile you must turn left or right. Turn left. The inn will be about four telephone poles south of the chapel.

Liberty Hall Inn
Pendleton, South Carolina 29670

INNKEEPERS: Lorett and Randy Hayes

ADDRESS/TELEPHONE: 621 South Mechanics Street; (864) 646-7500 or (800) 643-7944; fax (864) 646-7500

WEB SITE: www.bbonline.com/sc/liberty

E-MAIL: libertyhallinn@aol.com

ROOMS: 7; all with private bath, television, and telephone. No smoking in guest rooms.

RATES: $93 to $135 per room, includes continental-plus breakfast.

OPEN: Year-round.

FACILITIES AND ACTIVITIES: Full-service restaurant open to the public (except Monday), lounge; reservations appreciated; full liquor service. Located in Historic Pendleton, which is on the National Register of Historic Places. Nearby: golf, Lake Hartwell, Clemson University, many historic sites, Pendleton Playhouse.

BUSINESS TRAVEL: Telephone, computer and modem setup, excellent workspace in room; fax available; conference facilities.

*T*he inn, which was built around 1840, began life as a five-room summer home, became part of a dairy farm, then served as a boarding school. Operating as an inn since 1985, the rambling structure with the full-length, wraparound verandas on both floors features spacious, high-ceilinged rooms, heart-pine floors, antiques, and charm in abundance.

The inn is comfortably furnished with period antiques and lots of cheery reds and Charleston yellows in the draperies, bed covers, and linens; the beds

are still firm and comfortable. The owners have added to those basics lots of little personal items: books, family pictures, knickknacks, family needle-work, and quilts. And, being readers, they saw to it that every room has a good lamp on each side of the bed. The overall effect is that you can settle into a room as comfortably as if your own mother had fixed it up for your visit.

But let's talk about food, because the Hayeses are such good cooks. The menu changes regularly, but you can expect something like crab cakes or a spectacular beef tenderloin fillet marinated in a special sauce, plus chicken entrees and probably some other seafood choices. The owners say fresh ingredients and inspiration determine what they offer.

Randy continues to refine and expand his wine list while keeping the offerings in a price range that will not require you to take out a second mort-gage to buy a bottle of wine. The list changes often because he is always look-ing for a good value.

HOW TO GET THERE: From I-85, take exit 19B toward Clemson and follow U.S. 76/28 almost to Pendleton where Business 28 turns to the right. The inn is on the right, shortly after you turn. From U.S. 123, take 76/28 to Pendle-ton and turn left onto Business 28. Go past the town square. The inn will be on your left.

Woodlands Resort & Inn

Summerville, South Carolina 29483

INNKEEPER: Marty Wall

ADDRESS/TELEPHONE: 125 Parsons Road; (843) 875–2600 or
(800) 774–9999; fax (843) 875–2603

WEB SITE: www.woodlandsinn.com

E-MAIL: reservations@woodlandsinn.com

ROOMS: 19, including 9 executive suites, 4 junior suites, and 6 superior rooms; all with private bath, 2 telephones, television with VCR, alarm/radio, in-room safe, and robes; some with CD player, fireplace and/or whirlpool bath, and heated towel racks. Three rooms are accessible to the disabled.

RATES: $295 for superior rooms, $325 for junior suites, $350 for executive suites, all double or single occupancy; includes welcome champagne and roses, Evian water, afternoon tea, turndown service, valet parking, and leisure activities; meals and spa services extra. Numerous special packages available. Special arrangements for limousines, flowers, spa services, and additional dining can be arranged through concierge. Credit cards accepted.

OPEN: Year-round.

FACILITIES AND ACTIVITIES: Breakfast, lunch, and dinner in dining room; bar, conservatory, all-natural day spa; two English clay lighted tennis courts, professional croquet lawn, seasonally heated outdoor swimming pool with poolside food and beverage service; nature trails, bicycles. Facilities for weddings and small conferences. Nearby: Historic Summerville and Charleston, plantations, many golf courses, ocean beaches, seasonal theater, antiques shopping, galleries.

BUSINESS TRAVEL: Located 23 miles northwest of Charleston; executive conference center can serve 130 for dinner or 225 for a reception; boardroom for 8; private dining room for 12; fax; audiovisual equipment; food service.

*B*uilt in 1906 and a luxurious private home until 1993, Woodlands was renovated and expanded to become an exquisite inn in 1995. The original house provides space for a delightful formal parlor and sumptuous guest rooms. Wings added to both sides of the main house blend perfectly with the original structure and create room for suites, a restaurant, a lounge, and a conservatory. Elegantly appointed, without succumbing to the decorator look, public rooms and guest rooms reflect the Anglo-Indian and West Indian styles that so influenced the Low Country in past centuries. You feel that you are in a gracious home rather than a hotel.

You'll be thrilled with whichever lavish, spacious guest room or suite you're lucky enough to be assigned. Each has a distinct personality, but all are created with an eye to style and creature comforts with magnificent furnishings, four-poster or canopy king- or queen-size rice beds, upscale amenities, and all the modern conveniences. Fresh flowers—usually signature yellow roses—as well as a split of iced Perrier-Jouet champagne await you in each chamber, so kick off your shoes and relax in a deep chair while you imbibe this extravagant welcome. So enticing are the guest rooms that you may never want to leave yours, but the resort offers many inducements to tempt you out to explore and enjoy.

Created with the purpose of providing a restorative retreat par excellence for the body, mind, and spirit, the resort tempts guests with a variety of activities in the relaxed gentility of the countryside. Perhaps you can pamper yourself with the services of the spa: facials, manicures, pedicures, herbal body wraps or sea salt glows, or massage therapy. If your afternoon schedule

permits, request afternoon tea in the luxurious Winter Garden, a cheery conservatory furnished with wicker.

Dining while listening to the lilting strains emanating from the grand piano is a gastronomic experience at Woodlands and should be savored. Chef Ken Vedrinski's innovative, sophisticated, contemporary regional cuisine with an Asian influence has been recognized each year since 1997 with the AAA Five Diamond Award for Culinary Excellence—an award shared by only a few other restaurants in America; Woodlands is the only one so honored in South Carolina. *Condé Nast Traveler* recognized the dining room as one of the Top Three in North America. The stunning circular formal dining room offers many windowside or tucked-away tables perfect for lovers. Those who want to watch Chef Vedrinski at work may request a seat at the chef's table in the kitchen. Menus for three to five fixed-price courses change daily. Presentation and service are exemplary. Accompany your feast with a selection from the award-winning wine list. When you return to your bedchamber, you'll find that nightly turndown service includes chocolates or cookies handmade by Woodlands' pastry chef. Sweet dreams are guaranteed.

All this, as well as impeccable service and attention to detail, has earned the one-of-a-kind resort the designation as one of only seventeen AAA Five Diamond Resorts and Restaurants in the country. It is also a member of the prestigious world-renowned Relais & Chateaux collection of exquisite hotels—one of only four in the Southeast. It's little wonder that readers of *Condé Nast Traveler* voted Woodlands the Number Two small hotel in America in 2000.

HOW TO GET THERE: Take exit 199A off I-26 to Summerville (Highway 17A, Main Street). After you cross the railroad tracks, watch for the town square; turn right (north) onto Route 165 (West Richardson Avenue) and follow it to Parsons Road (on left). Turn left; Woodlands is on your left.

Summerville:
Flowertown in the Pines

During the eighteenth and early nineteenth centuries, the wealthy of the Low Country around Charleston escaped from the oppressive summer heat, humidity, and the threat of malaria by retreating 20 miles inland to the higher, drier, cooler pine forests of the town of Dorchester, now Summerville. This haven was their own closely guarded secret until 1886, when the International Congress of Physicians, meeting in Paris, declared Summerville to have one of the two most healthful climates in the world—especially for those with respiratory problems. Once the secret was out, almost overnight the tiny village became a world-renowned summer and winter retreat for the international elite.

Thus began the Golden Age of Summerville, and hotels and inns sprang up as well as grand mansions, which served as seasonal "cottages" for the wealthy. William Howard Taft and Theodore Roosevelt wintered there. Although the hotels and inns are long gone, many of the other architectural gems survive today, and there's no more delightful way to spend an afternoon than to drive up and down the tree-lined streets to admire the mansions and imagine the grandeur of the past. Downtown Summerville is a quaint village surrounding a manicured town square with charming gift shops and restaurants. During the springtime Flowertown Festival, more than 200,000 visitors descend on Summerville to admire the flamboyant azaleas and more restrained dogwoods, as well as to inspect the art being sold by local, regional, and national artists.

Select List of
Other South Carolina Inns

Holley Inn

235 Richland Avenue
Aiken, SC 29801
(803) 648-4265

Upscale old hotel/motel; 48 rooms; restaurant, bar, continental breakfast, afternoon tea.

Wentworth Mansion

149 Wentworth Street
Charleston, SC 29401
(843) 853-1886 or (888) INN-1886

1880s Second Empire town house—tallest in Charleston; 21 rooms and suites, some with fireplaces; evening wine tasting, restaurant.

A Cypress Inn

16 Elm Street
Conway, SC 29526
(843) 248-8199 or (800) 575-5307

Located at the water's edge; 12 rooms; most with whirlpool bath and/or fireplace; full breakfast.

The Inn on the Square

104 Court Street
Greenwood, SC 29646
(864) 223-4488 or (800) 231-9109

Historic warehouse building converted to an inn; 48 rooms; restaurant, bar, pool; caters to business travelers.

Litchfield Plantation

Litchfield Plantation—River Road (mailing address: P.O. Box 290)
Pawleys Island, SC 29585
(843) 237-9322 or (800) 869-1410

Eighteenth-century rice plantation on 600 acres; 1750 home, carriage house; 38 rooms and suites in a modern addition; restaurant, tennis, pool, beach.

Tennessee

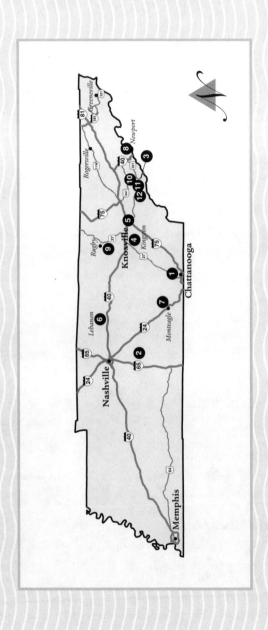

Tennessee

Numbers on map refer to towns numbered below.

* A Top Pick Inn

Adams Hilborne Mansion Inn and Restaurant

Chattanooga, Tennessee 37403

INNKEEPERS: Wendy and David Adams

ADDRESS/TELEPHONE: 801 Vine Street; (423) 265–5000;
fax (423) 265–5555

WEB SITE: www.innjoy.com

E-MAIL: innjoy@worldnet.att.net

ROOMS: 8, plus 3 suites; all with private bath, telephone, and cable
television; 1 room equipped for handicapped. No-smoking inn.

RATES: $125 to $195, rooms; $175 to $295, suites; single or double;
includes continental breakfast. Two-night minimum on weekends.

OPEN: Year-round.

FACILITIES AND ACTIVITIES: Restaurant; gift shop; free, lighted,
off-street parking. Nearby: Restaurants, University of Tennessee/
Chattanooga, The Challenger Learning Center, Erlanger Hospital.
Short drive to The Incline, a National Historic Site on Lookout
Mountain; Civil War battle sites; the Hunter Museum of Art; the
Tennessee Aquarium.

BUSINESS TRAVEL: Convenient to downtown and University of Ten-
nessee/Chattanooga. Meeting rooms, modem attachments, fax, good
work space in rooms.

*W*ell, Wendy and David did it again! Their Adams Edgeworth Inn
on the Monteagle Assembly Grounds in Monteagle is a notewor-
thy accomplishment that succeeded immediately. It never crossed
anyone's mind that having opened one inn Wendy and David would want
another, so their anouncement of the Adams Hilborne took us by surprise.

To the Adamses it makes perfect sense. They simply talk about having
"the country house" and "the city house." Wendy says, "Chattanooga's only
forty-five minutes away."

So, okay, the city house—with that Adams touch. This is a European-style
hotel in an 1889 Victorian building that looks like a castle. The exterior is
built of native mountain stone that makes it look almost fortified against

the storm troopers. Wendy and David found photographs and written descriptions of a twin house built in New Orleans that guided them in this renovation. The great oak staircase has been buffed to a soft gleam. There are hand-carved coffered ceilings, arched doorways, and Tiffany glass windows, all looking as splendid as they must have when they were new. The hotel is in the Fort Wood Historic District, a Civil War site, where buildings in a variety of architectural styles sit sedately amid the trees, giving you some sense of having stepped into a very good neighborhood at the turn of the century.

The rooms inside Adams Hilborne Mansion Inn have 16-foot-high ceil-

ings and hand-carved moldings. They are furnished with fine antiques and museum-quality art, then completed with such creature comforts as cotton sheets and an abundance of pillows. Some of the rooms have fireplaces adorned with their original mantels. The furnishings honor the history of the building.

In the public areas some of the outstanding features are 11-foot-tall pocket doors, original fixtures, antique chairs that are actually comfortable, a splendid stone fireplace, and tons of books everywhere.

The inn's restaurant has gone through several changes over the past few years but has now stabilized. Dinner is served Tuesday through Saturday evening in the gorgeous ballroom and in the Tiffany dining room. The cuisine is described as regional American and includes such dishes as baked-seared salmon steaks stuffed with crabmeat, crab-filled corn fritters, stuffed lobster tail (our personal favorite), at least one pork dish each day, and a catch of the day.

HOW TO GET THERE: From I-24, take Highway 27 north. Take the Fourth Street exit (1-C) from Highway 27. Go 1 mile and turn right onto Palmetto Street. Go 1½ blocks to the stop sign at the corner of Palmetto and Vine. Turn left onto Vine and left into the private parking lot.

Bluff View Inn ♥
Chattanooga, Tennessee 37377

INNKEEPERS: Julia Poston; Dr. and Mrs. Charles A. Portera, owners

ADDRESS/TELEPHONE: 412 East Second Street; (423) 265–5033, ext. 238 or (800) 725–8338, ext. 238; fax (423) 757–0120

ROOMS: 13 rooms and 3 suites, all with private bath, telephone with dataport, television, clock radio; some with coffeemaker, sitting area, balcony, fireplace, and/or whirlpool tub.

RATES: $100 to $200 for rooms; $225 to $275 for suites, double occupancy; includes full breakfast.

OPEN: Year-round.

FACILITIES AND ACTIVITIES: Restaurants, porches, gardens, boccie ball court. Nearby: Hunter Museum of American Art, River Gallery, Houston Museum of Decorative Arts, River Gallery Sculpture Garden.

BUSINESS TRAVEL: Renaissance Commons Conference Center offers meeting and banquet facilities; telephone with dataport.

We've discovered a wonderful little secret in Chattanooga. Yes, the city is the home of the famous Choo Choo, the Tennessee Aquarium, the historic Tennessee Valley Railroad, numerous important Civil War sites, Rock City Gardens, and Ruby Falls. But high up on the bluffs above the Tennessee River is an arts enclave—a delightful neighborhood of museums, working artist studios, galleries, parks and gardens, restaurants and cafes, and a great inn. Called the Bluff View Art District, the creative haven is anchored by the Bluff View Inn.

Such elegant accommodations are offered in each of the three mansions that together make up the inn, we don't know how you'd choose only one. Although they are of different styles, each house features high ceilings, large airy rooms, tall windows, beautiful hardwood floors, elegant fireplaces, and magnificent furnishings. Check-in for guests is at the English Tudor–style Maclellan House, so let's begin our tour there, where the dark-green front door opens into a world of bygone elegance. Built in the late 1800s, the house has been home to only two families. Many of the furnishings you'll see are one-of-a-kind heirlooms original to the house. Luxurious accommodations are found in six rooms and an exclusive penthouse suite. In the midst of all

Bluff View Art District

Fascinated by the artsy European/New Orleans–style ambience and wonderful old homes in the hilltop neighborhood surrounding the Hunter Museum of American Art, in 1991 Dr. and Mrs. Charles Portera began buying up and restoring homes and commercial buildings in what is now called the Bluff View Art District. They began small, with the building that now houses the River Gallery, but in just this short time they've created or attracted the Bluff View Scenic Overlook, River Gallery Sculpture Garden, Rembrandt's Coffee House, Tony's Pasta Shop and Trattoria, the Back Inn Cafe, the Renaissance Commons Conference Center, and the Bluff View Inn. Despite all these attractions, the area is a small, quiet 2-block cul-de-sac perfect for walking. You can spend an hour, a day, or a weekend there.

A feast for the eye, the nose, and the palate, Bluff View serves up visual and culinary arts, history, architecture, and landscaping. You might see a chocolatier hand-dipping truffles in the chocolate kitchen window; you'll surely get tantalizing whiffs of fresh bread just out of the oven at the bakery. For lunch or dinner, sample upscale Italian fare and rich desserts at the Back Inn Cafe, located in the rear of the C. G. Martin House. Located in the carriage house of the Bluff View Inn's Thompson House, Tony's Pasta Shop and Trattoria serves a classic Italian menu specializing in fresh house-made pastas, sauces, and rustic Italian breads. Rembrandt's Coffee House offers breakfast, lunch, and dinner as well as fine coffees, handmade chocolates, and freshly baked pastries. The very swanky Renaissance Commons Conference Center offers downtown's most elegant Sunday brunch.

Looking for art? The Hunter Museum of American Art houses an impressive collection of paintings, sculpture, and other art forms in a traditional building and a postmodern addition overlooking the river. You'll find an astounding array of glassware at the Annie Houston Museum of Decorative Arts. (The museum's array of pitchers is a hoot.) The River Gallery showcases the work of local and regional artisans, and their nearby River Gallery Sculpture Garden contains both permanent pieces of outdoor sculpture and traveling exhibitions.

Street fairs and musical performances keep the district hopping all year long. If for any reason you decide you don't want to spend every second of your visit on the bluffs, the historic neighborhood is conveniently connected to downtown and the North Shore on foot via Tennessee Riverwalk and the Walnut Street pedestrian bridge.

this old-world charm, however, you'll find all the modern comforts and conveniences: private bath, telephone, and cable television. Two rooms and the suite feature whirlpool tubs and Queen Anne–style handcrafted African mahogany vanities. Gardens surround the Maclellan House, and it offers spectacular views of the river and Maclellan Island. There's also a popular boccie ball court and a pleasant terrace.

Directly across the street is the traditional Colonial Revival–style C. G. Martin House, built in 1927. A full-length columned portico creates the quintessential Southern veranda. Double front doors lead into the main foyer, from which you can see the grand staircase and into the warmly paneled library. Upstairs, three spacious guest chambers are furnished with beautiful antiques complemented by carefully chosen traditional and contemporary art. Each of these rooms boasts a fireplace and whirlpool bath as well as cable television and a telephone. This house, too, offers splendid river views, and an addition in the rear houses the Back Inn Cafe, which offers indoor and outdoor dining.

Around on the next block is the 1908 Thompson House, a typical Victorian with a wraparound porch. It was the residence of an early mayor of Chattanooga. Today it offers four guest rooms and two apartment-size suites. Ideal for a longer stay, the suites offer a living room, bedroom, spacious bath with a whirlpool tub, and a fully equipped kitchen with a breakfast area. What's special about these suites, however, is that they boast gas-log fireplaces in both the living room and the bedroom.

Regardless of where you lay your head, a luscious gourmet breakfast is served in the lovely Audubon Room at the Maclellan House. In good weather the French doors may be thrown open to the herb garden and views. Breakfast choices might include French toast made from inn-baked baguettes topped with strawberry-kiwi glaze or an Italian sausage and portabello mushroom omelette. If you're in a hurry, you could always grab a muffin and a cappuccino at Rembrandt's Coffee House.

HOW TO GET THERE: From I–24, take exit 1C, the Fourth Street exit. Go 7 blocks on Fourth Street and turn left onto High Street. Go 2 blocks to East Second Street and turn right. Check in at the Maclellan House on the left.

Peacock Hill Country Inn
College Grove, Tennessee 37046

INNKEEPERS: Walter and Anita Ogilvie

ADDRESS/TELEPHONE: 6994 Giles Hill Road; (615) 368–7727 or (800) 327–6663; fax (615) 368–7933

WEB SITE: www.peacockhillinn.com

ROOMS: 7, plus 3 suites; all with king-size beds and private bath; some with whirlpool tub, all-around spray shower, and/or fireplace, TV, VCR, coffeemaker, minirefrigerator, ceiling fan, iron and ironing board, hair dryer; some with handicapped access.

RATES: $125 to $145 for Farmhouse rooms, $145 for McCall House rooms, $165 for Log Cabin Suite, $185 Grainery Suite, $225 for McCall House suites; all double or single occupancy; includes full breakfast, beverages, and snacks; $20 additional charge for extra people in room; $15 per night for horse stable, including feed. Candlelight Dinners on Friday and Saturday nights for $20; Bar suppers on Sunday through Thursday nights for $15; box lunches for $10 with 48-hour advance notice. Credit cards accepted. No smoking indoors.

OPEN: Year-round.

FACILITIES AND ACTIVITIES: Two parlors, dining room with hospitality bar, sunporch, books, games, television with VCR, good selection of videos, fitness equipment, riding and walking trails, stalls for those who bring their own horse, gardens. Fireside dinners or boxed lunches can be arranged. Nearby: Country music and other attractions of Nashville and Williamson County; Civil War sites and antiques shops of Franklin, including the Carter House and Carnton Plantation, Murfreesboro, and Lynchburg, home of the Jack Daniels Old Time Distillery; Natchez Trace Parkway; Henry Horton State Resort Park with eighteen-hole golf course; Ten-

nessee Walking Horse National Celebration in Shelbyville; Saturn Auto Plant in Spring Hill.

BUSINESS TRAVEL: Less than an hour's drive from Nashville; ideal for small corporate retreats.

We didn't actually see any of Peacock Hill Country Inn's three dozen peacocks, ancestors of which have inhabited the property for generations and which give the B&B inn its name, but we were assured that they were there and could be seen swaggering around the 1,000-acre working cattle ranch and farm during the day. The original 1850s farmhouse comprised only three high-ceilinged rooms connected by the same exposed, hand-hewn, red cedar beam and flanked by two brick fireplaces. Today these handsomely restored and cheerily decorated rooms serve as the inn's entry and two comfortable, inviting parlors. The Ogilvies have added a large wing that houses their kitchen, other public rooms, and five guest rooms. The warm, cozy breakfast room features clapboard walls, a checkerboard floor, and a brick fireplace as well as a hospitality bar where guests can get coffee, soft drinks, and snacks anytime day or night. French doors from the breakfast room lead onto an enclosed brick-floored sunporch with wicker furniture and ceiling fans. This is one of the most popular spots for relaxing at the inn.

Five spacious guest rooms in the Farmhouse, which are named for the Ogilvies' five grown children, vary in style and theme from country to Victorian to spring garden to Americana, but all sport all the modern amenities, including king-size beds, piped-in music controlled by bedside knobs, and wonderful bathrooms with whirlpool or claw-foot tubs and separate showers.

Although the exterior reveals little more than a rugged old farm building with a wagon port, the adjacent Grainery actually houses a handsome guest suite with a loft living room, a spacious Cottage Toile bedroom with a gas-log fireplace and whitewashed poster bed, and a European limestone bath with a double whirlpool and a separate shower. Other charming features include original poplar floors and painted beams as well as a fully furnished kitchenette. The old wagon port now serves as a private patio with bent-willow furniture. An old smokehouse has been converted to the Log Cabin Suite, where a fireplace dominates the exposed-log living room. There's an iron canopy bed in the loft bedroom, a claw-foot tub and separate shower in the bath, and private porch. Between the main house and the smokehouse, a trellised brick walkway and cottage garden provide another restful retreat.

Located in the hollow just a mile down the road is the McCall House, an antebellum farmhouse that has been completely restored and renovated to house three luxurious suites with private entrances, two with private screened porches, and one with a private deck. All these suites contain a king-size bed; fireplace; large, luxury private bath with a European all-around spray shower and double or claw-foot tub; TV/VCR; microwave; and small refrigerator. Premier among the suites is the Grand Suite, which gives the illusion of an English manor house, with a spacious log living room and original fireplace built in the mid-nineteenth century. Guests at the McCall House may fix their own breakfast or walk or ride over to the Farmhouse for a morning repast that includes a hot dish accompanied by freshly squeezed juice, fruit, and hot homemade breads.

HOW TO GET THERE: From I-65 North, take exit 46, Columbia/Chapel Hill, and go east on Highway 99 for $3\frac{9}{10}$ miles. Turn left on Highway 431 North and go $4\frac{6}{10}$ miles to Flat Creek Road. Turn right and go $6\frac{2}{10}$ miles to Giles Hill Road. Turn left and go ½ mile to the inn.

Buckhorn Inn 👪
Gatlinburg, Tennessee 37738

INNKEEPERS: Lee and John Mellor

ADDRESS/TELEPHONE: 2140 Tudor Mountain Road; (423) 436-4668; fax (423) 436-5009

WEB SITE: www.buckhorninn.com

E-MAIL: buckhorninn@msn.com

ROOMS: 9, plus 7 cottages, 2 guest houses; all with private bath; some with fireplace. Cottages and guest houses with television, refrigerator, coffeemaker, and fireplace. Cottages have whirlpool tub. Guest houses have 2 bedrooms, 2 baths.

RATES: $115 to $250, double; includes full breakfast and afternoon light refreshments. Credit cards accepted.

OPEN: Year-round.

FACILITIES AND ACTIVITIES: Fixed-price, set-menu dinner for guests by reservation, $25 per person. Spring-fed lake stocked with bream and bass. Located on 35 acres. Meditation labyrinth. Nearby: Hiking, swimming, tennis, racquetball, basketball, skiing, golf, shopping, and tourist activities. Close to Gatlinburg and Great Smoky Mountains National Park.

*T*he Buckhorn Inn sits atop a knoll where a log cabin once stood, overlooking the Smoky Mountains and, especially, Mt. LeConte. The inn was built in 1938 by Douglas Bebb; his brother Hubert, an architect, designed it. The inn remained in the family for many years.

Everything looks better than ever. And the short drive up the hill from the glitz of Gatlinburg, bringing you to the simple white building well settled into mature landscaping and woods, still soothes your jangled nerves, as does the view of the highest peaks of the Smokies.

Inside, the living room and dining room are divided from each other in one big, long room by a large stone fireplace in the middle of the front wall. The chairs and love seats are cool and summery looking in ivy-patterned upholstery.

From here, doors open out onto a narrow porch separated from a well-manicured lawn by a low hedge. From the lawn, stone steps lead to a groomed trail that meanders about the grounds.

The inn has always been known for its good food, and that, too, is better than ever. Everything is home cooked daily, from breads to desserts. A professional chef on staff creates sophisticated menus. At breakfast, for instance, your choices, in addition to standards such as country ham and eggs, might include a strawberry or walnut waffle with bacon or Buckhorn's own version of müesli. At dinner four-course gourmet dinners are served up with entrees ranging from marinated beef tenderloin to salmon Florentine en croute.

HOW TO GET THERE: Take U.S. 441 to Gatlinburg and turn onto U.S. 321 north at Gatlinburg Chamber of Commerce corner. Follow U.S. 321 north about 5 miles. Turn left at Buckhorn Road and go ¾ mile. Turn right at the BUCKHORN INN sign. The inn is ¼ mile on the right.

Eight Gables Inn 💗
Gatlinburg, Tennessee 37738

INNKEEPERS: Kim and Don Cason

ADDRESS/TELEPHONE: 219 North Mountain Trail; (865) 430–3344
or (800) 279–5716; fax (865) 430–3344 ext. 51

WEB SITE: www.eightgables.com

E-MAIL: 8gables@eightgables.com

ROOMS: 12 rooms and suites, all with private bath, cable television,
telephone; some with private patio or porch, gas-log fireplace,
whirlpool tub. No-smoking inn.

RATES: $119 to $189, double, includes full breakfast, complimentary
dessert, and beverage bar, turndown service on request. Each additional person, $15. All rates increase $10 in the month of October and
holidays. Off-season rates for January through March. Two-night minimum stay on weekends; 3-night minimum on holidays. Children welcome. Credit cards accepted.

OPEN: Year-round.

FACILITIES AND ACTIVITIES: Magnolia Tea Room serves lunch Tuesday through Friday and dinner Saturday; small gift shop. Nearby:
Trolley to Gatlinburg or Pigeon Forge; Great Smoky Mountains
National Park; golf, shopping, white-water rafting, hiking, motor
nature trails, horseback riding; Knoxville is 30 miles away.

*S*ituated in a semi-rural mountain setting at the foot of Great Smoky
Mountains National Park and conveniently close to but away from
the teeming hordes in Gatlinburg, Pigeon Forge, and Sevierville, the
four-diamond-rated Eight Gables Inn makes an excellent headquarters from
which to explore both the wilderness regions and the modern man-made
attractions.

Constructed to resemble some of the national park lodges of the early
twentieth century, Eight Gables was actually built in 1991 with all the comforts and conveniences today's discriminating travelers expect. First you'll
notice the peaked dormers, gables, and turret; then the deep wraparound
veranda with hammocks, swings, and a glider; then the small formal gardens, which all combine to create a welcoming ambience.

Inside vast public rooms burnished hardwood floors, paneling, and
moldings, along with enticing fireplaces and a sweeping grand staircase are
featured. The public rooms are ideal whether you want to socialize with your

fellow guests or curl up with a book. The common area has three separate seating groupings: one around a fireplace, one around a grand piano, and one around big-screen TV.

Furnishings were carefully chosen to complete the casual elegance. Good-quality period reproductions in the guest rooms include king- or queen-size Charleston four-poster rice beds, made of brass, iron, or wicker. The feeling of opulence is further enhanced by the fact that the majority of the rooms are spacious enough for a sitting area and perhaps a small table and chairs as well. Some of the upstairs rooms have a high pitched ceiling and big arched window and/or skylights in the bathroom.

You'll never go hungry at Eight Gables Inn. In addition to a full breakfast, hot and cold beverages are always available in the guest pantry off the common area, a coffee and juice bar is set out before breakfast, and complimentary desserts and coffee are offered in the evening. The Magnolia Tea Room serves lunch several days a week as well as a romantic candlelight dinner by the fireplace on Saturday evenings by reservation only.

HOW TO GET THERE: From Gatlinburg, drive north on U.S. 441. Turn right on Little Smoky Road and left on North Mountain Trail. The inn is on the left.

Whitestone Country Inn
Kingston, Tennessee 37763

INNKEEPERS: Jean and Paul Cowell

ADDRESS/TELEPHONE: 1200 Paint Rock Road; (865) 376–0113 or
(888) 247–2464; fax (865) 376–4454

WEB SITE: www.whitestoneinn.com

E-MAIL: moreinfo@whitestoneinn.com

ROOMS: 20 rooms and suites, all with private bath, fireplace,
whirlpool tub, television, king-size bed, VCR, telephone, refrigerator,
desk, iron and ironing board, coffeemaker; some with waterfall
shower; some rooms are wheelchair accessible. Children welcome.

RATES: $125 to $250; includes country breakfast. Credit cards
accepted.

OPEN: Year-round.

FACILITIES AND ACTIVITIES: Great room; recreation room with table
tennis, pool table, exercise equipment, and board games; restaurant;
private dining room; more than 8,000 feet of verandas and decks;
sauna; 2 tennis courts; croquet and lawn games; gift shop; wedding
chapel; 8 miles of walking trails; boating facilities with kayaks and
paddleboats; fishing. Nearby: Horseback riding, bird-watching, hiking,
water sports, Old Courthouse Museum, Fort Southwest Point; one
hour from Knoxville, Chattanooga, and Great Smoky Mountain
National Park.

BUSINESS TRAVEL: Conference facilities with state-of-the-art audiovisual equipment; in-room telephone with dataport, desk; copy service
available.

*N*ot just an inn, this elegant and delightful place is a destination in
itself—a true getaway. Far out in the country, the hilly, tree-
covered, 360-acre estate affords sweeping vistas of Watts Bar Lake
on the Tennessee River and is surrounded by a wildlife and waterfowl refuge.
We'd seen pictures of the attractive main inn, but weren't prepared for the
vastness of the property, the collection of other buildings, or the variety of
things to do. Obviously, Jean and Paul have a vision, and we probably haven't
seen the scope of it yet. Their work has certainly paid off—the inn has been

named one of the Ten Most Romantic Inns in America by *America's Historic Inns.*

Our introduction began by driving through a big red barn that serves as the entrance. Registration is in the little red schoolhouse next door, which also serves as a gift shop. From there we could look down over the hill to see charming gazebos and a bandstand, the main inn with Watts Bar Lake behind it, and in the distance on the next hill, the wedding chapel and adjacent conference center. We just simply couldn't resist whipping out the cameras—this is a photographer's paradise.

Traditionally Southern looking, the main inn is a two-story structure covered in white clapboard and topped with a green roof. An almost full-length, one-story veranda is supported by columns. The rear of the building features another veranda and a patio, both overlooking the lake.

Inside, although the style is traditional, the look is sleek and elegant. The small foyer sports a white and black marble fireplace, which turned out to be double sided. The other side faces into the great room, where vast windows overlook another veranda and the lake in the distance. Next door is the cheery restaurant; downstairs is a huge recreation room with kitchenette facilities. The covered patio boasts a sauna. The cozy third-floor sitting room also has a fireplace and is filled with books and videos.

In the main house, every one of the nine guest rooms, named for birds, is a work of art. Furnishings are high-quality reproductions designed for comfort. We got a kick out of the bird house headboard in the Blue Heron Room (this room is handicapped accessible) and the picket-fence headboard in the Blue Bird Room. Suites are to die for with a large sitting area and a luxurious gargantuan bathroom. In addition to the accommodations in the main inn, there are several more guest rooms in the barn, the schoolhouse, and the conference center.

Just a word about the chapel: It will seat 170 (we've always associated the word *chapel* with a place maybe seating twenty). The property is perfect for the whole shebang—the wedding, reception, and the honeymoon.

You may want to go on a diet before you visit. Breakfast is a substantial meal that might consist of an egg casserole or blueberry pancakes served along with fried potatoes, sausage, biscuits, fruit, and juice. Lunch and dinner are available by twenty-four-hour advance reservation at an additional fee. Iced tea and cookies are always available if you get an attack of the munchies.

For those who want to do more than just stay and play in their room or rock on one of the verandas, there are 8 miles of walking trails and 8,000 feet of lake frontage with canoes, kayaks, and paddleboats. Fishing and bird-watching are popular pastimes.

HOW TO GET THERE: I-75 South, take exit 72/TN 72 and travel west 9 miles. When you get into the crossroads village of Paint Rock, bear right onto Paint Rock Road. Follow it 9 miles to the inn. Signs clearly indicate where to go.

Maple Grove Inn
Knoxville, Tennessee 37923

INNKEEPERS: Curt Locket and Gina Buchanan

ADDRESS/TELEPHONE: 8800 Westland Drive; (865) 690–9565 or (800) 645–0713 for reservations; fax (865) 690–9385

WEB SITE: www.maplegroveinn.com

E-MAIL: mginn@usit.net

ROOMS: 8 rooms and suites, all with private bath, private telephone line with voice mail, television; some with whirlpool tub, fireplace, VCR; 1 with private porch. No-smoking inn.

RATES: $125 to $250; includes full breakfast. Children 12 and older welcome. Two-night minimum on weekends from March through November. Credit cards accepted.

OPEN: Year-round except the week following Christmas to January 3.

FACILITIES AND ACTIVITIES: Restaurant serving dinner Thursday through Saturday by reservation; swimming pool, tennis courts, gardens, fifteen acres. Nearby: Volunteer Landing, Gateway Regional Visitors Center, World's Fair Park, Women's Basketball Hall of Fame, James White's Fort, Blount Mansion and other historic house museums, Knoxville Museum of Art, East Tennessee Historical Society Museum, Museum of Appalachia, Ijams Nature Center, Knoxville Zoo, restaurants, galleries, shopping, hiking, biking, water sports.

BUSINESS TRAVEL: Formal meeting room with fireplace and audiovisual equipment; break-out rooms; fax; separate telephone lines.

*M*emories have been made at the Maple Grove Inn for more than 200 years, and now you can make your own. It seems only fitting that Knoxville's oldest house not only survives but serves as a luxurious inn. Although it is physically within the city, the Maple Grove Inn has a rural setting and sits on fifteen acres. The core of what is now a mansion was a basic two-over-two Georgian-style home. The intervening years have seen numerous additions that result in the rambling mansion you visit today.

Maple Grove Inn is lavishly appointed with magnificent hand-carved fireplaces and rich mahogany paneling and decorated with elegant antiques, colorful Oriental rugs, fine oil paintings, and family heirlooms. Guests can relax or socialize in the spacious formal parlor; cozy library; cheery sitting room; casual, clubby great room with big-screen TV; or the sunny wicker-filled Florida room.

Bedchambers are extremely romantic, especially the Maple and Oak Suites. In addition to its elegant king-size sleigh bed, the huge, opulent Maple Suite boasts a sitting area with a fireplace, what we can only describe as a "wow" bathroom with step-in Jacuzzi, and a small porch and larger screened-in porch. Other rooms and suites each have a distinct personality, whether it's formal or casual.

At least one night during a Thursday to Saturday stay, you'll want to make reservations to dine on Chef James Roger's upscale cuisine in the inn's dining room. For a very special occasion, you might want to consider enjoying the meal in the privacy of your suite. Entertaining is a specialty of the house, and many weddings, receptions, small meetings, and other events take place there. Overnight guests awaken to the tantalizing aroma of muffins baking and coffee being freshly brewed. There are no mundane meals at the Maple Grove Inn. A hearty breakfast might include eggs Benedict, an omelette, or crepes of your choice. Extensive dinner menus range from a chicken salad medley to beef tenderloin. All desserts are made fresh daily at the inn.

Although the Maple Grove Inn is convenient to all the attractions of Knoxville, with the swimming pool, tennis court, and extensive grounds,

you'd rarely have to leave the property.

The Maple Grove Inn is the créme de la créme among inns. Everything about it is top-drawer. It is filled with Southern hospitality, quiet charm, and gracious living. This is the type of place we love to stay.

HOW TO GET THERE: Take I–40 to the West Hills exit and turn left at the light. Turn right at the next light onto Morrell Road at West Town Mall. Go through five lights and turn right onto Westland Drive. Drive 2 miles to the Maple Grove Inn entrance on the left.

Cedarvine Manor 💚
Lebanon, Tennessee 37090

INNKEEPERS: Jack and Jackie George

ADDRESS/TELEPHONE: 8061 Murfreesboro Road; (615) 443–2211, (615) 443–2456, or (800) 447–9155; fax (615) 443–2123

WEB SITE: www.cedarvine.com

E-MAIL: mail@cedarvine.com

ROOMS: 8 rooms and 1 cabin, all with private bath, ceiling fan, clock radio; some with private outside entrance and/or porch; some with gas-log fireplace, whirlpool tub; some are wheelchair accessible. Telephone and television available in common areas. Children 12 and older welcome. Iron and ironing board, hair dryer available.

RATES: $155 to $265, single or double occupancy, includes full breakfast, cookies, coffee, tea, lemonade. Lunch and dinner can be arranged with prior notice at an additional fee. Credit cards accepted.

OPEN: Year-round except December 24 and 25.

FACILITIES AND ACTIVITIES: Formal parlors, dining room, porches, courtyard, gardens, twenty acres with pond, covered bridge, special events barn, helipad. Nearby: Cedars of Lebanon State Park, Pine Creek Golf Course, Stones River Battlefield Historical Site, outlets of Lebanon Antiques Shops and Mall, Prime Outlets Shopping Mall, hiking, horseback riding, swimming, NASCAR Superspeedway, Wilson County Fair, Wildflower Pilgrimage, sights of Nashville.

BUSINESS TRAVEL: Meeting facilities with state-of-the-art audiovisual equipment; telephone jacks in all guest rooms; copiers, fax.

*W*hat began as a two-story log home in 1865 has had many incarnations: private home, hospital, convalescent home, and now a fine 8,000-square-foot bed-and-breakfast with all the modern conveniences. The grounds were originally purchased through a Revolutionary War land grant in 1832, and the home was begun, although it wasn't completed until 1865. During the Civil War the home was commandeered as a hospital to treat the thousands of soldiers wounded at the Battle of Stones River. There was even a secret tunnel running from the kitchen to a cave across what is now U.S. 231. Previous owners tell stories of soldiers escaping through the tunnel and of valuables and cattle being hidden there when the Yankees came looking for them.

Several years ago a group of investors purchased the old home and began to turn it into a modern, state-of-the-art resort property. *Modern,* however, doesn't mean sterile or uninteresting. The new building incorporates and surrounds the original house—you can see its brick walls, fireplaces, and old beams in the master bedroom, front room, and dining room. The modified structure offers 5,000 square feet of guest rooms and common rooms with all the creature comforts and a definite country feel.

Our favorite room is the Honeymoon Suite, with its giant king-size bed and double whirlpool tub and shower combination, which should get newlyweds off to a swimmingly great start. There is also a more rustic honeymoon suite located in the 1832 reconstructed log cabin that sits in the courtyard—perfect for those who want a little extra privacy. Take it from us, you don't have to be just married to enjoy either.

Breakfast is served in the breakfast room, where you can enjoy watching the horses next door graze peacefully in their pasture that they share with the local deer and wild turkey. The manor's deluxe country breakfast includes fresh fruit; freshly baked breads, muffins, biscuits, and croissants; smoked pork chops; scrambled eggs; a potato-cheese casserole; Tomato Provincial; juice; and coffee or tea.

We saw the property as it was just opening and the grounds were still a little raw; however, all the ingredients, are there—gazebo-type covered bridge, small pond, pastures with horses happily cavorting, hidden verandas, and porches.

HOW TO GET THERE: From I–40, take I–840 south toward Chattanooga. Take exit 67 and turn left (east) onto Couchville Pike. Drive 4½ miles to U.S. 231 South. Cedarvine Manor is directly across the highway. From I–24, take I–840 north toward Lebanon. Take exit 67, turn right (east) onto Couchville Pike, and follow the directions above.

Adams Edgeworth Inn
Monteagle, Tennessee 37356

INNKEEPERS: Wendy and David Adams

ADDRESS/TELEPHONE: Monteagle Assembly; (931) 924–4000 or (878) RELAXINN; fax (931) 924–3236

WEB SITE: 1896-edgeworth-mountain-inn.com

E-MAIL: innjoy@worldnet.att.net

ROOMS: 12, plus 1 suite with kitchenette; all with private bath; some rooms with fireplace or wheelchair access. Smoking on verandas only.

RATES: Rooms $125 to $175, suites $175 to $250; includes full breakfast. Two-night minimum on weekends.

OPEN: Year-round.

FACILITIES AND ACTIVITIES: Five-course candlelight dinner by reservation; gift shop; on grounds of Monteagle Assembly. Nearby: Golf, tennis, Tennessee State Park, wilderness and developed hiking trails, Sewanee University of the South, Monteagle Wine Cellars.

Occasionally someone opens an inn that seems destined from the beginning to become a classic. Edgeworth is such an inn. The owners, David and Wendy Adams, put uncountable hours of study, thought, and travel into defining the kind of inn they wanted. Then they put at least that much into finding the right building in the right location. They wanted a good-size inn, in a rural setting, elegant but not formal. They wanted a full-service inn, serving dinner as well as breakfast.

The three-story Victorian house, nearly one hundred years old, on the grounds of the Monteagle Assembly (sometimes called "the Chautauqua of the South"), is perfect because it was built as an inn. Outside, David and Wendy expanded established perennial gardens to enhance the sense of rural seclusion. It looks like everything has been growing here forever.

Inside, they refurbished and brightened the interior without hiding the wood floors or changing the inn's warm character. They brought a large, eclectic collection of museum-quality art, as well as antiques and interesting mementos they and their grown children have picked up in world travel. Also, they have some wonderful items from the years Wendy's father spent as a United States ambassador. She has even found some of the antiques that were originally in the inn and returned them to their proper places.

Some of the guest rooms have been designed around quilts made by her mother and grandmother. The library and guest rooms overflow with books.

Classical music deepens the feeling of serenity in the sitting areas and floats out onto the shady porches.

The Treehouse, a third-floor suite, boasts a home theater for two, dinette, and a large bath with an antique footed tub and a separate shower.

If you prefer an active retreat to a sedentary one, the state park and wilderness areas offer more possibilities than you could explore in a lifetime, including swimming and walking.

After your daytime exertions, you definitely should plan on a dinner at the inn. Wendy dims the lights in the formal dining room and you dine by candlelight, often to live piano or guitar music. Some of the offerings are chicken Florentine, fresh salmon, and angel-hair pasta with Wendy's secret sauce. Wendy's cuisine includes lots of fresh herbs, lightly cooked and sauced fresh vegetables, fine cheeses, and delicate desserts. Each dish looks as good as it tastes.

HOW TO GET THERE: From I–24, take exit 134 into Monteagle. In the center of the village you will see a steel archway with a MONTEAGLE ASSEMBLY sign. Turn left through the arch. (There is a gate fee during the summer Chautauqua season, June 15 to August 15.) Once on the grounds, follow the green-and-white centennial celebration signs to the inn, 2/10 mile from gate.

Christopher Place ♥
Newport, Tennessee 37821

INNKEEPER: Drew Ogle

ADDRESS/TELEPHONE: 1500 Pinnacles Way; (423) 623–6555 or (800) 595–9441; fax (423) 613–4771

WEB SITE: www.christopherplace.com

E-MAIL: TheBestInn@aol.com

ROOMS: 4 rooms, 3 suites (1 suite has two bedrooms); all with private bath, CD player, radio, robes, toiletries, hair dryer, coffeemaker; some with whirlpool tub, television. Smoking on the veranda only.

RATES: $150 to $300, including breakfast, refreshments, and light snacks. Several packages available. Children 12 and older welcome.

OPEN: Year-round.

FACILITIES AND ACTIVITIES: Max's restaurant (reservations required 24 hours in advance), room service and concierge service 7:00 A.M. to 10:00 P.M., billiard room, heated outdoor pool, tennis court, fitness room, sauna, gift shop, laundry service, hiking and walking trails. Can arrange airport transfers with 24-hour notice. Nearby: Llama trekking, Great Smoky Mountains National Park, Gatlinburg, Pigeon Forge, Sevierville, white-water rafting, fishing, golf, Forbidden Caverns, Ober Gatlinburg Ski Resort, shopping.

BUSINESS TRAVEL: Message center, e-mail, copiers, fax, conference center, audiovisual equipment.

*S*eductive is the word that comes to mind when describing Christopher Place. We were seduced by the winding drive that wends its way up the mountain through heavy woods as well as by the colonial-style mansion with its soaring columns and magnificent view of the Smoky Mountains. From the moment we turned up the secluded drive, we knew life would be a little slower paced, but we weren't prepared for the luxury: the elegant interior, the furnishings, and the delightful staff.

Christopher Place perches atop a private mountaintop amid 200 acres at the edge of Great Smoky Mountains National Park. Although it was originally constructed just a few years ago as an extraordinary private home, it segued perfectly into use as a superb inn and romantic retreat.

The flying staircase circling its way up the three-story entry foyer is breathtaking. Crystal chandeliers are reflected in marble floors. Massive fireplaces, hand-carved furniture, gleaming hardwood floors and panel-

ing, and resort amenities satisfy even the most discriminating traveler.

Guest rooms and suites are limited in number but are unsurpassed in beauty, luxury, and comfort. Each is unique. The light and airy Roman Holiday Suite features a king bed elegantly draped in rich fabric. A woodburning fireplace and double whirlpool tub make this suite an outstanding choice for a honeymoon, anniversary, or other romantic getaway. The Lion's Den Suite is more masculine, with deep burgundies and dark woods. Its double whirlpool tub and his-and-her bath suite with sitting area combine to create another romantic retreat. Especially secluded, the Tournament of Roses Suite is located in the guest house. The decor in other rooms ranges from formal to country garden.

Max's restaurant, which is also open to the public by reservation, serves four-course gourmet candlelight dinners (additional charge) accompanied by soft music. County regulations prohibit the sale of alcohol, but you are welcome to bring your own. For a very special occasion, in-room dining can be arranged in select rooms. Four-diamond personal service and attention to detail are unobtrusive and unsurpassed. A hearty full mountain breakfast is served to order accompanied by gourmet coffees, teas, and fresh fruit. The staff can pack you a picnic lunch to eat poolside or on the nature trails.

Your days can be filled with activities or with none at all. A variety of sports options please the active; music, movies, books, games, or simply sitting in front of a roaring fire or in a rocker on the front veranda enjoying the ever-changing panoramic view appeal to others. Although close enough to the hustle and bustle of Gatlinburg, Pigeon Forge, and Sevierville for those who want the sights, entertainment, and shopping, Christopher Place is an oasis of tranquillity. Away from everyday stresses and strains or the hectic pace of many tourist destinations, you can relax, rediscover, and rekindle at this luxurious resort. You'll find it very difficult to leave.

HOW TO GET THERE: From I-40, take exit 435 to Highway 32 South for 2 miles. Turn right on English Mountain Road. Go 2 miles and turn right onto Pinnacles Way, which you will follow to the inn.

Newbury House
at Historic Rugby ¢¢
Rugby, Tennessee 37733

INNKEEPERS: Historic Rugby

ADDRESS/TELEPHONE: Highway 52 (mailing address: P.O. Box 8); (423) 628–2441 or (423) 628–2430; fax (423) 628–2266

WEB SITE: www.historicrugby.org

E-MAIL: rugbytn@highland.net

ROOMS: 3 rooms with private baths and 1 two-bedroom suite with one shared bath in the main house; 2 cottages, each with private bath. Cottages have sitting rooms and kitchenettes. One has a screened porch. No-smoking inn.

RATES: $65 to $90, single or double; $10 for each additional person; includes full breakfast at Harrow Road Cafe. No children under 12. Two-night minimum stay required weekends in October. Credit cards accepted.

OPEN: Year-round.

FACILITIES AND ACTIVITIES: Cafe open for breakfast and lunch daily; for dinner Friday and Saturday; closed Thanksgiving Day, December 24 and 25, January 1; brown bagging wine permitted. Guided tours of historic buildings, crafts commissary, print shop, "gentlemen's" swimming hole (now for ladies, too). Nearby: Village is at Boundary A of the Big South Fork National River and Recreational Area; hiking, rafting, fishing, horseback riding, Blue Heron Coal Mine, Big South Fork Scenic Railway, Tennessee's oldest winery.

For this place to make any sense to you, you need to know that once upon a time in England all the good jobs and positions of power went to the first sons in English families. Second sons didn't get much of anything. Thomas Hughes was a reformer who tried to change that by starting the Rugby colony in the wilderness of Tennessee as a cooperative, class-free agricultural community where second sons could create their own world and still enjoy British ways. Like most utopian attempts, it never quite worked, partly because no one prepared those younger sons for what they were getting into.

Staying here may not have been a lot of fun for those unprepared English sons, but it's great for a tourist today. Facilities are owned and operated by

The Haunting of Rugby

In the historic village of Rugby, current residents say that the past occasionally spills over into the present with otherworldly visits from spirits who cling tenaciously to their old homes. For example, if you stay overnight at Newbury House, you might be sharing your room with an unexpected guest. Some of the furniture in Newbury House was saved from the old Tabard Inn when it burned to the ground in the mid-1880s. The old hotel's manager had killed his wife there, and apparently these pieces of furniture carry some residue of their restless spirits. Guests have reported being awakened in the night to find the image of a man standing over their bed.

Mysterious goings-on keep life interesting at the privately owned Roslyn, which is often open for tours during the annual pilgrimage. In addition to hearing the tread of ghostly footsteps in the hall and seeing the vision of a woman in Victorian dress crying in the hall, it has been reported that the house frequently locked itself if the owner stepped outside. More than once there were the apparitions and sounds of a tally-ho carriage drawn by four horses racing up the driveway and disappearing into the woods where there is no road. Further investigation revealed that the place where the ghostly carriage disappeared was the location of the village's original High Street. Other people have been frightened out of their wits by the specter of a tall man in a black shroud or cloak hovering over the bed and surrounded by a luminous glow.

The town's impressive library was overseen by a fastidious, no-nonsense German named Mr. Bertz, who wouldn't let anyone borrow any of "his" books until they were properly cataloged. The staff often sense a presence in the library and wonder if he is checking to see that the collection is being properly taken care of. Even the founder's house, Kingston Lisle, has its own odd occurrences: The bedcovers won't stay straight. Ask about these stories and others when you're on a tour. For the most fun with ghosts, arrange a visit close to Halloween for the Ghostly Gathering.

nonprofit Historic Rugby, a museum/preservation organization. The National Trust for Historic Preservation calls Rugby one of the most authentically preserved historic villages in America.

In addition to getting a glimpse into the life of another time, you get the pleasures of a nicely kept inn with good beds, some exposure to the local mountain culture, and access to wonderful crafts.

Authentic historic accommodations are offered in three village buildings. Dormers peek out of the deeply overhanging mansard roof of Newbury House. Built in 1880, it was Rugby's first boardinghouse. Restored as a bed-and-breakfast inn, it features a large, inviting, book-filled parlor with a fireplace and offers three modest guest rooms with private baths and a two-bedroom suite with a shared bath. Lace curtains grace the windows, and antiques, some of them original to Rugby, give the cottage its charming Victorian character. Guests enjoy the veranda, sunporch, and the pond in the secret garden.

Pioneer Cottage was the first frame building constructed in Rugby, in 1879. It was originally called Asylum House because it was the place young men stayed when they arrived in the colony until they were able to build a house of their own. Founder Thomas Hughes stayed here himself on his first visit. Hand-planed poplar board-and-batten walls give this cottage a more rustic ambience than that of the inn. Rented to families or groups traveling together, the cottage's one downstairs bedroom and two upstairs guest chambers can accommodate up to ten people. Its large parlor, fully equipped kitchen, and screened-in porch make it ideal for family reunions and other small gatherings.

Newly constructed, but historically accurate, Percy Cottage is a picture-book Victorian Gothic with accommodations for three in a charming upstairs two-bedroom suite under the steeply slanting ceilings. Downstairs is a kitchenette/sitting room.

A stay in Newbury House includes hot beverages served in the parlor in the morning, a full breakfast at the Harrow Road Cafe (more about this in a moment), and hot beverages and cookies available all day. Breakfast and other refreshments are not included in stays at either of the cottages.

Although the inn is carefully attended by Historic Rugby staff, this is not the kind of place where

you lounge about chatting with the innkeeper. You'll find a letter on your bed telling you about the possibilities of the whole village. Your interaction is with the entire village and its staff, all of whom are educated to answer questions not only about Historic Rugby, but also about the surrounding area. Even breakfast is an interaction with the village, because it is served in the village cafe, where you have a choice of several Southern breakfasts, such as buttermilk pancakes with sugar-cured ham or scambled eggs with biscuits and gravy. It's all spelled out for you on a Victorian menu card.

The Rugby Commissary, now selling the work of about one hundred area craftspeople, has improved steadily in recent years and is considered by some visitors to be better than any other in the state. Much of the work is done by people who take the workshops Historic Rugby sponsors in weaving, quilting, making white-oak baskets, cornhusk crafts, and the like. Write for a full schedule. You may choose to plan your visit here to correspond with one of the workshops. The commissary also purveys British Isles food products, old-time Watkins extracts and spices, and books about Rugby's history as well as other Victorian-era literature.

A tour of Historic Rugby begins at the Schoolhouse Visitor Centre, where richly detailed interpretive exhibits chronicle the town's century-plus of history. Tours include the Bavarian-looking Thomas Hughes Free Public Library, which contains its original 7,000-volume collection of books as well as its original furnishings; Hughes's home, Kingston Lisle, which contains many of his personal furnishings; Christ Episcopal Church, a still active Carpenter Gothic church with original furnishings, organ, and stained-glass windows; and the Laurel Dale Cemetery, where early settlers, including Hughes's mother, are buried.

Lunch is served daily at the Harrow Road Cafe, newly constructed on the site of the original cafe of the same name. The cafe, which conforms to Rugby's historic architecture, serves meals in two wood-beamed dining rooms. The cuisine is a combination of Cumberland Plateau home cooking and British Isles specialties.

From Rugby, you can explore rugged gorges, trails down to the Clear Fork River, waterfalls, natural arches, and many other attractions.

HOW TO GET THERE: Rugby is on Route 52, between Elgin and Jamestown, Tennessee. From I–75, north of Knoxville, take State Highway 63 east, then go south on Highway 27 to Highway 52. Go west on 52 about 6 miles. From I–40, go north on Highway 127 at Crossville to 52.

Blue Mountain Mist Country Inn
Sevierville, Tennessee 37862

INNKEEPERS: Sarah and Norman Ball

ADDRESS/TELEPHONE: 1811 Pullen Road; (865) 428–2335 or (800) 497–2335; fax (865) 453–1720

WEB SITE: www.bluemountainmist.com

E-MAIL: blumtnmist@aol.com

ROOMS: 11, plus 1 suite; all with private bath; 2 with Jacuzzi; 4 with wheelchair access; 5 two-person cottages with Jacuzzi and fireplace. No-smoking inn.

RATES: $100 to $155, double; $10 less for single; includes full breakfast. Extra person in room, $15.

OPEN: Year-round.

FACILITIES AND ACTIVITIES: Television room, conference room, outdoor Jacuzzi, permanent horseshoe court, volleyball and badminton, walking trail. Nearby: Restaurants; short drive to Pigeon Forge, Gatlinburg, and Great Smoky Mountains National Park; Smoky Mountains Craft Community.

BUSINESS TRAVEL: Conference rooms, dataports, full audiovisual, fax, copier; good for small conferences.

Blue Mountain Mist is a Victorian-style farmhouse built in 1987 specifically to be used as a small conference center and B&B inn. Consequently, the interior is bright, cheerful, and spacious, escaping the sense of gloom and spaces being forced into unnatural uses that sometimes afflicts old mansions converted to inns.

The inn is in the foothills, where you find lots of rolling farmland and can see in all directions. The Balls have built the inn on a portion of the farm belonging to Sarah's parents, and the family feeling pervades the operation. Quilts and furniture from Sarah's family are part of the inn's decor, and a picture of the inn drawn by Sarah's son, Jason, in 1987 when he was in kindergarten, hangs framed in a position of honor at the foot of the stairs near the front door. Sarah's mother stops in regularly with fresh flowers for the inn, and folks do a lot of visiting.

Visiting is encouraged by cozy upstairs and downstairs sitting areas, each with a fireplace, and by the rocking chairs on the big wraparound porch, from which you have a great view of the surrounding countryside as well as the inn's nicely kept grounds.

The guest rooms, furnished with country antiques, are as airy and pleasing as the common areas of the inn. The Rainbow Falls Room, however, stands in a class by itself. It has a huge hot tub set up on a platform behind a stained-glass window in a rainbow falls design created by a local stained-glass artisan. The carpet, drapes, and bedding pick up deep greens and blue-greens from the stained glass, producing a stunning effect.

The Sugarlands Room, usually used as the bridal suite, catches your imagination, too. The hot tub in this room is on a platform in a windowed turret, with a view of the mountains. The room is decorated in white, mauve, and mint green.

The five cottages in the wooded area behind the inn offer more seclusion. Designed for two people, each cottage has a queen bed, fireplace, kitchenette, two-person Jacuzzi, porch with swing, and a grill and picnic table in the yard.

HOW TO GET THERE: From I–40, take exit 407 onto Highway 66 South, proceeding to Sevierville. Turn left onto Highway 411. At the fourth traffic light, turn right onto Lower Middle Creek Road. Go 3⁹/₁₀ miles and turn left onto Jay Ell Road. The inn is 1½ miles on the left.

Richmont Inn
Townsend, Tennessee 37882

INNKEEPERS: Susan and Jim Hind and Jimmy and Hilda Hind

ADDRESS/TELEPHONE: 220 Winterberry Lane; (865) 448-6751 or (866) 267-7086 (toll-free); fax (865) 448-6480

WEB SITE: www.richmontinn.com

E-MAIL: richmontinn@aol.com

ROOMS: 12 rooms, all with private bath, robes, piped-in music, coffeemaker, hair dryer, refrigerator; most with double-size whirlpool tub, fireplace, and balcony; one room with wheelchair access.

RATES: $115 to $220; includes full breakfast, afternoon coffee and tea, and evening gourmet desserts.

OPEN: Year-round.

FACILITIES AND ACTIVITIES: Sitting room, dining area, potting shed, greenhouse, chapel. Nearby: Great Smoky Mountains National Park, hiking, biking, fishing, horseback riding, white-water rafting, golf, swimming, historic tours, antiques and mountain crafts shopping.

BUSINESS TRAVEL: Meeting facilities for up to twenty-five.

*W*e remember driving through deep woods and pulling up in front of what appeared to be an unusual weathered gray barn—not just any barn, but one where the square upper story overhangs the smaller lower story. In fact, the B&B inn is modeled after the Appalachian cantilever barn, which is a hallmark of nearby Cades Cove and indigenous to the mountainous areas of eastern Tennessee and western North Carolina. With its ideal, secluded location facing Laurel Valley and towering Rich Mountain, for which it is named, we knew the inn would make a perfect getaway.

We were warmly greeted by Susan and Jim Hind, who explained the barn's style to us and told us that farmers often chose that design because the overhang provided shelter for animals in bad weather.

Our first impression was that the interior would be as rustic as the exterior, but we were partially wrong. True, the main living/dining area does have mortar-chinked barn-wood walls, the 13-foot-high ceilings are open to the exposed beams, and broad planks and gray slates cover the floors. But the fireplace wall is formally paneled in white and is embellished with fine moldings and a graceful mantel. Antiques, traditional furnishings, comfortable overstuffed sofas and chairs, original sculpture, and French paintings create an upscale total look.

A huge corner window in the dining area permits an unparalleled panorama of the valley and mountains. The stunning view from here is ever changing, depending on the time of day, the

season of the year, and the weather. What a perfect place to enjoy a gourmet breakfast, which might be something scrumptious such as an egg-and-sausage casserole or apple-cinnamon pancakes with fresh fruit and maple syrup. When darkness settles, candles are lit and the room is transformed into a romantic scene for sinful desserts.

Considering that the exterior of the inn gives the impression that there are few windows, you might be surprised to find that each guest room actually has windows that permit an amazing amount of light as well as stunning views. Guest chambers are named for obscure and unselfish men and women who made major contributions to the history and culture of the Great Smoky Mountains. Each of these chambers is decorated in a manner that pays homage to its namesake. Old barn paneling, folk art, canopy beds, a stained-glass window, log walls, and Native American art set each room apart from every other. Each, however, brims with modern comforts and conveniences. The Nancy Ward Room, which features a wet bar and refrigerator, is large enough to double as a conference room or special events room. Two new deluxe suites done in French Country style occupy the lower level of another building, lending them a much more private air.

The Hinds recognize that many visitors love the property and its surroundings so much that they'd prefer not to leave at all, so they can provide some other meal options at an additional fee. An adjacent building serves as a casual cafe where you can enjoy a fondue dinner most evenings with reservations. They will also provide dinner baskets so that you can enjoy a private "picnic" in your room. This basket might be filled with such delicacies as cold chicken breast, smoked trout, salad, fruit, Brie, and bread. They'll prepare similar picnics for you to take on hikes and other outings.

HOW TO GET THERE: As you enter Townsend at Mile Marker 26 from Maryville on U.S. 321 North, take the first right onto Old Tuckaleechee Road. Turn right on Laurel Valley, the next paved road, and go 8/10 mile through the stone wall entrance. Go to the crest of the hill and turn left.

Blackberry Farm 🖤
Walland, Tennessee 37886

INNKEEPERS: Matt Alexander, general manager; Kreis and Sandy Beall, owners

ADDRESS/TELEPHONE: 1471 West Millers Cove; (865) 984–8166 or (865) 380–2260; fax (865) 977–4012

WEB SITE: www.blackberryfarm.com

E-MAIL: info@blackberryfarm.com

ROOMS: 23 estate rooms, 16 cottage suites, and 5 rooms in two separate cottages (Cove Cottage, 3 rooms, Gate House, 2 rooms), all with private bath, king- or queen-size feather bed, television, VCR, and telephone; suites with whirlpool bath and fireplace. Some wheelchair accessible.

RATES: $395 to $845 for rooms, $695 to $895 for cottage suites (more during holidays); includes all meals, afternoon tea, and recreational equipment and amenities; deduct $100 for single occupancy; deduct $100 during winter months; a two-night minimum is required for all stays; Friday and Saturday may not be split unless reserved one week prior to arrival and space is available; a three-night minimum is required for the month of October on weekends. Spa and other packages available.

OPEN: Year-round.

FACILITIES AND ACTIVITIES: Restaurant, spa, gift shop, wine cellar, outdoor heated pool, tennis courts, stocked fishing ponds, hiking and nature trails, bicycles, fully equipped fitness room. Nearby: Great Smoky Mountains National Park, antiques and crafts shops.

BUSINESS TRAVEL: 25 minutes from Knoxville; facilities for small conferences: wood-paneled boardroom, three meeting rooms in Chestnut Cottage, conference equipment.

After traveling several miles of winding mountain highway, we turned off onto a country road and meandered through a valley, or cove, of neat-as-a-pin farmsteads before we came to the stately Virginia fence and gateway to Blackberry Farm. Our anticipation mounted as we drove up the heavily wooded hill to the stunning frame-and-stone country house perched at the top. We were welcomed at the front door and escorted to our room in the elegant Guest House next door, which blends so perfectly with the restored manor house that you'd swear they were built at the same time. Recently, Holly Glade Cottages, which are suites, were added, scattered throughout the grounds. In all, the resort boasts forty-four luxurious accommodations, including those in the historic main house.

This sophisticated and gracious country inn is the centerpiece of an 1,100-acre estate bordering Great Smoky Mountains National Park. A stylish ambience reminiscent of great English country houses is achieved in all the public rooms and guest chambers by the lavish use of English and American antiques, period reproductions, floral chintz fabrics, opulent window treatments, and carefully selected art. Sumptuous guest rooms are spacious, comfortable, and lavishly decorated, but the new, knock-your-socks-off Cottage Suites are even larger and boast a king-size feather bed, whirlpool bath, wood-burning fireplace, entertainment center, stocked refrigerator/pantry, and covered porch.

Our favorite activity is simply to pull up a pair of rocking chairs from the ones lined up across the stone patio so that we can gaze out at the vast expanses of forests and rolling lawns. More likely than not, early morning reveals a heavy mist draped over the peaks, educating you as to why Native Americans called the ridges the Smoky Mountains. Gradually the veils of mist lift, revealing not only the forests but also birds and wildlife. If you've forgotten binoculars, borrow a pair from the collection sitting on the windowsill. On the occasional inclement day or during the winter season, the public lounges are filled with books, magazines, and games to help you enjoy your time of utter relaxation by a blazing fireplace.

Although the attractions of the national park, as well as several small towns filled with antiques and crafts shops, may entice you off the property, you may opt not to leave it at all. A splendid restaurant specializing in creative Southern cuisine allows you to eat all your meals on the property. Jackets are required for gentlemen at

dinner. Until recently the inn was unable to serve any alcoholic beverages due to local laws. However, with the institution of the Blackberry Mountain Club, a private club, guests can purchase a minimally priced membership that permits them to buy wine and spirits in the dining room. A pool, tennis courts, fishing ponds, shuffleboard, and bicycles attract more active guests, as do hiking along secluded mountain trails crossing burbling streams and canoeing. Orvis-certified instructors provide free fly-fishing demonstrations on Saturday, and all fly rods and flies are provided. Cooking schools are scheduled periodically throughout the year. Christmas at Blackberry Farm is a never-to-be-forgotten experience.

HOW TO GET THERE: From I-75, exit onto U.S. 321 east to Walland; just past Walland, watch for West Miller Cove Road, turn right, and follow the signs to the inn.

Select List of Other Tennessee Inns

Hachland Hill Inn
1601 Madison Street
Clarksville, TN 37043
(931) 647-4084

1790 house; 6 rooms, 3 cottages; some with fireplaces; restaurant.

Mountain Harbor Inn and Restaurant
1199 Highway 139
Dandridge, TN 37725
(865) 397-3345

Sprawling lakeshore inn on Douglas Lake; 4 rooms and 9 suites; patios and verandas; restaurant.

The Spence Manor
11 Music Square East
Nashville, TN 37203
(615) 259-4400

Favorite with recording professionals; 24 suites; pool.

Parish Patch Farm and Inn

1100 Cortner Road
Normandy, TN 37360
(931) 857–3017 or (800) 876–3017

Working cattle and grain farm on the Duck River; 18 rooms and suites, some with fireplaces; pool; restaurant in historic flour mill; bar.

Little Greenbrier Lodge

3685 Lyon Springs Road
Sevierville, TN 37862
(423) 429–2500 or (800) 277–8100

Rustic 1939 mountain lodge; 10 rooms; breakfast.

Pin Oak Lodge

567 Pin Oak Lodge Lane
Wildersville, TN 38388
(901) 968–8176

Rustic lodge; 20 rooms, 18 cottages; some with fireplace or kitchen facilities; pool, tennis, restaurant, lake.

Indexes

Alphabetical Index to Inns

Inns on the Ocean, Bay, Lake, or River

Alabama

Florida

Georgia

Louisiana

Mississippi

Inns for Business Travelers

(downtown location*, meeting/convention facilities,
and/or special guest room facilities)

Secluded Inns

Inns in Restored Historic Buildings

(* denotes historic home)

Inns with Provisions for the Disabled

Inns with Restaurants or Where Other Meals Can Be Served by Special Arrangement

About the Authors

CAROL and DAN THALIMER have been associated with the travel industry for twenty years, and for seven of them they owned travel agencies. During those years they've inspected dozens of cruise ships and hundreds of hotels, inns, and bed-and-breakfasts and reported on them for travel agent publications and guides such as *Travel Agent Magazine* and *ABC Star Service*. For the past fifteen years they have written about travel for fifty magazines and newspapers and for several guidebook publishers. They are the authors of *Quick Escapes from Atlanta, Fun with the Family: Georgia, Recommended Bed & Breakfasts: The South,* and *Romantic Days and Nights in Atlanta,* all from The Globe Pequot Press, as well as ten guidebooks for other publishers.